MW00668943

Tigers I and II

The Spielberger German Armor and Military Vehicle Series

Tigers I and II

and their Variants

Walter J. Spielberger

Hilary L. Doyle

Schiffer Military History
Atglen, PA

Photo credits: Dipl.-Ing. Willi Esser 4, Federal Archives/Military Archives 12, Dipl.-Ing. Theodor Icken 10, Col. Robert J. Icks 1, Thyssen-Henschel 232, Walter J. Spielberger 271
Scale drawings: Hilary L. Doyle and D. P. Dyer.
Color illustrations: Anthony J. Kaye and Patrick B. Loughran.

Book translation by Dr. Edward Force, Central Connecticut State

Book Design by Ian Robertson.

Library of Congress Control Number: 2007930641

Printed in China.
ISBN: 978-0-7643-2780-3

This book was originally published in German under the title
Der Panzer-Kampfwagen Tiger und Seine Abarten by Motorbuch Verlag

We are interested in hearing from authors with book ideas on related topics.

Published by Schiffer Publishing Ltd.
4880 Lower Valley Road
Atglen, PA 19310
Phone: (610) 593-1777
FAX: (610) 593-2002
E-mail: Info@schifferbooks.com.
Visit our web site at: www.schifferbooks.com
Please write for a free catalog.
This book may be purchased from the publisher.
Please include $3.95 postage.
Try your bookstore first.

In Europe, Schiffer books are distributed by:
Bushwood Books
6 Marksbury Avenue
Kew Gardens
Surrey TW9 4JF, England
Phone: 44 (0) 20 8392-8585
FAX: 44 (0) 20 8392-9876
E-mail: Info@bushwoodbooks.co.uk.
Visit our website at: www.bushwoodbooks.co.uk
Free postage in the UK. Europe: air mail at cost.
Try your bookstore first.

Contents

Foreword

Seldom has an armored vehicle aroused the spirits of specialists and laymen in such a fashion as the German *Wehrmacht's* World War II "Tiger" tank, which is now almost legendary. In the postwar era, volumes appeared from professional writers, and alas, also from non-professionals, who reported on the development and action of these vehicles. How difficult it really is to tackle this unique achievement of German industry objectively is something even the responsible development chief, Dr. Erwin Aders, had to experience, as he reported at the end of January 1945:

"As early as September or October 1942, the *Panzerkampfwagen* Tiger Type E was called a 'crippled cart' by someone in an influential position, and the cylindrical turret, designed by Krupp after ample consideration, was compared to a fruit can. Its first, perverted action provided the reason. After several months, to the amazement of all involved, that admiration began to appear in the press that had to move us just as unpleasantly in its exaggeration as the previous belittlement."

This disagreement still continues today. The few remaining "genuine" Tiger people, to whom this vehicle had given a real chance to survive, are still convinced that the "Tiger" was the only useful armored vehicle that there was. Far beyond subjective experience, it was therefore our job to grasp the technical development of this vehicle in as many details as possible, and thus preserve them for the future.

If one cautiously estimates the total cost of "Tiger" development and production at about 500 million *Reichsmark*, and then compares it with the actual results, the question arises whether this vehicle really was what the troops needed. Hitler's influence, recorded in detail, is also made clear again and again. That technical ventures into the borderland were being made was very soon made clear to everyone involved in the development. The accomplishment of industry, which created the first test vehicles out of nothing within twelve months, is undeniable. Thereby the troops were finally provided with a vehicle that could take part in every tank battle with a good chance of success. Shortages of raw materials, and the effects of the Allied air superiority also prevented a really sufficient supplying of the troops. "Tiger" tanks were not only feared by the enemy, but were also regarded by our own troops as very rare and extremely valuable vehicles that were never available in sufficient numbers. The war history writing of today too often overlooks the fact that in reality fewer than 2000 of these vehicles were produced. Compared with the production statistics of enemy tanks from east and west, that is truly a modest number. The fact that its reputation lasts to this day is recognition of the achievement of the industry that created it, and of the crews that gained success with it. For both, this book is meant to bring a piece of past history to memory.

I am grateful to the Thyseen-Industrie AG, Henschel Wehrtechnik in Kassel, for the kind sharing of the memoirs of Dr. Erwin Aders, and above all, to Mr. H. H. Schmidt for his encouragement. A large number of the pictures of "Tiger E" production were also made available by Henschel. Information and pictures from my archives came partially from my time at the Nibelungenwerke, or were gathered from original documents, whereby thanks are due to the Federal Archives/Military Archives in Freiburg for their decisive support, when a wealth of information, drawings, and photos can for the first time be presented to the public herewith. Colonel Robert J. Icks and Hofrat Dr. Friedrich Wiener have helped very much. Also, retired Major Dipl.-Ing. H. Sculteus and retired Colonel Dipl.-Ing. Theodor Icken contributed a great deal. Messrs. P. Chamberlain and U. Feist have, through years of effort, gathered important material, which now enriches this book. And finally, as again and again, the contributions of Hilary L. Doyle are worthy of mention, for his drawings make the book complete. Such a document always arises only through the cooperation of many, whereby we hope that our readers will also take part in this research, in order to make future editions even more complete. Every bit helps, no matter how little it may be.

Walter J. Spielberger

The Life of Dr.-Ing. habil.Dipl.-Ing. Erwin Aders

Paul Erwin Aders was born in Düsseldorf on May 7, 1881. He studied at the Technische Hochschule in Aachen, where he passed the State Examination in 1906. After that he was active as a designer for firms that built machines and motor vehicles.

During World War I he served with the motor vehicle troops, and later with the Motor Vehicle Testing Department in Berlin.

In 1919 he joined the Maschinenfabrik Augsburg-Nürnberg (MAN) as a senior engineer, in 1925 the Vogtländische Maschinenfabrik (Vomag) in Plauen, and in 1929 the Daimler-Benz AG. In 1933 he became a private instructor at the Technische Hochschule in Aachen. In 1936 he became the Director of the Development Department of the Henschel & Sohn firm in Kassel, and took charge of tank development there. The high point of his creative career was the development of the Tiger tank.

Development

The production of German armored vehicles in World War II concluded with the "Tiger" and "Panther" tanks.

Influential progress in tank building was and is dependent on the availability of suitable components, including high-performance motors that produce as much energy and take up as little space as possible. For that reason, the development of tank motors in the thirties will also be portrayed here.

From 1935 on, the Ordnance Office was already busy with the creation of high-performance motors for use in heavy armored vehicles. On October 28, 1935, a technical discussion took place in the Army Ordnance Office that concerned itself with, among others, "600 HP machines for the Large Tractor." The Daimler-Benz AG then suggested their "M 71" aircraft motor (later DB 600) for use in tanks. Designed for a sustained production of 550 HP and a maximum of 600 HP at 2200 rpm, this machine was to be rebuilt in the form of standing cylinders. Fuel injection and conversion to Diesel fuel were foreseen in its further development. The powerplant being considered for use in tanks was designated "MB 503" when running on gasoline; its Diesel version was "MB 507." On June 3, 1937, WaPrüf 6 ordered two test motors, with their delivery, on test benches ready for acceptance, planned for the spring of 1938. The use of these test motors, though, had changed repeatedly in the course of time, in the face of other, more urgent tasks (Rheinmetall-Borsig "Device 040"). Finally, two were rebuilt as "MB 507" Diesel motors, and planned for installation in the "VK. 3001 (DB) tank. Early in 1937, new requests were made of the industry in terms of the proposed tank development. The Henschel & Sohn AG thus received, as its area of the work, the development of the heaviest armored vehicles. As a result, Henschel created the first research vehicles of their own design. Drawings of tanks in the 30-ton class were delivered by the Daimler-Benz, Henschel, and MAN firms as of 1937, under contract to the Ordnance Office. At the end of 1939 the Dr.-Ing. h.c. F. Porsche KG was also contracted to participate in this development.

While the designs of the MAN and Daimler-Benz firms later developed into the "Panther" tank, the experience gained with the Henschel and Porsche firms' prototype vehicles created the first prerequisites for the later "Tiger" vehicle. Corresponding to the instructions given by the Army high command, at first the 7.5 cm KwK L/24, and later the 10.5 cm KwK L/28 were foreseen as the armament for the Henschel heavy tank. This necessitated a turret diameter of 1650 mm.

The setting of tasks for the "DW" 1 (Durchbruchswagen 1) vehicle was done by Baurat Kniekamp of the Army Ordnance Office at the end of January 1937. The vehicle, planned to have a weight of 30 tons, had a two-part hull. Its rear section was connected by screws, since the rolling works were not yet capable of producing a one-piece sidewall of that length. Emergency hatches were planned for the right front of the hull by the radioman's seat, and in the engine compartment at the left rear. A skirting plate had been designed for the track-driving wheel, which could be started by hand crank and gear transmission.

The shooting tests gave no usable results. The armor thickness was 50 mm all around. A chassis was built and thoroughly tested.

Panzerkampfwagen DW 1

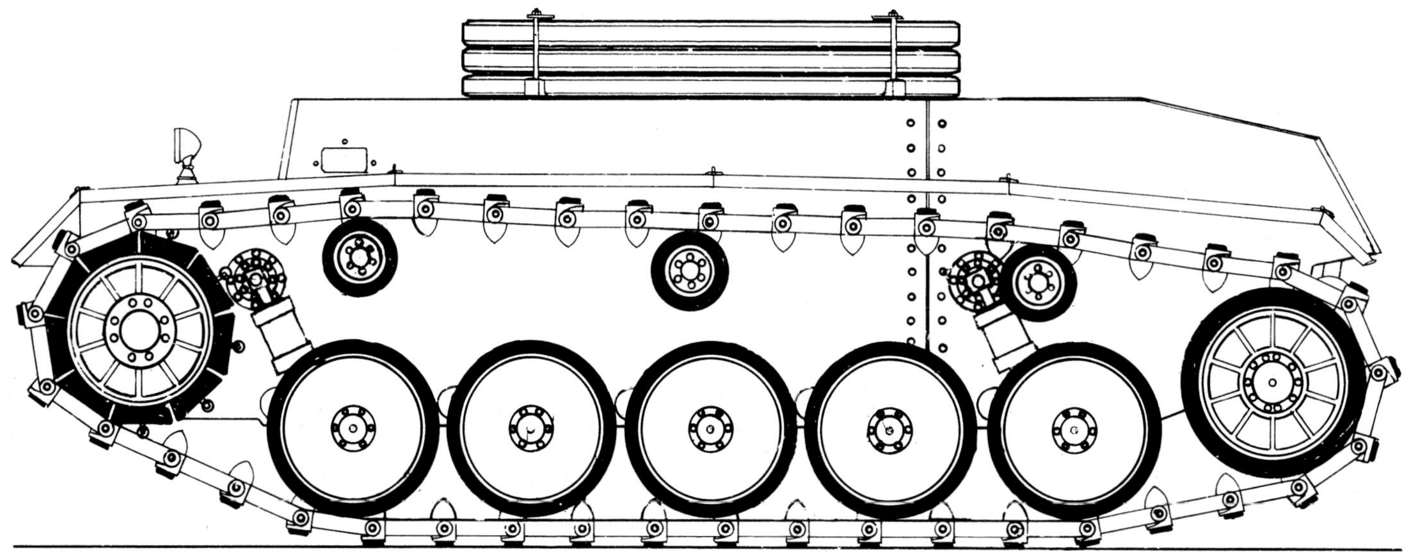

Its tracks had 300 mm divisions, and the track bolts were mounted in needle bearings and lubricated. The later addition of rubber pads was planned. The powerplant was the Maybach "HL 120" motor, which produced 280 HP. The turret drive was to operate via screw wheels, driven directly by a built-in piece of the main shaft cable. For gear shifting, a Maybach "Variorex" gearbox was installed. The steering gear had three successive, connected Cletrac steps. The steering drive, fitted with six brakes and four Ortlinghaus clutches, proved to be a failure, and had to be developed completely anew. The hydraulic pressure-transmitting system was delivered by the Teves firm. The reduction of the track drive, which was geared internally, was set at 1:21.5. Henschel used external shoe brakes of their own make, with Jurid linings. Because of unbearable smoke development during braking, a Götze hard-cast addition had to be turned to. Activating the brakes was done hydraulically. The suspension of the cast steel disc road wheels with complete rubber double tires was done by a torsion-bar system, in which spring bars with a full cross section and hollow springs (Röchling) were aligned one after the other (spring constancy ca. 12-13 kg/mm). Spring breaks were not determined. The road-wheel cranks were singly forged pieces, with tapered gudgeons for the road wheels. In the hull itself, they were mounted in Novotext boxes. The running gear also had external front and rear special shock absorbers made by the firm of Boge & Sohn attached. The axles of the leading wheels were mounted inside the hull, and their adjustment was done from inside. The leading wheels were made of cast steel, and had complete rubber bindings. The backward-running upper track return was directed by three rubber-tired jack rollers. The vehicle attained a top speed of 35 km/h.

On April 2, 1937, at a discussion with the In. 6, a successor model to the "DW 1," to be called "DW 2," was called for. The vehicle was to be a further development of the Panzer VI. The actual contract for it was given only on September 9, 1938. Compared to the "DW 1" vehicle, there were changes in the steering gear, reduction gears, brakes, tracks, drive wheels, and torsion-bar suspension. The triple-radius steering gear worked with magnetic clutches. The direction of running had been reversed, which necessitated changes to the track drive and the brakes, as well as the mounting of the gearbox and the torsion-bar suspension. Since the originally used steering gear of the "VW 38" (Panzer III) had proved itself on but not off the road, the two big radii were eliminated, and only the first Cletrac step, which was shifted mechanically with a shift lever, was kept.

The tracks of the "DW 2" vehicle had lubricated links with needle bearings for the bolts.

The prototype of the "DW 2" tank with its drive wheel removed.

The drive of the tracks was accomplished with simple crown-wheel reduction through a planetary drive. A Lorenz-Sykes gearing was used, and the reduction ratio of 1:12 was less than that of the "DW 1." The lubricated tracks now had 260 mm links, which provided considerably greater quiet running of the vehicle. The drive wheels were revised for the 260 mm links, and various mountings of the drive wheels, with needle bearings and Novotext boxes, were tried experimentally. Now simple torsion-

***Panzerkampfwagen* DW 2**

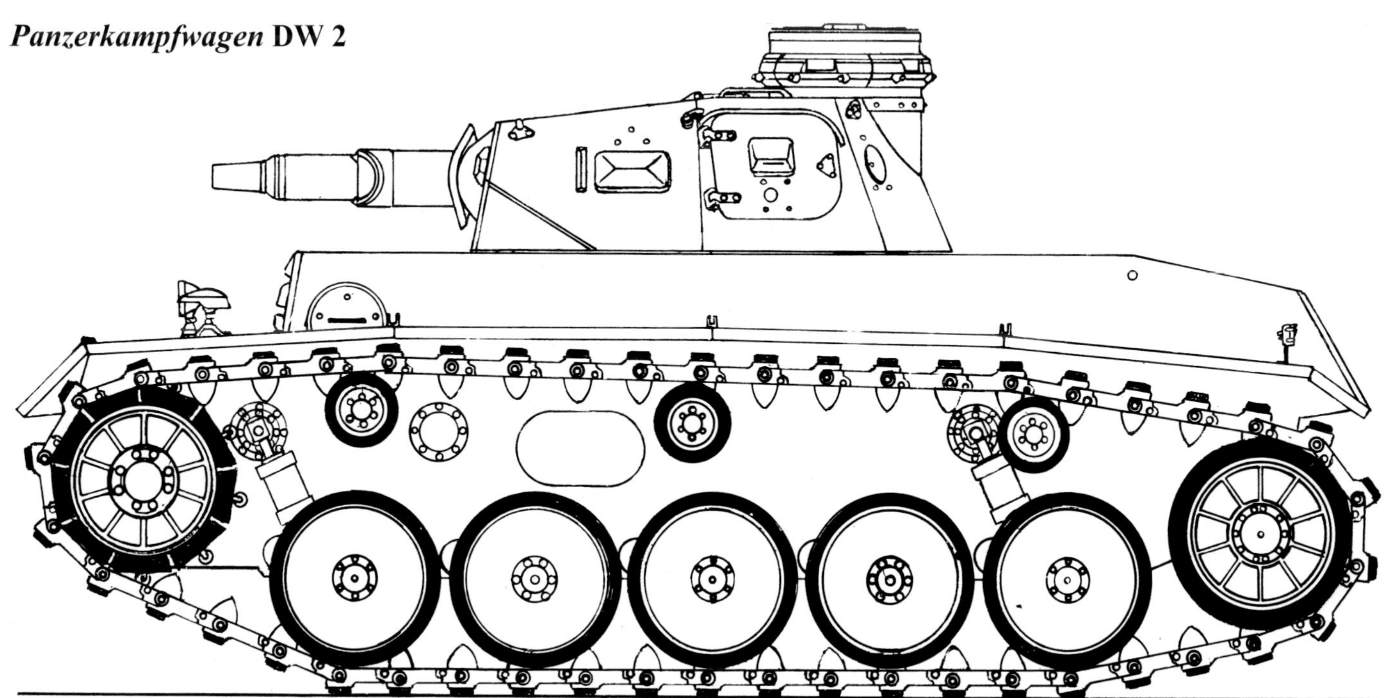

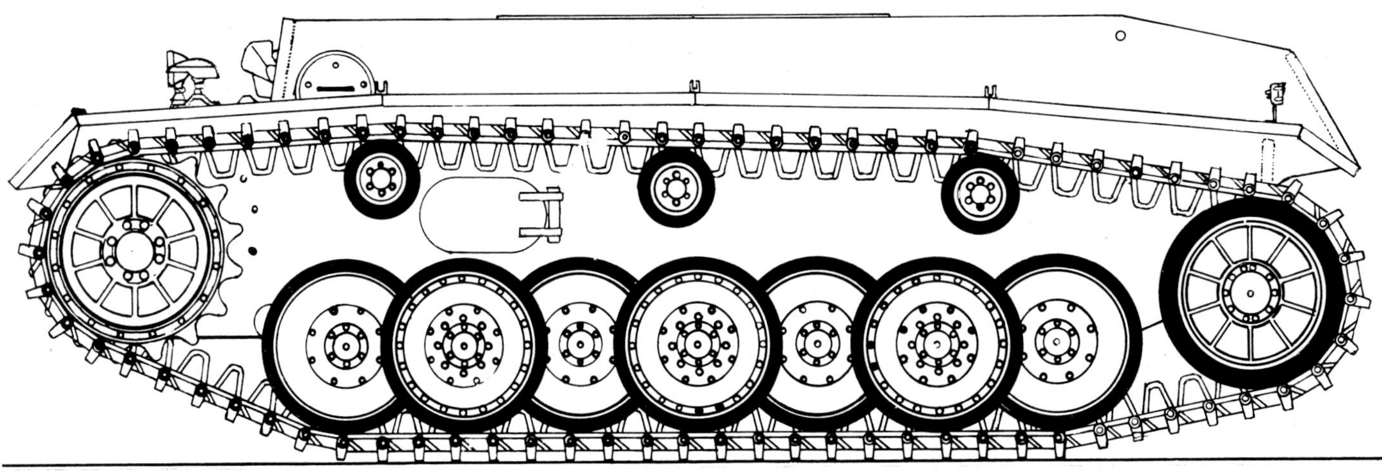

Panzerkampfwagen VK 3001 (H)

bar suspension was installed, which did without a spring softness (spring constant of 32 kg/mm). A chassis of this 30-ton vehicle with a top speed of 35 km/h was built and tested. The successor model VK. 3001 (H) had a one-piece hull with side hatches at the right and left front. On the sides were extensions for the cool air intakes. Admitting air into the engine- compartment cover through diagonal louvers was also tried. The armor was 60 mm thick at the front and 50 mm on the sides. Now unlubricated tracks with 520 mm width and 130 mm division were used. The guiding tooth of the track was in the middle. The power package was a Maybach "HL 116" 6-cylinder gasoline engine, which produced 300 HP at 3000 rpm. To cool the motor, there were two radiators with four ventilators situated behind the motor. They were driven by V-belts that were mounted on tension rollers with springs. As before,

The VK 3001 (H) vehicle with the attached digging-in plow.

In tests, the wall had been formed easily with four forward runs.

The soil is heaped up before the vehicle after it has moved three lengths.

The VK. 3001 (H) tank pushes masses of earth ahead of itself at a speed of about 2.5 km/h.

The strongly packed mass of earth presses against the box-shaped plow blade.

Left: The heaped up masses of earth rise as high as the driver's visor.

Below left: This picture shows the vehicle from behind after the fourth forward run. The success of the trenching operation is minimal.

Despite moving a lot of earth, the vehicle has scarcely dug itself in.

Left: The same VK. 3001 (H) vehicle is being tested with the LP 500 plow made by the Scheid firm. Below: Rear view of the vehicle with the plow installed.

The plow is being prepared for plowing.

The plow hangs on the attachment, in order to dig itself in through short forward and backward runs as far as the pressure bars can be set.

The pressure bars are being set.

Now the trenching plow is ready for action.

The trenching begins. For a depth of up to 60 cm, depths of up to 80 cm can be formed by using the earth plowed to the sides.

At a speed of 9 km/h, endless trenches can be dug.

This picture shows the tank with the trench plow moving at a speed of 14 km/h. At increasing speeds the trench became less neat.

With the plow mounted rigidly, trenches of constant depth, not less than 90 meters in radius, could be plowed out.

a Maybach "Variorex" gearbox was used. The Type "L 320 C" steering gear, with three radii and oil-pressure steering, had five clutches in oil baths.

In the track drive, a change had been made from flange pins. The change was made by using the body as a carrier. The crown wheel had straight flanks, and the planetary drives, one behind the other, had a reduction ratio of 1:10.75. The mechanical Perrot inside-lining brakes were largely taken from the "ZW 38" vehicle. There were seven disc road wheels on each side, in an alternating arrangement. As before, three jack rollers with rubber tires and ball bearings were used. The road-wheel cranks were one-piece forgings, since there was no room for a combined construction. They were mounted in Novotext boxes in the hull. On the left side of the hull they were set up to push, on the right to pull. Simple torsion bars with unequally strong heads (Porsche patent) linked the spring elements. The torsion bars and running cranks could be adjusted precisely (Nonius effect), the spring constants being different, 33 or 28 kg/mm. Hemscheidt shock absorbers were

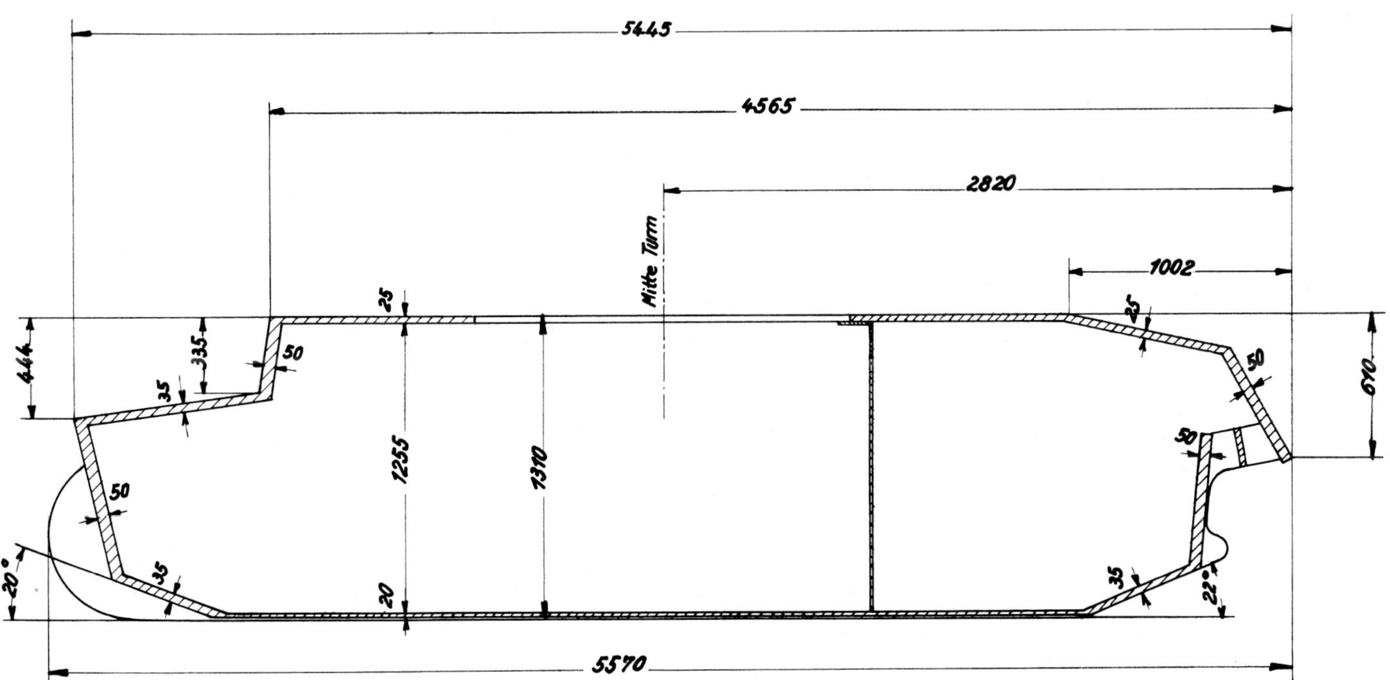

The layout of the VK. 3001 shows the typical stepped front end and the armor thicknesses.

planned for the front and back on each side, set directly on the crank pins. The leading wheels were also of cast steel, while the rubber bindings had been dropped again. The total weight of the VK. 3001 (H) was thirty tons; its top speed was 35 km/h.

In all three test chassis were built, and eight more vehicles prepared. From Krupp came a turret with a short 7.5 cm cannon. A Maybach OLVAR Type 40 12 16 gearbox was installed for testing. This was originally developed for a motor producing 400 HP (40 = 400 HP/12 = Md 120 mkp/16 = I=16). It had eight forward speeds and one reverse gear. For the 7th and 8th vehicles, a new steering gear of Type SMG 90 was planned. In September 1942 the hastened production of four of these vehicles had been ordered as school vehicles.

One of the VK. 3001 (H) chassis ran until the war's end at the Henschel test center in Haustenbeck i. L. Tests of the most varying kinds were made with it. Among others, it was fitted with a digging-in apparatus planned for the Panzer III. This consisted of an upper plow blade and a lower shovel with ripping teeth welded on the front. By driving the tank back and forth numerous times, a depth was supposed to be reached that would offer the vehicle protection up to the level of the skirting plates. The device was made by the firm of W. & J. Scheid, of Limburg on the Lahn, but could not establish itself.

Also made by the Scheid firm was a running trench plow (Type LP 500) which, unlike the digging-in device, was only attached to the back of the vehicle. The test vehicle was once again the VK. 3001 No. 2 chassis (without a turret), which was stationed at Haustenbeck as a recovery and towing tractor. A mounting bar, which was attached to the rear of the hull by two long bolts, served to hold the actual plow, which could be mounted on it at various heights. Trenches up to 80 cm deep could be plowed. The tests carried out in January 1944 showed that the vehicle could drive only very wide curves while plowing a running trench. The depth of the trench was also insufficient. A movable attached plow was promised by the Scheid firm for mid-February 1944. This was also planned for installation on a Panzer III tank, but the device was not introduced.

On May 25, 1941, Hitler had urged the development of self-propelled mounts for 10.5 and 12.8 mm guns, which were intended for fighting against bunkers, and for defense against heavily armored tanks, which were expected from Britain and America. While the 10.5 cm gun was mounted on a Panzer IV chassis, a variant of the Henschel "V.K. 3001" had been chosen for the 12.8 cm gun. The size of the gun required a special version of the armored hull, with 30 mm armor on the sides. The body was open on top.

The first test model of the 12.8 cm Armored Self-propelled Mount V was supposed to be delivered in August 1941, and be accepted by the General Army Office in reference to the need for connection. The 12.8 cm gun, with a caliber length of L/61, was the strongest antitank weapon used by the troops during WWII. Originally developed as an anti-aircraft weapon, this "Device 40" was produced by Rheinmetall as of 1936. The first production models were delivered to the Ordnance Office in 1938. The muzzle velocity (Vo) of the gun was 910 m/sec, the shot weight was 26 kg, the traverse of the weapon was 14 degrees in all, and the elevation went from -15 to +10 degrees. The gun weighed 7.5 tons. A five-man crew was planned. The vehicle carried 18 rounds of separated ready ammunition. Because of the increased total weight of some 36 tons, compared to the VK. 3001, eight road wheels were installed on each side. The series of outside and inside wheels (size 700/98-550) was set up so that, in front and in back, there were 1300 mm for the section of track running in each direction. Unlike the VK. 3001 (H), the tracks had to be lengthened appropriately. Every track had 85 links. With a track width of 520 mm, the ground contact was 4750 mm. The last two road wheels on each side of the vehicle had stronger torsion bars added later, since it was shown that in firing tests, strong nodding movements made it impossible for the gunner to observe the shot.

Two of the VK. 3001 chassis were lengthened at the back, and fitted by Rheinmetall with an open armored body to hold the 12.8 cm *Kanone* 40. The lower picture shows the gun at its highest elevation.

These two pictures show further details of the Armored Self-propelled Mount V.

12.8 cm Self-propelled Mount L/61 (Pz.Sfl. V).

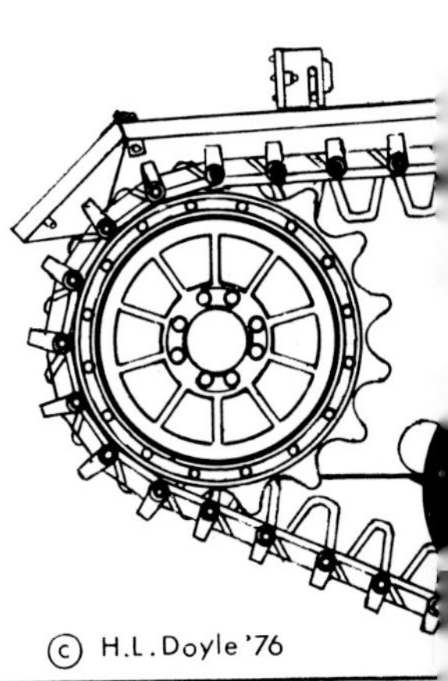

The three pictures show details of the open-topped fighting compartment of this self-propelled mount. The stowing of the ammunition is easy to see. Cartridges and shells were stored separately.

At the left in the fighting compartment is the gunner's seat, while at right is that of the commander. The aiming and observing devices are mounted over them.

The VK 3000 test vehicle developed by the Porsche firm is seen during testing in the country. The vehicle had gasoline-electric drive; the drive wheels were at the front.

The power was provided by a special version of the Maybach "HL 116" six-cylinder gasoline engine. It was mounted higher than the radiator. The belt drive for the cooler and the duct for the cooling air had to be changed. The track drives were built lower because of the higher steering power needed for the lengthened tracks. A dry three-plate clutch carried the power to a six-speed ZF "SSG 77" Aphon gearbox. The fuel tank held 450 liters, and the external measurements were 9800 x 3180 x 1670 mm. A top speed of 19.6 km/h was reached. Two vehicles of the "12/8 cm Self-propelled Mount L/61" (Pz. Sfl. V) were built by Rheinmetall-Borsig in Düsseldorf. Both vehicles, despite their original use, saw action in Russia. One is known to have fallen into Russian hands in the autumn of 1943.

The vehicle also known as "Leopard," is seen turning off the main road in the vicinity of the Nibelungenwerk.

From the Porsche firm came their first developmental vehicle to reach the newly built Nibelungenwerk, the "Sonderfahrzeug I," with the Porsche works nickname "Leopard." The official Army designation was "VK. 3001 (P)," while the Porsche type number was "100." Two test vehicles were finished, but the expected turrets from the Krupp firm were never mounted on them. Two side-by-side Porsche motors of Type "100," built and tested by the Simmering-Graz-Pauker AG in Vienna, and each producing 210 HP at 2500 rpm, were connected to a dynamo. From there the power was carried to two electric motors for the front-mounted drive wheels. The aircooled powerplants each had a fan. These gasoline engines, with a 72-degree V-10 form, had a bore of 105 mm and a stroke of 115 mm, for a displacement of ten liters. Steering and speed regulation were done electrically in connection with a "NITA" special gearbox with transformer built by the Voith firm of Heidenheim. Road wheels and jack rollers were planned for the running gear. The road-wheel suspension worked via bell-crank links on longitudinal torsion bars. Both chassis were submitted to

***Panzerkampfwagen* VK 3001 (P)**

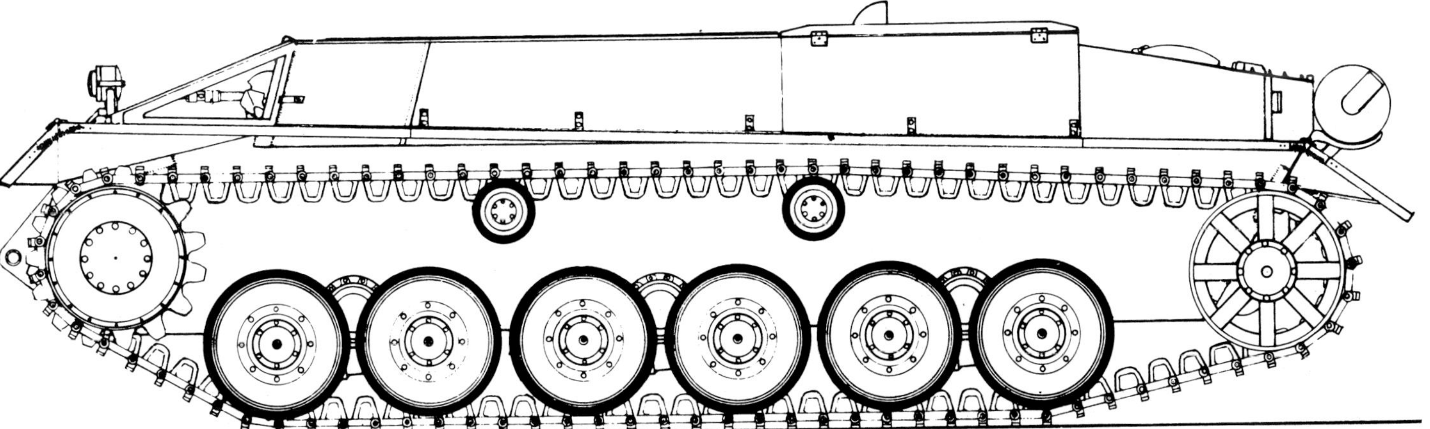

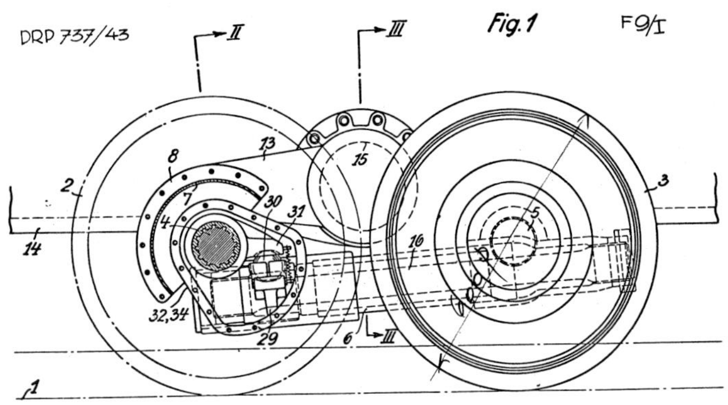

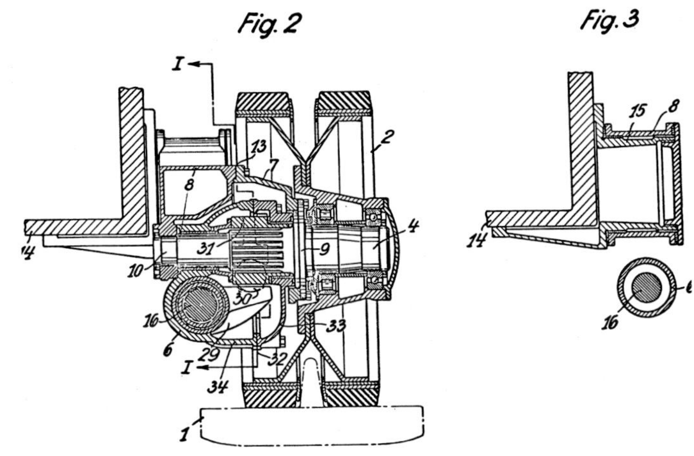

For the suspension of the VK. 3001, Porsche used a patented longitudinal torsion-bar system. The sketches show the technical structure of the wheel trucks.

thorough testing in 1941-42, and the motors in particular caused constant difficulties.

A Diesel powerplant was also supposed to be developed for this vehicle, likewise with an aircooled V-10 motor. A pre-combustion chamber burning system was planned. This powerplant was never built. The Porsche type designation was "200."

In the meantime, Henschel had started to work on a further development of the "*Panzerkampfwagen* VI" with the emphasis on "heaviest armor," the "*Panzerkampfwagen* VII" (VK. 6501), contracted for by the Ordnance Office on September 1, 1939. By the contract for a pre-production series, Henschel was to prepare the chassis and body, while Krupp was responsible for the turret. The Henschel factory code for this vehicle was "SW." When the tasks were set, nobody saw a possibility of building a vehicle of that size that would fit into the railroad loading profile. It was thus planned to separate the vehicle into three pieces, and use mobile cranes to take it apart and put it back together. A time period of three weeks between action at various places was expected.

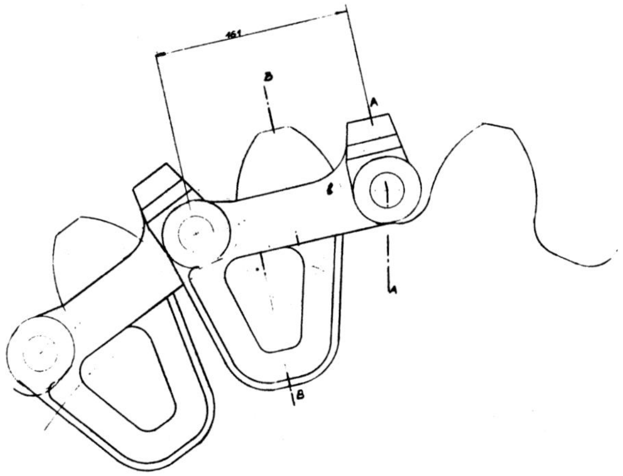

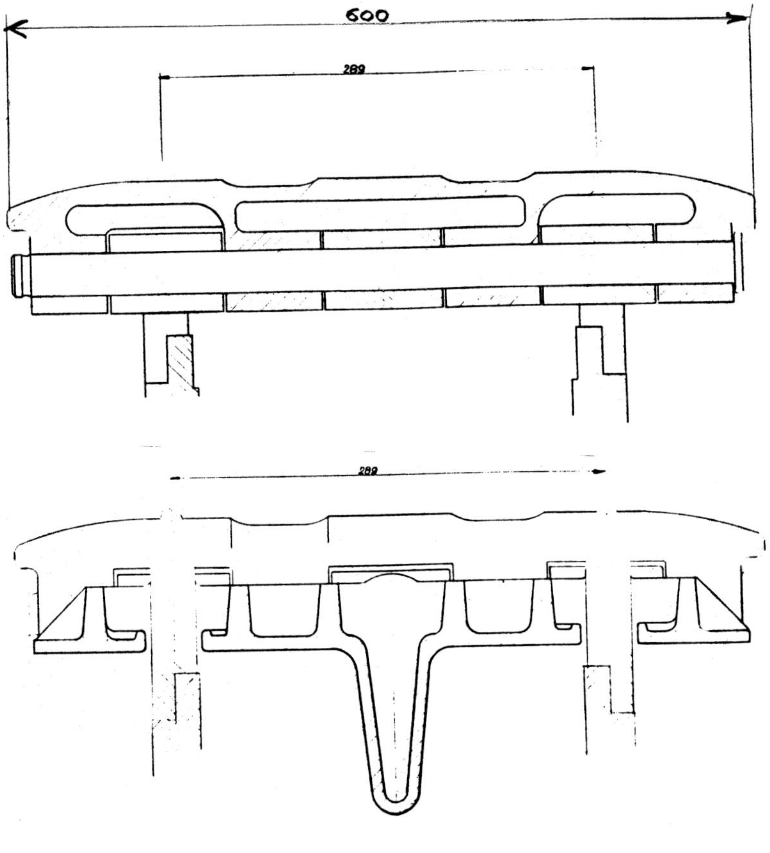

The track design on the Porsche Type 100 (VK. 3001).

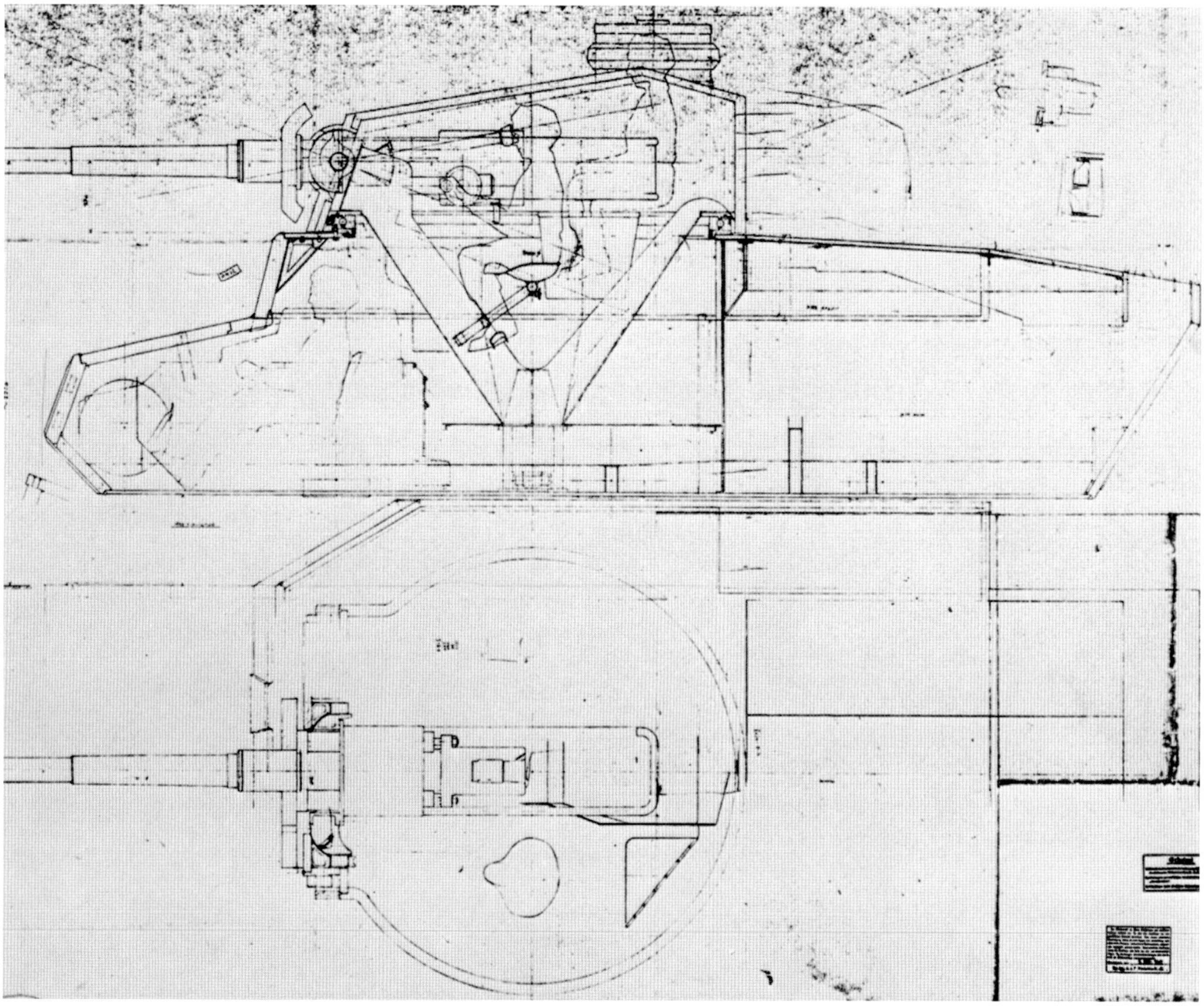

The layout of the hull of the Porsche VK. 3001. The turret was never mounted.

Panzerkampfwagen VK 6501 (H), 3/26/1941

SW Turret (80 mm all around), AW Turret (100 mm all around)

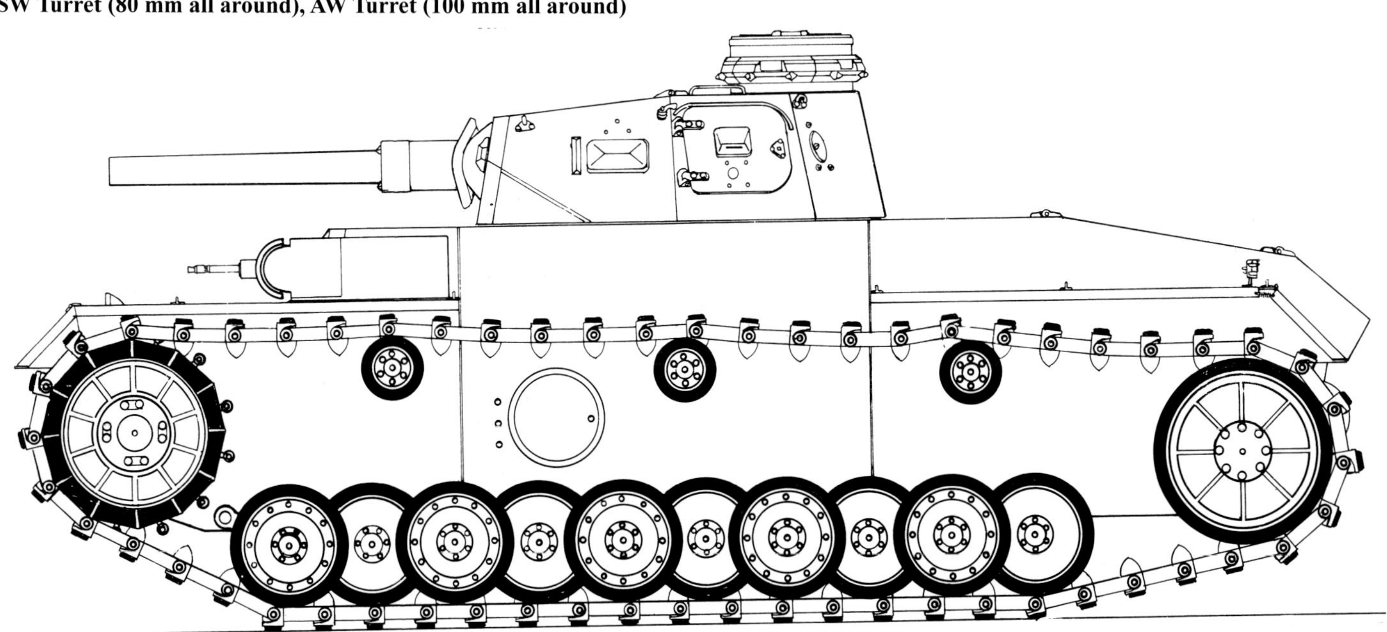

The mobile cranes by Faun of Nürnberg, with bodies by Demag of Benrath, were Faun Type L 900 D 567, which the Ordnance Office had contracted for in 1938 as Road-Rail Crane (LK 5 S). The first test model of the crane was tested in 1939, and seven models of a first series were built. Individual vehicles were sent to the test center at Sennelager, and later also to Kummersdorf. Two together are said to have been able to lift weights up to 20 tons. The hull of the VK. 6501 was laid out in three parts, with side armor plates 80 mm thick. They were connected with tie-bolts, yokes, and bolts with conical seats in the sidewalls. (They look from the inside something like a Hussar's uniform decorations.) The sealing for fording was done with caulking cement. Lateral forces, such as when being fired on, were absorbed by cylindrical blocks, arranged one on top of another, in grooves cut in either side. The thickness of the armor in front of the driver was 100 mm. Alkett had developed the 80 mm visor cover in double-slider form. A 12-cylinder Maybach Type "HL 24" motor that produced 600 HP at 3000 rpm was planned as the powerplant. Cooling air came in from the side, warm air was ducted out through a wide louver in back. The exhaust pipes were not supposed to pass through the rear wall, but over it. The gearbox was newly developed by Maybach. Transmission took place through parallel shafts in a way so that one shaft would be driven without interrupting the driving power when shifting. The other shaft was disconnected and shifted to the desired gear. Then the first shaft was shifted, while the second shaft had to take over the work. The drive of the steering gear with three radii took place via two bevel gears. This design was created by four Henschel designers, who had spent over a year with Maybach, in Friedrichshafen, to develop it. The VK. 6501 was braked by mechanical Perrot brakes. The track drive worked backward at first, like that of the "DW 2," so that not a pin, but the covering cast steel housing had the cutting off of the track drive to transmit to the sidewall. This arrangement was a model for all future designs, not only of Henschel, but also of other firms. The drive wheel was made for the first time as a protective bell of cast steel.

The stepped running gear had nine steel road wheels with rubber tires. The road-wheel cranks were drop-forged. Drop-forged parts from the Krupp firm were planned for production. For the first time it was tried to allow the road wheels a drop by using elastic shape-changing parts. The torsion bars were massively built, and their gearing at the ends was formed in different strengths. On each side, there were four shock absorbers made by the Boge firm at the front and back, set directly on the pins of the road-wheel cranks. Sheet metal attachments for the road-wheel cranks with rubber buffers were planned for all the wheels. The leading wheels consisted of cast steel with forged armor-steel hubs.

The VK 6501 heavy vehicle conceived by Henschel was to be broken down into three loads for transport. Road-rail cranes were to be contracted for by the Ordnance Office. The picture shows the Faun Type "L 900 D 567" that was planned for this project.

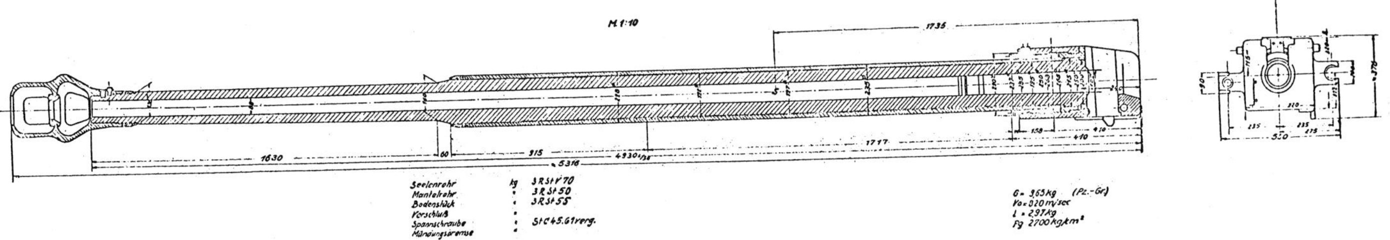

At the end of May 1941 it was decided to use the 8.8 cm Flak gun as a tank gun too. This drawing shows a longitudinal cut through the 8.8 cm KwK L/56 for the Porsche firm's VK. 4501.

A rod spring 70 mm in diameter was provided for the axle of the leading wheel. Changing positions no longer took place by swinging, but by pushing the entire leading-wheel axle. The leading wheel had a rubber tire.

The 65-ton vehicle was planned for a top speed of 25-26 km/h. The five-man crew were to have a 7.5 cm KwK L./24 and an MG 34 at their disposal in the turret. Another MG 34 was planned; it would be in a ball mantlet near the radioman. Two test vehicles were planned. The hulls were made out of soft steel. Many parts, such as suspension arms, were worked, or created as raw parts. Due to the burdens of the factory and the testing department by the production of the VK. 4501 (the Tiger tank), at the end of 1942 WaPrüf 6/III gave permission for all the remaining components to be scrapped, and not to do any testing of the VK. 6501.

On May 26, 1941, Hitler hosted a discussion at his Berghof, in which basic weaponry questions were brought up. Among others, an armored vehicle was promoted that could serve as the "spearhead" of armored units, with some twenty of them per armored division, and should have the following features:

- a greater penetration capability than enemy tanks,
- a heavier armor than previous tanks,
- a speed not to exceed 40 km/h.

In evaluating previous war experiences, and on the basis of the requirements stated by Hitler for greater penetrating power, it was decided to produce—with production starting in May or June 1942—a Vehicle 4501, Porsche type, with 8.8 cm tank gun, as well as a Vehicle 3601, Henschel type, with the 0725 weapon with a conical barrel.

It was required that both vehicles being developed—Professor Porsche's and Henschel's—should continue, so that in the summer of 1942 their use in the planned numbers (six of each) could be reckoned on. The Porsche version was favored for the use of the 8.8 cm gun, the effect of which was to be upgraded, so that 100 mm armor could be pierced at a range of 1500 meters. Since the 8.8 cm gun had been developed originally as a pure anti-aircraft gun, a planned further development for antitank use appeared to be possible and favorable. There was no objection to the use of the 0725 gun in the Henschel version, but this gun could be produced in large numbers only if a satisfactory source of tungsten could be found. Mounting the 8.8 cm gun on the Henschel tank was to be tried. The contract with the Krupp firm for designing the turret with the 0725 weapon was given on May 26, 1941. The first 0725 barrel—provided other work could be postponed—was to be ready for firing on November 1, 1941. Developing ammunition for it was supposed to be finished by the beginning of 1942. The effect of expediting the first twelve vehicles was still to be reported on.

The Ordnance Office indicated that new territory was going to be entered for both versions. In the Porsche solution, the aircooled tank motor and the gasoline-electric principle were not yet tested. The Henschel firm had been able to gain a lot of experience with the motor and running gear of the 30-ton vehicle in two years of running, but further test work was still necessary. Hitler declared again that both versions were to be developed independently of each other.

The full size wooden dummy of the Porsche VK. 4501 shows the driver's seat with the control levers. In the middle are compressed-air tanks to support braking.

By using experience gained in building the VK. 3001 (P), the Nibelungenwerk built the first prototypes of the "VK. 4501 (P)," in which the installation of the 8.8 cm KwK L/56 was planned in the course of upgrading the tank gun. The turret for it had just been ordered by Porsche from Krupp, and was being developed by the two firms in direct cooperation. The Ordnance Office, because of other obligations, had not given a development contract to the Krupp firm.

Originally, a test series of ten of the "Special Vehicle II," the Porsche Type "101," had been planned. With a total weight of some 59 tons, the "*Panzerkampfwagen* VI, VK. 4501 (P) Tiger (P)" was to have two parallel V-10 gasoline engines of Type "101/1" installed. The two-engine arrangement was chosen to produce as much power as possible in the limited engine compartment. The crankshaft of each motor was connected directly to an electric generator, which in turn had a cooling fan for the motor built in. The "101" motor type was an aircooled four-stroke gasoline engine with magneto ignition. The cylinders formed a 72-degree V and had drop valves, operated by tappets. Other details were: Motor type 101/3 A, Porsche design, made by Simmering-Graz-Pauker.

The removal of the mechanical transmission parts and the movement of the powerplant to the rear provided an unusual amount of space in the front of the vehicle. At upper left is the driver's visor, at upper right the MG 34 operated by the radioman.

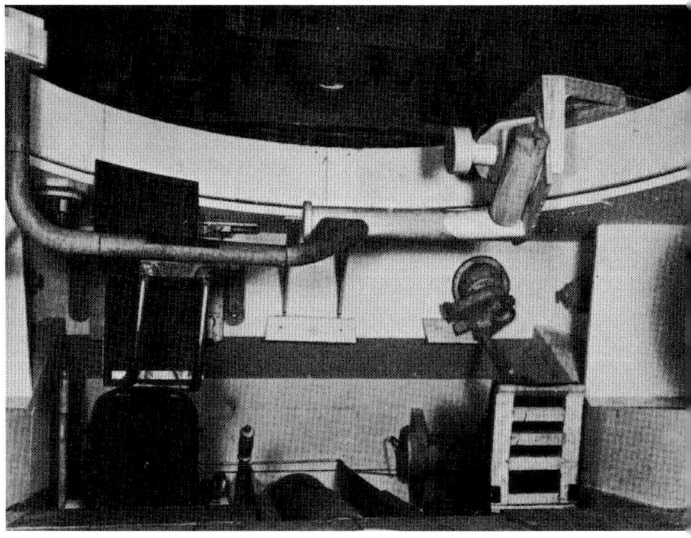

A look from the fighting compartment toward the turret turning circle.

Parts of the vehicle's electric equipment.

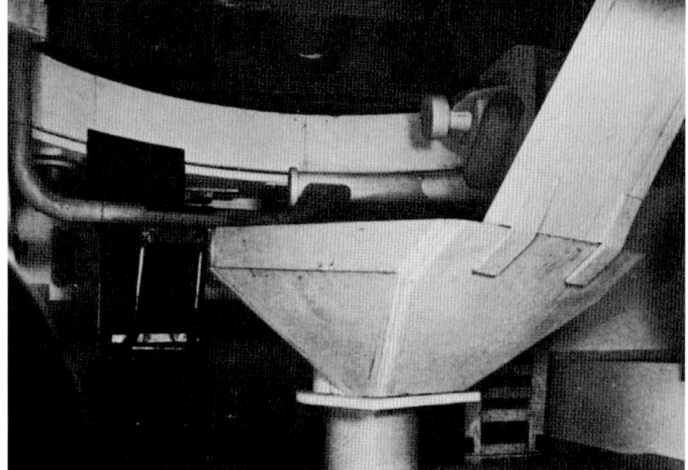

The seat for the gunner.

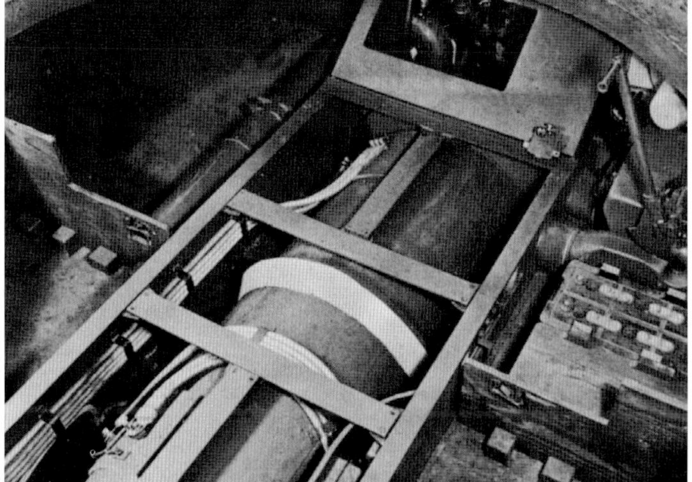

Left: A look at the breech of the dummy gun. The machine gun is at far right.

The ammunition was stored in the bays of the tank's body.

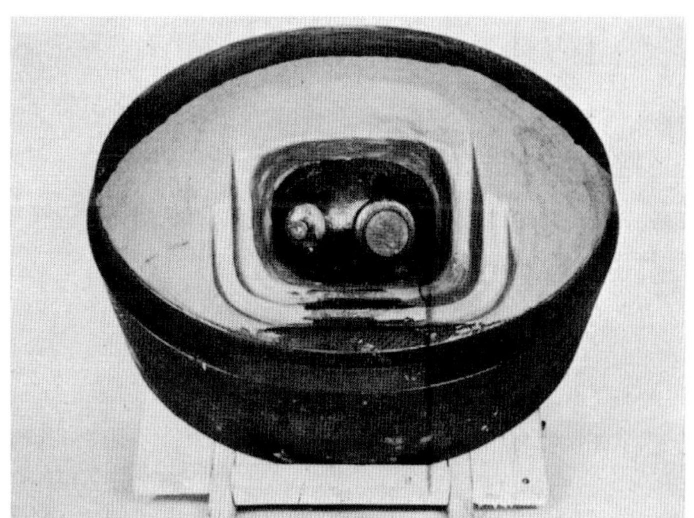

The suggested mount of the radioman's machine gun in a ball mantlet.

Panzerkampfwagen VK 4501 (P)

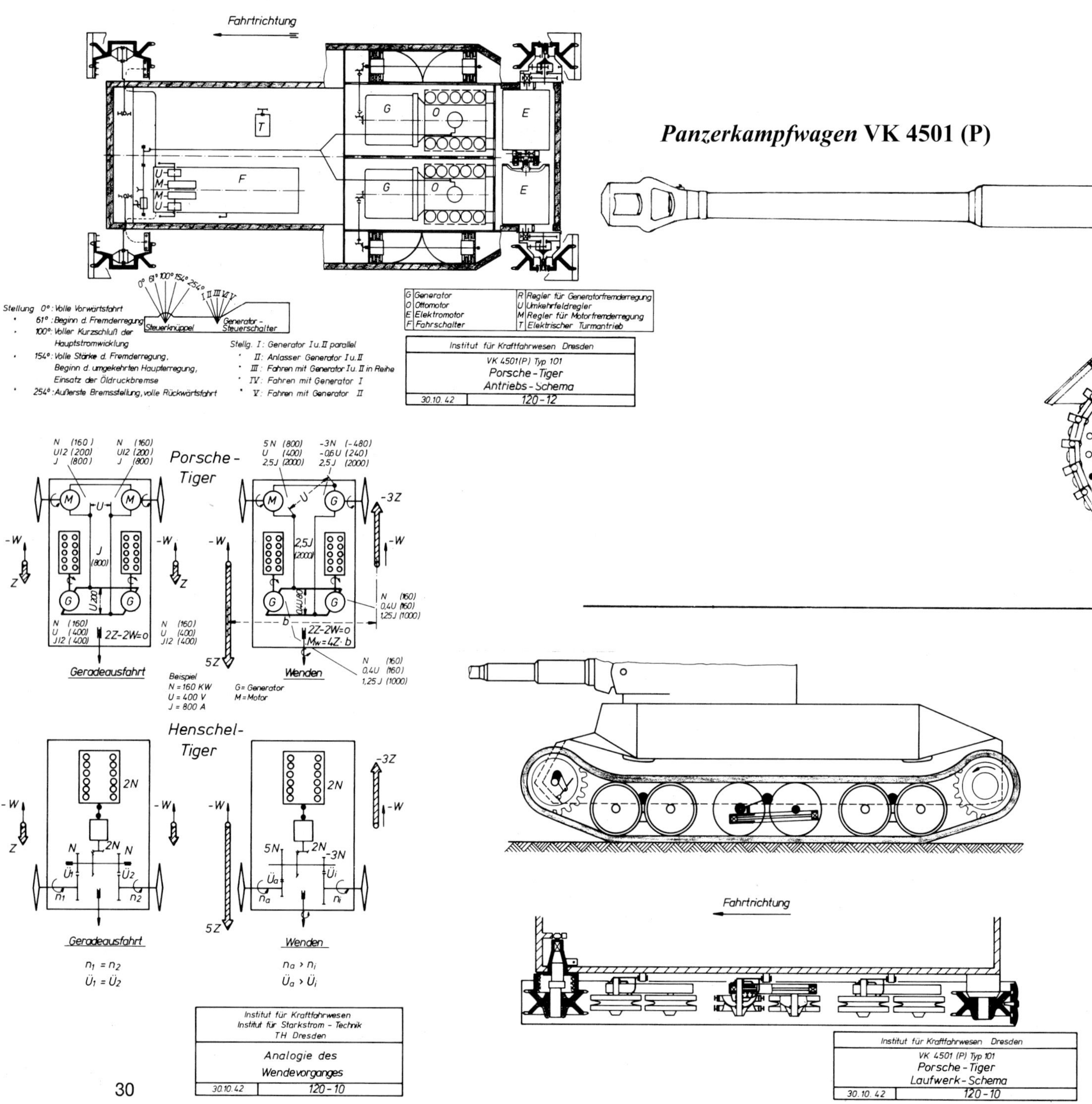

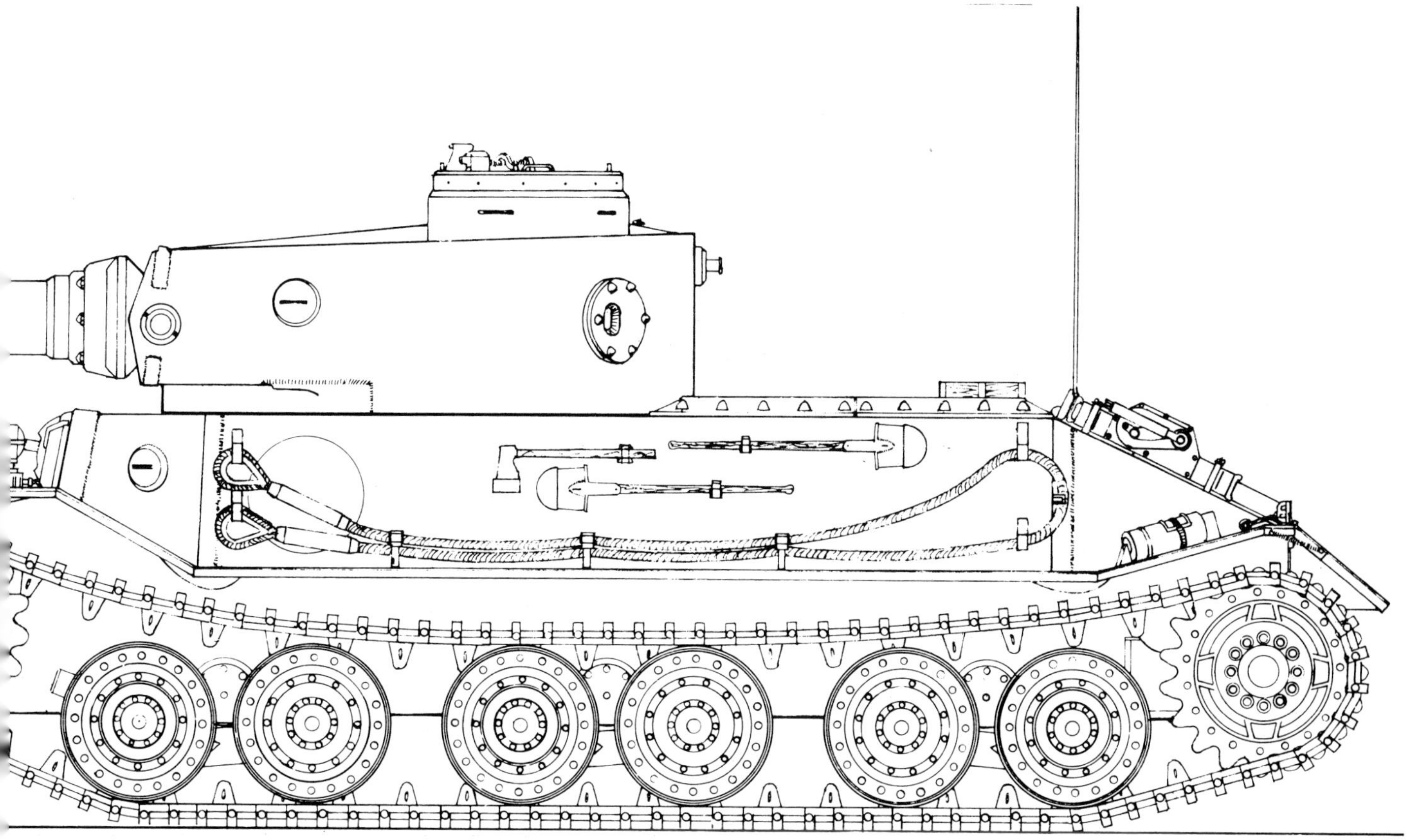

Engine power (per motor)	320 HP at 2500 rpm
Fuel consumption	250-270 g/hp/hr
Piston speed	12.1 m/sec at 2500 rpm
Torque	105 m/kg at 1900 rpm
Bore	115 mm
Stroke	145 mm
Displacement	15,060 cc
Cylinders (per motor)	10
Compression ratio	5.9 : 1
Cylinder heads	aluminum
Valves	drop, with tappets and rockers
Crankshaft bearings	6 journal bearings
Motor mountings	3
Spark plugs	Bosch W 25
Carburetor	1 Solex 50 JFF 2
Cooling	air-cooled by fans
Total weight of motor and Generator	1500 kg
Motor weight (dry)	450 kg
Weight with cooling fan	80 kg
Firing order	1-8-3-10-5-9-4-7-2-6

The dummy motor shows the connection with the generator. Over the generator are the engine cooling fans.

In the first Type 101 motors, the belt connections of motor, generator, and cooling fan are easy to see.

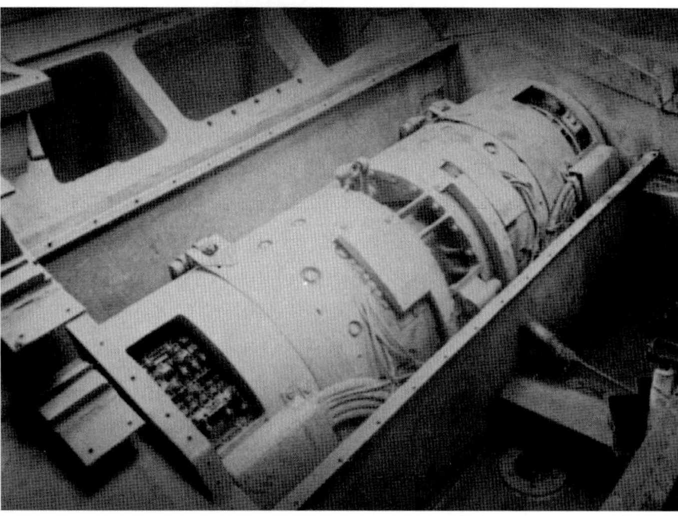

The two electric drive motors were mounted transversely in the vehicle.

The generator also served as the starter, and was fed by two 12-volt batteries. The motors were started one after the other. Long-term tests of the aircooled motors were carried out at the Simmering-Graz-Pauker AG in Vienna. The starter in the subsequent series of 35 vehicles was to be half of a Volkswagen motor (Type 141). This produced 9 HP at 2200 rpm. To start a main engine, though, at least

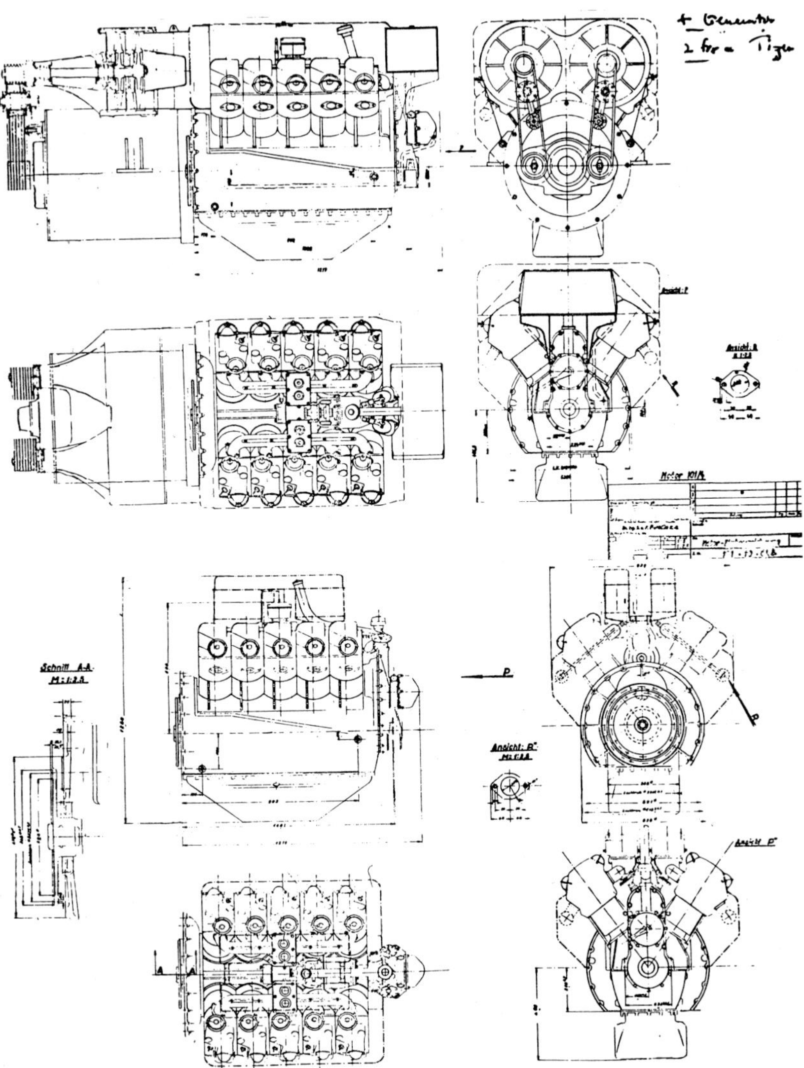

The drawings show the structure of the 101 motors.

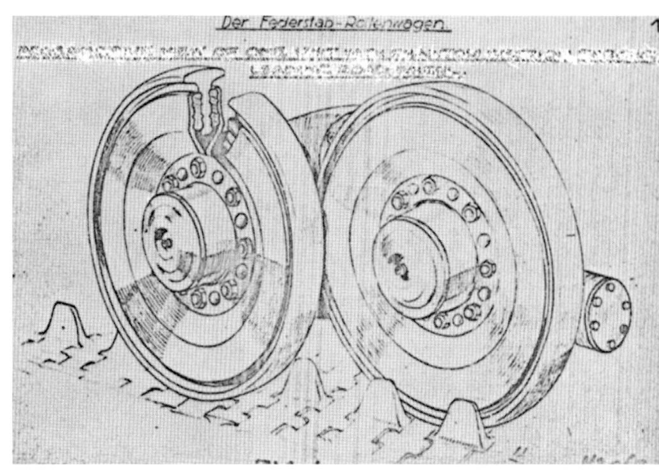

Above: Drawings of the Porsche wheel trucks, which were also used for VK. 4501.

Above left: The picture shows one of the first VK. 4501 hulls. At the front is the turret turning circle, and behind it the engine compartment with the front mounts for the two motors.

Left: The hull of the second prototype as seen from the front. The openings for the driver's visor and the ball mantlet for the machine gun can be seen.

18 HP was needed. Thus, a Bosch "AL/SED" centrifugal starter was used. The electric power transmission parts were supplied by the Siemens-Schuckert firm. Electric power passed from two direct-current generators to two electric motors, which directly operated the rear mounted drive sprockets. The power ratio was 1 : 15, and the diameter of the sprocket was 794 mm. A top speed of 35 km/h was expected. The running gear included 12 double steel road wheels on each side, mounted in pairs on longitudinal torsion bars. The pressure was 4250 kg per road wheel. To attain a bearable ground pressure of about 1 kg/cm^2, the tracks had to be widened during development from an original 500 mm to 600 mm, then to a final width of 640 mm (track type Kgs 62/640/130). The links measured 130 mm.

The main fuel tank, mounted over the generators, contained 520 liters, making the range only 50 km. Since Hitler wanted particularly to use these tanks in Africa, an action radius of at least 150 km was required, but there was no space in the vehicle.

The aircooled motors of these vehicles had problems from the start of development. To be able to test the VK. 4501 prototypes built in the interim, the VK. 3001 (P) was used as a power producing vehicle. The pictures show how the VK. 3001 (P) supplied the electrics of the VK. 4501 (P) with power by cable.

The VK. 4501 (P) is seen in rough country with an experimental turret. Professor Dr. F. Porsche is on the turret.

The central series of pictures shows a VK. 4501 (P) during dust checking. As one can see, the engine compartment is completely filled by the two motors.

Reich Minister Speer often visited the *Nibelungenwerk* to check on the progress made on the Porsche Tiger vehicles. Here a ladder makes his entry into the vehicle easier.

Speer thoroughly examined the vehicles himself. Here he takes an initial test drive on the factory grounds. In the background is a Panzer IV.

A prototype on which a turret has been mounted is being road tested on a paved road.

The second series of 35 vehicles was to be delivered by January 1943, with the remaining 45 expected by the end of April. The last series was to have the Type "101/2" motor, in which both oil coolers were mounted at the back of the motors. The magneto was also located in the "V" of the motors.

Along with the aircooled Type "101" engine, which could not be put into production because of technical problems, Porsche also worked on the development of water cooled gasoline engines for this vehicle. The Type "130" was planned as a V-10 motor with bore and stroke of 130 x 145 mm for electric drive, while the Type "131," with the same dimensions, was to be used for a vehicle with hydraulic drive. With a displacement of 19.3 liters, a performance of 400 HP at 2500 rpm was expected. A double arrangement of the powerplants was planned again. For the "101" vehicle, a pre-ignition chamber Diesel engine with air cooling was also planned, likewise to be used with electric drive. In the one-cylinder Type "191" test motor, a cylinder size of 120 x 145 mm gave 1.64 liters. The Simmering pre-ignition chamber burning system was supposed to be used, and a V-10 "190" powerplant with a displacement of 16.4 liters was expected to produce 400 HP at 2500 rpm. None of these motors was built, and all studies in favor of a 16-cylinder "X" Diesel engine were halted.

Only a few of the prototypes were fitted with Krupp turrets, which held the 8.8 cm KwK L/56, plus a coaxial MG 34. Another

The high ground pressure of the VK. 4501 (P) often led to such problems. Here two other Porsche Tigers are needed to tow out the stock vehicle.

MG 34 was installed in a Ball Mantlet 80 in front of the radioman's seat. An ammunition supply of 70 rounds was carried, 50 of them at hand in the hull, with the others just over the hull floor. The usual five-man crew operated the vehicle.

For the vehicle already in production, 25 mm floor armor was ordered. As for weapons, the option of installing a 15 cm KwK L/37 or a 10 cm KwK L/70 was to be tried. Professor Porsche announced the delivery of the first production vehicles for May 12, 1942.

In 1940 and 1941, Henschel redesigned and enlarged the armored body at Works III in Mittelfeld. The effect of this expansion, though, did not come into use until 1942-43. Henschel production included not only the working of the armored housings of the running-gear parts, delivered from the steel works, but also the track drive, the track guiding—with adjusting of the track tension, when planned—the jack rollers, the steering gear, the gears for turning the turret, the driver's seat and controls, the ammunition storage, the drive for the radiator fan. the exhaust system, the entry and servicing hatches, and all the assembly work until the vehicle was ready for use. The welded and tempered armored body, the tracks, the ready-to-use turrets, the optical devices, the rubber tires for the running gear, all the bearings, driveshafts, radiators with fans, motors, gearboxes, suspension elements, shock absorbers, and other pieces of equipment, such as tools and measuring instruments, were delivered or provided by sub-contractors or army service agencies.

In the meantime, Henschel had worked on Wagen 3601*, which was supposed to be built, after acceptance by the Ordnance Office on May 26, 1941, by Henschel (chassis) and Krupp (turret), and for which the following building requirements were defined: 100 mm armor in front, 60 mm on the sides; top speed 40 km/h; weapon with 100 mm piercing power at 1400 meters; and great explosive effect of the shells. Henschel was under contract to build one plus six test models of this "VK. 3601," which were to be delivered from April 1942 on. With a weight of 36 to 40 tons, a gun with a Type 0725 conical barrel was first planned as the primary armament. The armor thickness of the turret had been set at 80/60 mm. Changed running gear now had large disc wheels with flat sheet-steel discs without spokes, which made jack rollers unnecessary. Although it turned out very quickly that the "VKL. 3601" could only be seen as an intermediate step toward further development, the "Panzer Program 41," which was set up on May 30, 1941, included the equipping of the Panzer troops with the "*Panzerkampfwagen* VI-VK. 3601" in great numbers. A first stage of 116, and a final total of 172 vehicles of this type were foreseen. Variations of the vehicles were also to be produced: "*Panzerbefehlswagen*" and "*schwerster Betonknacker.*" Since the turret for this vehicle—on account of the Führer's order that conical barrels could no longer be used—was not developed any farther, it was decided in September 1942 to prepare four of these chassis, other than the one test chassis for Oberbaurat Kniekamp, quickly as towing tractors for Tiger tanks. The chassis had to be

* Officially also called *Panzerkampfwagen* VI, Type B.

***Panzerkampfwagen* VK 3601 (H)**

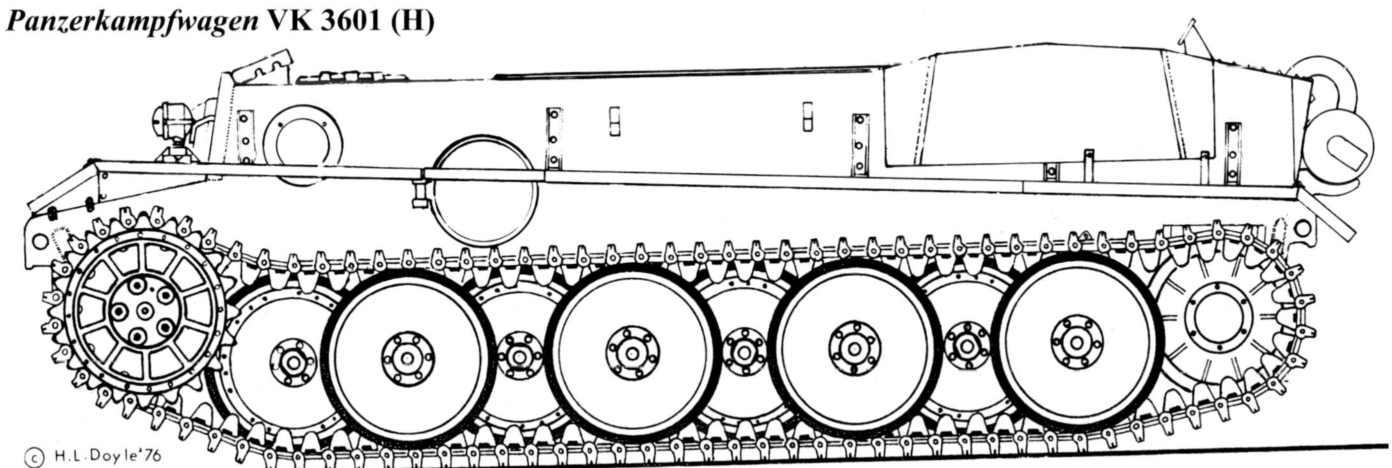

adapted to carry a 40-ton cable winch made by FAMO-Ursus. In particular, the winch drive from the gearbox had to be developed. The chassis would also be fitted with the Maybach HL 210 motor, instead of the originally planned Maybach HL 174. The chassis were finished—without interrupting Tiger production—in 1942, since Hitler had objected that there was no towing vehicle available for the Tiger.

The insufficient piercing ability of the primary weapon used until then required new solutions.

At the Berghof on April 26, 1941, Hitler had given the following instructions:

"If from a smaller caliber than 8.8 cm (such as 6 or 7.5 cm) an equal penetrating ability can result, then for reasons of ammunition supply and turret weight this can be advantageous. The chosen caliber must be suitable for attacking tanks, ground targets, and bunkers."

After testing by the Ordnance Office, an 8.8 cm gun allowed an operating diameter of 1850 mm, as opposed to one of 1650 mm for the Weapon 0725. The larger turret diameter alone, with 80 mm front and 60 mm side armor, gave a turret weight of 2.2 tons.

In mid-1941 the request was made for armor-piercing performance of 100 mm at a range of 1500 meters. In mid-July 1941, the Ordnance Office gave the Rheinmetall firm a contract for a turret whose shells had an armor-piercing ability of 140 mm at 1000 meters, without specifically requesting that the caliber be 8.8 mm.

The contract for the 8.8 cm KwK was also given in June 1941 to the Friedrich Krupp AG, which developed this weapon out of the 8.8 cm Flak. The barrel length was 4930 mm = L/56, and the weight of the weapon was 1310 kg.

Rheinmetall tried to attain the required firing performance by using a KwK with a cylindrical barrel, which was supposed to arise on the basis of the Pak 44 that Hitler wanted. The use of such barrels, though, was very much dependent on the raw material

As an interim stage of development, the VK. 3601 of the Henschel firm got nowhere. The pictures below show a prototype driven offroad by Minister Speer. Professor Porsche sits on the side of the hull. The slim upper body made it impossible to carry an 8.8 cm gun.

But since Henschel had to install the 8.8 cm gun, there arose the VK. 4501 (H), in which the armored upper body now hung over the running gear.

Removing the turret from the first VK. 4501 test vehicle at the Henschel test site in Haustenbeck i. L.

The turret is being taken off by an 18-ton towing truck with a 10-ton crane (Sd.Kfz. 9/2). In the right background is a 22-ton low-loader trailer (Sd.Anh. 116).

situation. Germany could no longer afford to buy large amounts of tungsten for gun production without risking the industry's need for tool steel. Minister Todt had at this point referred to the supply of some 700 tons on hand, of which about 260 tons were available for armaments. The need for the Weapon 0725 was calculated as about one kg of tungsten per shell. As long as this need was not met, or an equally good substitute was not found for industry, the development and improved performance offers that did not depend on tungsten were given priority. A further directive of Hitler ordered that conical barrels must no longer be needed. Therefore, the Henschel firm had to take over, with minor modifications, the turret developed by Professor Porsche at Krupp, since with the shortness of time no other solution was possible anymore. This measure compelled a change of the chassis being developed by Henschel, so that the Henschel type also became a 45-ton vehicle (VK. 4501 (H)). Front armor 100 mm thick was regarded as necessary. On the sides, 60

This picture shows the removed turret with stage and turning gear.

The turret is set on a prepared wooden frame.

mm sufficed for the Porsche and Henschel vehicles. At the same time, and above all else, tracks and drive sprockets were to be protected by armor in front. The contract with the Henschel firm for a new design of the vehicle with track and sprocket protection, and the possibility of mounting a turret with the 8.8 cm gun, was issued on May 5, 1941.

The track and sprocket protection required by the *Führer* was supposed to be attached so it could be raised and lowered. The required laborious hydraulic apparatus and its vulnerability to disturbance, plus the fact that no sufficient protection from diagonal side shots could be expected anyway, led to this feature being dropped at the time of the first showing.

Production

The "VK. 4501 (H)" consisted of the chassis and 360-degree-turnable turret. The turret, with the commander's cupola, armor shield, and gun, set on the armored hull, and turned on ball bearings. To hold the larger turret diameter, a new hull with side extensions was needed, in which the cooling system was also located. The armored hull was divided into fighting and engine compartments by a wall, and held the powerplant, power transmission, and running-gear bearings.

The first 250 vehicles had the Maybach "HL 210 P 30" motor installed, which produced 600 to 650 HP. From chassis no. 250 251 on, the "HL 230 P 45," producing 650 to 700 HP, was used. This was a water-cooled V-12 gasoline engine with two rows of cylinders and dry-sump lubrication. The circulation pump cooling consisted of two radiators, set one behind the other in the cooling water circulation; the ventilator casings, with two ventilators for

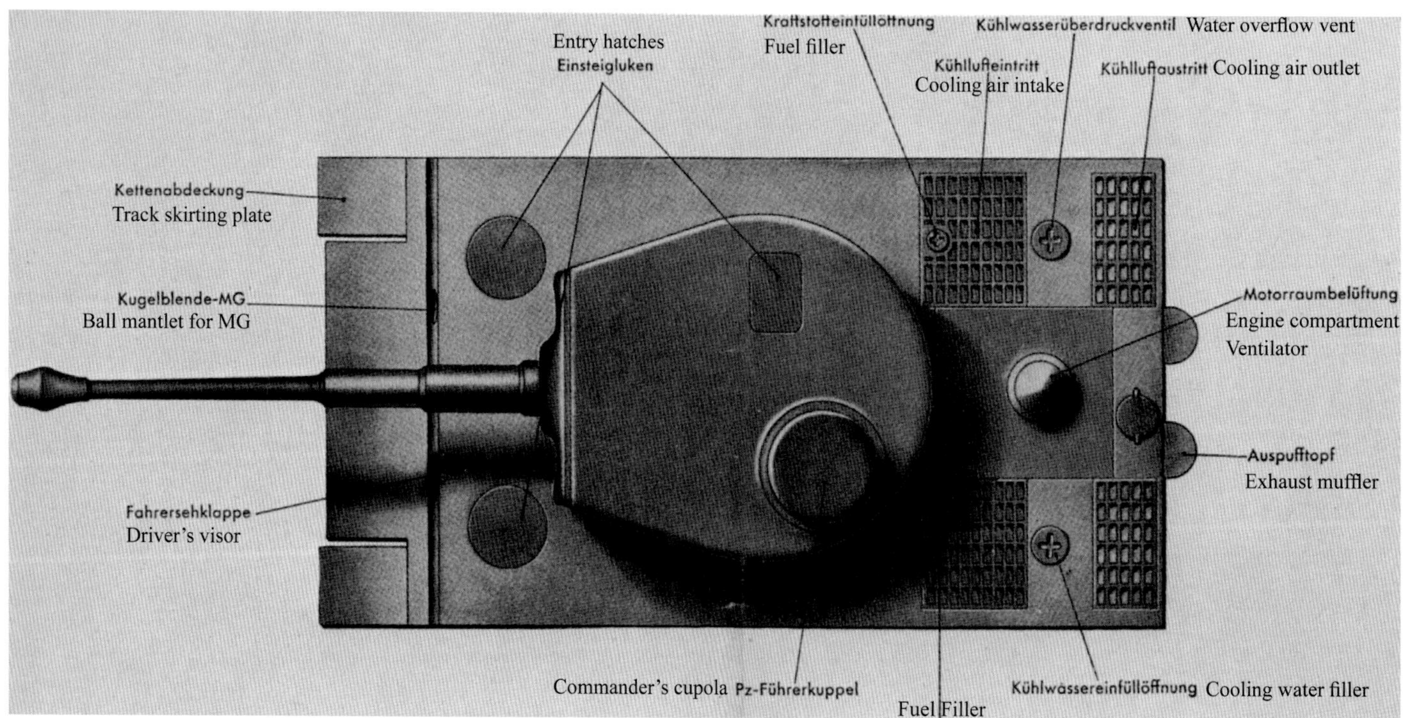

This top view shows the general layout of the vehicle.

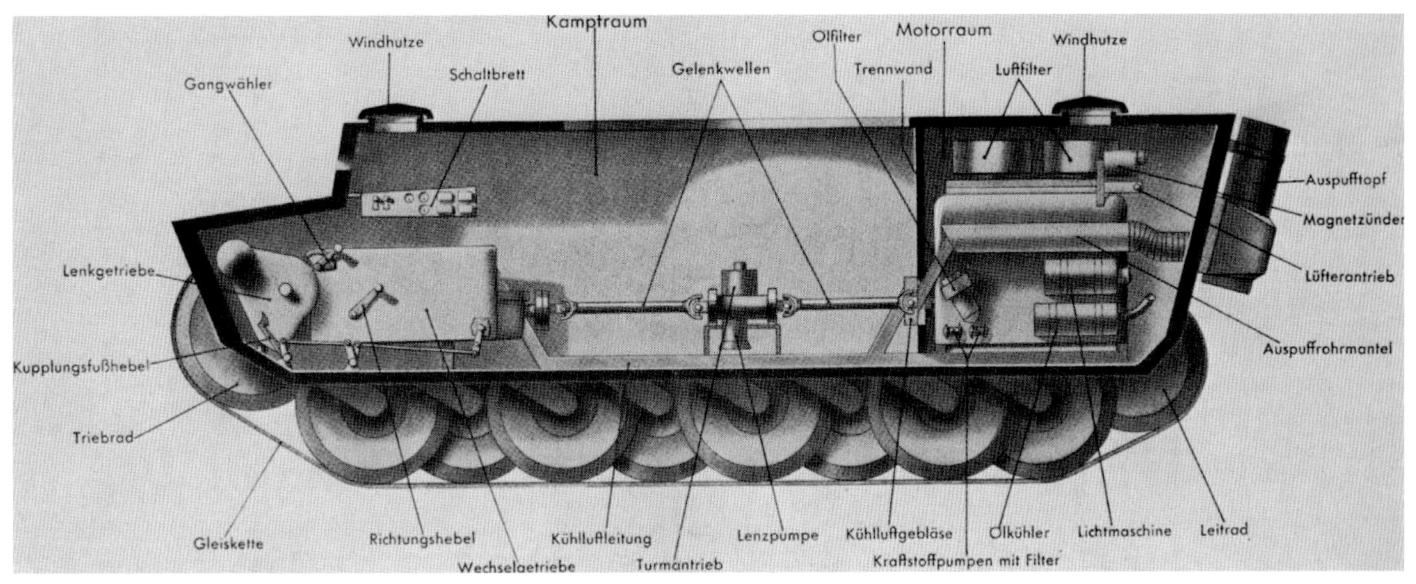

A longitudinal cut through the chassis.

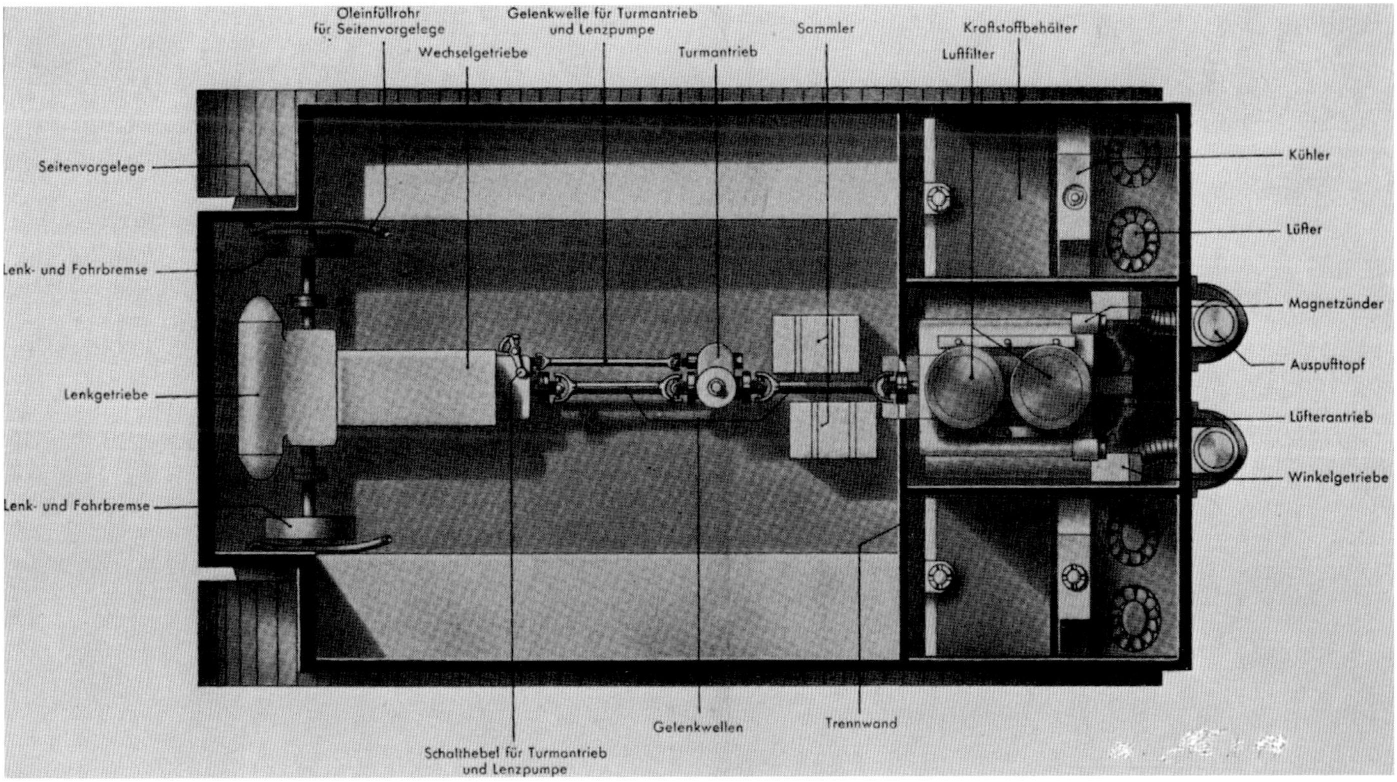

Top view and power flow, schematically depicted.

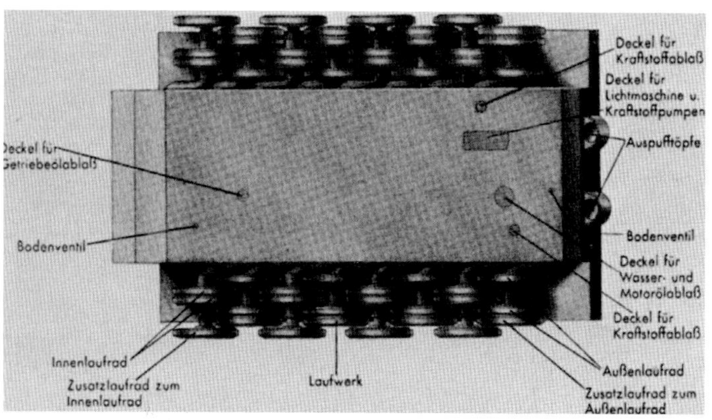

The armored hull from below.

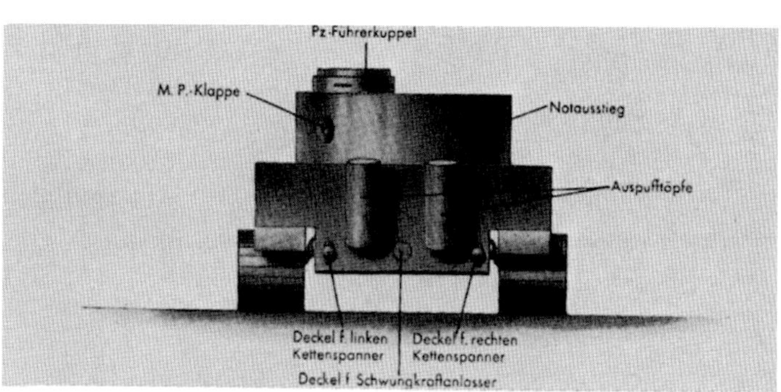

A schematic rear view of the "Tiger."

The engine compartment before the engine was installed.

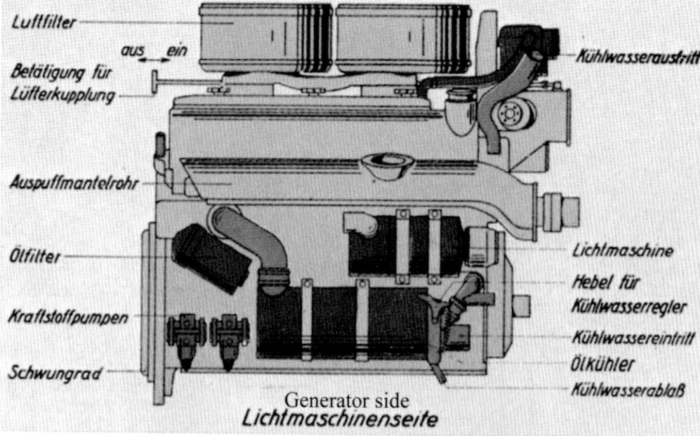

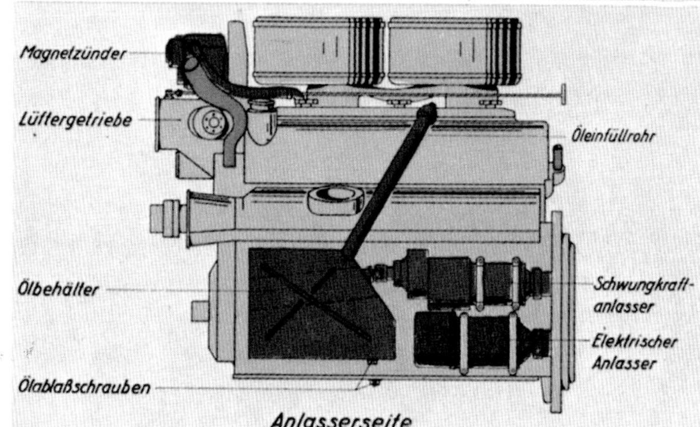

A schematic portrayal of the Maybach "HL 230" motor.

The motor seen from the flywheel side (left).

The motor from behind.

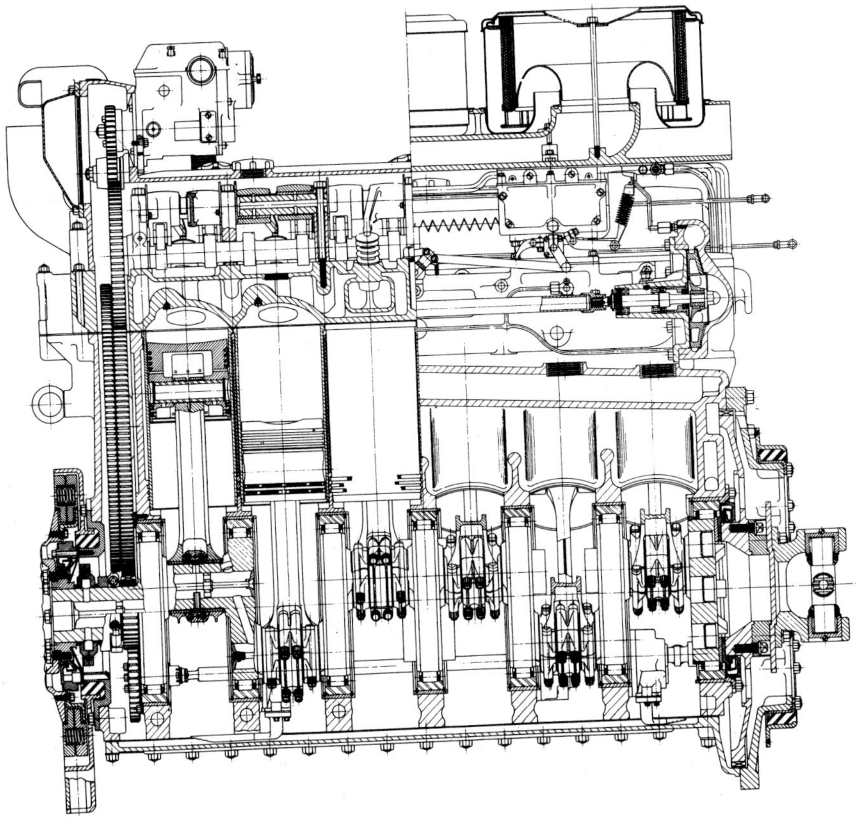

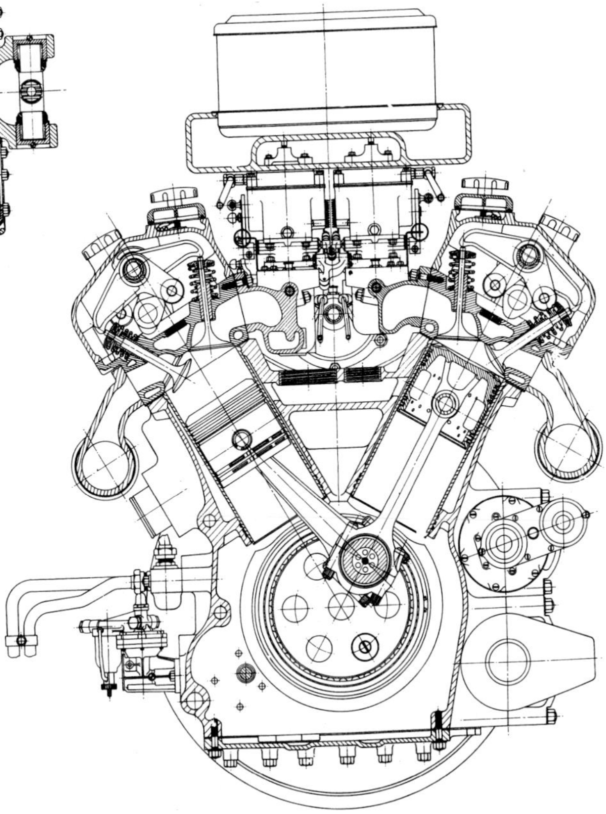

Longitudinal and transverse cuts through the "Tiger" motor.

The crankcase of the motor, with the opening for the camshaft drive.

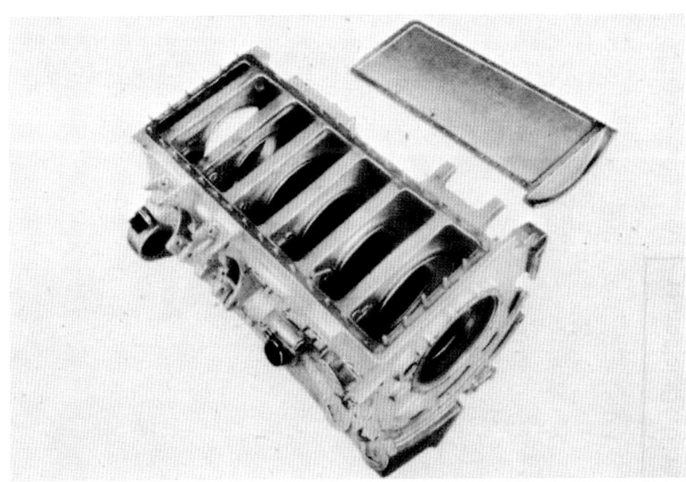

The crankcase from below.

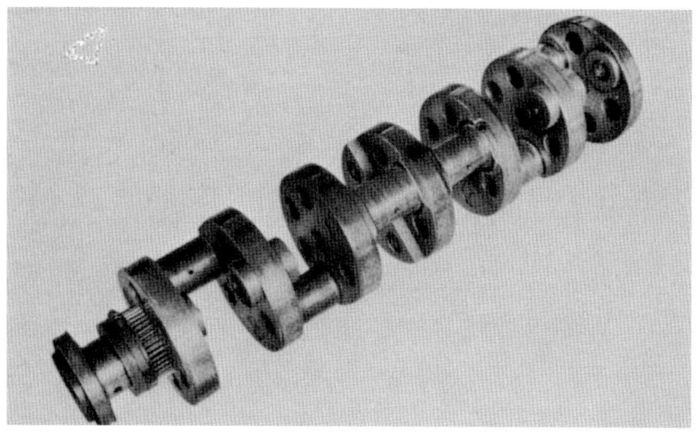

The crankshaft

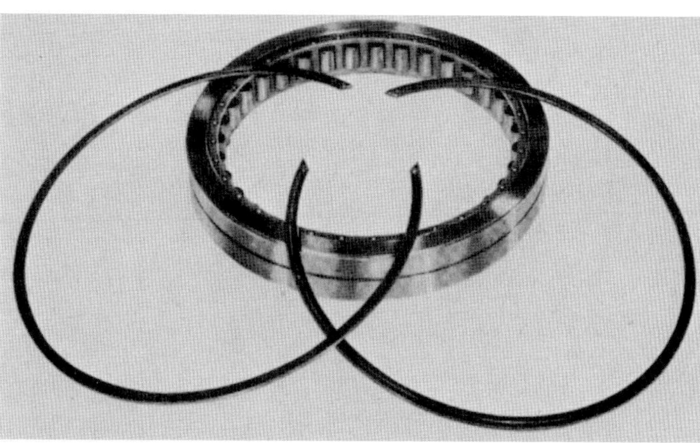

One of the seven main roller bearings.

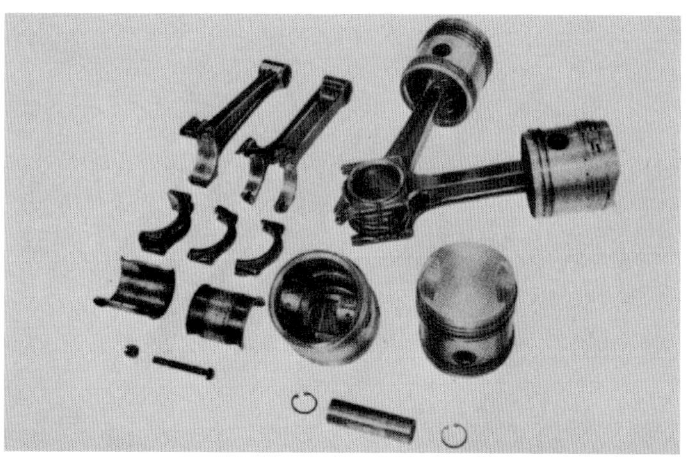

Pistons and connecting rods, with bolts and bearing shells.

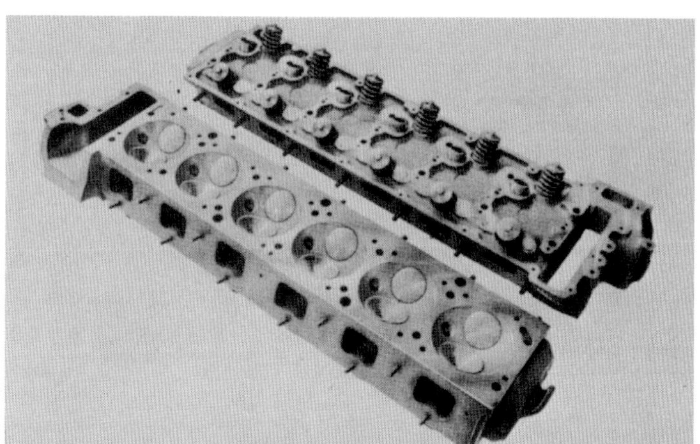

The cylinder heads with camshafts and rockers removed.

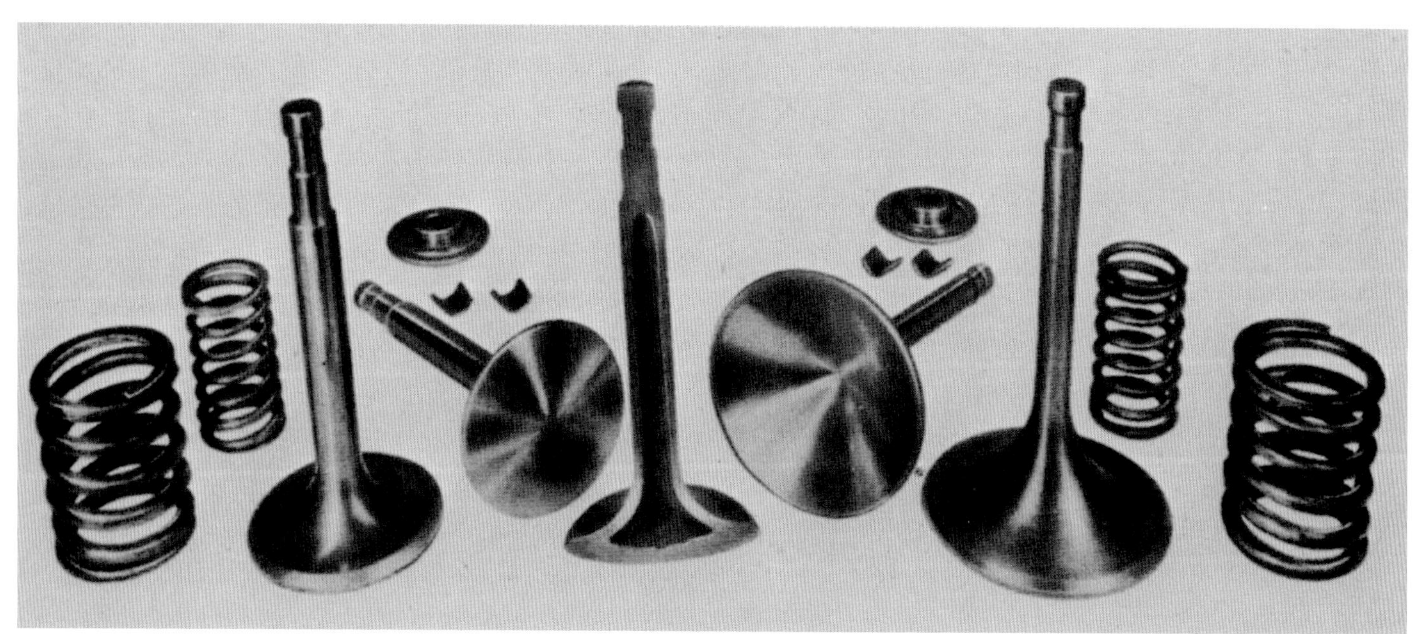

The valves and valve springs. One of the exhaust valves, filled with natrium, is cut open.

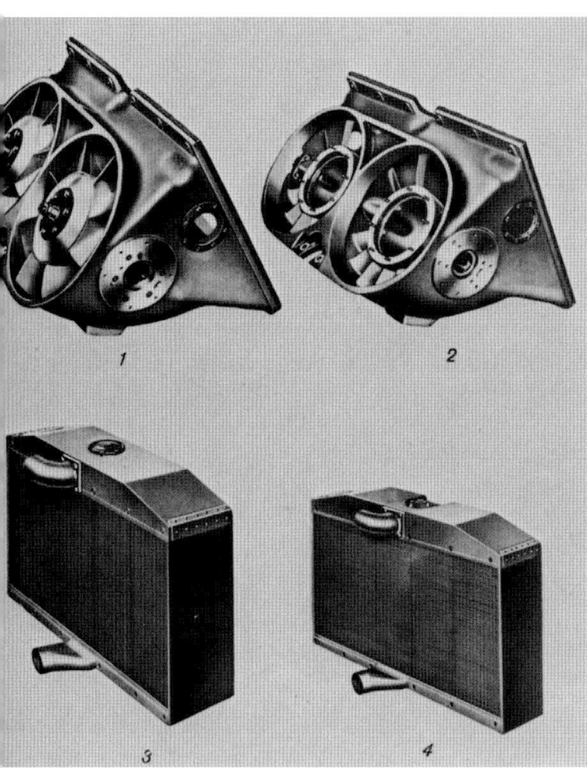

Parts of the cooling system: the complete right and left ventilators (1, 2) and the radiators (3, 4).

each radiator, the oil cooler, the water pump, and the connections and the thermostat for transmitting cooling water. The ventilators were driven by the motor via a two-speed gearbox, a two-plate clutch, a bevel drive, and one angular gear each.

In all, 19 gears were required. In the first 250 series vehicles, a simplified two-stage cooling system was installed. A blower mounted on the compartment wall cooled the gearbox, as well as the exhaust system. A flow regulator limited the top speed to 2500 rpm. The four built-in fuel tanks held some 534 liters. The reserves of the pairs of tanks were enough for about 30 km of on-road driving. The fuel was pumped by two Solex double tappets pumps to the carburetors. Four Solex double offroad carburetors created the mixture of gasoline and air. The oil strainer air filters

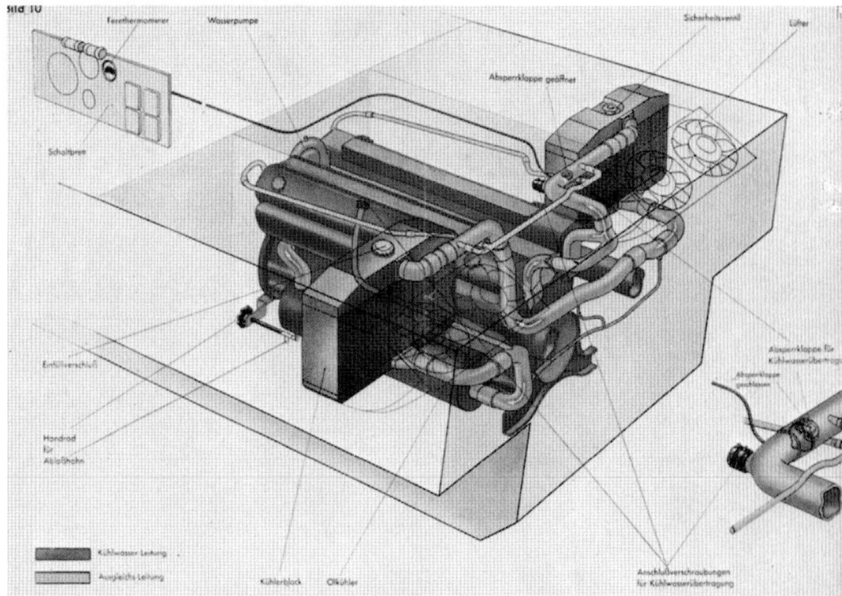

The cooling system of the "Tiger" tank.

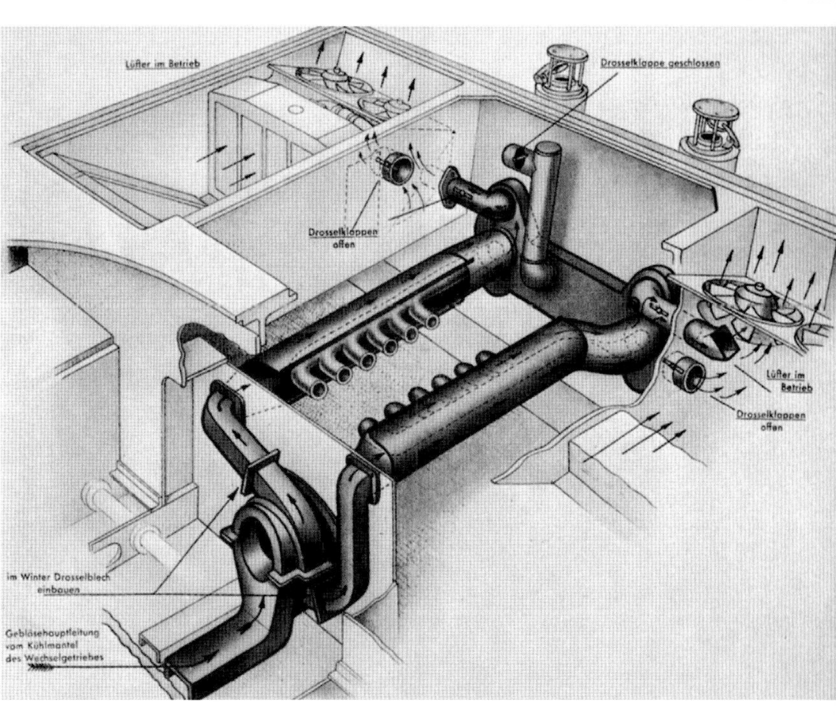

A schematic drawing of the ventilation system.

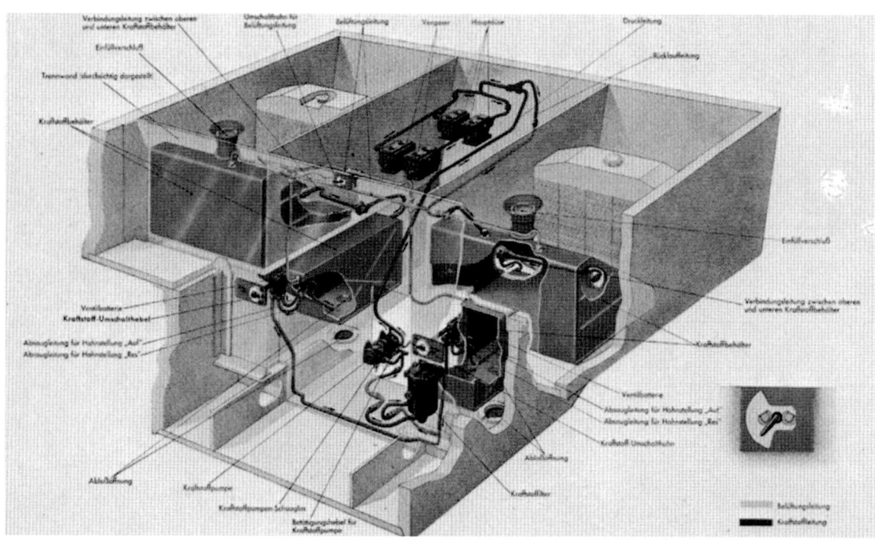

The fuel system with the four tanks.

were mounted on the motor. The use of the vehicles in Africa and southern Russia led for a long time to an additional arrangement of "Feifel" dry filters. These were attached to the outside of the rear hull wall, and connected by flexible tubes to an added air louver. These added filters were dropped at the start of 1944.

The motor was connected with the gearbox by two driveshafts. They were mounted in the turret drive housing. The turret drive was powered by an auxiliary shaft in the gearbox via a driveshaft, a conical clutch, and the second pair of bevel gears in the turret drive housing. From there on, the drive was carried via a plate clutch to the fluid drive, and by a driveshaft to the turning machine.

The Maybach "Olvar" gearbox, Type "OG 40 12 16," was semi-automatic. It was an eight-speed wheel gearbox with claw shifting and built-in main clutch. All eight forward and four reverse speeds were chosen with the selector lever located on the gearbox. The self-acting shift functioned with the aid of oil pressure.

The mail clutch was a wet-plate type. It was built into the gearbox, and served to interrupt the power flow between the motor

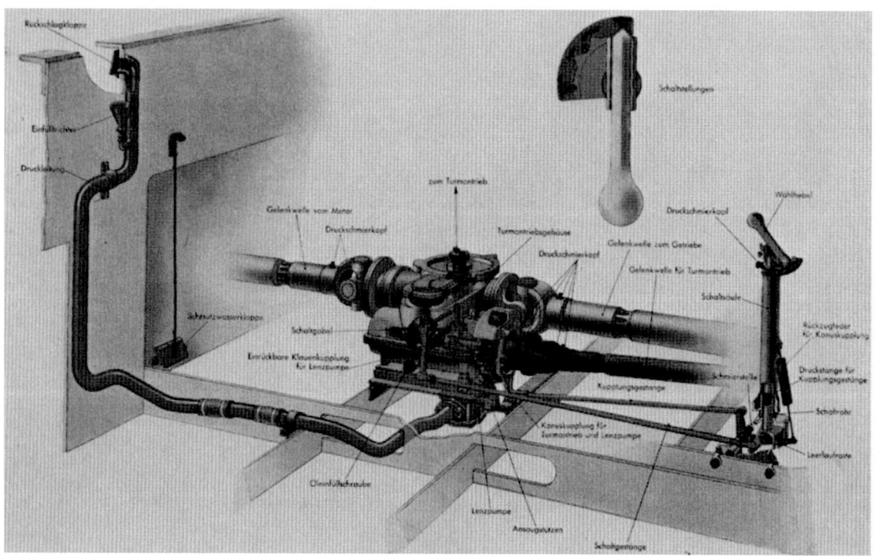

The turret drive with drain system.

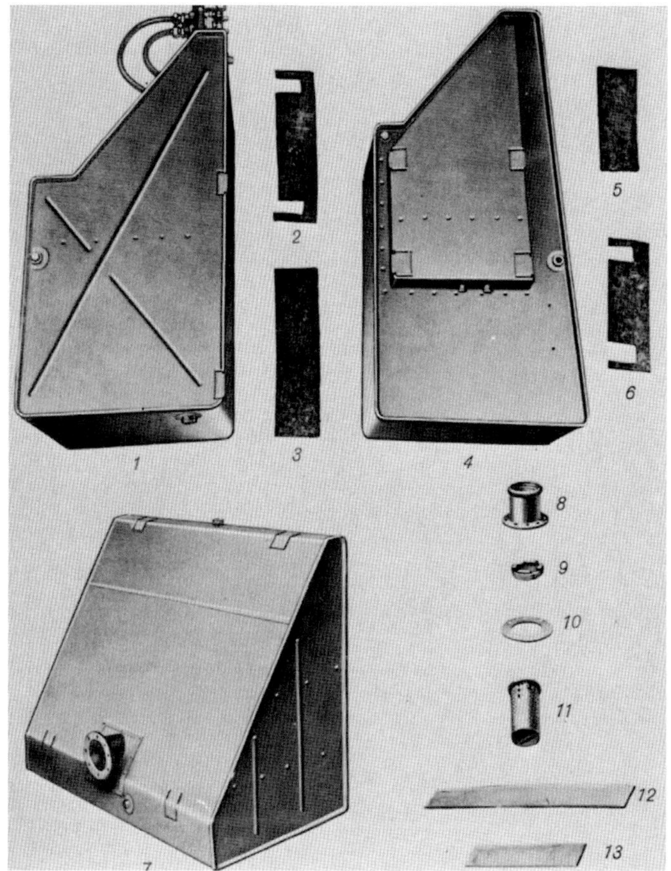

The fuel tank with installation parts.

and gearbox. The gears of the gearbox were diagonally toothed, and always engaged in pairs. By using the pre-selector, the channels of the oil pressure net in the gear selector were opened or closed as necessary for carrying out the desired gearshifting. The declutching, shifting, and clutching took place fully automatically. The possibility of an emergency shifting by hand was given. The whole reduction of the gearbox was 1:16. The two-radius steering

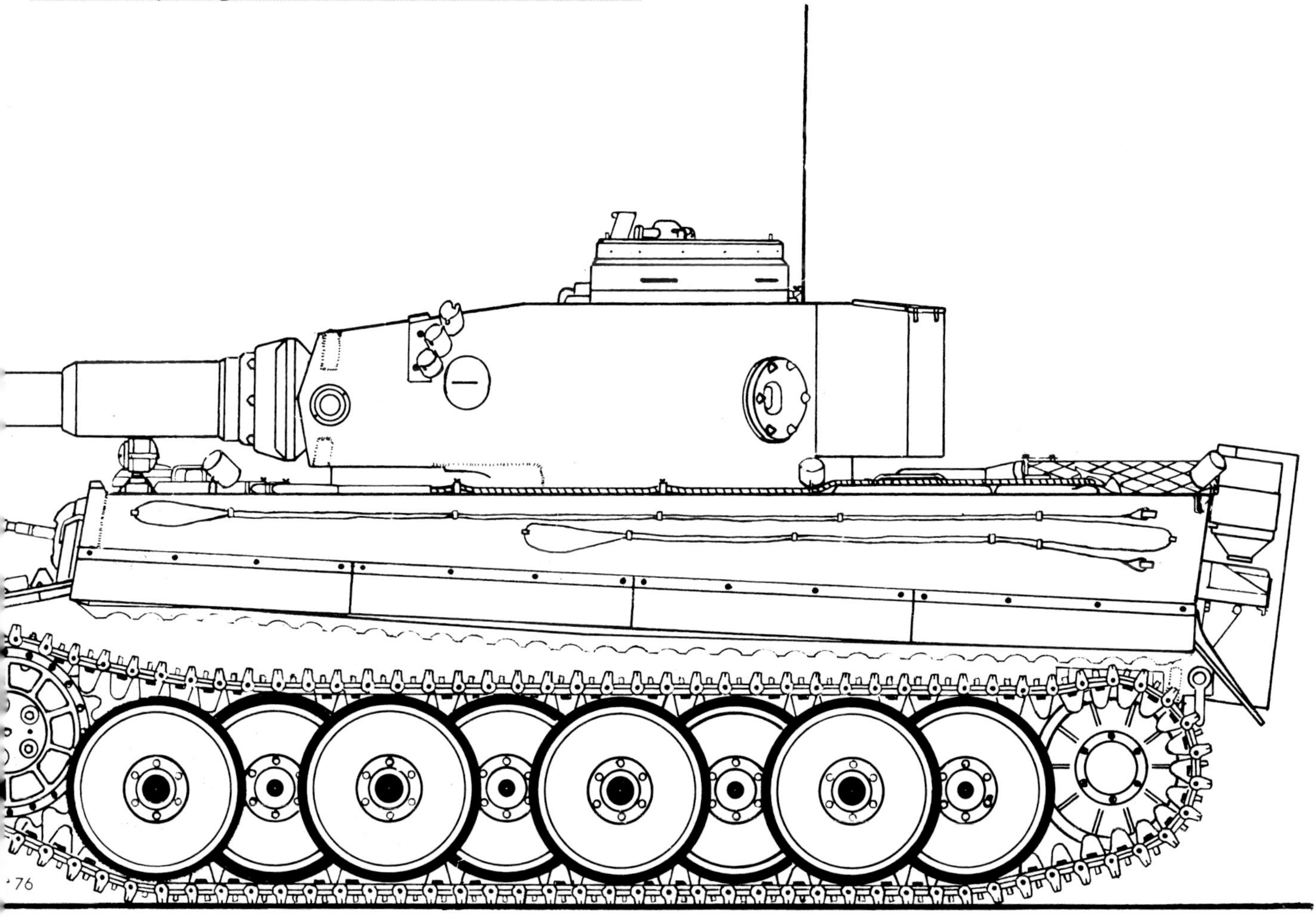

Four-side views of the *Panzerkampfwagen* VI Tiger, Type E.

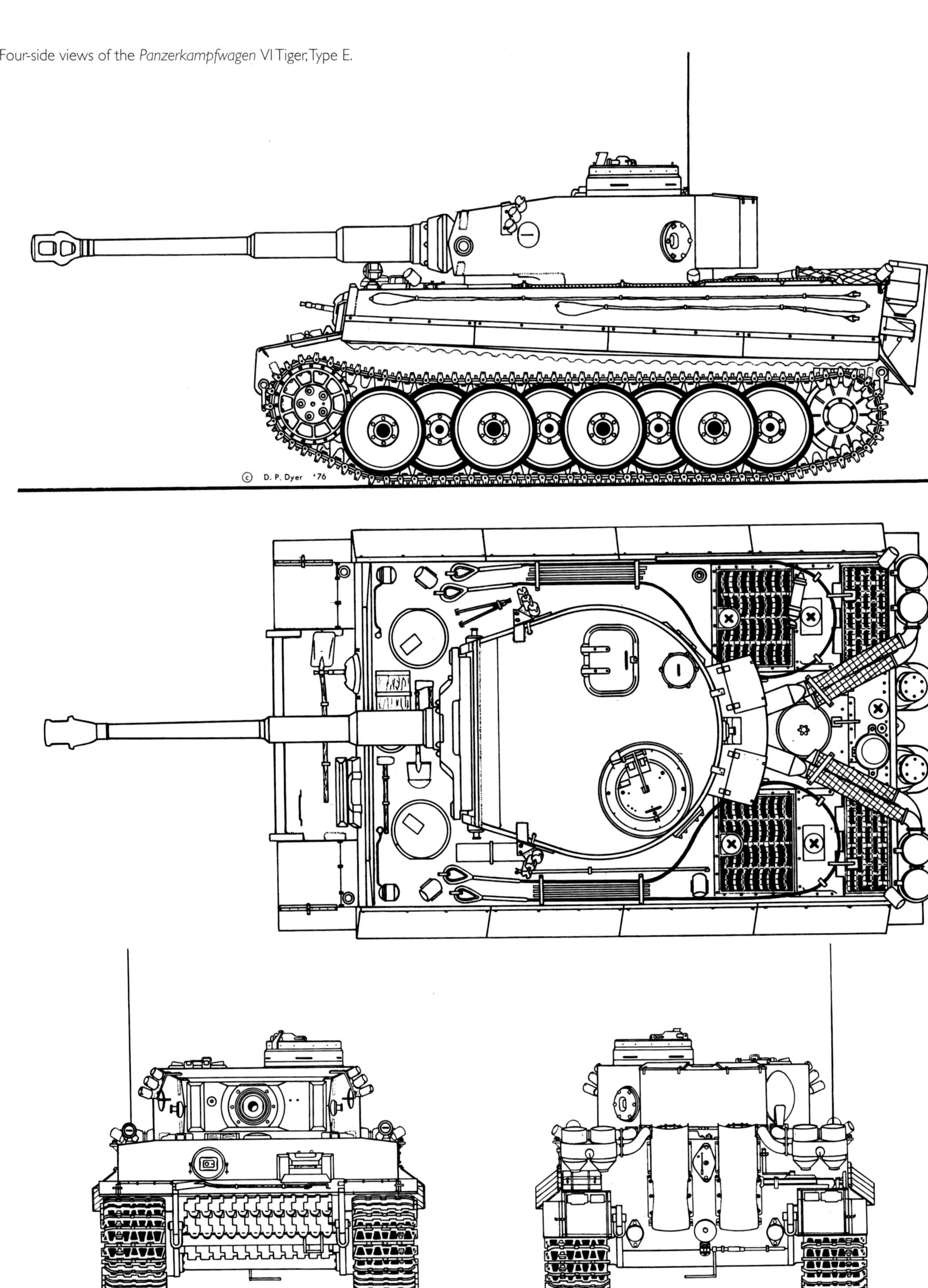

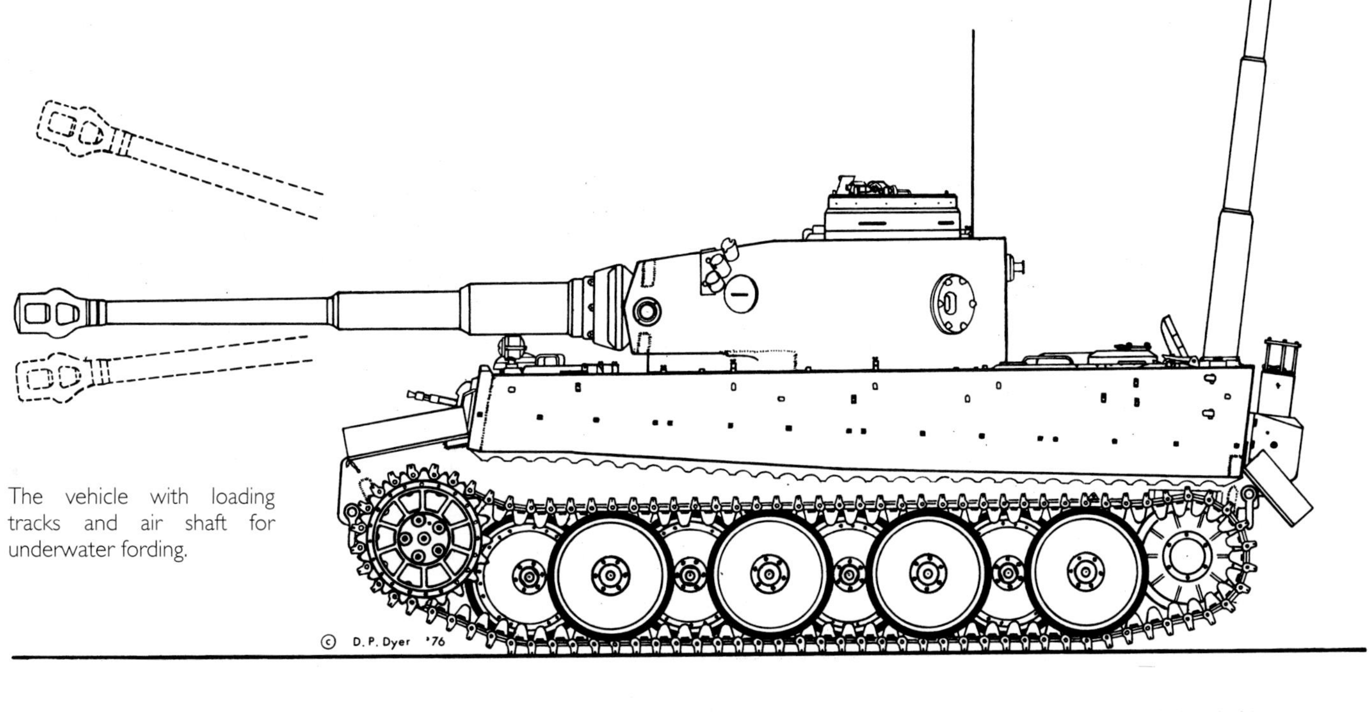

The vehicle with loading tracks and air shaft for underwater fording.

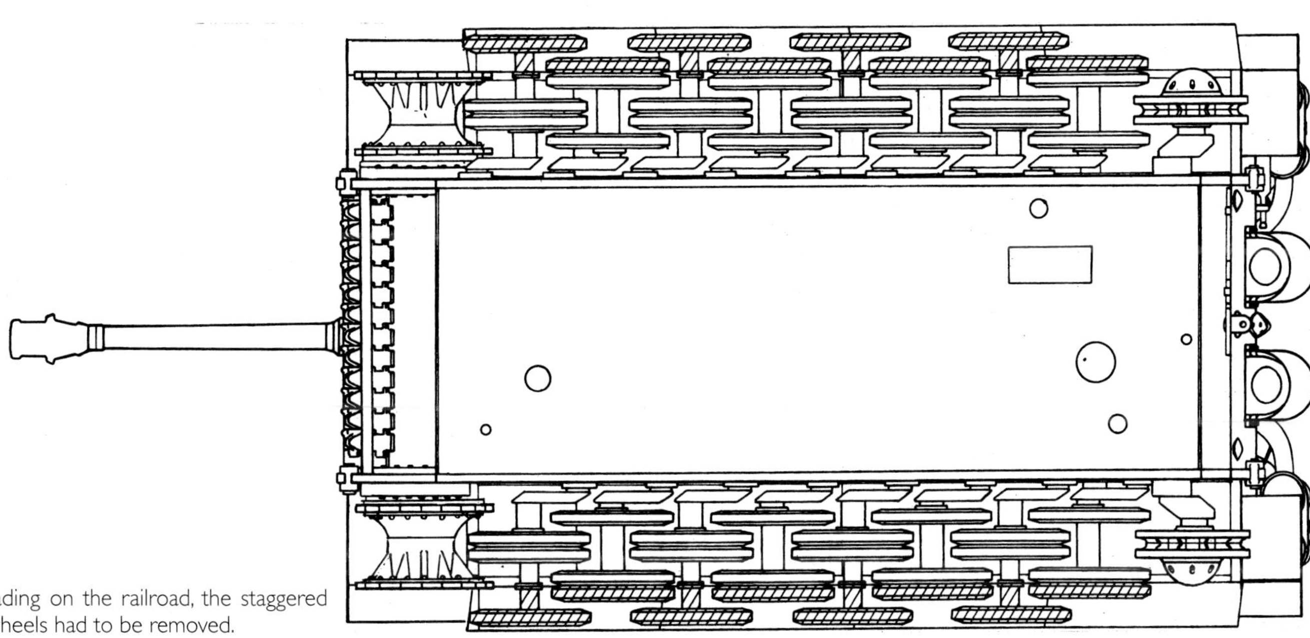

For loading on the railroad, the staggered road wheels had to be removed.

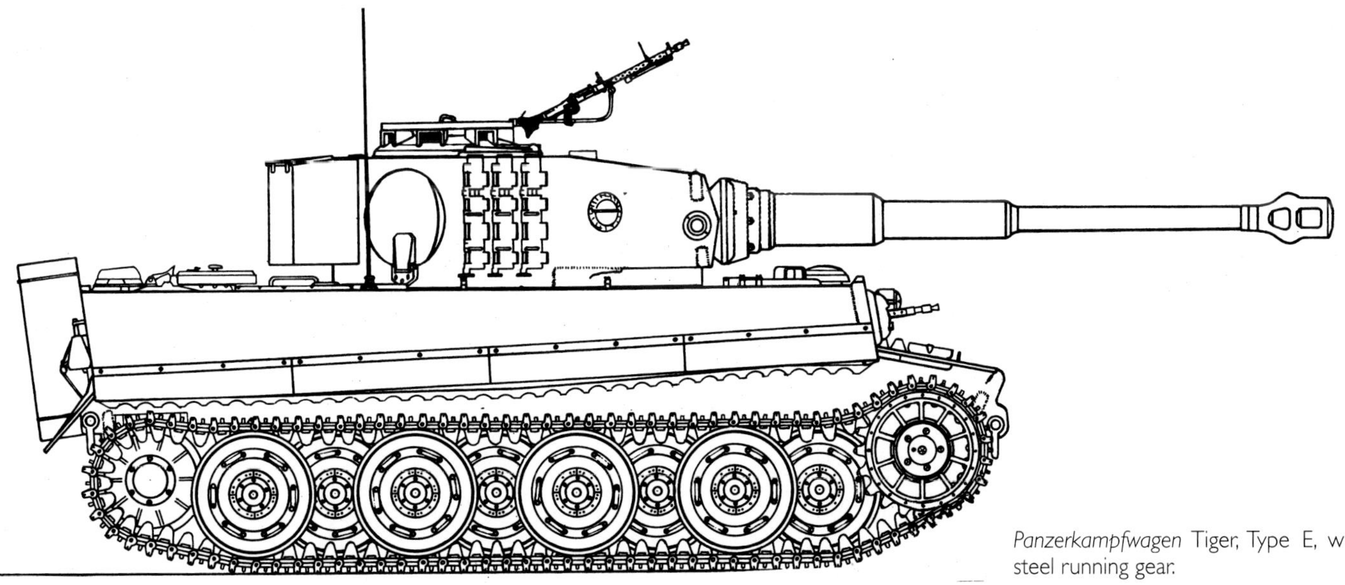

Panzerkampfwagen Tiger, Type E, with steel running gear.

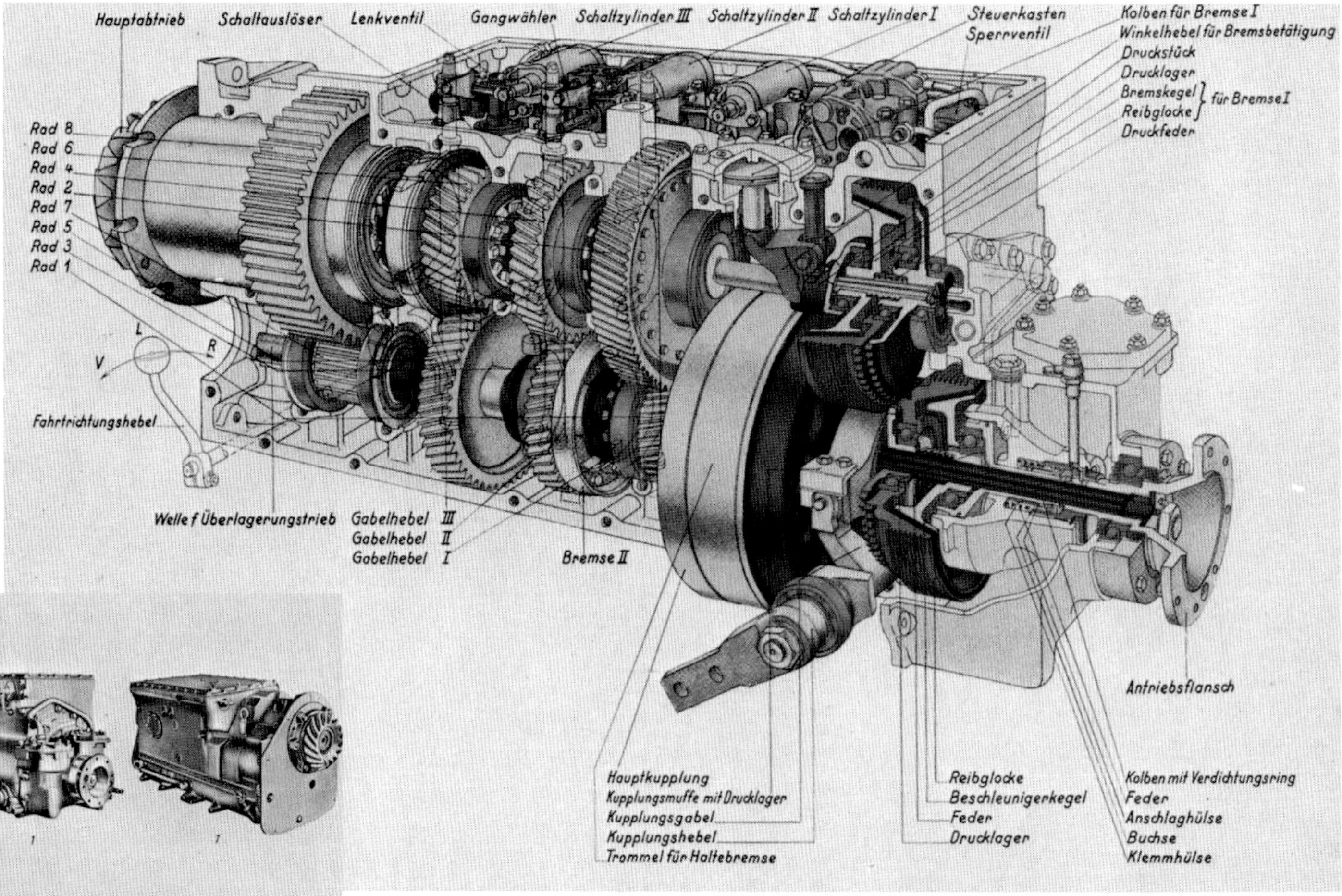

Hauptabtrieb
Schaltauslöser
Lenkventil
Gangwähler
Schaltzylinder III
Schaltzylinder II
Schaltzylinder I
Steuerkasten
Sperrventil
Kolben für Bremse I
Winkelhebel für Bremsbetätigung
Druckstück
Drucklager
Bremskegel
Reibglocke
für Bremse I
Druckfeder
Rad 8
Rad 6
Rad 4
Rad 2
Rad 7
Rad 5
Rad 3
Rad 1
L
R
V
Fahrtrichtungshebel
Welle f Überlagerungstrieb
Gabelhebel III
Gabelhebel II
Gabelhebel I
Bremse II
Antriebsflansch
Hauptkupplung
Kupplungsmuffe mit Drucklager
Kupplungsgabel
Kupplungshebel
Trommel für Haltebremse
Reibglocke
Beschleunigerkegel
Feder
Drucklager
Kolben mit Verdichtungsring
Feder
Anschlaghülse
Buchse
Klemmhülse

The Maybach "Olvar" gearbox.

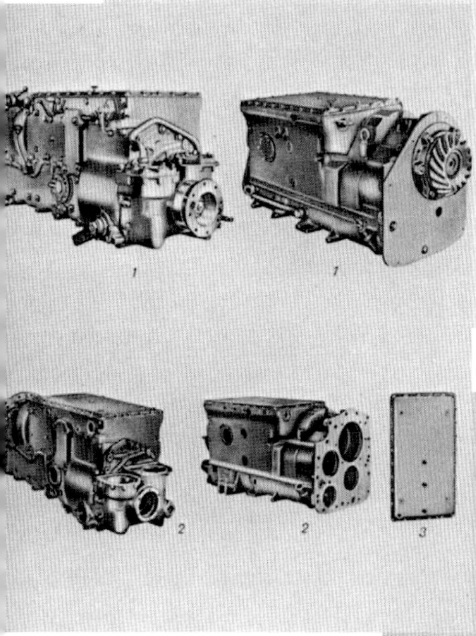

1
1
2
2
3

The gearbox with clutch.

Gehäuse Gr. a
Kegelritzel (Abtrieb) Gr.
Lagerbüchse Gr. e
Abtriebswelle Gr. e
Rad 7 mit Lagerung Gr. l
Rad 8 Gr. e
Doppelklauenring Gr. e
Rad 5 Gr. h
Einfachklauenring Gr. f
Schaltteile Gr. d
Rad 3 Gr. h
Radgruppe 6-4-2 Gr. f
Gleitsegment Gr. d
Bremstrommel Bremse II Gr. h
Rad 1 Gr. h
Hohlwelle Gr. g
Deckel z. Bremser I Gr. g
Kupplung u. Beschleuniger Gr. j
Zylinder-Bremser I Gr. g
Winkelhebel Gr. g
Gabelwelle Gr. k
Bremser I Gr. g
Kupplungsbetätigung Gr. k
Kupplungsmuffe Gr.

Fahrtrichtung
Antrieb zum Geschwindig
Kupplungsverzögerer
Vorwählapparat
Antrieb zum Drehza
Getriebenum
Richtungshebel
Schaltauslös mit Hauptsch u. Servo-Sch
Druckknopf für Haltebremse
Lenkventil
Rückschlagv
Akku
Schaltzylinde mit Steuersch u. Rätsch-Ser
Gasgeber
Gangwähler
zum Offnungskolben
Schaltzylinde mit ....
Gestänge für Kupplung u. Kuppl.-Verzögerer
Olrücklauf
Überbrückun
Schaltzylinde mit ....
Steuerkasten Kupplungssc Druckregulie Feder, Sperrschiebe u. Steuerschie
Entkuppler
Druckstange
Kupplungswelle
Schmierventil
Olablaufroh
Doppelsperr
Olfüllung
Olfilter
Kupplungskolben
Hinterer Deckel
Getriebelagerung
Turmantrieb

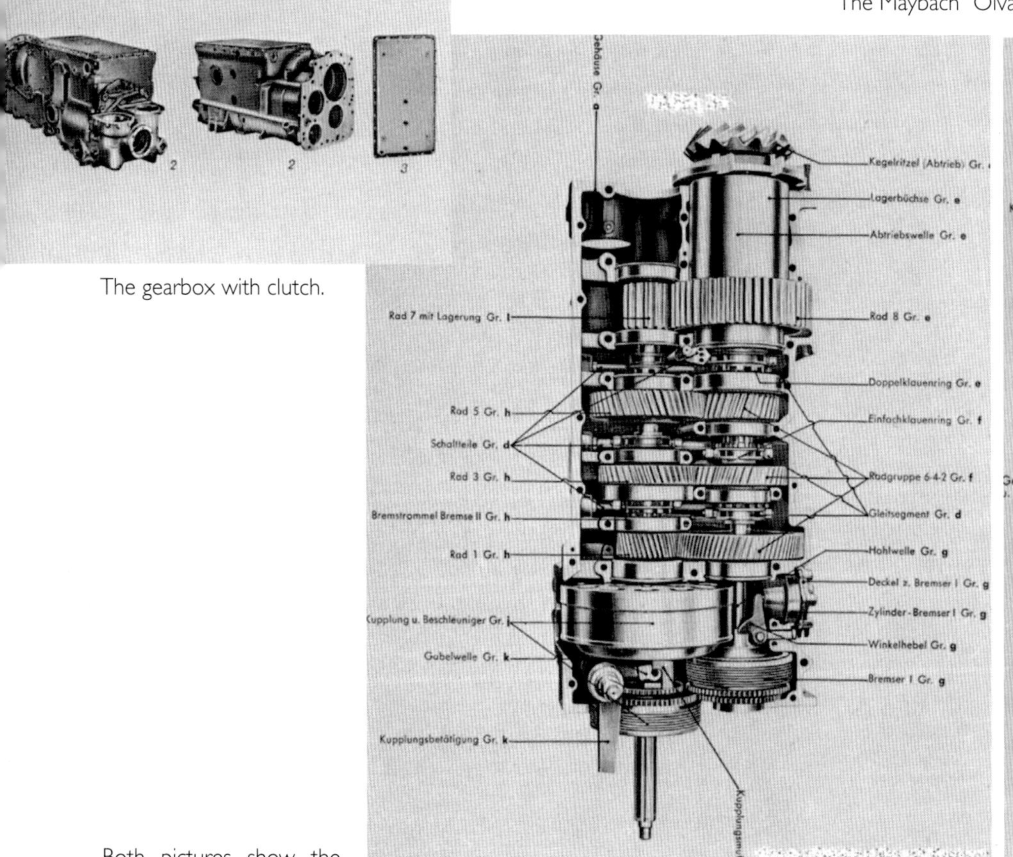

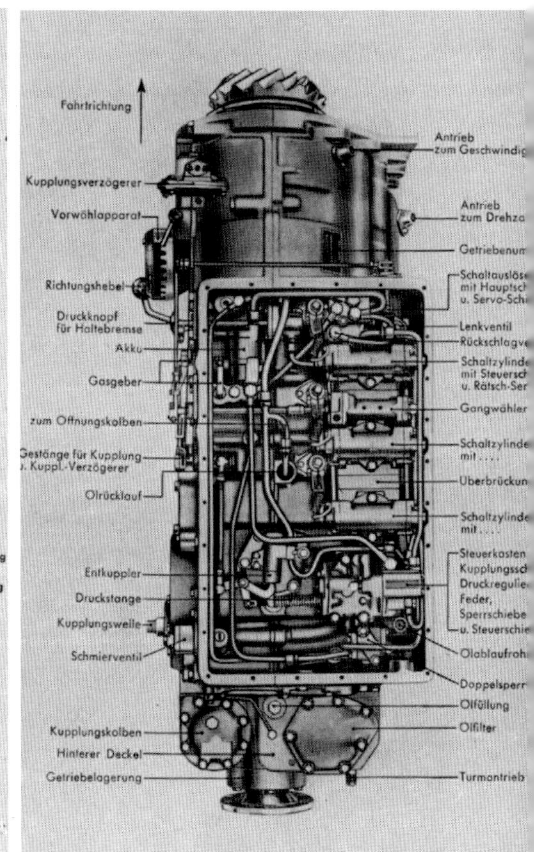

Both pictures show the details of the gearbox.

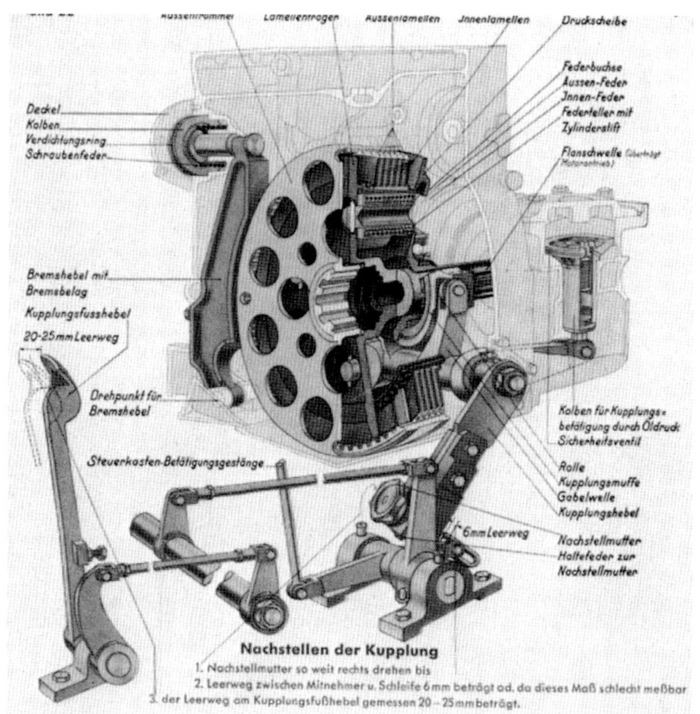

The main clutch of VK 4501 (H).

The steering pattern of the "Tiger" tank.

gear, Type "L 600 C," made by Henschel, was flanged onto the gearbox. Originally three radii were foreseen, but because of a weak spot in the drive the smallest radius had to be omitted. Similarly to the "L 320 C" steering gear of the "VK. 3001," the various radii were shifted by lamellar clutches and oil pressure. For emergency steering of the vehicle, a steering lever was attached to each of the two brakes. Steering itself took place, unlike the lever steering customary in tanks, by a steering wheel connected to the steering apparatus. The steering of the oil pressure originally took place on a large number of vehicles via a Henschel tube slide. Later, for reasons of simplification, a steering apparatus made by the South German Argus Works had to be used. The steering apparatus types were interchangeable. From the steering gear, the power was

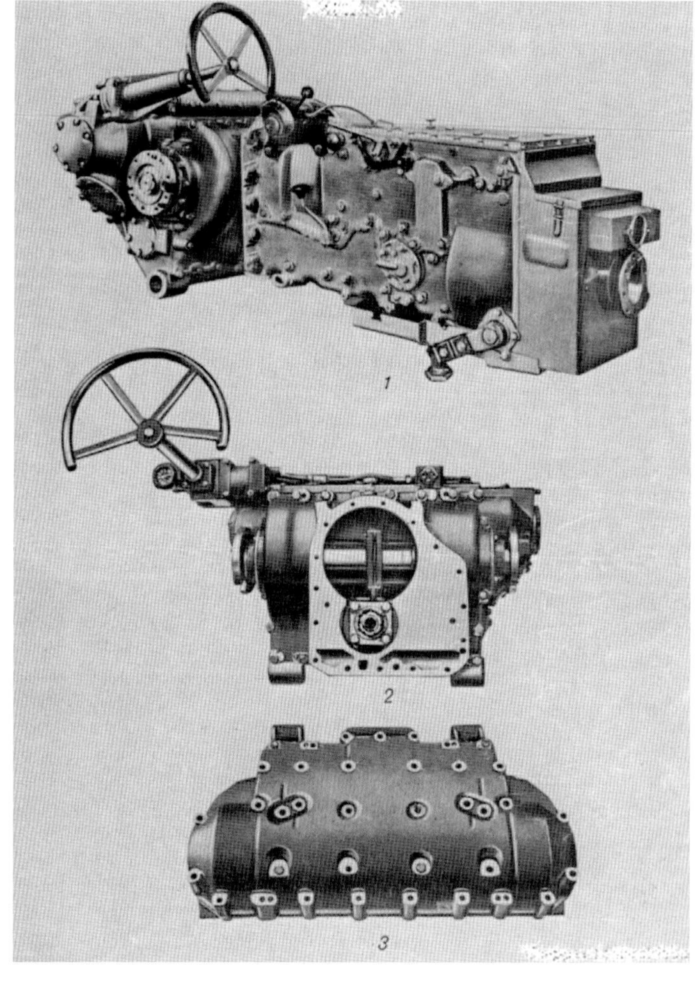

The steering gear, seen when removed.

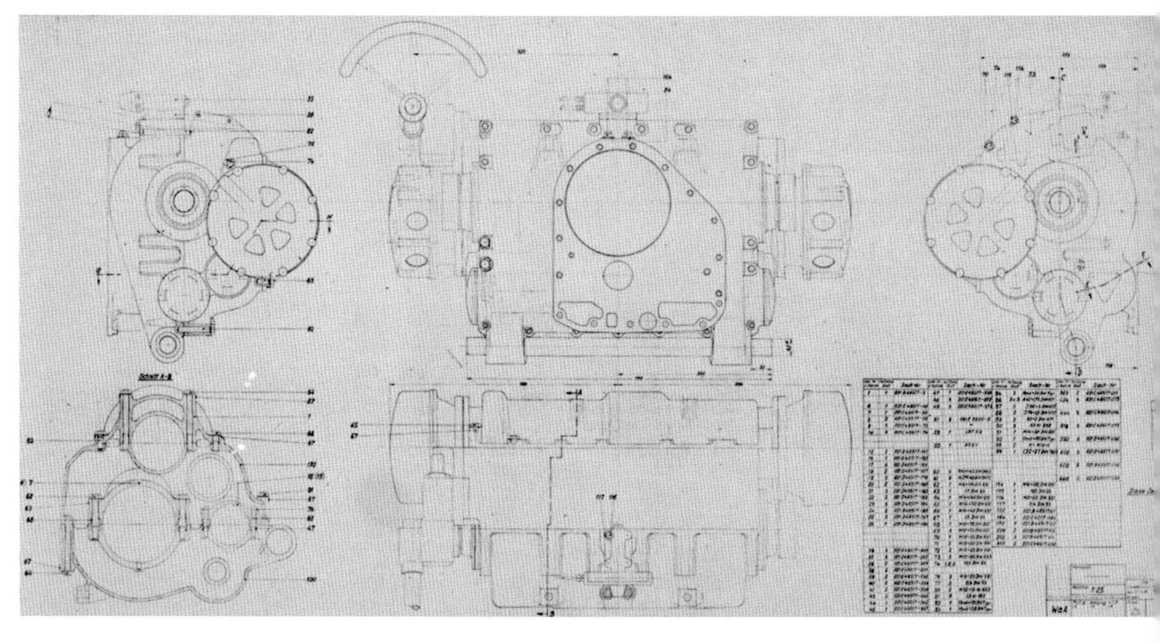

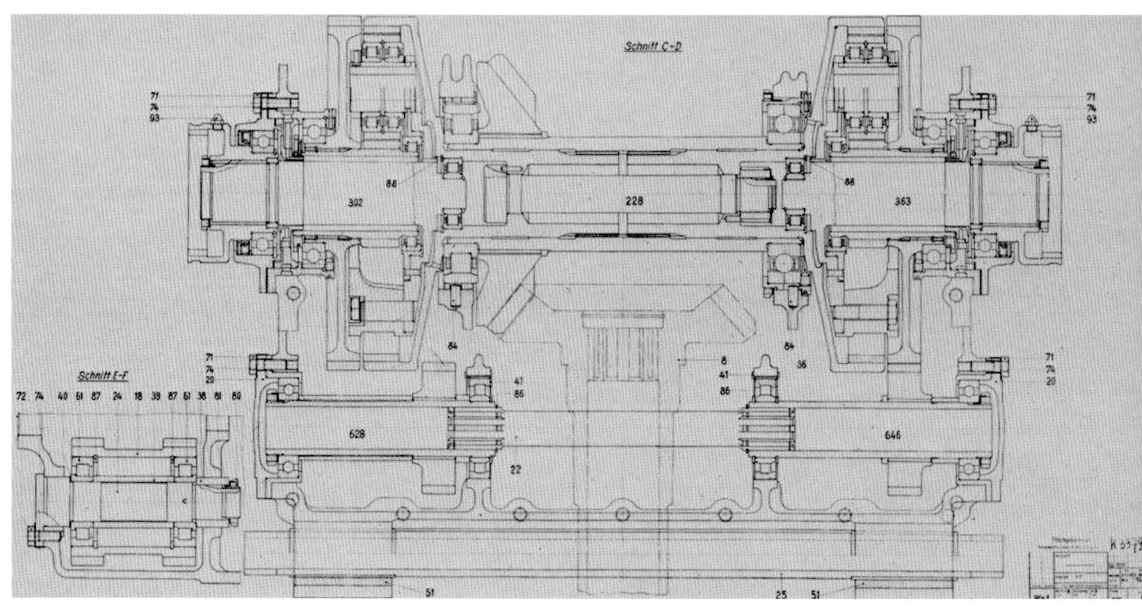

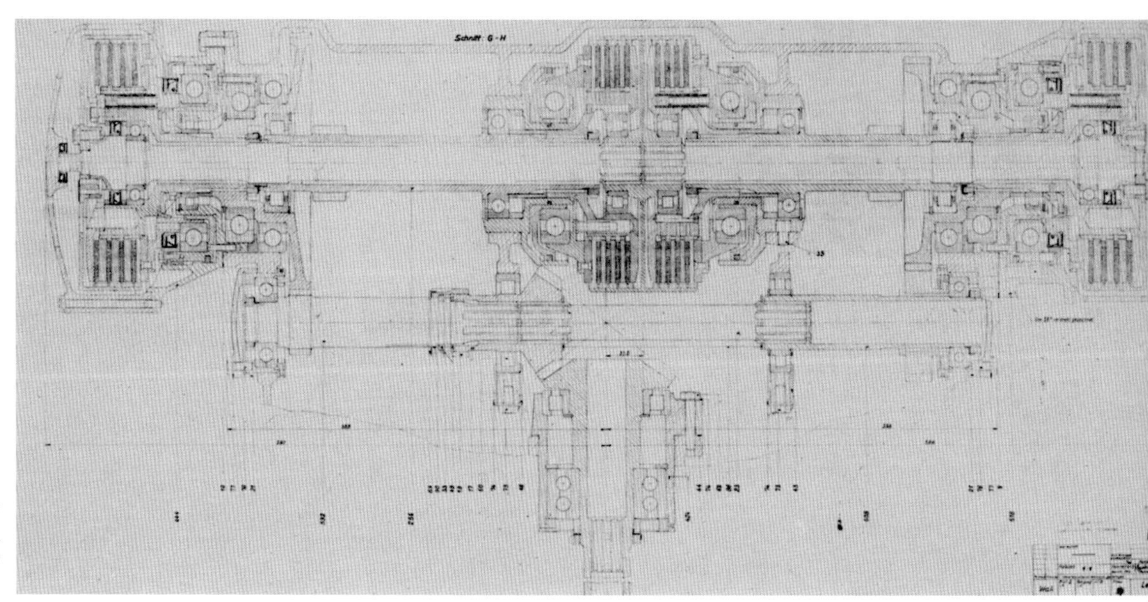

These three drawings show the structure of the "L 801" steering gear made by Henschel.

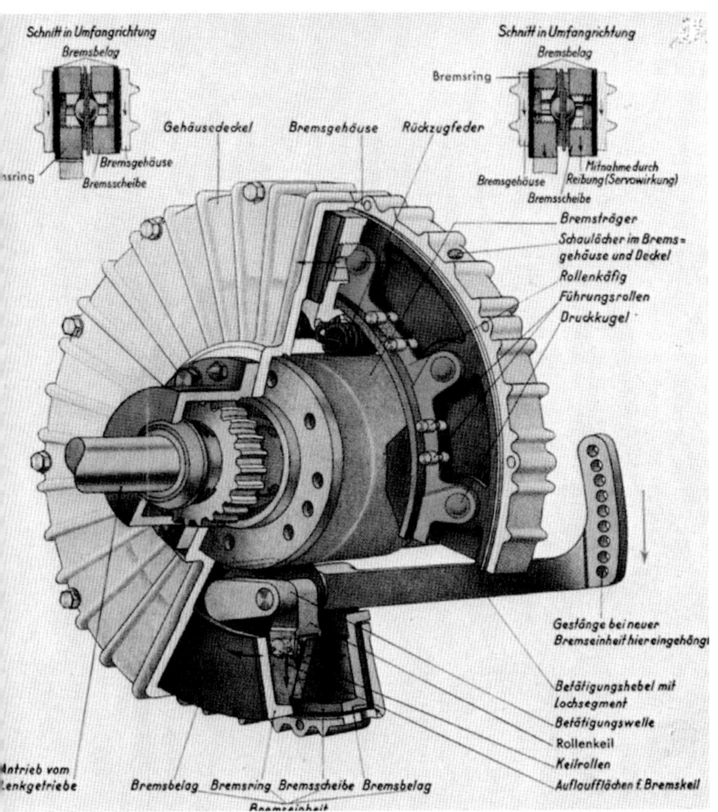

Above: The brakes developed by Dr.-Ing. Klaue and by the Argus firm.

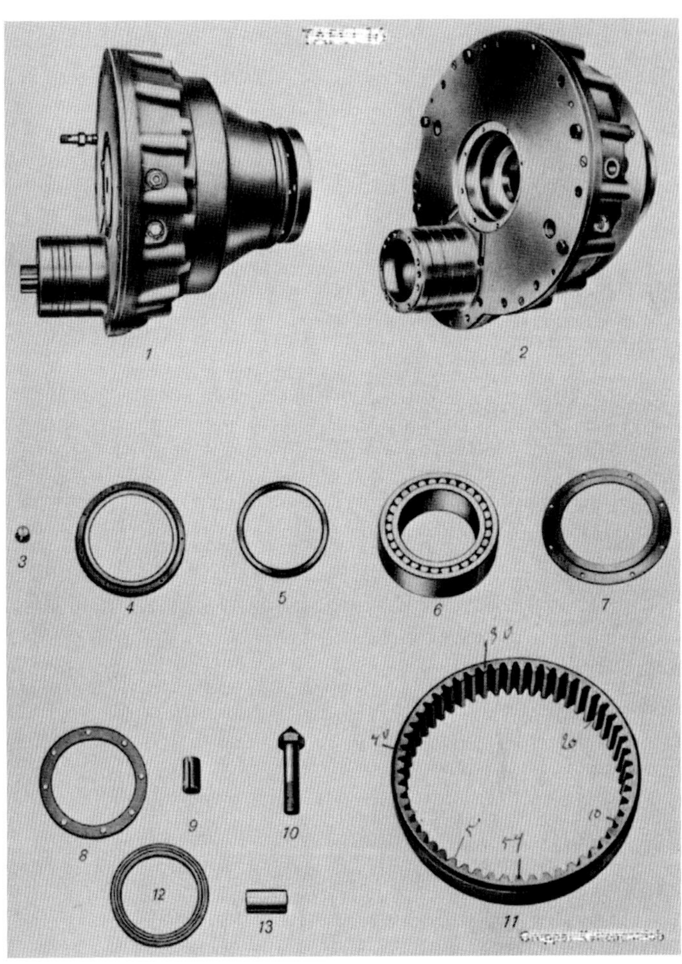

Right: The track drive with individual parts.

Below: A depiction of the final drive.

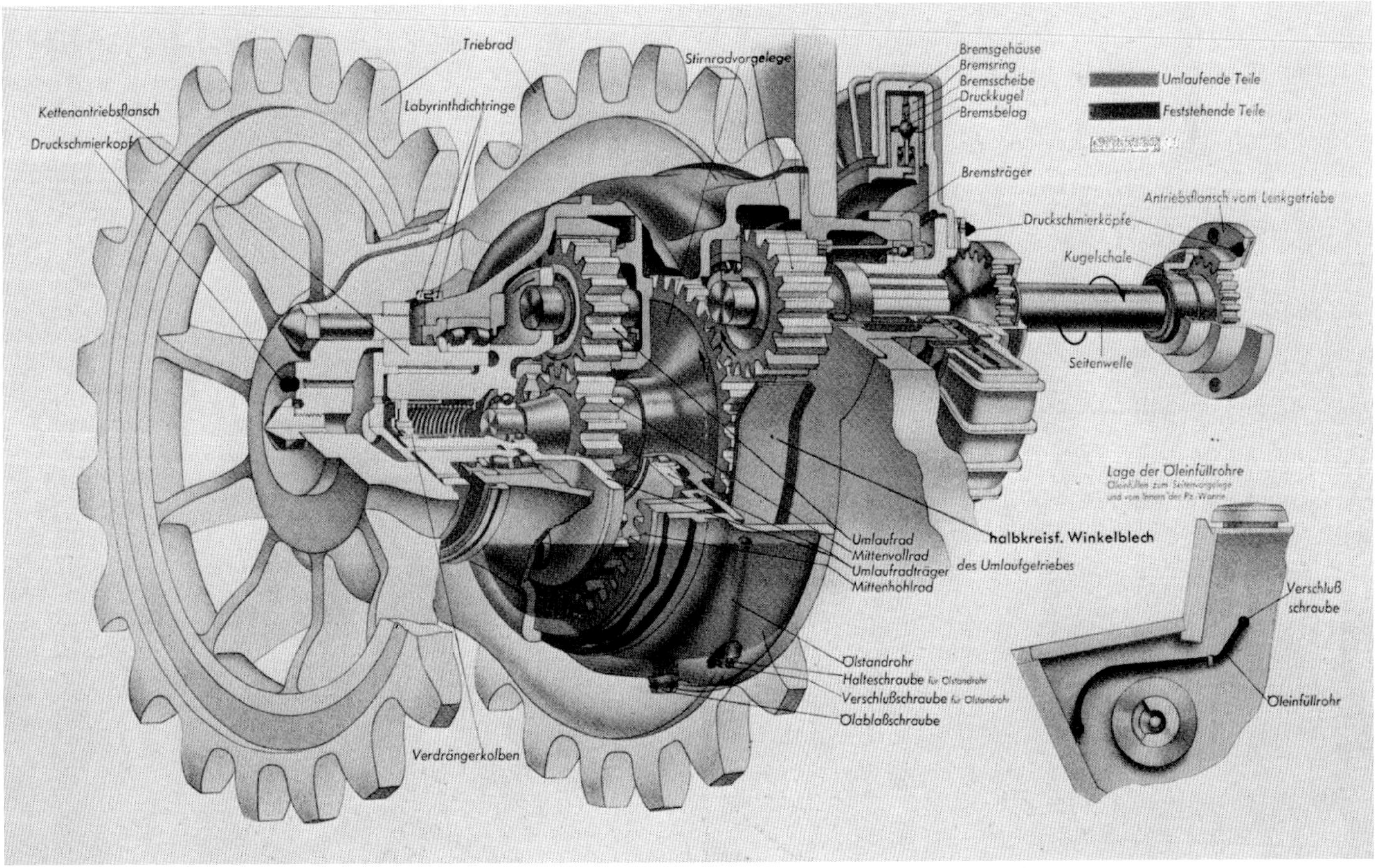

The drive wheel with hub and toothed ring.

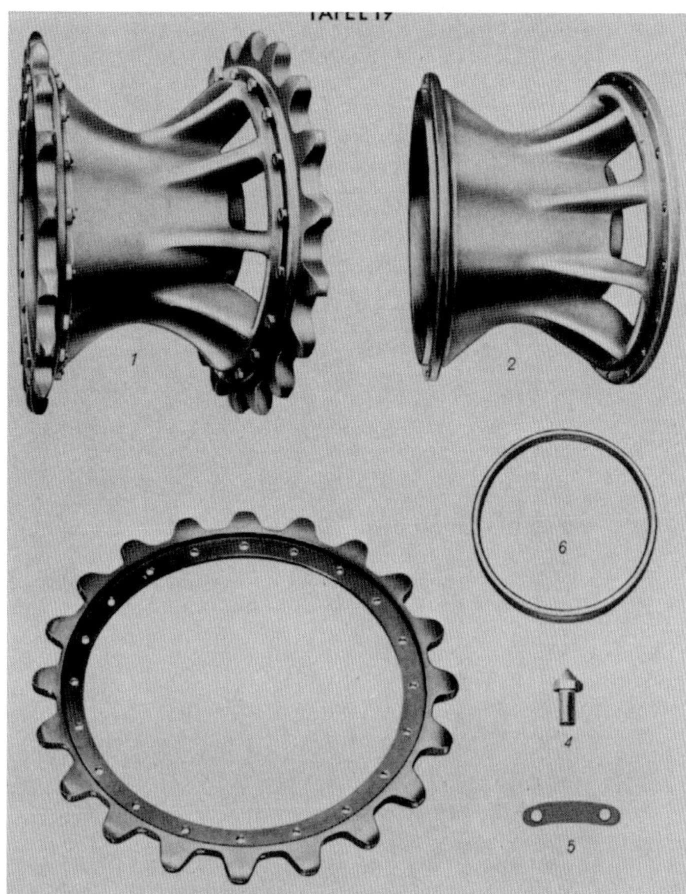

carried by a shaft on each side to the forward final drives. In the process, toothed couplings with little mobility were used. The driving and steering brakes were disc brakes, in which the braking effect automatically increased. The braking material was Buna, with cast-in steel threads. The brakes were originally supposed to be operated hydraulically, but numerous problems with this type caused mechanical activation to be introduced.

The final drive, like that of the "VK. 3001," was reduced by a crown wheel and planetary gear to a ratio of 1 : 10.75. The running gear consisted of the drive sprocket, four inner and four outer road wheels, eight auxiliary wheels, torsion-bar suspension, shock absorbers, the leading wheel with tension adjuster, and the track on each side.

The drive sprocket was attached to the drive flange of the final drive. The geared rings were interchangeable. The road wheels were interleaved. After the beginning of the developmental work it appeared that the expected total weight far exceeded the carrying limit of the rubber tires. Thus, outside road wheels had to be added. The road wheels (size 800 x 95 E) themselves had been taken from "VK. 3601," and were disc wheels with rubber tires. The development of the new hard rubber rims with wire inlays, not yet developed at that time, inspired many complaints from the troops. The life span of the rubber tires was too short, and required constant changing of the road wheels. The interleaved running gear thus gained a bad reputation. The road wheels had rings to guide the track teeth. Each pair of road wheels, with its auxiliary wheel, was mounted in two roller bearings on a crank arm. These pointed backward on the right side—forward on the left—and were mounted on the hull with two boxes of pressed material. After some 800 "VK. 4501" vehicles, the original road wheels were replaced by rubber tired steel wheels made by the Deutsche Eisen-Werke.

The suspension of the road wheels was composed of suspension arms and a torsion bar. The heads of the torsion bars

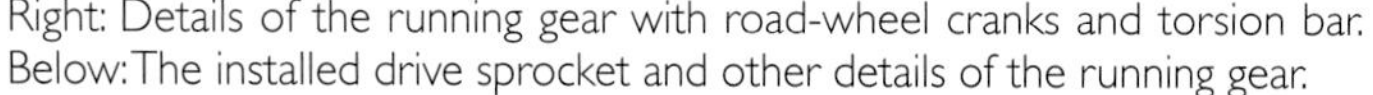

Right: Details of the running gear with road-wheel cranks and torsion bar. Below: The installed drive sprocket and other details of the running gear.

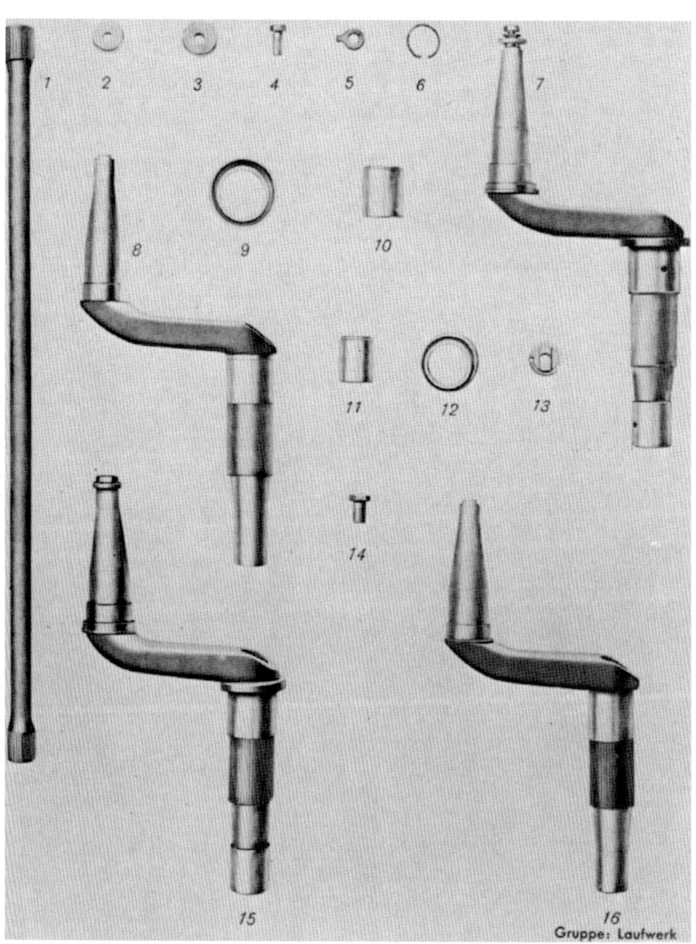

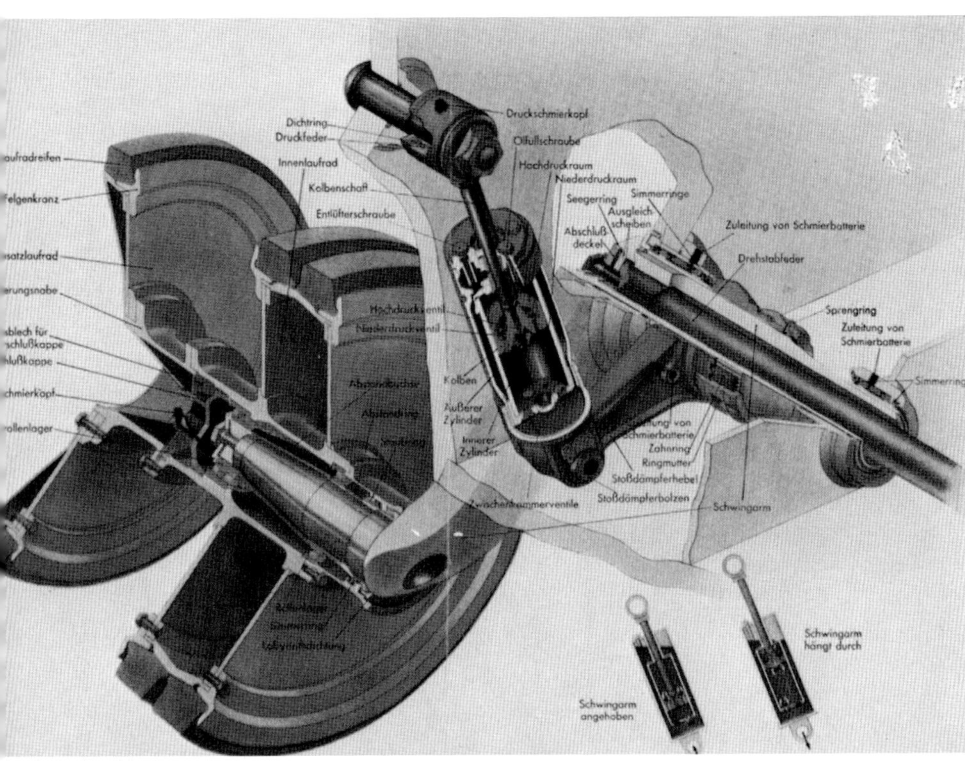

The road-wheel suspension and shock absorbers are shown.

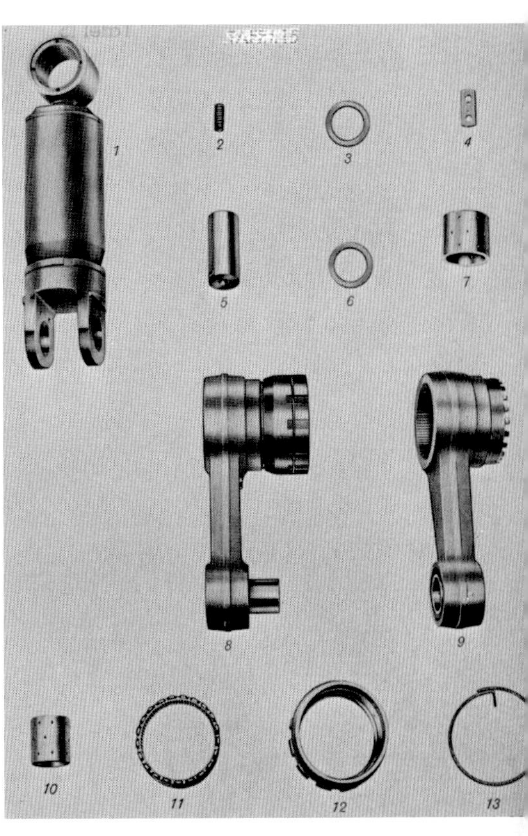

The shock absorber and its mount, with all the pieces.

Below: The leading wheel with track-tension adjuster.

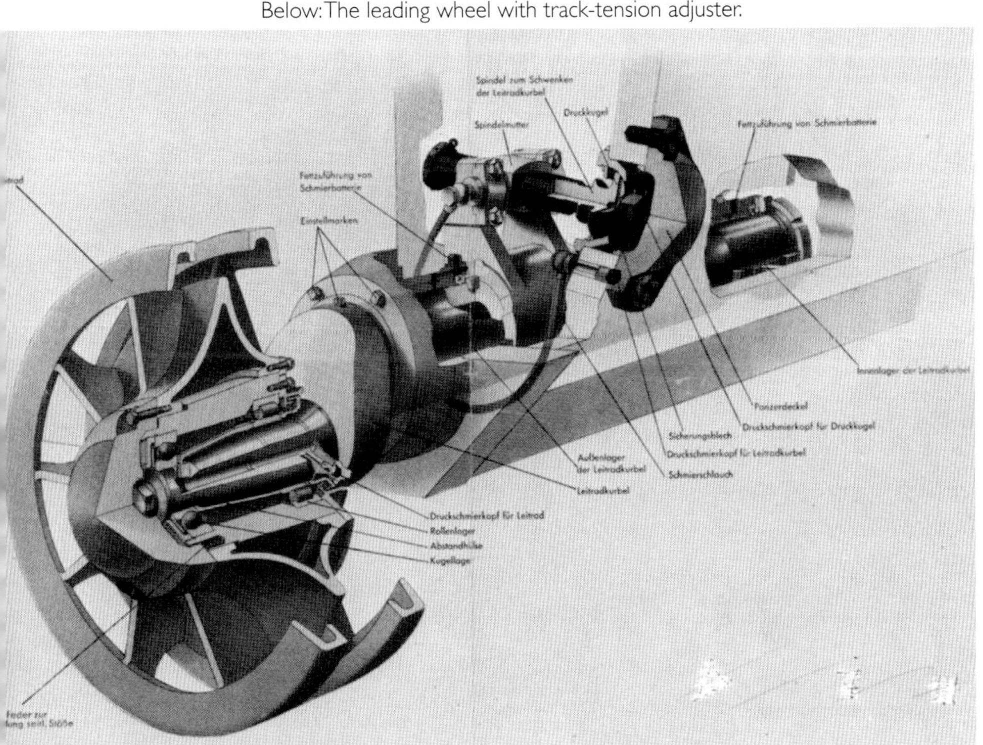

Below: Details of the leading wheel.

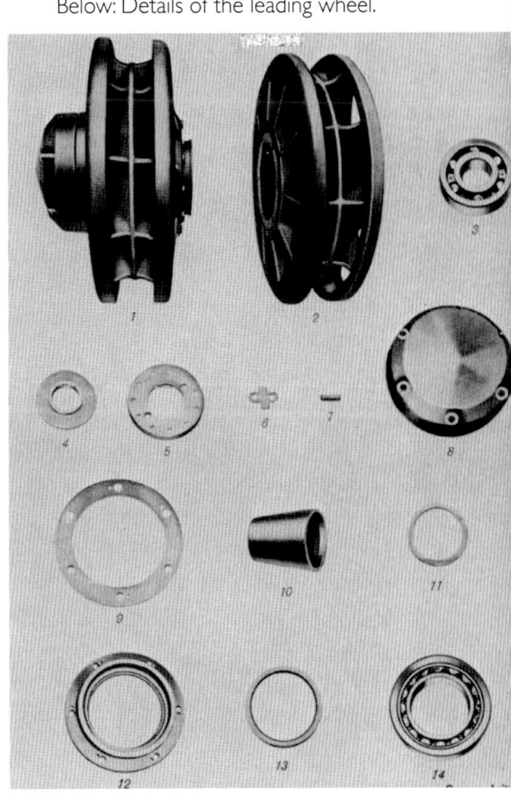

The road wheels of the original running gear.

Later these rubber-padded steel wheels were used.

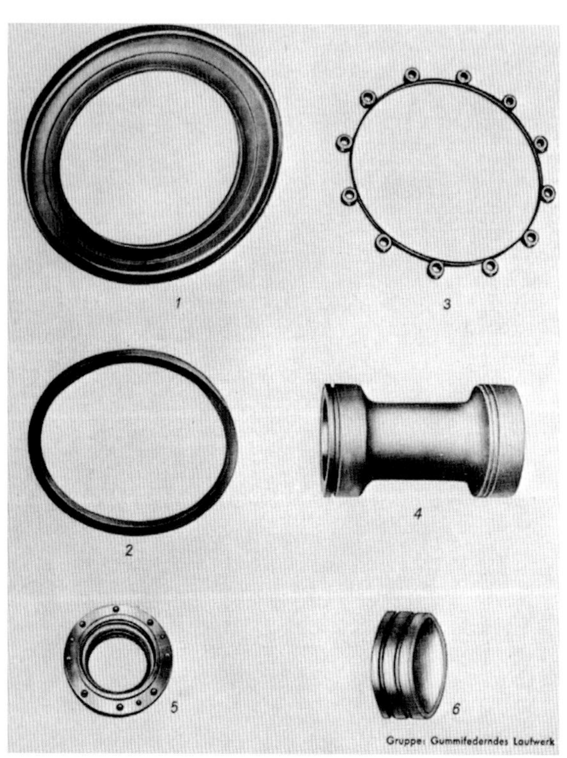

Parts of the rubber-tired steel running gear.

***Panzerkampfwagen* Tiger Type E (Sd.Kfz. 181), final version.**

Ⓒ D

were equipped with toothed gearing, and attached to the crank arms, and to a flange on the wall of the armored hull.

The first and last crank arms on each side were fitted with stronger torsion bars. To dampen the vehicle's movements, shock absorbers working in one direction were attached to the first and last suspension arms inside the hull. The leading wheel with the tension adjuster was doubly mounted on the hull. To tighten the tracks, the leading-wheel crank was swung to the rear.

Originally, a 520 mm wide track with 130 mm links was planned. As the total weight increased, a widening of the tracks to 725 mm took place. This exceeded the railroad loading profile. Henschel suggested two tracks running side by side, but the Army Ordnance Office insisted on two different tracks, one offroad and one loading type. They consisted of 96 links, which were connected by ungreased track bolts. When the loading tracks were put on, the outer auxiliary road wheels had to be removed. (The transport tracks were "Kgs 63/520/130," the battle tracks "Khs 63/725/130.") In the engine compartment, an automatic fire extinguishing system was installed. If the temperature went over 160 degrees Celsius on the electric heat sensors, a certain amount of extinguishing material was sprayed on especially endangered positions for about seven seconds.

Also required, because of the high total weight, was a fording capacity up to 4.5 meters. All openings and joints on the vehicle had been made watertight with rubber seals. A three-part tube could be assembled to form a pipe about three meters high, which

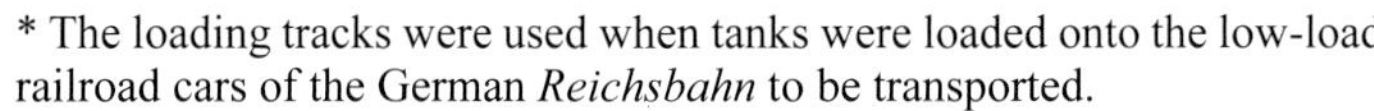

* The loading tracks were used when tanks were loaded onto the low-load railroad cars of the German *Reichsbahn* to be transported.

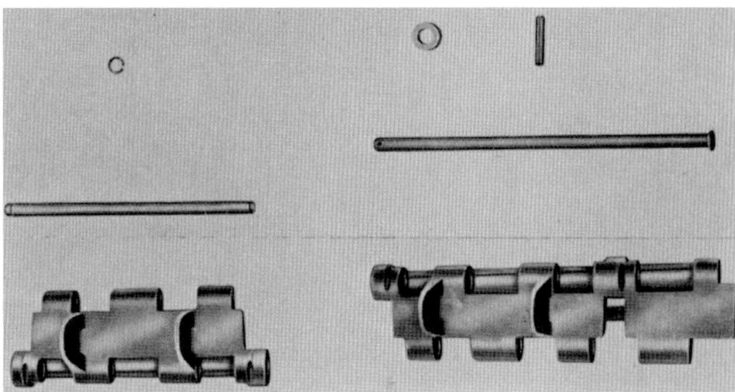

The tracks of the "Tiger" tank. The loading* tracks are shown at left, the battle tracks at right.

The final version of the running gear.

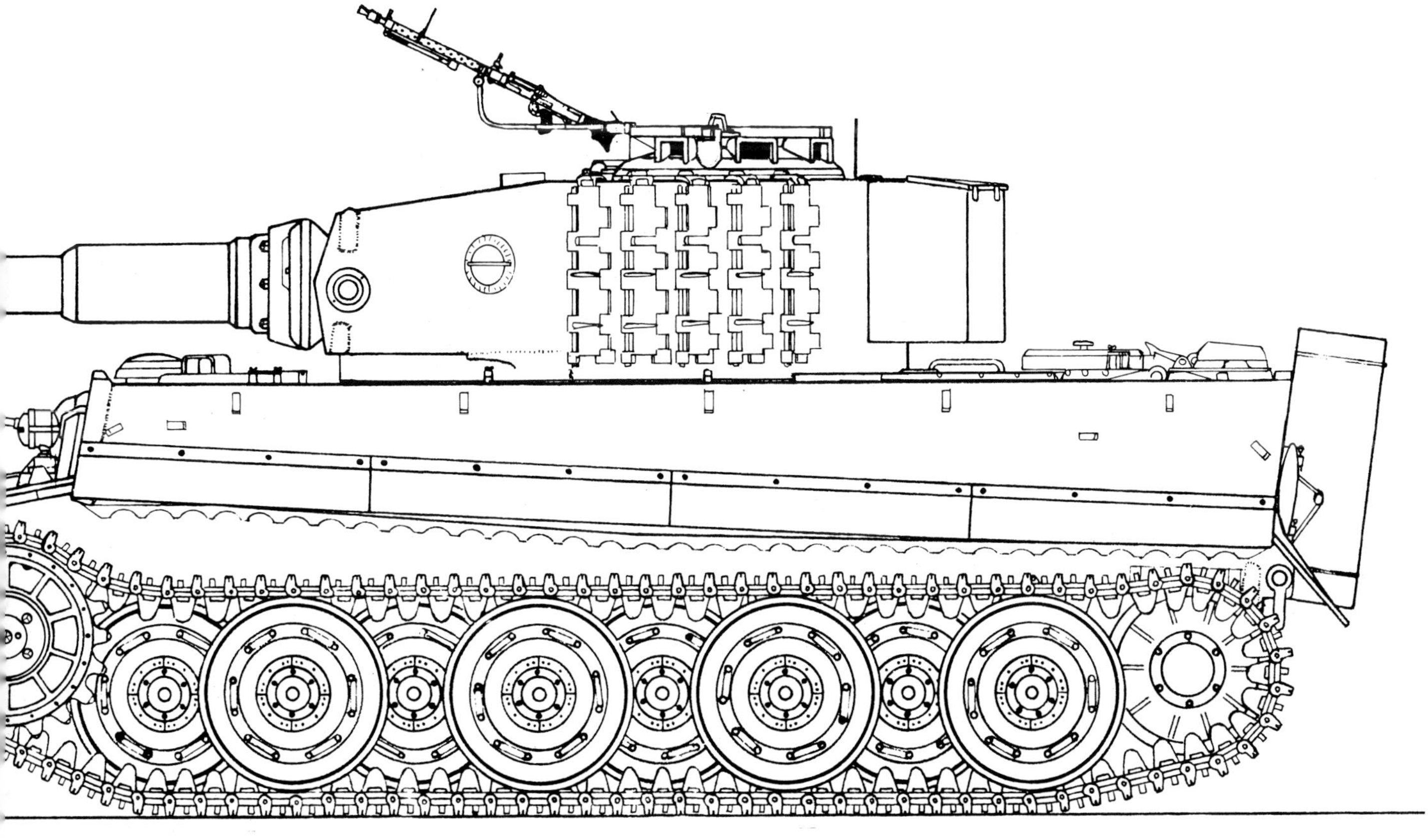

A Tiger E is ready for fording, with its air pipe in place.

The Henschel firm's fording pool in Haustenbeck (seen while under construction) was built to test Tiger tanks. The pool was 60 meters long, 18 meters wide, and 6.66 meters deep.

The pool is shown, with command bridge and observation cabin. At the lower left were two heavy drain plugs.

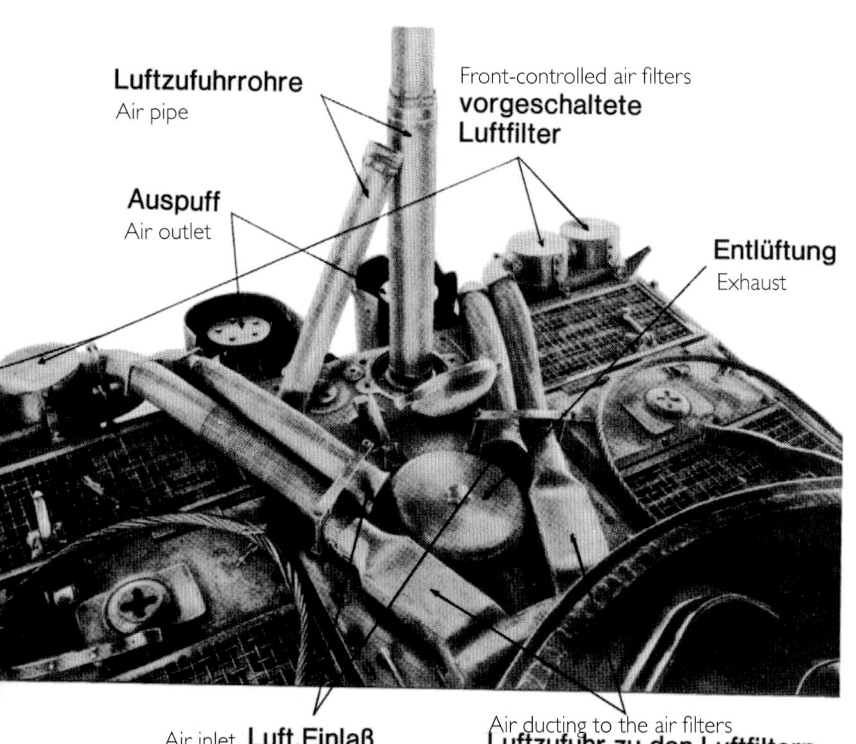

The engine compartment of the vehicle, with the air pipe attached for underwater fording.

If necessary, the pool could be drained quickly.

The crew is equipped with life jackets.

A Tiger is seen just short of the deepest part of the pool.

On the 19th fording test in 4.1 meters of water, heavy white smoke suddenly appeared above the surface. The two drain plugs of the pool were opened. After 6 minutes and 20 seconds the commander's cupola was above water,, and after nine minutes the pool was empty. For unknown reasons the automatic fire-extinguishing system had come on. The pictures show the vehicle afterward, still putting out a lot of smoke.

Above and below: The V3 test vehicle was set up for underwater driving. The ball mantlet for the radioman's machine gun was covered with a special cap.

The telescope, with its direction indicator, can be seen above. Before it on the turret is the flash signaling device.

The vehicle enters the water, the depth of which is 4.3 meters.

The exhaust gases make waves on the water's surface.

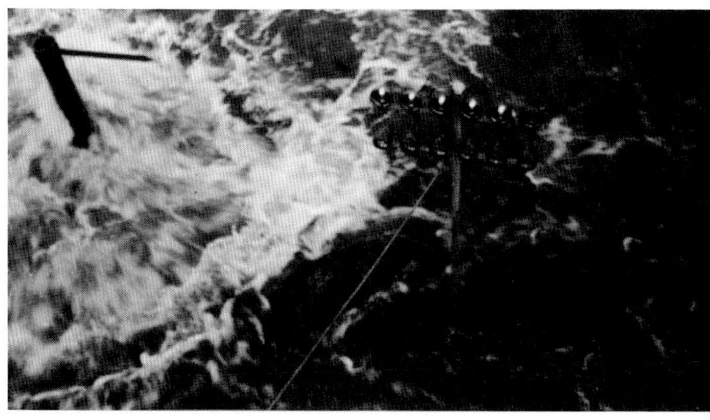

The flash signal served mainly to indicate a CO buildup in the submerged vehicle during testing.

On July 12, 1943, the first fording tests in an open lake were made. The pictures show the tank entering and crossing the body of water.

The tank comes out of the water after finishing the test. The steam buildup was caused by the hot, wet exhaust pipes. These pictures show the tank in the water after making several turns, and as it comes out of the water.

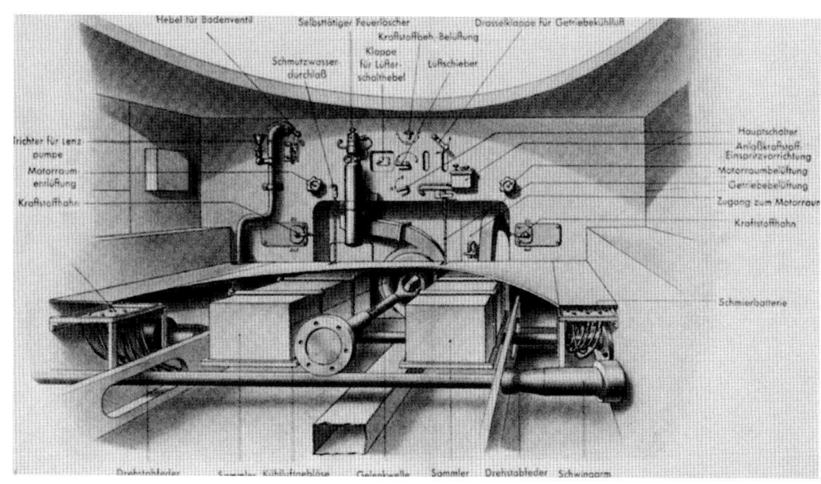

The wall between the engine and fighting compartments.

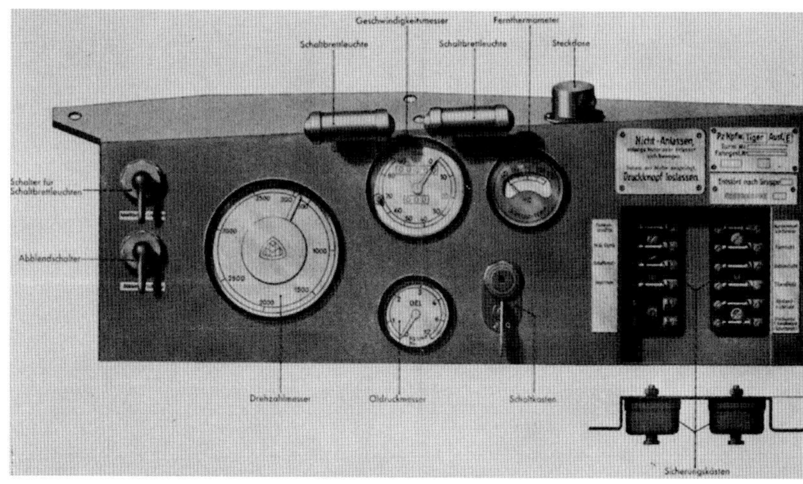

The instrument panel of the 'Tiger E."

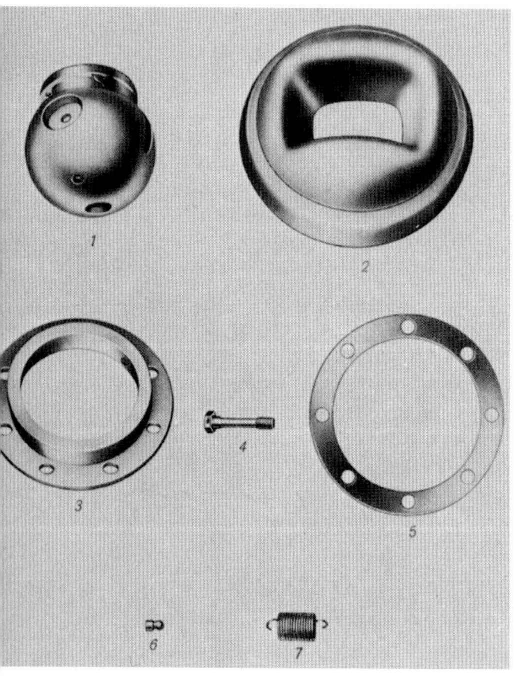

The ball mantlet for the machine gun mounted on the body plate in front of the radioman.

The pictures show the ammunition racks for the 8.8 cm shells.

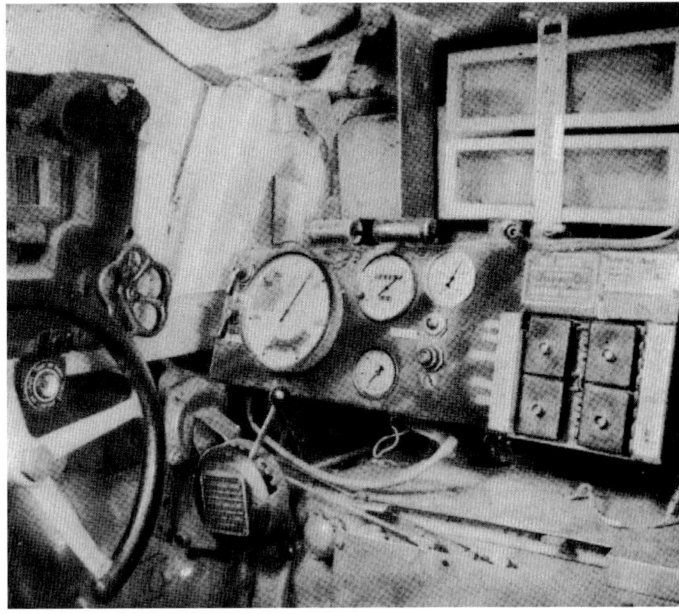

The two pictures show the driver's area of the "Tiger." Over the steering wheel is the driver's visor. At left front is the course indicator. To the left of the seat the front shock absorber can be seen. Under the instrument panel is the pre-selector for the gearbox.

The picture shows the opened driver's hatch from outside; the drawing completes the picture.

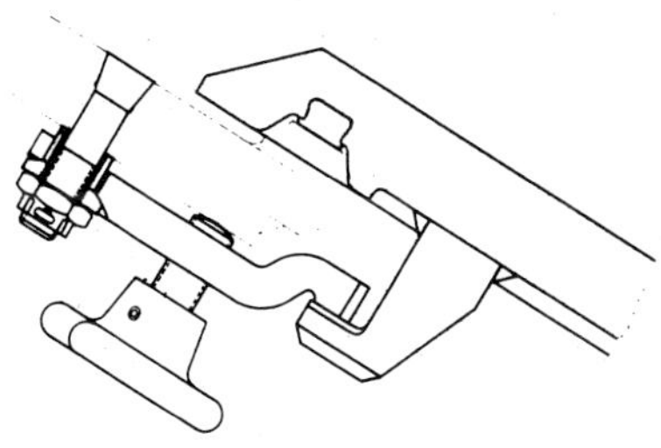

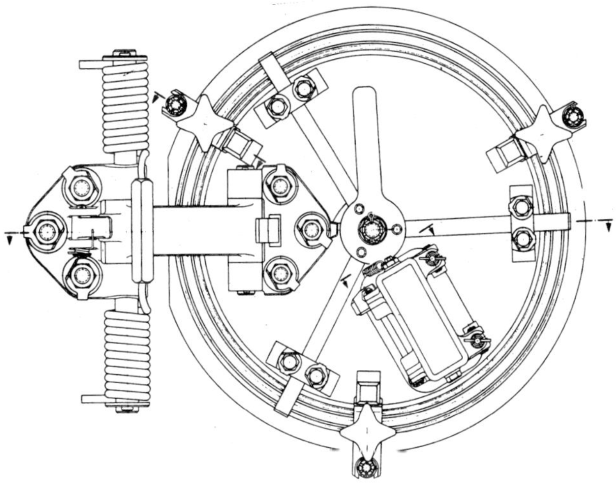

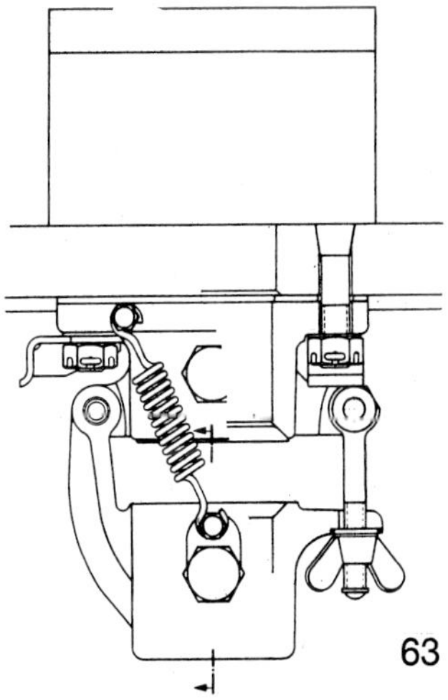

63

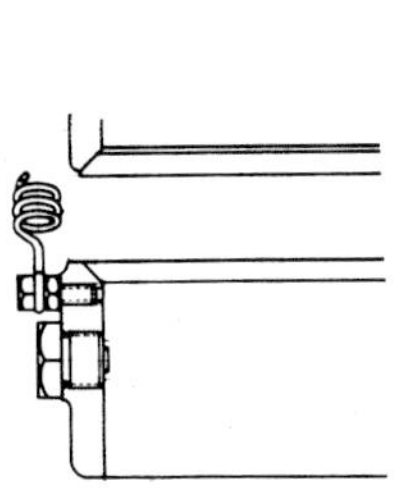

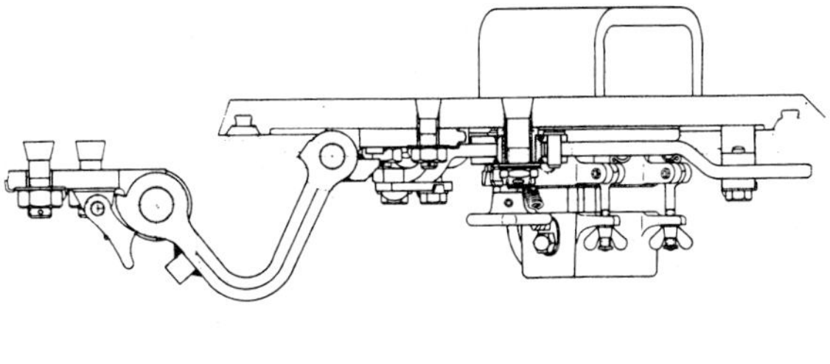

could be screwed onto the engine cover to assure its supply of air for combustion. The exhaust gases were piped into the water through jointed covering plates.

A bilge pump got rid of unwanted water. The sealing of the engine compartment wall was done especially carefully, to make the entry of CO into the fighting compartment impossible. Month long tests made sure that vehicles could stay underwater with engines running for up to 2.5 hours. Only the first 495 tanks were fitted with this fording apparatus.

For the fording tests, a concrete pool was built at the Henschel test center in Haustenbeck; it allowed diving depths of up to 6.66 meters. The total water volume of the pool was about 4400 cubic meters. The entrance and exit had an incline of 15 degrees. At the deepest spot in the pool were two heavy drain plugs for draining, which could be done within 9 to 11 minutes. Above the pool was a command bridge, with an observation cabin behind it containing measuring instruments, telephone, and radio sending and receiving equipment. During fording tests, a special flashing device, which could send 18 different signals, was attached to the tank.

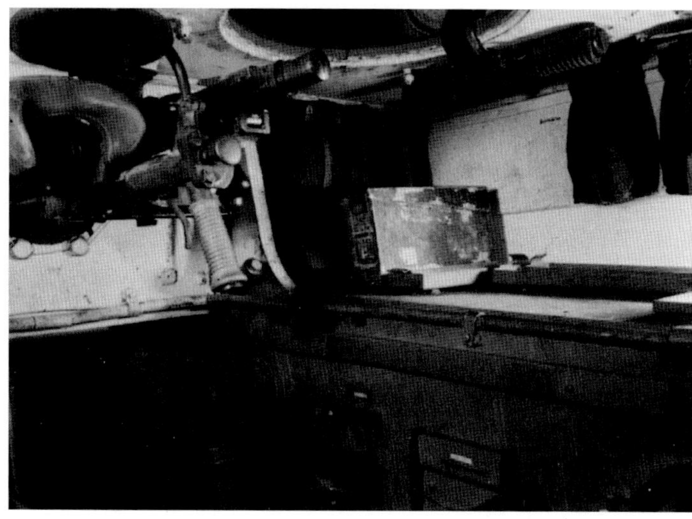

The radioman's seat with the MG 34 built into the bow plate. The hatch can be seen above it. The machine-gun ammunition is stored in the side extension at right. The radio sets were to the radioman's left, above the gearbox. The right front shock absorber is visible behind the brake housing.

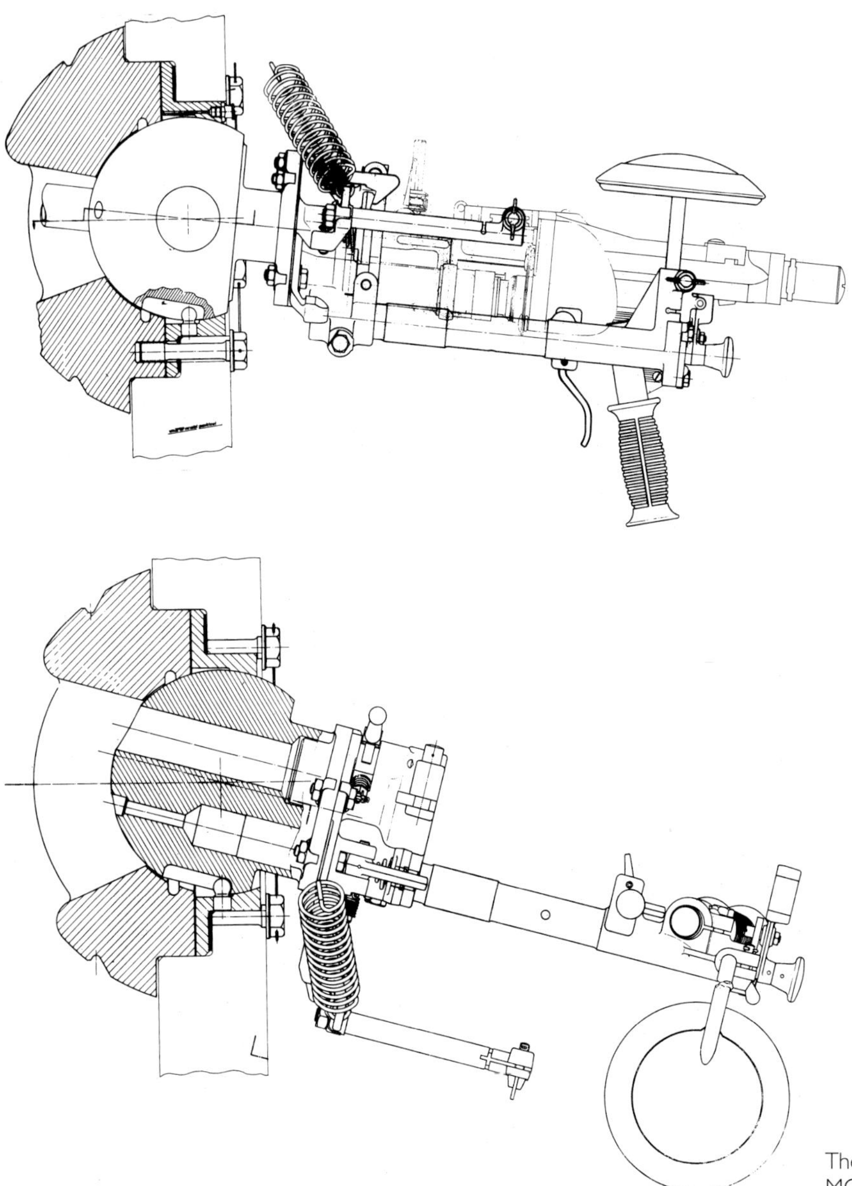

The drawings show details of the ball mantlet for the radioman's MG 34.

On July 12, 1943, the first fording tests took place in a lake on the grounds. Divers were on hand who could, in an emergency, connect the towing cable already attached to the tank to recovery (Panther) vehicles. The whole fording time during these tests was one hour and 33 minutes. In the vehicle, water depths averaging 1.5 to 3 cm were measured. The air in the tank was good, with the temperature somewhat lower than the temperature outside.

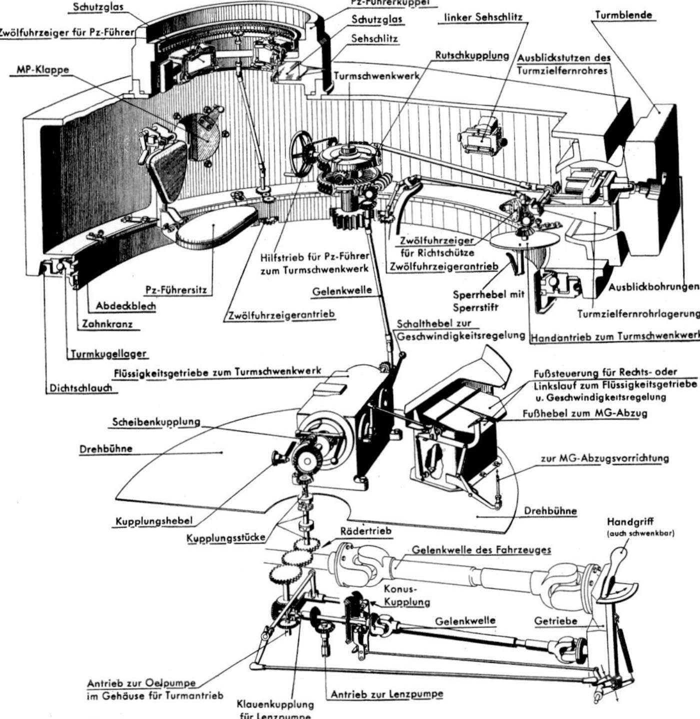

The schematic drawing explains the turret-turning mechanism.

The turret, which could turn 360 degrees, was supported on its turning ring by ball bearings. It consisted of the turret mantle, the roof with the commander's cupola, and the rounded shield with the tank gun and MG. The turning stage was directly connected to the turret. Underneath was a sliding-ring connector for the electric power to the turret. Elevating the gun was done by hand with an elevation machine. Traversing was done with the turret traversing mechanism, which was operated by hand or hydraulically. With hydraulic drive, the turret could be turned 360 degrees in a minute at an engine speed of 1500 rpm.

The turret of the "Tiger E" tank with the new commander's cupola. Below is the turret body without the gun mount.

A look at the left side of the turret.

A look into the turret toward the left front.

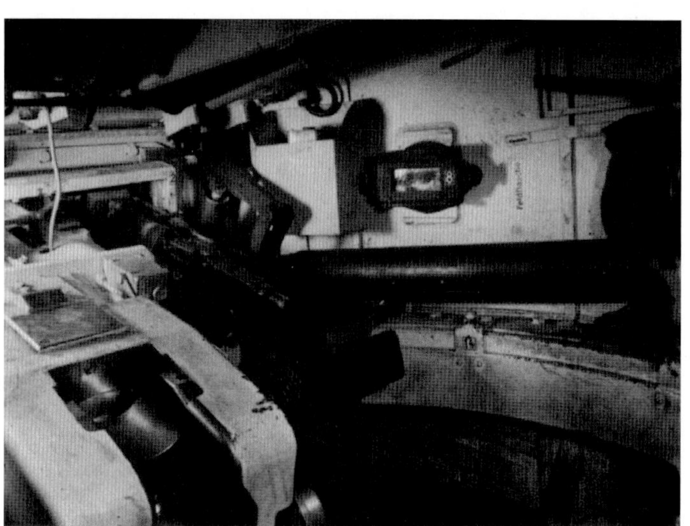

A look into the turret toward the right front.

A look at the rear wall of the turret. The ventilator is in the roof at the upper left.

The right side of the turret with the emergency hatch.

A look under the breech of the gun. At the upper left is the port for the turret visor.

The original shape of the commander's cupola.

A look at the gunner's seat and the turret-turning mechanism.

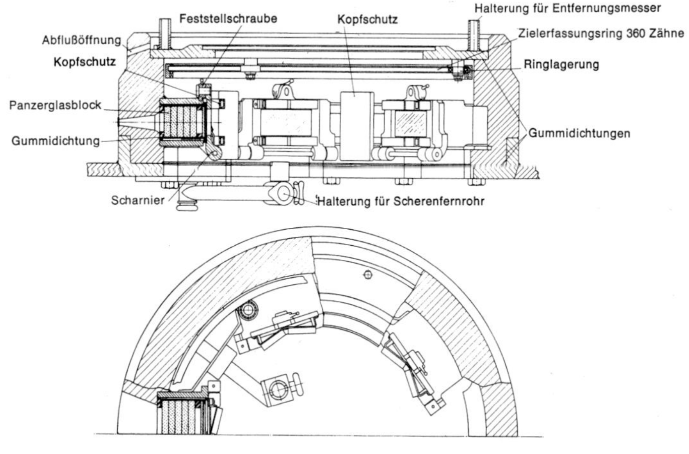

A cutaway view of the commander's cupola.

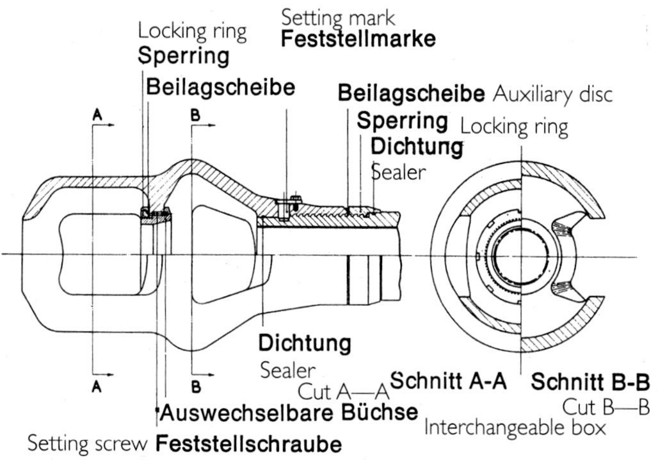

Einzelheiten der Mündungsbremse der 8,8 cm KwK 36 L/56.

Details of the muzzle brake of the 8.8 cm KwK 36 L/56.

The drive of the turret-turning mechanism led from the gearbox through a driveshaft to a friction coupling, which was turned on by the radioman by pushing down the turret-drive handle. From there, the power passed through several crown wheels and bevel drives to the disc clutch attached to the fluid drive. This was turned on by the loader as soon as the turret was to be turned. The fluid drive drove the lower spiral of the turret-turning mechanism via two bevel gears and the upper driveshaft. By a spiral wheel and a bevel-gear turning shaft, the driving pinion in the turret's turning ring was thus driven.

Activating the turret-turning mechanism by hand was done with a handwheel in front of the gunner's seat, which operated the upper spiral in the turning mechanism via two bevel gears and a driveshaft. This turned the upper bevel gear of the turning mechanism via a sliding coupling and, through the drive pinion, the turret gears. An auxiliary drive for the commander also turned the upper spiral in the turning mechanism, but the gunner could lock this by releasing a click on his handwheel. The sliding coupling in the turning mechanism and an overflow valve in the fluid drive prevented damaging the turret drive if the gun should hit an obstacle.

The locations of equipment on the outside of the vehicle.

Loading plan—outside

1. Close defense weapon
2. Towing cable
3. 15 mm cable for pulling the tracks on
4. Barrel-cleaning device
5. Covering for air intake to engine compartment
6. Sledge hammer
7. Shovel
8. Cable dispenser
9. Spade
10. Axe
11. Wire cutters
12. Baggage rack
13. TETRA fire extinguisher
14. Antenna shield
15. Spare track links
16. 15-ton winch
17. Track tool
18. Towing shackles
19. Starting crank
20. Crowbar
21. Headlight
22. Smoke-cartridge launcher
23. Openings to attach camouflage canvas (as truck or bus)

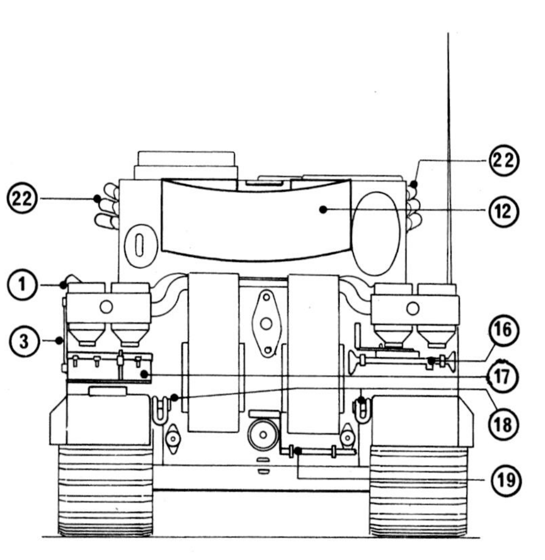

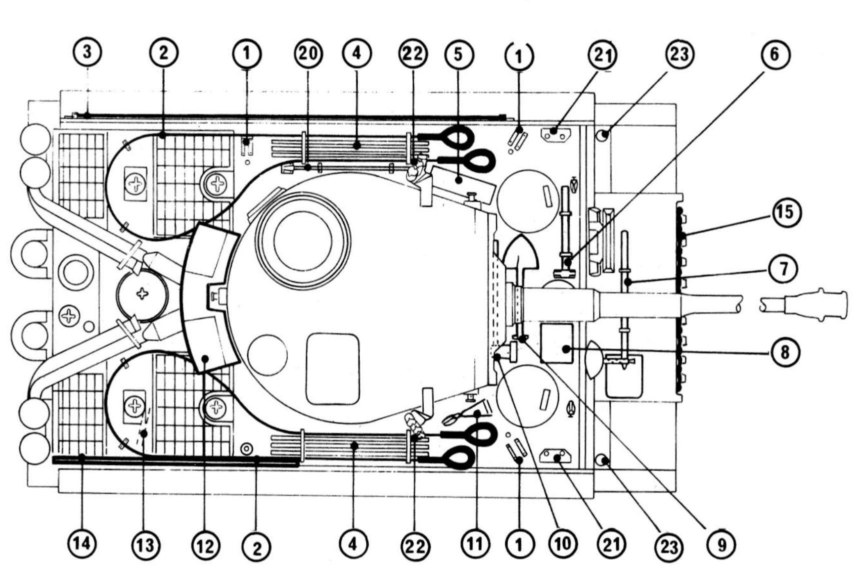

The fluid drive (Böhringer-Sturm oil drive) consisted of two identical pumps with casings around them, from which one was operated, and the other worked as an oil motor. They were united through a sucking and pressing canal in a fixed tube body to form a closed circulation system. The regulation of the drive speed of the oil motor, and thus the turning speed of the turret, was done by regulating the amount of pump pressure. By adjusting the outer extent of the housing, the work space of the pump, and thus the amount it could pump, were changed, and the pumping direction and thus the swinging direction were changed. This adjustment was made by tipping the gunner's foot rest. The greatest turning speed that the fluid drive could produce could be set with a lever on the drive housing, which changed the outer extent on the oil motor. The winter equipment of a tank consisted of the following items:

- Cooling water heating device with a blow-lamp. The device was mounted in the lower left corner of the engine compartment. It was heated from outside with the blow-lamp. The blow-lamp was housed in the fighting compartment next to the radioman.
- Attachments and locking flap for cooling-water flow (omitted from vehicles with built in cooling-water heaters).
- Crank-starting mechanism.
- Starting fuel pump (attached to the firewall).
- Collector-isolator box; by turning on the heating plate that was attached to the bottom of the isolating box, the collector could be kept warm by the generator while on the move. The lighting of the green indicator light showed that the heating plate was turned on.

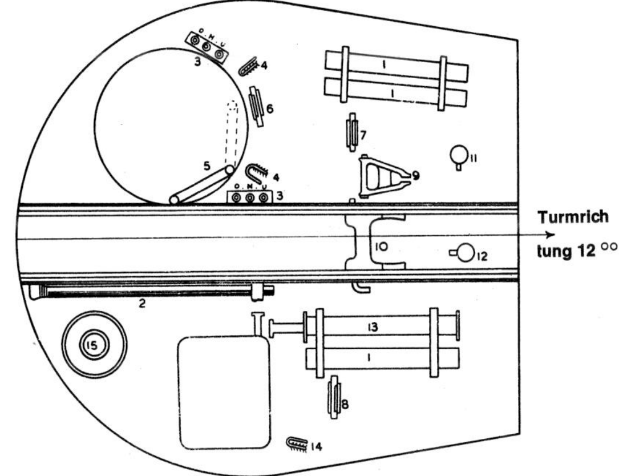

The location of equipment on the turret roof
Loading plan turret roof underside
1. Respiratory tube
2. Watertight cover for turret MG (for deep fording)
3. Smoke-cartridge trigger
4. Commander's handgrip
5. Bracket for commander's shear scope
6. Commander's reading lamp
7. Gunner's reading lamp
8. Loader's reading lamp
9. Bracket for turret targeting scope
10. Bow for elevating barrel
11. Socket for targeting scope and elevation indicator
12. Socket for firing mechanism
13. Equalizer for loading lid
14. Loader's handgrip
15. Exhaust ventilator, 12 V, 10 Amp.

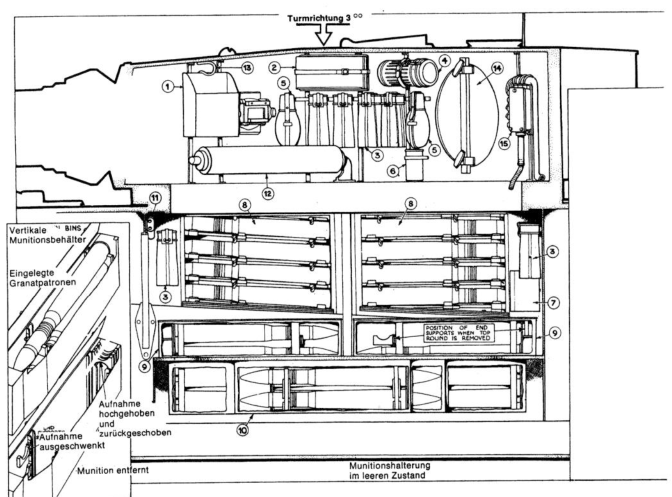

Loading plan—right side of turret and fighting compartment
1. Baggage box
2. Standard and legs for turret machine gun
3. Machine-gun belt bag, 6 x 150 rounds
4. Gas mask
5. Field flask
6. Unloader
7. Machine-gun tools
8. Ammunition box, 16 rounds
9. Ammunition box, 4 rounds
10. Ammunition box, 6 rounds
11. Spare jacket for turret MG
12. Turret equalizing spring housing
13. Smoke cartridge release
14. Emergency hatch
15. Turret securing box

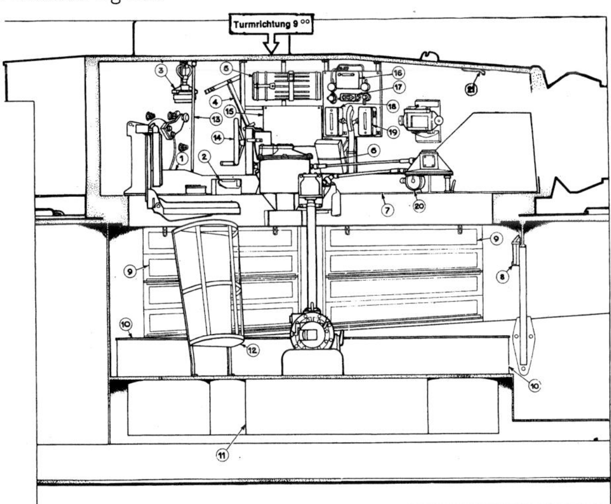

Loading plan and ammunition storage on the right and left sides of the turret. Loading plan—left side of turret and fighting compartment
1. Map rack
2. Telescope
3. Watertight machine gun cover (for deep fording)
4. Flare pistol
5. Gas mask
6. Barrel and cradle book
7. Gunner's position
8. Prism socket
9. Ammunition rack, 16 rounds
10. Ammunition rack, 4 rounds
11. Baggage box
12. Cord basket (for flags, etc.)
13. Shaft for direction indicator in cupola
14. Commander's turret handwheel
15. Directions for sealing turret
16. Emergency battery for firing
17. Emergency net
18. Wall socket for commander's communication
19. Wall socket for gunner's communication
20. Turret direction indicator
21. Smoke cartridge release

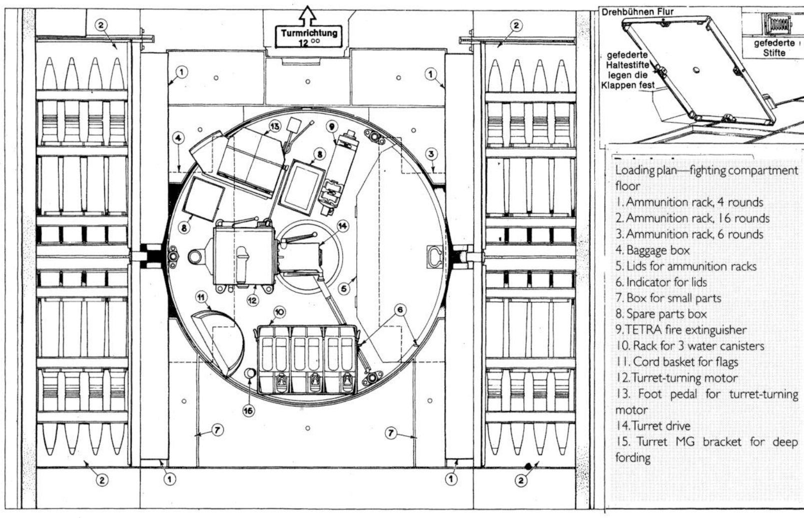

Ammunition storage and details of fighting compartment floor

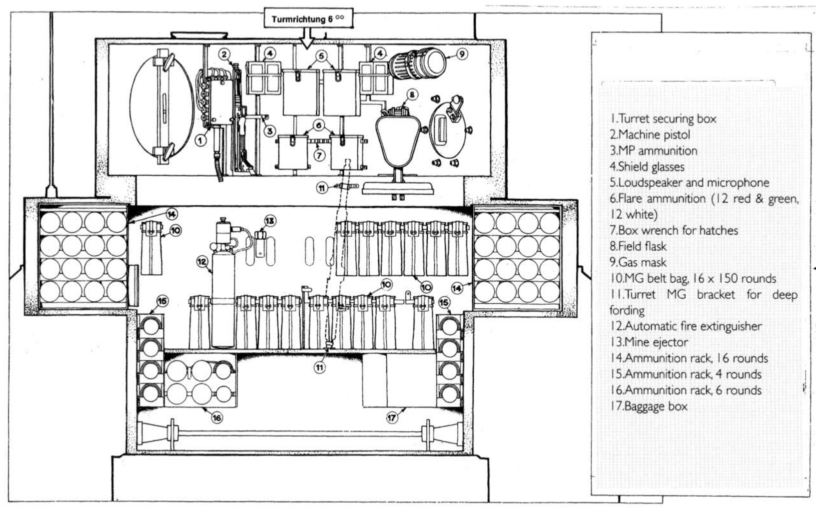

Storage of equipment and ammunition, cutaway view

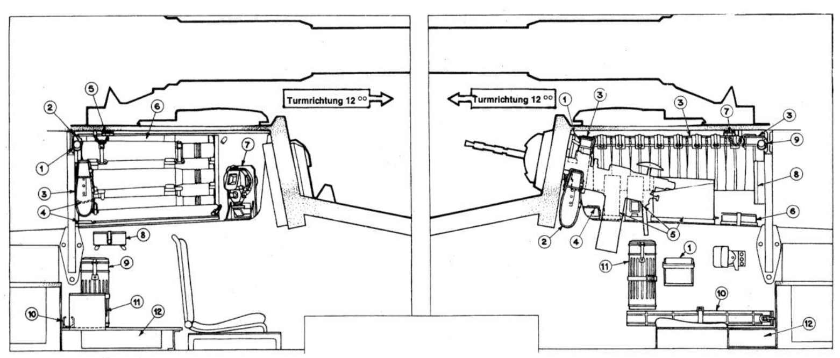

Location of equipment and ammunition in driver's and radioman's space

Loading Plan—Driver's Space
1. Respiration tube
2. Prism socket
3. Field flask
4. Magnetic lamp
5. Headlight
6. Ammunition rack, 6 rounds
7. Course gyrocompass
8. Telescope equipment
9. Gas mask
10. Space for oil can
11. Loudspeaker and microphone
12. Small container for adjusting tools

Loading Plan—Radioman's Seat
1. Prism socket
2. Field flask
3. MG belt bag, 16 x 150 rounds
4. First-aid kit
5. MG equipment
6. MG standard and legs
7. Headlight
8. MG tools
9. Respiratory tube
10. Two spare MG barrels
11. Gas mask
12. Tool kit

- Connection plate for connecting an outside generator to load and quickly heat the battery. The plate had a negative terminal, a positive terminal (middle terminal) for loading and warming, and a positive terminal for fast heating.

Dr.-habil. Dipl.-Ing. Erwin Aders, who had worked for the firm since 1936, was responsible for the technical development of armored vehicles for Henschel. Henschel had planned two different versions of the vehicle, and Krupp built the turret with the 8.8 cm KwK 36 L/56 for the "H 1" version. The "H 2" version was supposed to use the turret suggested by Rheinmetall-Borsig, with the 7.5 cm KwK 42 L/70. The wooden model of this turret had a ball mantlet on the rear wall for an MG 34. The turret was not finished.

Because of the urgent need for vehicles of this type—above all, at the beginning of the Russian campaign—the VK 4501 built by Porsche and Henschel were released for series production without testing in advance. At Henschel, a series of 60 tanks in two series had been planned in mid-1941. Parts were ordered for 100 tanks. Without even one

Panzerkampfwagen Tiger Type H 2 (suggestion)

While Henschel fitted the 8.8 cm KwK 36 L/56 into the turret, Rheinmetall-Borsig developed a turret with the 7.5 cm KwK 42. The Tiger with this turret was to be called Type H 2. The turret was not built.

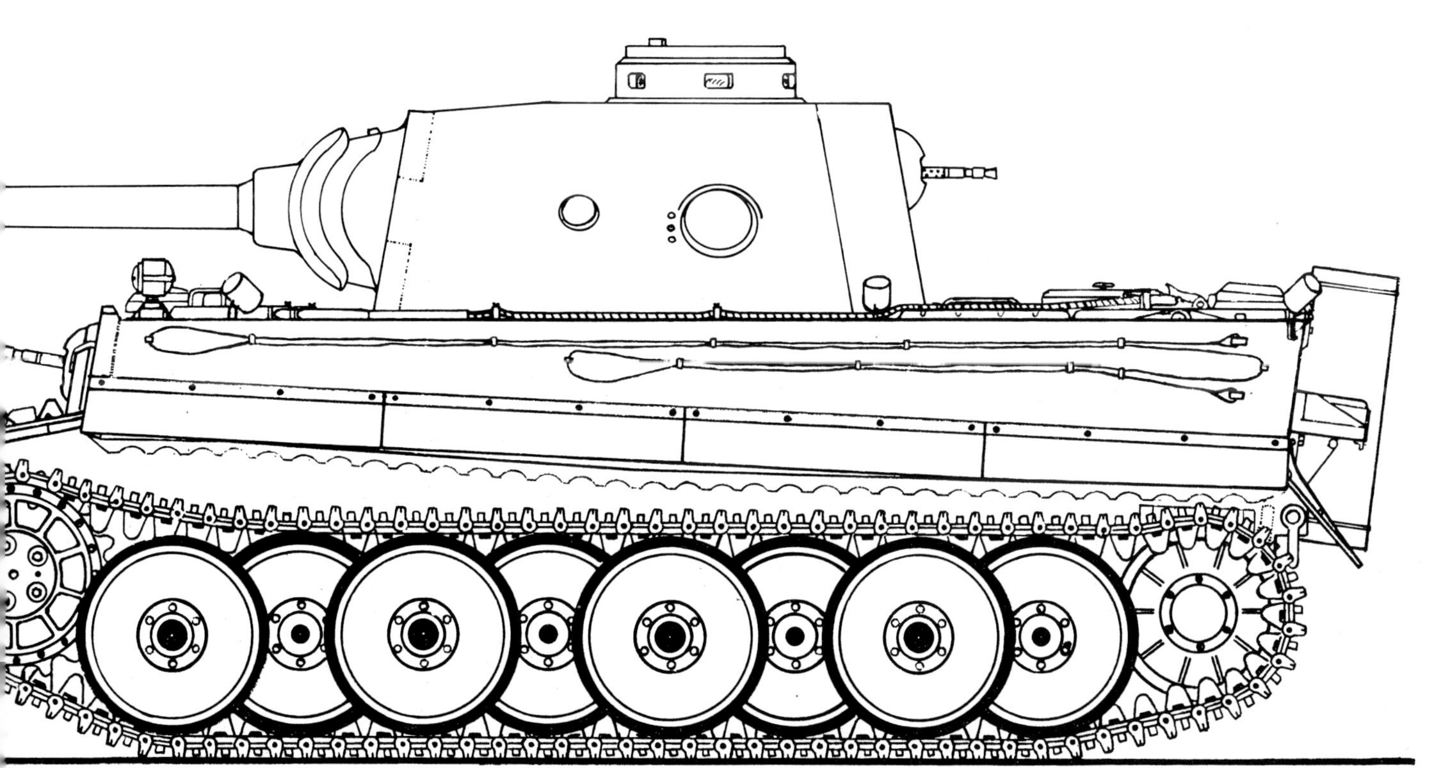

vehicle having been built or tested, orders for parts plus tools for a mass production of at least 1300 vehicles resulted, as well as for the necessary supplies of spare parts. On April 4, 1942, Hitler ordered the development of an antitank shell (*Panzergranate* 40) with increased piercing power for the 7.5 and 8.8 cm guns for the "Tiger" tank. At least ten of these shells had to be present in every tank.

On October 26, 1940, a design for a tank transport and recovery vehicle for the "VK 3601" had been requested from the

* *Amtsgruppe Kraftfahrwesen*, Inspektion 6 of the Army high Command.

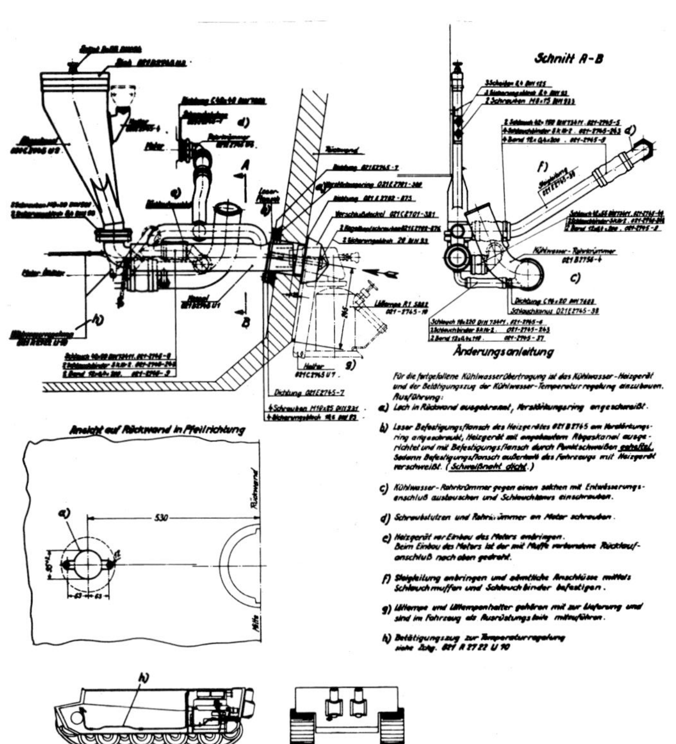

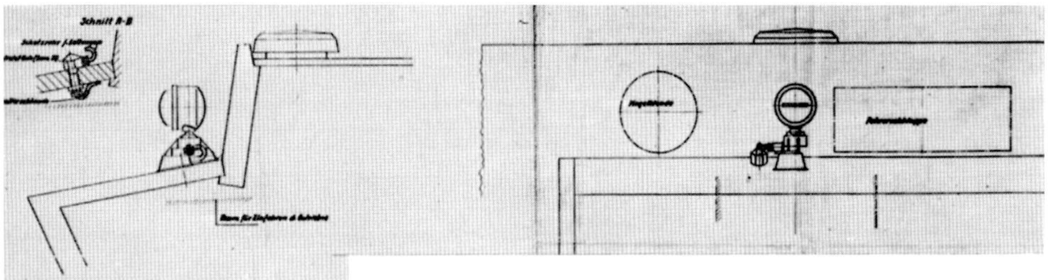

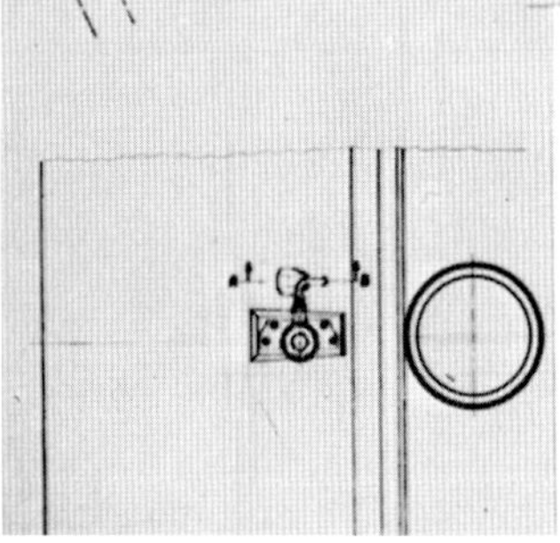

After the cooling-water transmission, a cooling-water heater could be added later. This drawing shows how it was to be installed.

This drawing shows a headlight attached to the last version of the Tiger E.

Tank transport vehicle (Porsche Type 142)

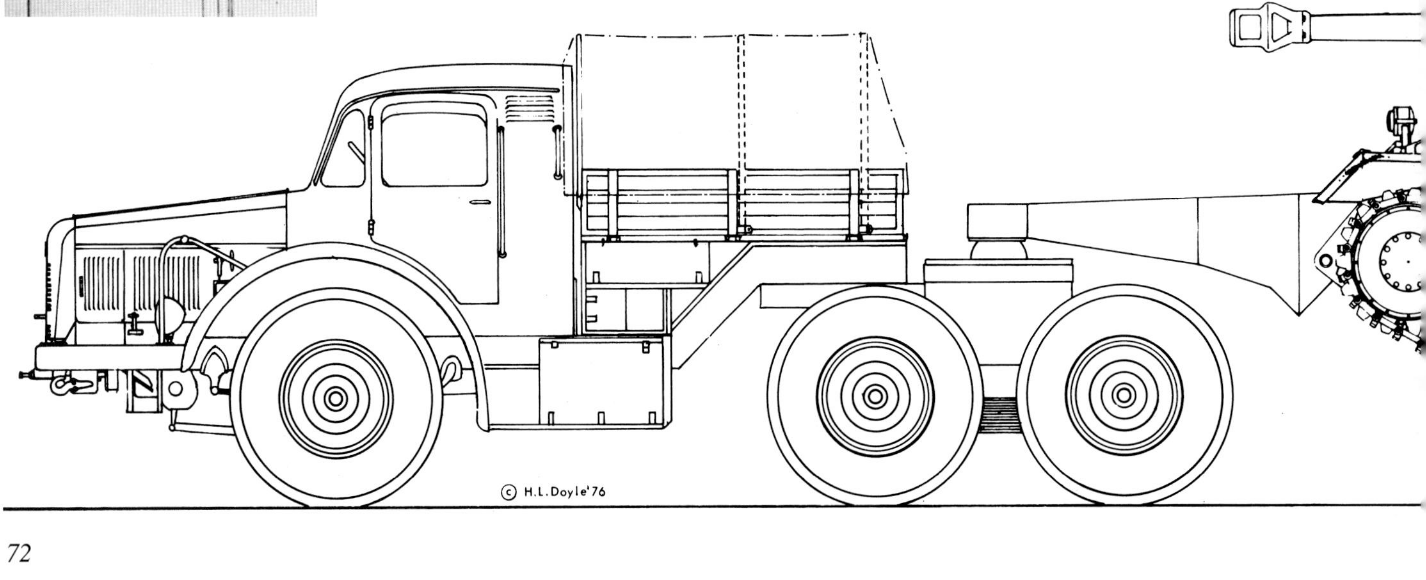

© H.L.Doyle'76

Kämper-Motoren AG through the AG K.In 6.* The Kämper firm was responsible for the Diesel engines and the assembly of the vehicles, while the electric motors were to be provided by the firm of Brown-Boverie & Co. The hydraulic system came from the firm of A. Teves; Trucks and trailers had all-wheel drive in the form of equal uniform drive pairs, each with one electric motor per wheel. Two of the Kämper 150 HP "6 D 13 E" (6 cylinders, 13.5 liter displacement) Diesel engines were coupled with BBC generators, and made a top speed of 40 km/h possible. The weight of the truck was about 20 tons, and that of the trailer about 18 tons. The vehicle had rubber tires, and a 4- to 6-man crew was planned. Two test vehicles were built in 1942; a pre-production series of 30 was being prepared. Hitler did not consider it necessary on May 25, 1942, that just as many heavy transporters as Tigers should be built. He considered a series of, at first, 60 to 80 of these vehicles to be sufficient. He also considered a ratio of 1 : 2 to be quite appropriate. He also required that these transporters must also be usable for other heavy loads.

Independently of this solution, the Porsche firm busied itself from 1941 on with the development of a heavy transport vehicle for tanks and materials. The Porsche design "142" was a five-axle transport vehicle with Diesel-electric all-wheel drive. The three-axle towing vehicle was designed as a truck tractor. In principle, the load was supposed to be carried hanging between the tractor and a two-axle trailer. For this, uniform suspending apparatus was needed on all armored vehicles to be moved in this manner. The distance between the tractor and trailer could thus be varied, which was especially important for armored vehicles of different sizes. A steering apparatus on the trailer, working by means of two steering levers, allowed electric steering as on the tank itself. The two trailer axles were electrically driven. The total length of the tractor and trailer was 17.4 meters.

On October 9, 1942, the Daimler-Benz AG announced that a model "MB 819" test motor for the heavy transporter project had been delivered in 1941. So if the first tests worked out well, perhaps series production could begin later. The 12-cylinder Diesel engine, originally developed for tanks, produced 450 HP.

Then on December 3, 1942, it was announced that a heavy transporter was being developed for the "Organisation Todt" at the Technische Hochschule in Berlin-Charlottenburg. To drive its

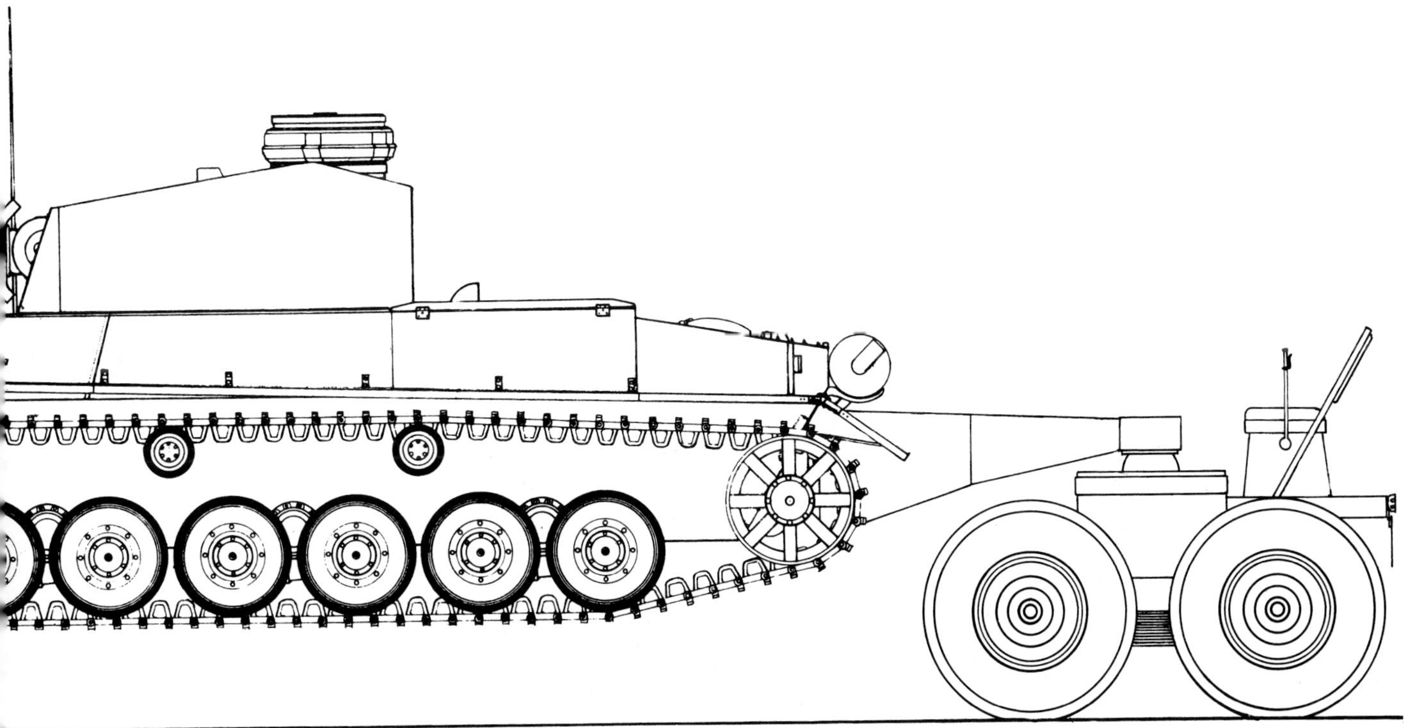

A low-loader trailer with a load limit of 60 tons for transporting vehicles of the Tiger class had 40 all-rubber tires of 670 x 170 size. It was made by Karl Kässbohrer of Ulm. Factory number 17 498, built 1944, weight 23,000 kg, load limit 68,000 kg, compressed air brakes.

generators, two of the "MB 819" test motors were made available. A future need, as before, would depend on the test results. But the project was not completed. Only a few individual heavy-load trailers that could carry up to 60 tons were built to carry the "VK 4501."

In March 1942, Hitler emphasized his interest in getting the first Tigers to the front at once. Testing could take place simultaneously with front action. The new vehicles were to become available from May 1942 on in, if possible, increased numbers. Their possible action would be of the greatest importance.

On March 19, 1942, Hitler took note of what numbers of Tigers would be available by October 1942 and March 1943. It was pure theory when he was promised 60 Porsche and 25 Henschel Tigers by the end of September 1942, and another 135 Porsche and Henschel Tigers by the end of February 1943. It was to be decided as quickly as possible whether the Porsche or the Henschel vehicle was to be built, so that just one could be produced in large numbers. A decision in advance was possible under circumstances—if the Porsche tank were extraordinarily successful.

On March 2, 1942, Hitler asked for additional cooling for the desert use of these vehicles, but at the same time, also for vehicle heating. Professor Porsche declared that these problems would be solved, and that he had already found a solution for his vehicles.

To be able to show the Tiger tanks to Hitler on his birthday (April 20, 1942), Henschel and Porsche (at the Nibelungenwerk) worked day and night. Each firm produced a Tiger. The pictures show the first Tiger at the Nibelungenwerk.

The first vehicle is seen before being transported to Rastenburg. At the left front on the hull side, the welded opening originally planned as an exit hatch can be seen.

For the Henschel Tiger, other railroad transit had to be halted, as the vehicle exceeded the loading profile.

Dr. Aders, in the writings he left, described the introduction of the first "Tiger" vehicles in a way that we do not want to keep from our readers:

"...while work was done with all available and obtainable forces, and the preparation for production already was planned for several hundred vehicles, there came the Hauptamtsleiter Otto Saur to the—then frightening—conclusion that the first vehicle should be introduced to the Führer on 20 April as a birthday present. With extra workers on several shifts, disregarding all economic factors, the realization of this bold venture finally succeeded; but there was no longer time for road testing. The vehicle may have been driven 500 meters before it was put on a flatcar. That was on 18 April. The tracks hung over the railroad profile by 50 mm on each side. The railroad directors therefore closed the Kassel-Rasteburg (East Prussia) line to all other traffic, so that meetings would be avoided. At a secondary depot near the headquarters, the transport arrived on 19 April. A 70-ton Reichsbahn crane stood ready under steam at 9:00. We were not allowed to drive immediately to the headquarters on a public street, but had to wait along with our "rival" (Porsche) to use the blocked-off street.*

Professor Dr. h. c. F. Porsche had, in fact, also received a contract from Hitler (omitting the WaA), and apparently had not wanted to decline. For his 50-ton vehicle with the same turret (which Krupp built) he preferred two motors, and in fact Diesels, air-cooled, with electric power transmitted to two electric motors at the rear end of the vehicle. The steering was to be electric.

We had an hour to wait, and used it for test drives and adjustments; we also gave explanations to a group of officers from the headquarters, the younger ones in particular, showing a transfigured mood. The transport from St. Valentin (Nibelungenwerk) arrived around 10:00. A flatbed truck with a generator was there; they had obviously still been doing welding work on the way. The tracks were lying there; they were stretched out, and the vehicle was set onto them. By chance, and unfortunately, it was now crossways to the rail line. The first trip under its own power had to begin with a right-angle turn. That did not succeed; the tracks gradually dug in more and more deeply during the stubbornly repeated attempts, and after an hour they were on the ballast of the pavement. Designer Reimspiess asked us for help, but his colleague from electric planning (Zadnig) forbade it. Porsche stood there and let everything happen. Then we received instructions to drive to the entrance of the headquarters and park our vehicle in the woods. Only later did we learn that after our departure the steam crane had been warmed up again, and turned the Porsche vehicle in the right direction to drive off. On a paved street it lived up to expectations, and also reached the parking place in the woods.

The next morning (4/20/1942) the two tanks drove into headquarters. About 10:30 A.M. the 'great ones' of the Reich assembled. Goebbels and Göring were missing. When Hitler appeared about 11:00, the representatives of industry were introduced in order: Krupp—Nibelungenwerk—Henschel. Porsche then received the Kriegsverdienstkreuz FirstClass. After that, Hitler had the design of the Porsche vehicle and turret (by Senior Engineer Heerlein of Krupp) explained to him for half an hour. It was obvious that all prejudices were already in favor of Porsche. Hitler had only two or three minutes left for Henschel. In any case, he got onto the Henschel tank, struggled to think of a question, which dealt with the cooling system (because he saw the grille for the cooling system in the roof), and climbed back down. By this time I already had the feeling that Hitler sensed my rejection and my cool attitude, and was probably hindered by it. The actual showing took place that morning on the straight exit road for vehicles to the good hard road that led past the 'Wolf's Den'; both tanks soon disappeared in the distance, but neither one

* Chief Office Manager = State Secretary in the *Reichministerium* (Speer).

came right back. For Henschel, the still untested brakes had to be adjusted; from Porsche we heard nothing. While we then waited at headquarters for further instructions, it became known that a second showing, to Göring, would take place in the afternoon.

The Reich Marshal arrived around 3:00 P.M. in absolutely operetta-like manner, with great glory and splendor. He handed his marshal's staff with his dress sword to a comrade from St. Valentin to hold, and climbed into the Porsche tank with Hitler. Again it was explained, but this time the Henschel vehicle was not looked at. When the Porsche vehicle had gone off on driving practice, Hauptamtsmeister Otto Saur insisted, to my horror, that the Henschel tank make haste to the fallow field beside the road. I was all set to make a catastrophic refusal, but was disappointed in a somewhat "triumphal" manner. As if the showing had been practiced, our tank drove away, crossed a gravel-covered field path without delay, as if it was a matter of course, and got back onto the road in the distance."

In June 1942 tests were begun to see if the "Tiger" vehicle could be fitted with 120 mm front armor.

On June 23, 1942, Hitler was informed that by May 12, 1943, a total of 285 "Tigers" would be available. He showed himself to be pleased.

Minister Speer, on the basis of test results, pointed out the weaknesses of these heavy vehicles, whereupon Hitler made the following demands:

- The "Tiger" had to be ready for the front this year, and in fact, in September at the latest.
- A gentler way of driving had to be provided, or else every vehicle would become unusable.

These comparison models show the difference between the Henschel and Porsche versions of the Tiger (dark: Porsche; light: Henschel).

- It was planned to use the tanks in France at first, and since the rough conditions in Russia were ruled out there, the easier conditions of use in testing the vehicles would likewise be taken into consideration.
- The heaviest Russian tank (KW II) was to be subjected to long-term testing under the same conditions. It was then to be seen that the Russian tank, in terms of materials as well, would not live up to the highest demands.
- Heavy vehicles had to be driven with feeling.
- Both "Tiger" vehicles would then be tested according to the eased test conditions.

Chronic problems with the motors delayed preparation of the Porsche vehicles, which had been laid out at the Nibelungenwerk in the meantime.

Henschel began series production of the "*Panzerkampfwagen* VI—Tiger E" (Sd.Kfz. 181) in August 1942. The assigned chassis numbers ran from 250 001 to 252 000. The following numbers were made by Henschel as the sole builder:

Month	**1942**	**1943**	**1944**
January	--	35	93
February	--	32	95
March	--	41	86
April	1	46	104
May	--	50	100
June	--	60	75
July	--	65	64
August	8	60	6
September	3	85	--
October	11	50	--
November	25	60	--
December	30	65	--
Total	78	649	623

A look at the production of Type E "Tiger" tanks is provided by this series of pictures:

A look at major component production.

The suspension-arm section of the mechanical department.

Turning the turret seat during hull preparation.

Cutting the grooves with a special machine during hull preparation.

Boring holes with the eight-drill boring machine during hull preparation.

Making the steering-gear housings.

Below: Boring out the hull under the roof borer.

Below: Checking the steering-gear housing.

The assembly line for the final drive housings.

Scouring a suspension arm on its line.

The finest boring of the planetary beam in the final drive.

Above: Boring a suspension arm on its line. Below: Boring out a suspension arm with a four-drill horizontal borer.

Checking a planetary beam.

Finished suspension arms are turned over to production.

The installation of the leading-wheel crank on the assembly line.

Assembling road wheels in pre-assembly.

Installing the suspension arms on the assembly line.

In pre-assembly, the Maybach motors are made ready.

The torsion-bar suspension is attached to the suspension arms.

Mounting the road wheels on the suspension arms.

Now the chassis are driven, powered by bottled gas.

In Step 8 the tracks are put on.

An almost finished chassis on the assembly line.

During production, single vehicles are taken for testing with weight rings.

The turret, made by Wegmann, was mounted on the chassis by Henschel.

Then the Tigers were completely equipped.

Finished vehicles ready to be accepted. At the far right are two "Panther" tanks, also made by Henschel.

These four pictures show a brand new vehicle being taken over by a tank crew. It is using loading tracks.

This comparison shows the vehicle with loading tracks in the foreground, while the one in back has combat tracks.

	Number	Purchase Contract	Army Contract	Notes
Test vehicles	2	424 047	SS 006-6307/41	
Test vehicle	1	424 048	SS "	
Series	30	420 437	SS 4911-210-5904/41	
Series	30	420 438	SS "	
Series	40	420 439	SS "	
Series	200	420 442	SS 4911-210-5910/41/42	
Series	124	420 480	SS "	
Series	250	420 520	SS "	
Series	490	420 560	SS "	Chassis # 250675-251164
Series	128	420 660	SS "	Chassis # 251165-251292
Series, later	45	420 750	SS "	

By July 9, 1942, the test vehicle had covered 320 kilometers at Kummersdorf. Motor damage appeared; the first front road-wheel cranks were very bent, and had to be replaced. The gearbox could be shifted only to 6th gear. The fuel consumption was 5.5 liters per kilometer.

Tigers and Panthers being loaded onto Syms cars in the Henschel firm's railroad depot.

At this point, Henschel still urged that tank production should be transferred from the Kassel works to Berlin-Marienfelde in favor of locomotive production.

At a meeting of the Tank Commission on July 14, 1942, it was decided that two more Henschel and Porsche Tigers should be delivered to Kummersdorf at once for testing. Of them, one was to be tested under easy and one under severe conditions. On the subject, it was stated that except for the torsion bars of the Tiger, no highly stressed chromium-alloy steel was used. On July 15, 1942, it had been decided that the second series of Henschel Tigers should also be fitted with the 8.8 cm KwK L/56 gun. Until May 1, 1943, 145 units were listed as the minimum production total, which had to be not only produced in the factory, but ready for action, meaning driven in, equipped, and accepted. From

Four-side views of a new Type E Tiger tank.

Tiger Type E, seen from above with opened and closed hatches.

A Tiger with a snowplow attached (July 1942).

Type E during snow testing in the Grossglockner area, under the direction of Major (Ing.) Dipl.-Ing. Th. Icken.

Changing tracks was thoroughly practiced in training. With a track weight of about three tons, it was no easy task (and took 25 minutes).

This picture of changing from loading to marching tracks was always seen at the unloading depots.

The two pictures show the different widths of the loading and marching tracks (the difference was 400 mm).

Servicing these costly vehicles was accorded great importance.

Recovery was also practiced thoroughly. Below is the 18-ton towing vehicle, used especially for tank recovery. Some were equipped with a 40-ton winch and listed as Sd.Kfz. 9/6.

Kummersdorf there came a report on July 16, 1942, that the test vehicle had covered 209 kilometers offroad. Colonel Thomale, who drove it himself, showed his satisfaction. By July 22, 1942, 960 km in all had been covered by the vehicle, whose fighting weight was 56.7 tons. In medium-heavy country the average speed was 18 km/h, with a fuel consumption of 430 liters per 100 km. The vehicle was not yet combat-ready in its form at that time. The equipping of a combat-ready group with some 25 vehicles could not be expected before October 1, 1942.

In comparison drives with the Porsche vehicle at Kummersdorf on July 27, 1942—in heavy country and sand—the latter broke down completely. The Henschel vehicle fulfilled all the requirements. Porsche was then given three more months for testing. The final drive was to have 1 : 19 instead of 1 : 15 reduction, and the diameters of the drive sprockets and leading wheels were to be made smaller. Only every other track link was to be fitted with a driving tooth. Because of the breakdown of the Porsche Tiger, Henschel was instructed to build at least 210 of its vehicles by May 1, 1943.

The Führer called for a Tiger company with nine vehicles, completely equipped, accepted, and ready for action at the Kassel works on August 26, 1942. For it, the Henschel Tiger was declared ready for action in the west and east, with a marching speed between 15 and 20 km/h. Bad seals on the motor caused oil losses up to 15 liters in 100 kilometers. This was accepted in the bargain as bearable. Damage to the tires of the road wheels led Colonel Thomale to call for a new, improved running gear as of the 101st vehicle. This could not be developed. For winter use, Henschel cooperated with Wegmann to turn out nine Panzer III with attachments for cooling-water transfer. In action, every Tiger was to be accompanied by a "ZW" vehicle. Firing tests were carried on in Fallingbostel.* Driving-school instruction for the crews took place at Kassel-Wilhelmstal.

* Tiger *Abteilungen* 1 and 2 were formed there.

Colonel Thomale declared that the Porsche vehicle had to be rejected, on account of a too-short radius of action, oil leaks in the motor and resulting seriously worsened motor performance, and basic faults in the running gear.

The nine Henschel vehicles prepared for the troops had front suspension arms made of improved material, and the belts for the ventilator drive were changed. For underwater driving, butterfly valves were mounted between the engine and radiator compartments, as well as flanges for the attachment of cooling-water exchange with the accompanying "ZF" vehicles. These were not provided by Wegmann (for lack of the 5 cm KwK L/60), but rather by Alkett or Daimler-Benz. Internally, the Henschel Tiger was designated Device "c 10," and the improved version "c 11," The latter was to begin with five vehicles in January. The "c 10" production envisioned a total of 185 units. At the beginning of September 1942, the production capacity at Henschel was set at 50 "c 11" devices and 30 "c 10."

On August 19, 1942, General of the Artillery Leeb, as chief of the Ordnance Office, expressed his thanks to the Henschel firm for filling the quota of Tigers so urgently requested by Hitler. The request to install the Panther motor in the tiger forced Maybach to suggest that they build a transitional type between the VK 4501 and the planned VK 4503, so that as of vehicle no. 200, a VK 4502 could be equipped with the Panther motor, including the Panther cooling system. According to Maybach, it was only necessary to tilt the rear wall of the hull about 2 degrees out of the vertical. Henschel began tests in this direction. For the first nine "c 10" devices the water transfer was omitted. It was to be installed later.

The delivery date for the first four production Tigers was advanced to August 18, 1942. Devices 5 and 6 were sent to Fallingbostel on August 27, 1942. As before, the Maybach OLVAR gearbox gave a lot of trouble, mainly through the failure of the oil-pressure pump drive, and the breaking of the pressure cylinder in the upper part of the drive. The oil-pressure regulator valve also got dirty constantly.

The first four Tigers of *Panzerabteilung* 502 saw service near Mga on August 29, 1942. Here a Tiger is recovered by two 18-ton towing vehicles. The replacement motors had to be flown directly into the combat area by Ju 52 planes to make the tigers ready for action again. The picture shows the unloading of a tank motor.

These original photos of the first Tiger action came from retired Colonel Th. Icken. Of the four tanks in action, all of which broke down, three could be recovered; the fourth one was blown up.

Below: This picture shows the battlefield supplying of ammunition by the Medium *Schützenpanzerwagen* (Sd.Kfz. 251).

Reich Minister Speer decided at the end of August 1942 to issue Henschel another contract, this one for 300 Tigers. As for the question of type definition, it was decided to produce the earlier version of Tiger I up to vehicle no. 140. Vehicles 141 to 300 were to be delivered unchanged, but with an angled bow. The introduction of an intermediate type with a Panther rear, motor, ventilator, and cooling system, suggested by Maybach, was rejected.

The Zahnradfabrik Friedrichshafen had meanwhile developed an electric gearbox, which according to a document of September 2, 1942, was to be tested first in VK 3601, and then in VK 4501.

On September 10, 1942, instructions were given for the Tiger to be fitted with heating for the fighting compartment.

The first action of Tiger vehicles produced by Henschel took place on August 29, 1942, in the vicinity of Leningrad. The badly prepared attack came to grief in unfavorable terrain, and led to a premature revelation of the secret. In mid-September 1942 the first reports from the front told of damage to the shifting and steering gears, which made Colonel Thomale think that the tiger had to be refused as not ready for the troops. He requested a check as to whether the ZF gearbox used in the Panther could not also be used in the Tiger. Colonel Thomale said literally that he would refuse to send German men into combat with such a vehicle. A representative of the Maybach firm replied that the firm had always been told the vehicles did not necessarily have to be ready for the troops to use. All efforts were simply to be made to send the tanks to the front, so they could be tested there in the field. The Maybach gearboxes were also made by the Adler firm in Frankfurt, on the Main. Henschel reported to *Oberbaurat* Kniekamp on September 21, 1942, that the ZF all-claw gearbox could be installed in the Tiger.

On September 23, 1942, two "12 E 170" electric gearboxes were finished by ZF and ready for installation in Tigers. The new steering gear, available since the end of September 1942, was built in series by the firms of AVOG in Holland and Mühlschlegel of Bühlerthal, Baden.

At the beginning of September 1942, Hitler wanted the first series of the still unavailable Porsche Tigers sent to Africa at once, since he considered them, with their air-cooled motors, to be especially suitable for that area.

In these lifting tests with hydraulic telescopic lifts, Type Hydrovis, for 15 to 30 tons, easily recognizable details of the running gear and tracks of the Henschel Tiger can be seen.

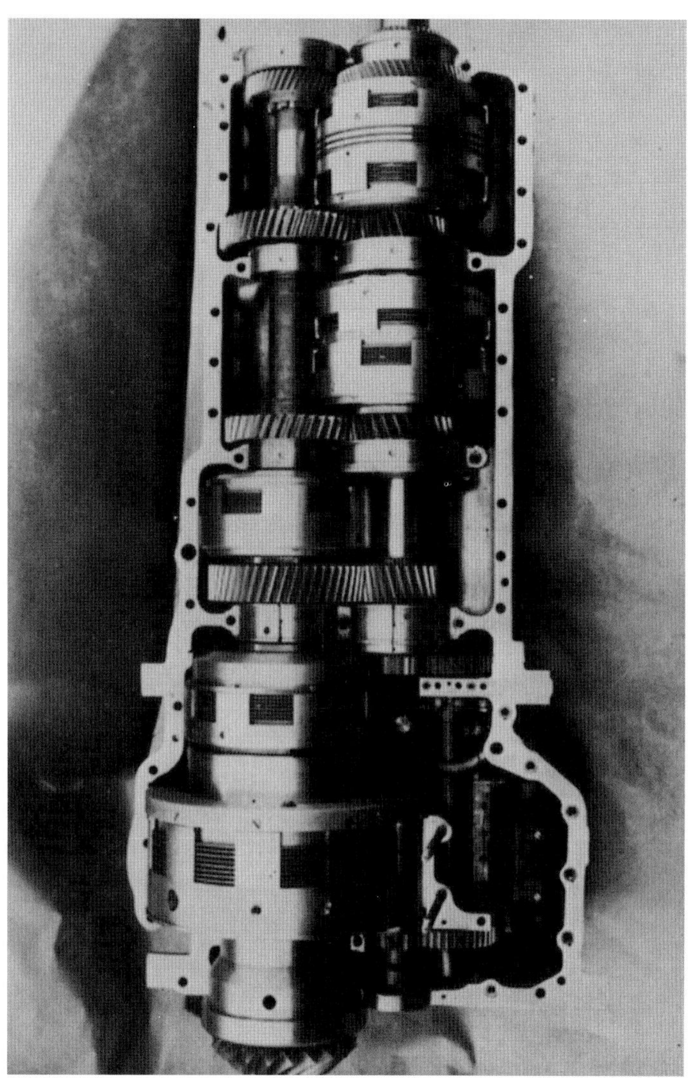

The 2 x 6-speed (12-speed) electric clutch and gearbox, Type 12 E 170 test model.

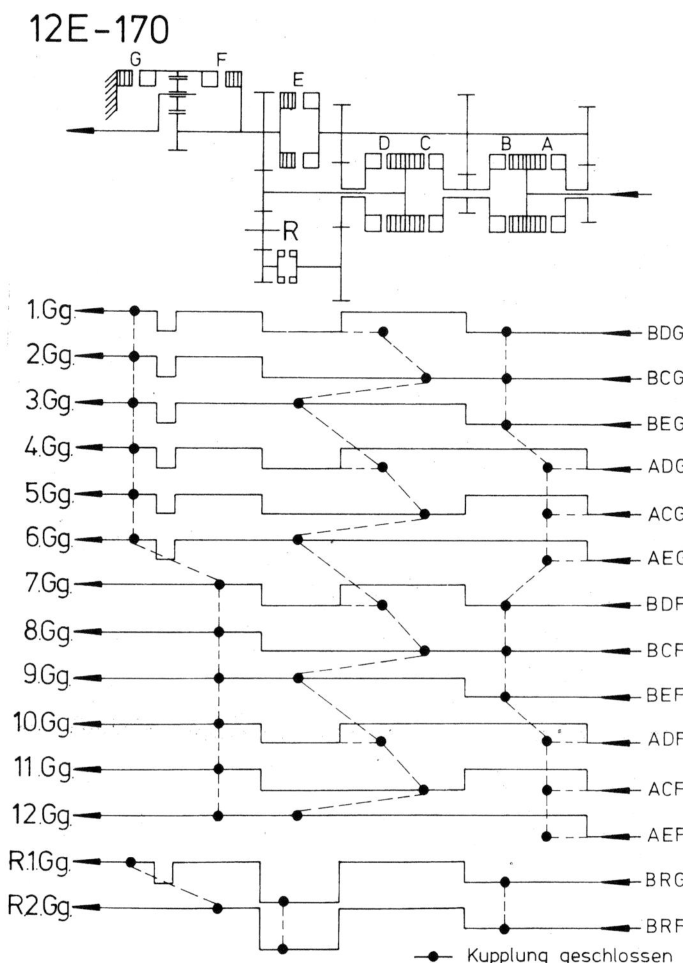

The shifting scheme for the Type 12 E 170 electric clutch-gearbox.

From October 1942 production three vehicles were to be made available for testing purposes. Chassis 250 017 was to be sent to Döllersheim, Austria, for comparison tests with the Porsche Tiger. Vehicle no. 6, chassis no. 250 018, which was driven in on 6 October, was fitted with the ZF electric gearbox and, without turret and equipment, also sent to Döllersheim. The vehicle with chassis no. 250 019 was delivered to the troops for winter testing. In addition, one vehicle was requested for underwater testing.

At the beginning of October 1942 the delivery plan for the VK 4503 was made up. The large number of 424 Tigers still called for at the beginning of production was declared to be impossible. A transition to the VK 4502 was recommended, with 170 vehicles, and increases of Series 1 and 2 to 500, so that Type 3 could be built as of vehicle 501. Clonel Thomale rejected this plan to stick VK 4502 into the middle. He approved the beginning of VK 4503 production for September, and declared his acceptance of the approximately 100 Tiger 3 available at that time for the 1944 [1943?] spring offensive. The VK 4502, moreover, should have a front plate inclined at less than 40 degrees.

In October 1942 Speer created a Tiger Commission, which was to choose the final model. Colonel Thomale expected that Henschel as well as Porsche could show two of the best and most competitive Tiger models to the Commission. It would examine them thoroughly for six days, and test them without the industry. Finally, the leading men "as attorneys for their factories" would have the chance to indicate the special advantages of their designs.

In October 1942, a contract was given for a tropical version of the Tiger.

In all vehicles that were driven in by mid-October there were shifting troubles. The carburetor setting drew criticism. The VK 4501 was absolutely not safe for driving and operating at that time because of the unreliability of the Maybach gearbox.

On October 12, 1942, it was noted that in June 1943 the Tiger vehicles were first supposed to be fitted with Panther motors. As of October 15, 1942, no vehicle was allowed to be delivered without winter oil.

During testing of the VK 4501/V 3, the track came loose from the drive sprocket during backing and turning.

The left track had come loose from the sprocket teeth. The final drive was torn out of line for up to five centimeters.

Here it can be seen that the track has run onto the outer rim of the sprocket.

On October 12, 1942, Henschel announced that from vehicle 170 on, the Panther motor was to be installed in the Tiger. This interim solution would require the installation of a so-called zig-zag gearbox with arc gearing. The designs for this gearbox were finished in mid-November 1942.

In the period from October 26 to 31, 1942, the Commmission for Approving the Tiger Tank met at Eisenach and Berka.*

Chairmen	a) technical: Prof. Dr. Eberan von Eberhorst Technische Hochschule, Dresden	
	b) military: Colonel Thomale Chef. H Rüst u BdE/Stab	
Members	Colonel Dipl.-Ing Esser	WaPrüf 6
	Colonel von Wilcke	WaPrüf 6
	Min.Rat Dipl.-Ing. Baier	Wa J Rü-WuG
	Lt. Col. Dipl.-Ing. Bolnrinker	AHA/In 6
	Lt. Col. Dr. Körbler	AHA/In 6
	Captain Ohrloff	Chef H Rüst u BdE/Stab
	Ob.Reg.Baurat Röver	Wa Chef Ing. 4
	Reg.Baurat Grosser	Wa Chef Ing. 4
	Dr. Dipl.-Ing. Freyberg	ALKETT
	Ing. Rosenfeld	ALKETT
	Ob.Reg.Baurat Knönagel	Wa Chef Ing.
	Ing. Wittmann	Wa Chef Ing.
	Dipl.-Ing. Mann	Wa Chef Ing.
	Dir. Dipl.-Ing. Welge	Panzer branch
	Dir. Aureden, Krupp	Panzer branch
	Lt. Col. Post	Cdr. Pz.Abt. 503
	Major Lueder	Cdr. Pz.Abt. 501

In the comparison tests, the clear superiority and the decision in favor of the Henschel version resulted.

Of the Henschel Tigers produced by October 16, 1942, 424 were to be delivered as Type 1, the remaining 176 as Type 3.

The "c 10" device with ZF electric gearbox left the works on the evening of October 20, 1942, after being test driven only ten kilometers. This drive, though, showed very favorable results. The steering gear of vehicles 1 to 10 were not made of spare parts.

*Location of a training camp.

After removing the first outer road wheel, the track had to be cut through with a welding torch.

The two batteries were installed in Flender heating cases. The cardan shaft ran between the two batteries.

The picture shows the case with the inlaid heating panel to warm the batteries.

They had to be replaced by newer types during repairs. In mid-November 1942 testing of the fording ability of the tiger was begun. Because of the great development of flames from the exhaust, a covering was suggested. Tests were begun to carry additional fuel for some 50 to 60 kilometers. In November 1942 most of the difficulties were just assembly problems that arose from unexpected disturbances. There were engine fires, repeated leaks from cooling-water ducts, and short circuits in the electric lines, as well as defective gearboxes. In addition, a higher number of assembly problems were clearly noticeable because of the heavy strains on the workers.

Both batteries are covered. At the bottom center is the turret-drive flange.

The heating panel with connecting wires.

Here a battery is being taken from the heating case.

In a discussion on November 20, 1942, it was determined that the planned increase in Tiger VK 5401 production would run in conjunction with the introduction of VK 4503. According to the existing production schedule, the contracted 424 (+3) VK 4501 should be finished in September 1943. The start of VK 4503 production should begin with one vehicle in the same month, and reach the full monthly number of 50 only in May 1944. Thus, from September 1943 to and including April 1944, a production of at least some 250 vehicles would result. Therefore, it was decided to give the Henschel firm an additional contract for some 250 VK 4501. Accordingly, Henschel was under contract for 424 + 250 = 674 VK 4501 chassis and 176 VK 4503. There were also three VK 4501 test models for WaPrüf 6. As already noted, Vehicle 018 had an electric gearbox installed, and this vehicle was back at the Zahnradfabrik Friedrichshafen. It was now to be renumbered as Test Vehicle no. 2. In its place, the V 2 vehicle delivered to Pz. Abt. 501 was given number 250 018.

The cranks for the track adjustment were changed as of the 26th vehicle. As of the 37th, an improved 8-speed gearbox, which showed numerous improvements, was installed. Up to the 50th vehicle a floor vent was installed. In mid-December 1942 the suggestion was made to run the vehicles in on bottled gas, which the Alkett firm had already begun. Master Schlickenrieder developed a similar device for use in trucks, and it proved itself at once. Previously, some 800 to 900 liters of gasoline were used for driving in (120 km). It was reckoned that at least 500 liters could be saved if the driving-in could be done with bottled gas, and only the acceptance trip (some 25 to 30 km) needed gasoline. With a production of 80 vehicles per month, this would save about 40,000 liters of gasoline!

At the end of January 1943, the "Adolf Hitler" program of tank production was published; it called for the following numbers of tanks to be produced:

Name	**Tons**	**Armament**
Panzerkampfwagen II *Luchs*	12	2 cm KwK 38
Panzerkampfwagen III, Type M	23	5 cm KwK 39 L/60
Panzerkampfwagen IV	23	7.5 cm KwK 40 L/43
Panzerkampfwagen Panther	45	7.5 cm KwK 42 L/70
Panzerkampfwagen Tiger (H 1)	57	8.8 cm KwK 36 L/56
Panzerkampfwagen Tiger (H 3)	65	8.8 cm KwK 43 L/71
7.5 cm *Sturmgeschütz* 40	23	7.5 cm StuK 40 L/48
8.8 cm *Sturmgeschütz* 42	40	8.8 cm StuK 42 L/71
Sturmgeschütz Ferdinand	65/70	8.8 cm StuK 42 L/71
leichte Selbstfahrlafette	11	7.5 cm Pak 40 L/46
leFH 18 *auf* Panzer II	11	10.5 cm leFH 18 L/28
sIG 33 *auf* Panzer 38(t)	11	15 cm sIG 33 L/11
sSfl *auf* Panzer III/IV *Hornisse*	24	8.8 cm Pak 43 L/71
sSfl *auf* Panzer III/IV Hummel	21	15 cm sFH 18 M L/28
sSfl *auf* Panzer Panther	40	15 cm sFH 43 or 12.8 cm K

In addition to the Tiger tank, Henschel was also to build the 8.8 cm *Sturmgeschütz* 42. This vehicle was called "ss. Sfl" (super-heavy self-propelled mount) at the works. There were constant changes in Tiger production that had to be switched into the process; for example, the brake holder for the track brakes and the whole brake jacket were basically changed from the 151st tank on. As already noted, as of vehicle 251 the Maybach HL 230 P 45 motor was installed. Thus, the left and right radiators for the cooling system also had to be changed. Up to the 28th vehicle, when repair work was done on the steering gear, the main shaft had to be exchanged. As for vehicle 301, the front shock-absorber attachment was changed. The mounting and attaching of the fuel tanks was updated as of chassis 250 231. The construction of the turret structure for the Tiger I was also carried out by the Siemens-Schuckert works in Mülheim, on the Ruhr. The turret was basically changed as of vehicle 391. A new commander's cupola, taken from the Panther tank, was also installed. The escape hatch, the firing process, the turret bearings, the prismatic mirror mount, and the barrel lashing were also changed. So were the turret machine-gun mount, the clock drive, the direction indicator, the seats for the crew, and the spring equalizer, as well as the turret equipment and its storage places.

The Rhorleitungsbau firm of Unna, in Westphalia, sent in a drawing for a turnable smoke cartridge on June 11, 1943. Whether this device could be attached to the tiger turret behind the loader was to be tested. For questions of space, a rough wooden model was finished by Jnue 23, 1943. The device was installed in the Tiger B.

On July 6, 1943, *Hauptdienstleiter* Saur required that the Henschel firm stick to the monthly output of 65 vehicles as called for in the schedule. A third Tiger body production facility, in addition to the Dortmund-Hoerder Huttenverein and Krupp, had to be found. Witkowitz was to take over the SM steel delivery and the rolling and heat treatment, while the Skoda works did the working and assembly of the body.

As of June 1943, the installation of an improved anti-aircraft device for MG 34 began to be attached by the commander's cupola.

In mid-1943, 13,600 tons of raw steel were available to the Krupp firm. They needed, at the top of the list:

For 140 Tiger II	95 tons each = 13,300 tons
For 120 BW (Panzer IV)	23 tons each = 2,750 tons
For 5 Maus	280 tons each = 1,400 tons

On orders from HDL Saur, Wegmann was to make haste to fit an H 1 turret with an 8.8 cm KwK L/71 in August 1943. The turret was delivered by Krupp at the end of September. As of vehicle 391. turret joint protection was also planned, so that shots hitting the turret joint could no longer enter. In October 1943 eleven Tiger command tanks stored at Magdeburg were converted into normal tanks.

Production of the H 1 test turret with L/71 gun was delayed. The barrel meant for it was sent out from the Kummersdorf test center to Unterlüss, and was supposed to arrive on October 10, 1943. For October 1943 production only four command turrets were needed. The housing for the L 600 C steering gear was changed as of vehicle 425. As of chassis 250 501, the engine compartment wall was designed anew. As already noted, after the production of about 800 vehicles, the rubber-tired running gear was replaced by a rubber-sprung type. Finally, the vehicle was fitted with left and

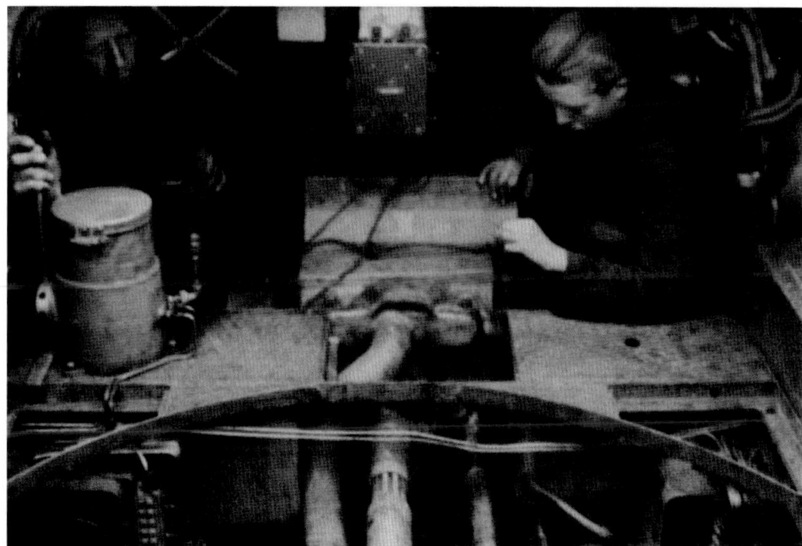

A Helios hydraulic-automatic high-pressure central lubrication system, Type "HA", was installed in VK 4501/V 3 for testing. It was mounted behind the driver's seat, as can be seen in the picture.

The distributors are visible to the left and right, near the firewall, and near the batteries under the fighting compartment platform.

For winter use, track grippers that extended out 20 to 24 mm over the actual track had to be created

right upper fuel tanks as of chassis no. 251 201.

On May 10, 1944, the following contracts for Tiger 1 were about to be filled: 3 test vehicles for WaPrüf, 1292 series vehicles for WaJRü, and 54 more for the same office. The three test vehicles were also delivered by Henschel; their turrets, made from rebuilt Krupp turrets, came from Wegmann. For the series, Henschel had delivered the vehicles up to number 1201 by May 31, 1944, and needed the turrets for them by May 24, 1944. Henschel requested 18 more turrets for the June production, up to no. 1219. In June Henschel delivered those up to no. 1276, and in July the rest, up to no. 1292. For the 54 vehicles in the new contract, there was no final completion date; their production was planned for July 1944. At the beginning of December 1942, Speer had already let Hitler know that divided use of Henschel Tigers could bring considerable

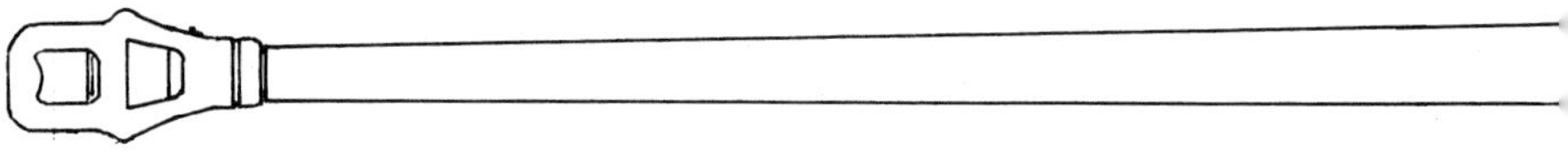

After some 800 vehicles had been built, the running gear was converted to rubber saving steel road wheels (chassis no. 250 82).

Panzerkampfwagen **Tiger Type E (Sd.Kfz. 181), tested with an 8.8 cm KwK 43 L/71.**

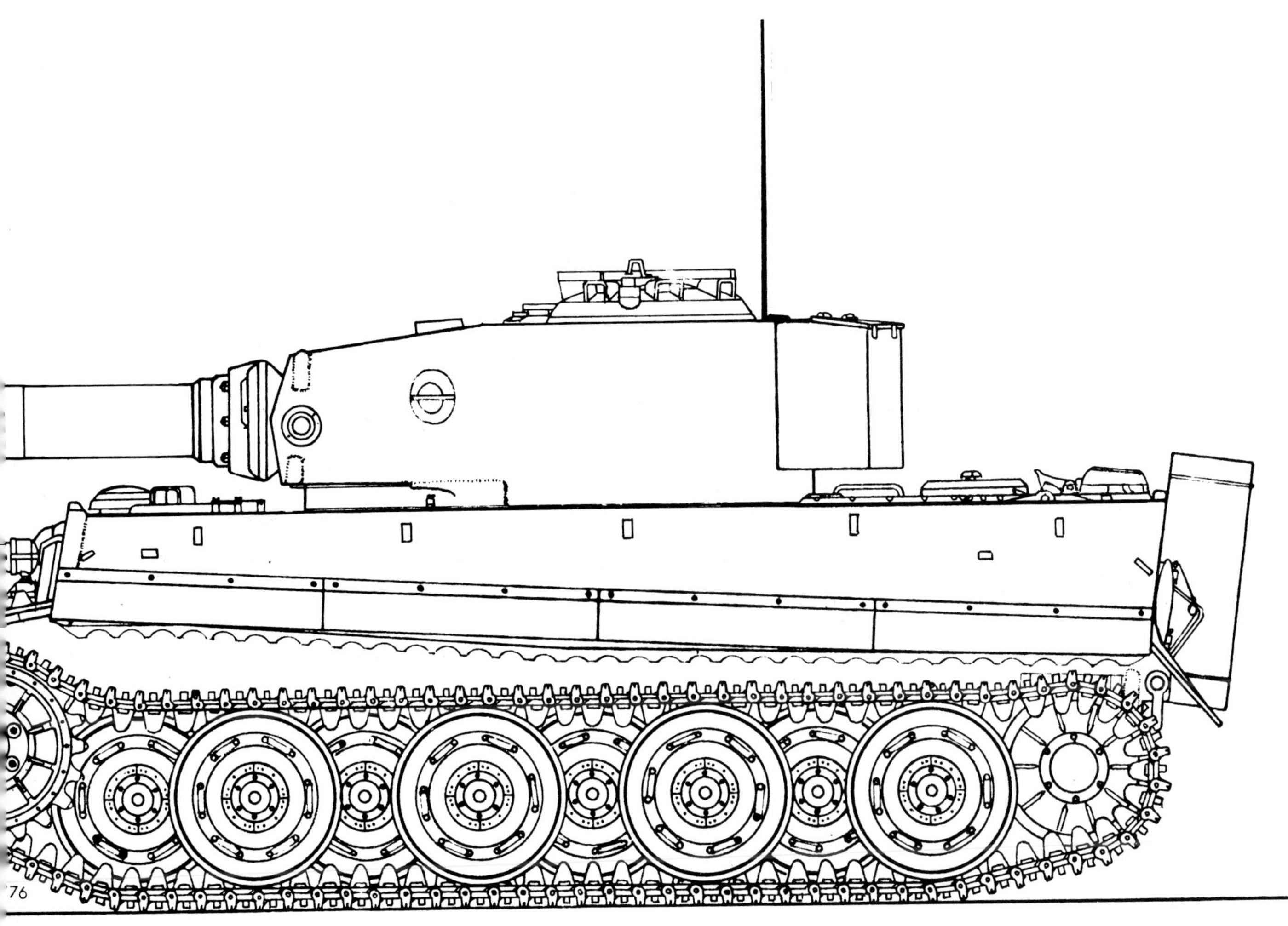

disadvantages. For such a new vehicle, gathering into larger bands would mean:

- the exchange of experience for eliminating or avoiding faults would be much better,
- the use of workshop components would last longer, and
- the quality of the assigned works masters would be better.

In addition, the supply of replacement parts was at first too meager. Only for every tenth vehicle could a motor and a gearbox be delivered, if the output of new vehicles was not to be harmed. In divided action, the insufficient spare parts supply led at first to a complete loss of vehicles that needed repairs. Yet Hitler insisted that the vehicles should be divided up more strongly for service in the east, while concentrated use was planned for Africa.

At last the German armored troops had a vehicle that could take on any enemy tanks with good prospects of success. This was due mainly to the outstanding primary weapon, which was produced by the firms of R. Wolf of Magdeburg-Buckau and Dortmund-Hoerder Hüttenverein. The often changed ammunition storage consisted of four ammunition racks, arranged in front, in back, and at the left and right center. In addition, near ammunition racks 1 and 2 there was still another available under the stage. In all, 92 rounds of 8.8 cm ammunition were carried.

The cooling-water exchange system was dropped when the Fuchs motorized heater was installed.*

The designation "*Panzerkampfwagen* VI" was abolished by the Führer's order of February 27, 1944. The official designation was now "*Panzerkampfwagen* Tiger," Ausf. E. The last vehicles of

* The inventor was *Kriegsverwaltungsrat* Fuchs.

this series left the Henschel factory in August 1944. The price per vehicle was RM 250,000.

Originally, the Wegmann Waggonfabrik AG of Kassel was also supposed to assemble the "Tiger," but this factory was too cramped in space, and thus switched to assembling the "Tiger" turret. The turrets were delivered to Henschel in a finished state.

At the very beginning of "Tiger" development, Porsche had expressed doubts as to whether the use of mechanical gearboxes was still advisable for such heavy vehicles. Out of these considerations came the Porsche Type "102," which was supposed to be fitted with an electric gearbox made by the Voith firm in Heidelberg. The vehicle itself was unchanged from the Type "101." Fifty of these gearboxes were ordered at first, but only one was actually delivered. It took up a great deal of space, and worked much worse than mechanical gearboxes. It was expected, though, that its functioning would resemble that of an electric gearbox that was being tested then. Two hydraulic torque converters were planned for each motor.

The steering of the Type 102 consisted of a superheterodyne gear with only two differentials. They were activated hydropneumatically. Plans were made to equip vehicles 91 to 100 with this system. The first installation took place in March 1942 at the Nibelungenwerk, where test runs of up to 2000 km were made with it. In view of chronic motor problems, the transfer of the vehicle to Kummersdorf was delayed until March 1944. A variant of Type "102" was made by using a "NITA" gearbox made by the Voith firm. Whereby the motors of the vehicle now called Type "103" were fitted with two cooling fans.

On September 22, 1942, Hitler requested the rebuilding of a number of Porsche "Tigers" as assault guns with 200 mm front armor. They were to be armed with the 8.8 cm L/71 gun. The possibility of installing a captured French 21 cm mortar was also to be tried. The hull and roof were to be made stronger. Hitler agreed that the armor plates could be taken from naval supplies.

The order to rebuild into an assault gun without a turret was

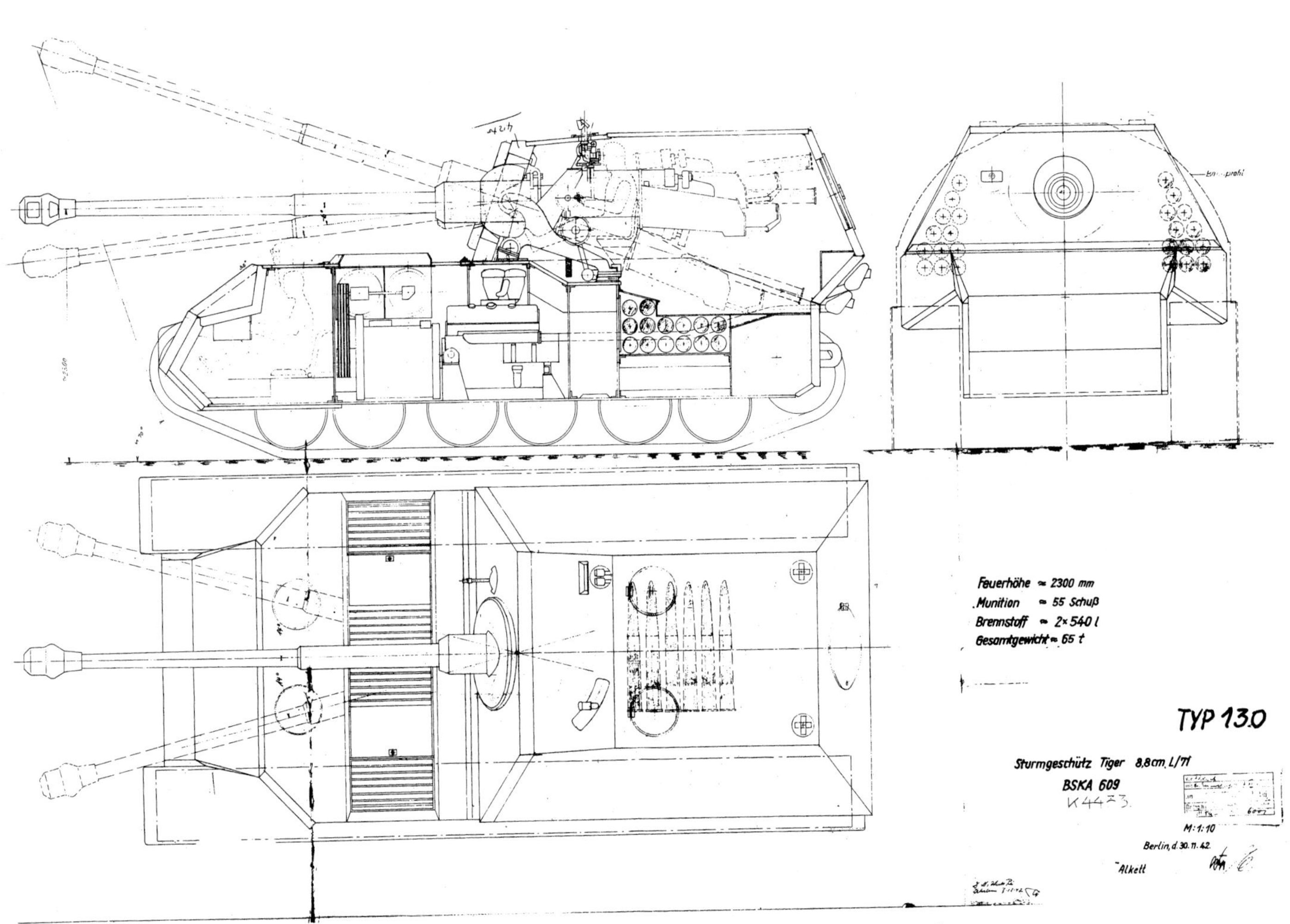

In September 1942, Hitler requested the rebuilding of a number of Porsche tigers as assault guns. The drawing shows the original Alkett design for this vehicle.

officially issued to the Porsche firm on September 26, 1942. On October 14, 1942, Hitler declared that if the heavy infantry gun could be mounted on a Panzer IV chassis, then the necessity of an assault gun on the Porsche "Tiger" with the long 8.8 cm gun or the 21 cm mortar would no longer have the same degree of urgency. Therefore, only constructive suggestions should be worked on for the time being.

On January 5, 1943, Hitler requested the trial of a Porsche "Tiger" with an 8.8 cm L/100 gun.

The spare parts supplying of the Henschel "Tiger" was causing much difficulty at this time.

On July 23, 1941, Colonel Fichtner, as representative of the Ordnance Office, had already told Professor Porsche that he would not have any luck with the Krupp turret, and should look for a better long-range solution. By a message of June 21, 1942, the Porsche firm was empowered to try installing the Flak 41 instead of the 8.8 cm KwK L/56 in the "Tiger" turret. On 10 September the firm reported that, for the time being, only the L/56 gun was a possibility for the "VK 4501." But in the same month, the Krupp and Rheinmetall firms were contracted to present a design for a turret—armed with the 8.8 cm Flak 41—for use on the *Panzerkampfwagen* 4501 (Porsche and Henschel). In August 1942, Hitler ordered immediate information as to how quickly the long 8.8 cm gun could be installed in the "Tiger." An armor-piercing ability of 200 mm was called for.

On May 19, 1943, WaPrüf 6 informed the Henschel firm that Japan, in the process of its armament buildup, planned to copy German weapons, equipment, and ammunition. The "Tiger I" and "Panther" tanks were planned. Henschel was asked to send two complete sets of design drawings to Japan. The drawings were sent on microfilm. On September 1, 1843, the A.G.K. (the Ausfuhrgemeinschaft für Kriegsgerät in the Reichsgruppe Industrie) informed Henschel that, according to information from the OKW, a "Tiger I" tank out of Army stocks, with a supply of ammunition, should be sent to Japan. The vehicle chosen for Japan was to be taken from the Army Armored Arsenal at Magdeburg-Kömigsborn. It was indicated that it was presumably to be sent, along with a "Panther" tank supplied by MAN, from Bordeaux to Japan. Along with the prices, there were long discussions about the prices of licensing, patent, and copyright rights. The German and Japanese businesses entrusted with the shipping also did not want to miss out on their rightful shares. At the end of September 1943 Japan insisted on the prompt delivery of the vehicles. Discussions were begun about the extent to which the vehicles could be shipped in dismantled condition. There were the following possibilities for the 'Tiger":

- Hull with all equipment and running gear, but without turret and tracks: 36 tons,
- Hull as before, but without running gear and drive sprockets: 29 tons
- Turret with gun, sent separately: 11 tons; gun could be separated from turret,
- If running gear was separated from the hull, weight of the running gear without tracks, 7 tons; drive sprockets, about 1 ton,
- Weight of both combat tracks: 6 tons; loading tracks, 5 tons.

On October 1, 1943, the Ausfuhrgemeinschaft für Kriegsgerät informed the Henschel firm that the price set for a complete "Tiger," Type E, with equipment (92 rounds of 8.8 cm ammunition, 4500 rounds of MG and 192 rounds of MG ammunition, Fu 2 or Fu 5, and optics) would be RM 300,000. An export price of RM 645,000 was suggested. On October 7, 1943, this price was put on the bill.

The Army Armored Arsenal in Königsborn sent a "Tiger" tank, chassis no. 250 455, to the railroad depot in Bordeaux for shipping to Japan. The vehicle arrived there on October 27, 1943, after having been held up for several days for exceeding the profile. On February 28, 1944, Henschel confirmed the receipt of the selling price of RM 645,000. The prices of the various components are of interest: (figures are in Rehichsmark): Motor 13,000, gearbox 8,300, hull 54,000, turret (with cupola and mounts) 26,000, turret assembly 20,000, chassis assembly 124,000, tracks 7000, gun 22,000, ammunition 9000, optics 2900, radios 3000, two MG 34 1100, and one machine pistol 75.

After subtracting the *Wehrmacht* price of RM 300,000 and

the costs of packing, loading, and shipping (RM 33,166), there remained the amount of RM 311,834 to be shared. The *Wehrmacht* received 80% (249,467), while Henschel got 2.5% (7795.85) for its efforts, and the three development firms of Henschel, Krupp, and Maybach got 17.5% (54,570.95). According to the shares for development, Maybach got 7.1%, Krupp 22.7%, and Henschel 70.2%.

According to a message from the OKH *Chef* H Rüst und BdE AHAStab Ib (2), no. 11646/44 g, of September 21, 1944, the "Tiger" intended for Japan was not shipped out. The vehicle was turned over to the German *Wehrmacht* on loan.

For the sake of completeness, a Type F of the "Tiger" tank must also be mentioned, although all other details of it are lacking.

In the meantime, the Type E Tiger tank, formerly also called "Tiger I," had proven itself despite its more than typical size and weight. The technical problems had also been reduced to a bearable extent, especially after replacing the original running gear. Further large-series construction was therefore wanted. But the Ordnance Office insisted on a new development.

Henschel tried to persuade the Office to accept an interim solution in the autumn of 1942. In it, the Type E "Tiger" was to be equipped with a curved bow plate. By retaining the earlier "L 600 C" steering gear, an interim solution between the stepped hull and the suggested "Tiger II" hull was to be created. This solution was rejected.

In January 1943 Hitler decided that the new "Tiger" then being planned was to be fitted with the long 8.8 cm gun, and to have 150 mm front and 80 mm side armor. The inclination of the armor plates resulted in a vehicle similar to the "Panther." The

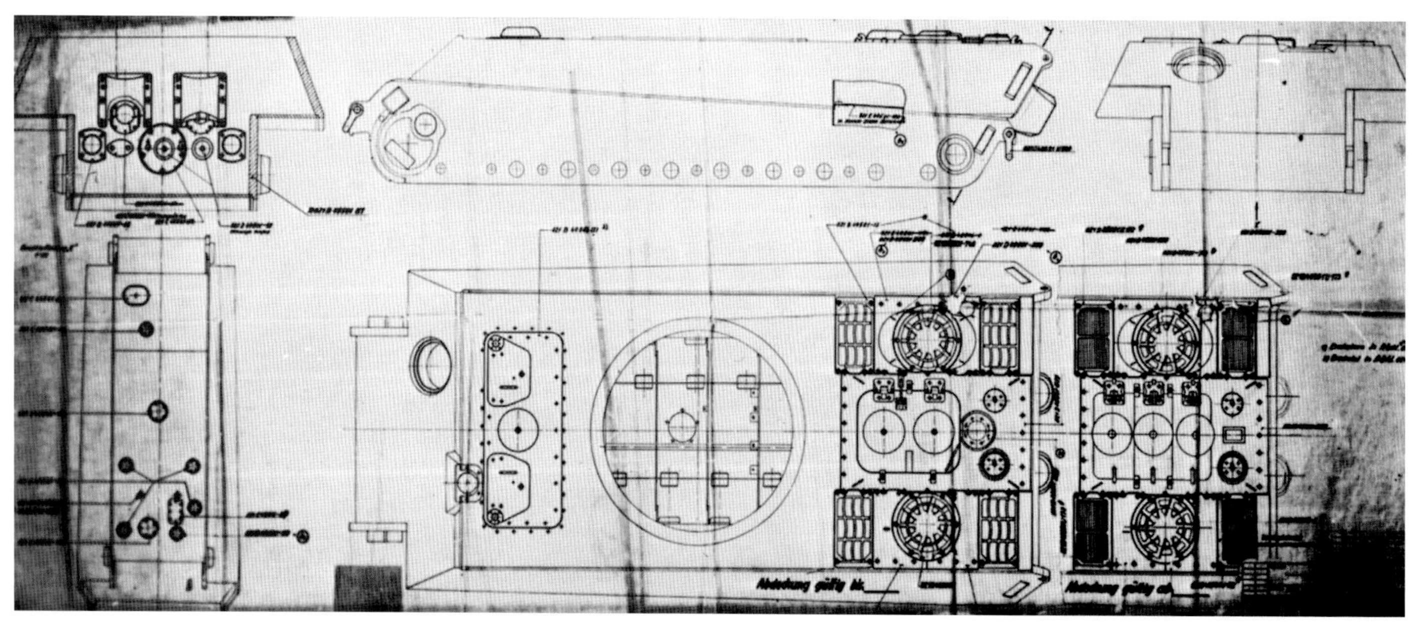

The new hull layout for the Tiger Type B tank. At the lower right is the new cover for the engine compartment, which was used in the last series of these vehicles.

front plates were tilted at 35, and the side plates at 65 degrees. The plates were toothed. A new track, 800 mm wide and divided into 130 mm links, was developed. It was comparatively light (2.8 tons per track), and consisted of leading links of cast steel, plus forged intermediate links. The improved track, available as of July 1944, was developed by MIAG and Skoda. The links (without guiding teeth) were cast in one piece. Their rigidity against lateral forces was significantly improved. The weight per track, though, had climbed to 3.2 tons. Once again, loading tracks (600 mm wide) had to be used. The vehicle's width then measured 3300 mm. The whole running gear, with drive sprockets and leading wheels, had to be created anew. For the first time, a staggered running gear with nine pairs of rubber-sprung road wheels (800 mm diameter) on each side was used. These rubber saving road wheels, developed by the Deutsche Eisen-Werke, consisted of two strong sheet steel rims attached to a wheel disc of steel between two rubber rings under very high pressure. The drive sprocket was similar to that of the "Tiger E," but more strongly laid out. The road wheel cranks were single drop-forged pieces and much strengthened. The crank attachments resembled those of the "Panther" without rubber, but with layered conical springs. There were four attachments. Compared to the "Tiger E," the torsion bars were strengthened and fitted with toothed heads. They no longer differed in diameter, so they could not be finely tuned.

The powerplant was the Maybach "HL 230 P 30" motor already used in the "Panther"; it produced up to 700 HP at 3000 rpm. The cooling system of the "Panther," with four radiators arranged in two groups to the right and left, was also used. On either side there was also a horizontal cooling wheel. The turret drive was done by bevel gears, which were constantly in contact. From there the power flowed to the Maybach "OLVAR OG 40 12 16 B" gearbox, which was a new type, in which the driving bevel gear was no longer mounted in the gearbox. A new steering gear, Type "L 801," also had to be developed by Henschel. Dry clutches

The wooden model of the Tiger B and 8.8 cm ammunition are being shown to Hitler and Speer. Ammunition could not be exchanged between the two Tiger types.

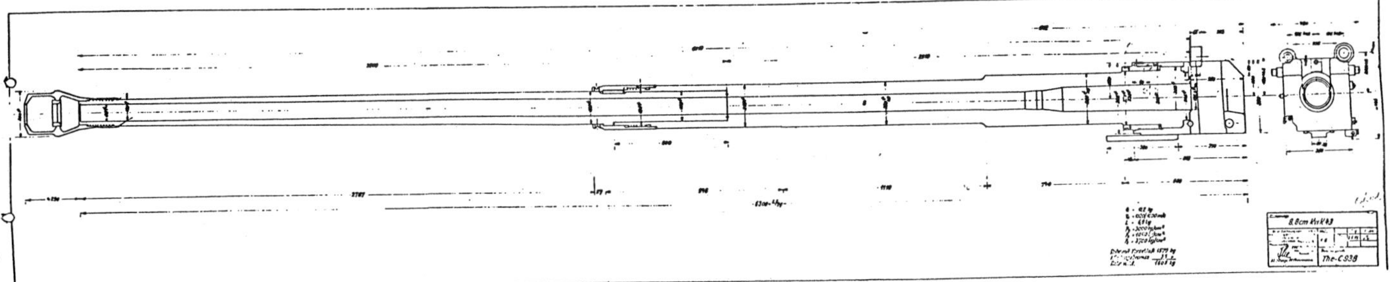

A longitudinal cut through the 8.8 cm KwK 43 L/71 planned for the Tiger B. The gun could destroy any enemy tank at 2000 meters.

The interior of the hull of the VK 4503 shows the attachments for the torsion bars. In the middle is the turret drive, with its connecting flange for the cardan. The left and right pipes are parts of the lubricating battery for the running gear.

Here all the carrying arms of one side of the chassis are installed; likewise, the adjustable spindle of the track adjustment on the leading wheel. The arms pointed in opposite directions on the two sides of the vehicle.

Now the road wheels are mounted, as well as the drive sprocket in front and the leading wheel in back.

The pictures show the running gear cranks with the heads of the torsion-bar suspension. Between the arms is the mount of the opposite torsion bar.

The drive sprocket is attached.

The covers for the track adjusters were attached with four nuts.

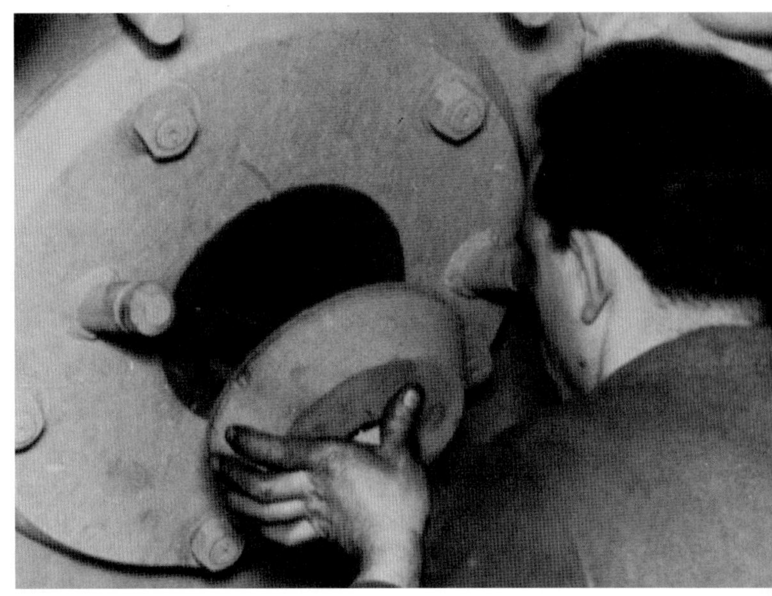

The large servicing port in the rear panel was made in two parts.

After the cover was removed, the track tension adjuster could be reached.

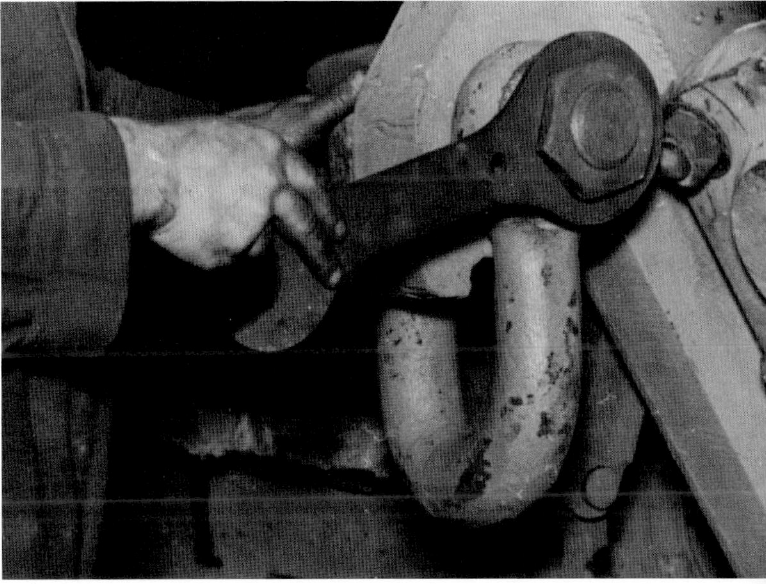

Here one of the two towing shackles is attached to the rear plate.

Below left: The opening for the starting crank. Below right: The tracks for the Tiger B were basically changed. This picture shows the first version.

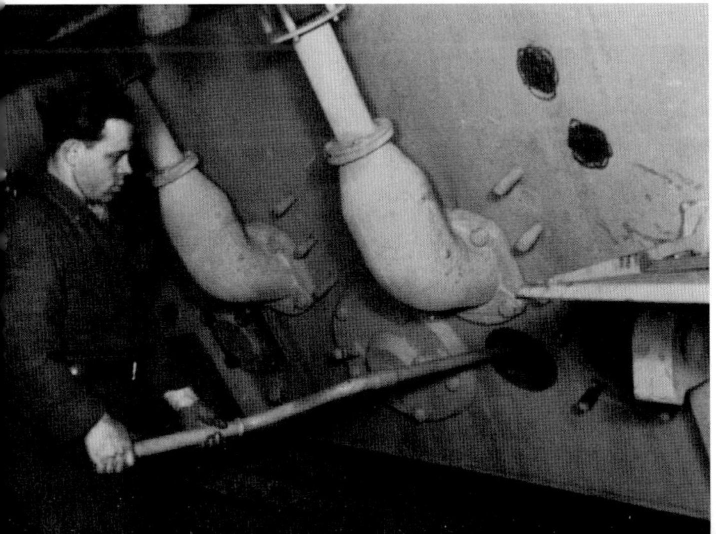

These pictures show the tracks being put on and closed.

for the steering had originally been planned, with only the clutches for setting the steering radii running in an oil bath. This approach was given up. Both drive bevel gears were mounted in steering gears. Corresponding to the first and eighth speeds, there was a smallest turning circle diameter of 2.4 meters and a largest one of 114 meters.

The OLVAR gearbox required a shifting process that was just like that of a manual transmission with power interruption. Its trouble free operation depended largely on the ability and calm (even in combat) of the driver. Major damage was done to the overhaul clutches and accelerator, as well as the brake couplings. During development they could be decreased, but never completely eliminated. Thus, the gearbox, which had worked well under simpler conditions in ordinary vehicles from its conception—and which needed a good, calm driver to operate it as an undeniable prerequisite—was only somewhat suited for the heavy technical and human requisites of a very heavy tank. All the same, the easily shifted OLVAR gearbox and easily steered two-radius steering gear were a very decisive easing of the driver's job.

Turning on the road was possible for both "Tiger" versions. An emergency steering device using a tiller was again planned. The steering apparatus and the disc brakes were made by the Süddeutsche Argus-Werke. They could be mainly taken over from

A track bolt is driven in.

The complete running gear without skirting plates.

Details of the Tiger B running gear are shown.

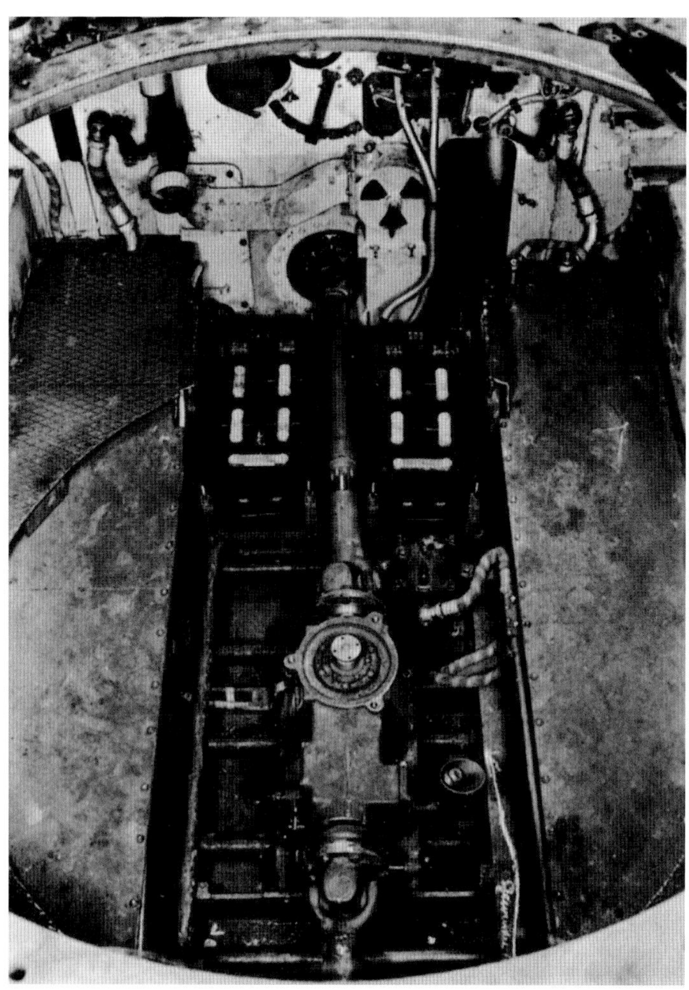

This picture shows the fighting compartment, seen through the turret ring, with a look toward the firewall between the engine and fighting compartment. In the center is the cardan drive with subsidiary turret drive. To the left and right of the cardan are the two batteries.

Details of the turret drive. The turret platform can be seen at the top.

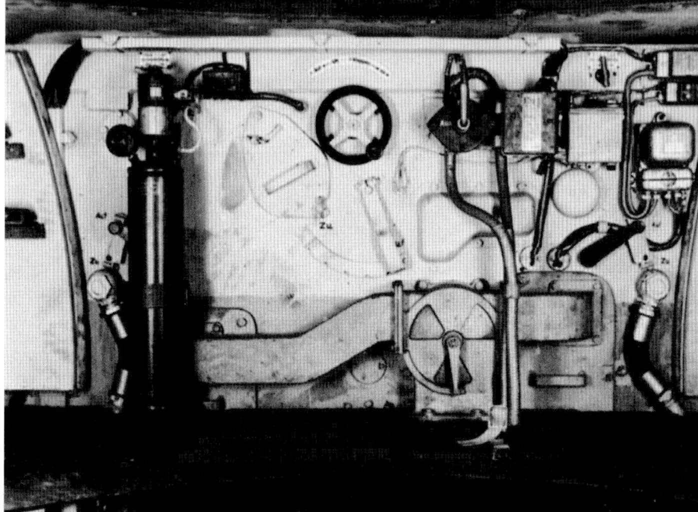

The firewall divided the fighting compartment from the engine compartment.

This picture shows the front of the hull, with the driver's and radioman's seats. In between is the gearbox, linked to the motor in back by a cardan.

Panzerkampfwagen Tiger, Type B (Sd.Kfz. 182).

"Tiger on the Eastern Front": watercolor by the well known military sketcher and painter Mahteyko.

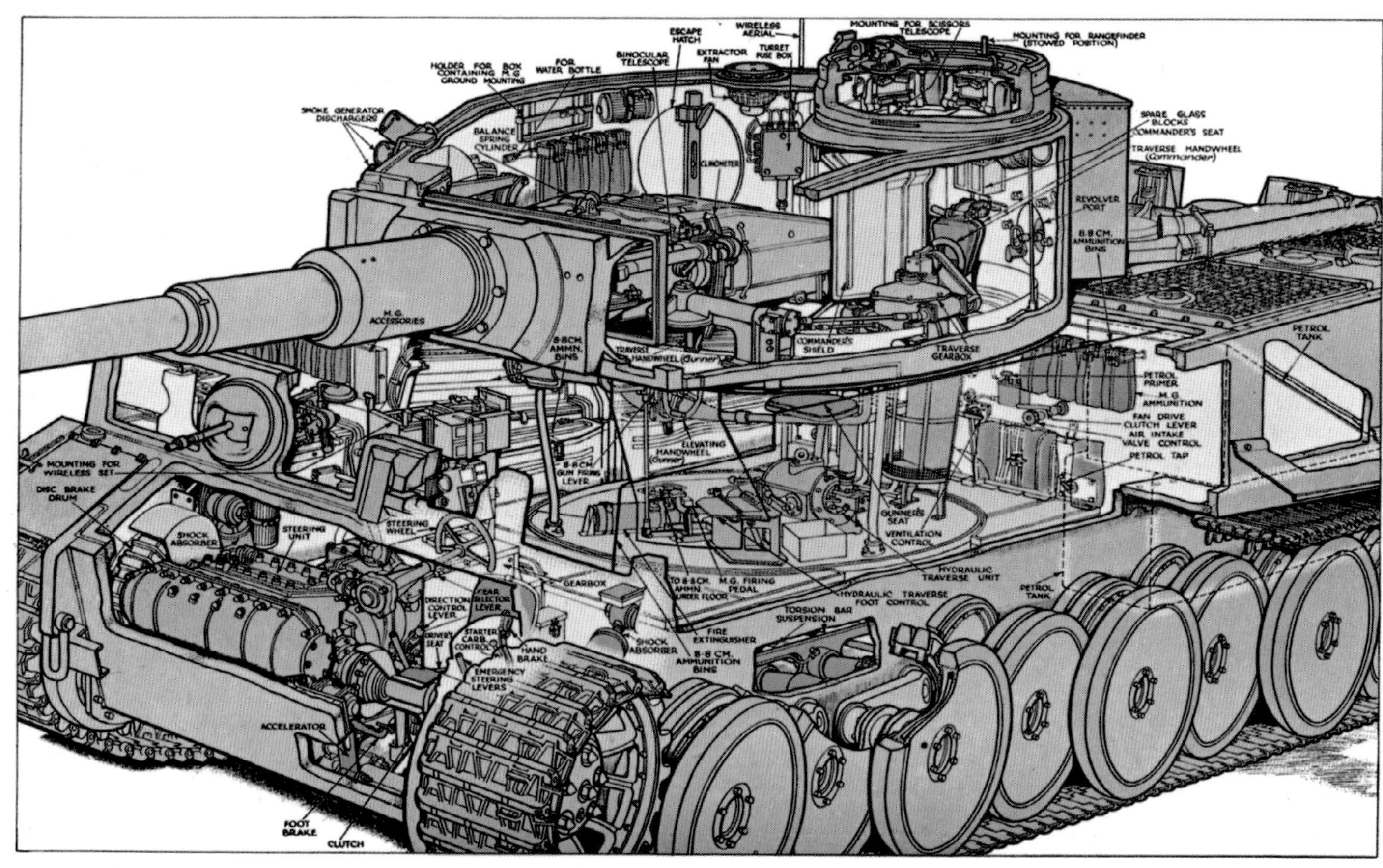

smoke generator dischargers = Nebelmittelwurfgerät
holder for box containing MG ground mounting = Behälter für MG-Zweibein
for waterbottle = für Feldflasche
binocular telescope = Zielfernrohr
escape hatch = Notausstiegluke
extractor fan = Rauchabzugsanlage
wireless aerial = Antenne
turret fuse box = Turmsicherungskasten
mounting for scissors telescope = Halterung für Scherenfernrohr
mounting for range finder (stowed position) = Halterung für Entfernungsmesser
balance spring cylinder = Ausgleichsfeder
clinometer = Höhenrichtanzeiger
spare glass blocks = Ersatzsichtblöcke
commanders seat = Kommandantensitz
traverse handwheel (commander) = Seitenrichtrad für Kommandanten
revolver port = MP-Schießöffnung
8.8 cm ammunition bins = Halterung für 8.8 cm Munition
MG accessories = MG-Zubehör
traverse handwheel (gunner) = Seitenrichthandrad (Richtschütze)
commanders shield = Abweisblech für Kanone
traverse gearbox = Turnschwenkwerk
petrol tank = Kraftstoffbehälter
petrol primer = Aniaßpumpe für Motor
MG ammunition = MG Munition
fan drive clutch lever = Kupplungshebel für Kühlgebläse
air intake valve control = Bedlenung für Ansaugluftventil
petrol tap = Kraftstoffabsperrhahn
mounting for wireless set = Halterung für Ansaugluftventil
disc brake drum = Scheibenbremsengehäuse
shock absorber = Stoßdämpfer
steering unit = Lenkgetriebe
steering wheel = Lenkrad
8.8 cm gun firing lever = Abfeuerungshebel für 8.8 cm Kanone
elevating handwheel (gunner) = Höhenrichtrad (Richtschütze)
accelerator = Gaspedal
foot brake = Bremspedal
clutch = Kupplungspedal
Direction control lever = Fahrtrichtungshebel
gear selector lever = Getriebegangvorwählung
drivers seat = Fahrersitz
starter carb. control = Starklappenknopf
hand brake = Handbremse
gearbox = Schaltgetriebe
emergency steering levers = Notlenkhebel
to 8.8 cm ammun. under floor = 8.8 cm. Munition unter Drehbühne
MG firing pedal = MG Abfeuerung
fire extinguisher = Feuerlöscher
torsion bar suspension = Drehstabfederung
hydraulic traverse unit = hydr. Turmschwenkwerk
ventialtion control = Schalter für Rauchabzugsanlage
gunners seat = Richtschützensitz
hydraulic traverse foot control = Fußpedal für hydr. Turmschwenkwerk

Here the driver's and radioman's seats are easy to see. At left is the steering wheel, and over it is the driver's visor. At right is the built-in machine gun for the radioman. Over the gearbox is the pickup for the radios. The back of the driver's seat is folded down.

Another view of the driver's seat shows the left disc brake and the foot pedals.

This detailed picture of the driver's space shows the emergency levers, foot pedals and, at the lower left, the front shock absorber. At right is the pre-selector lever on the gearbox.

On the radioman's side the disc brake is covered, and the attachment for the front shock absorber is easy to see.

The steering gear of the Tiger B.

The vehicle's gearbox, with the driveshaft at right.

The two pictures show the installation of the gearbox through the servicing hatch above the driver and radioman.

The air filters are mounted over the motor.

The removable headlight was fastened onto the bow plate.

This picture shows one of the first Tiger B tanks with the Porsche turret.

The turret had a hatch in its roof, as well as open hatches for the driver and radioman.

The front and back of the Type B Tiger tank.

Here are details of the turret roof, with the commander's cupola and ventilator. Behind the loader's hatch is the close-in defense weapon. Below and opposite: A look from the turret at the driver's and radioman's hatches.

The engine cover still shows the attachment for the fording equipment.

These pitctures show the close-in defense weapon inside the turret, both closed and opened.

Comparison of the Tiger B with Porsche turret (above) and production turret.

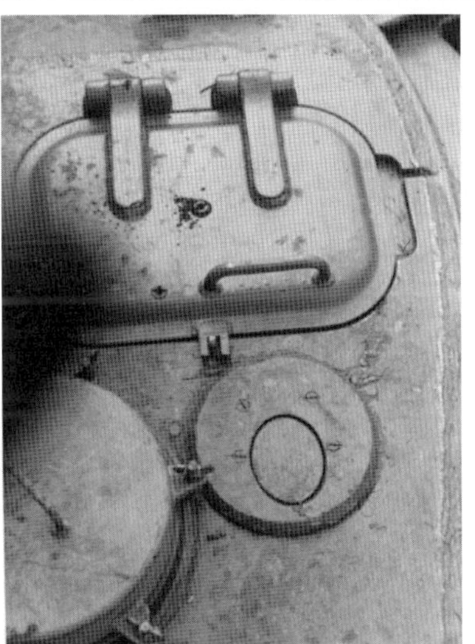

The close-in defense weapon, which could also be used as a smoke launcher, also closed and opened.

the "Tiger E."

In February 1943, WaPrüf 6/III called for an extensive unification between the "Tiger B" (VK 4503) and the improved "Panther II". It was expected that important components should match, for the sake of spare-parts supplying. These efforts delayed the development work at Henschel for several months, without the "Panther II" ever getting out of the test stage.

The engine compartments and cooling systems of the two vehicles were alike. The drive shafts were taken from the "Tiger E," but laid out so that by pushing them together, they could also be used in the "Panther II." The engine compartment cover of the "Panther" proved to be unhandy and had to be redesigned. The hatch was now made in three pieces to improve access to the motor. The driver's and radioman's hatch covers, balanced by springs and swingable to the side, were also taken from the "Panther." The WaA expressed the opinion that this arrangement, especially when the vehicle was at an angle, would cause considerable difficulty; thus, they called for lids that were eased with springs, and could be thrown away if necessary. They were not introduced. The driver's visor was dropped completely. The driver's view was provided by a swingable and turnable angled periscope developed by Henschel. The driver's seat height could be adjusted, so that on the march the driver's head stuck out the entrance hatch, giving him an unbroken view. The primary weapon intended for this vehicle was the successor to the 8.8 cm KwK 36, the 8.8 cm KwK 41. The development contract for it was issued to the Friedrich Krupp AG in Essen in November 1941. Mass production of this gun, extended to the length of L/71, was planned for October 1942. As the 8.8 cm KwK 43 (L/71), it was produced mainly by the Fr. Garny firm of Frankfurt on the Main.

The turret, armed with this weapon and one MG 34, was located in the center of the tank. The barrel, with brake and pneumatic recuperator, the MG 34, and the telescopic sight (TZF 9b/1) were mounted in the gun cradle. It was moved by the handwheel of the

The optic opening for the turret telescopic sight.

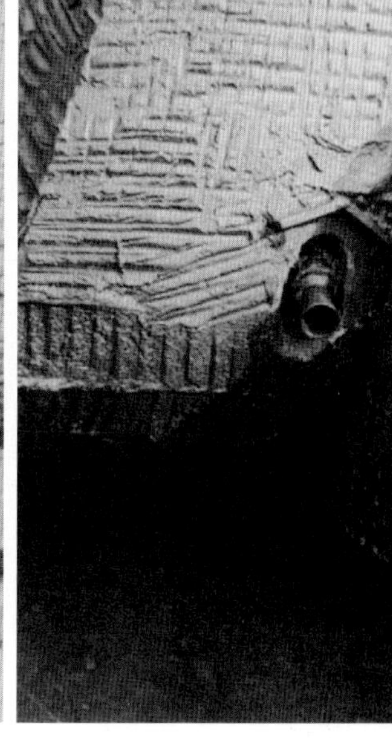

The turret MG was mounted near the tank gun.

The machine gun near the radioman was mounted in a ball mantlet. The protective coating of Zimmerit was supposed to prevent the attachment of magnetic charges.

In the first Tiger B test vehicle there was no leading-wheel limit. Thus, the hub diameter of the leading wheel could be pressed against the outer ring of the last road wheel.

The folding protective hood for the telescope shaft of the UK (underwater combat) equipment was planned for only a few vehicles.

The front shackle was installed as seen here.

These pictures show part of the pipe in the fording shaft.

These pictures show the driver's hatch, and the driver in his raised seat on the march.

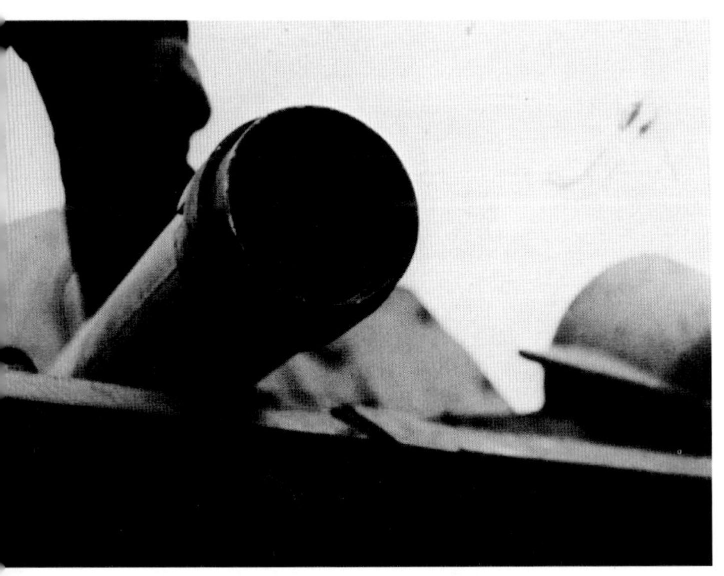

The vehicle is seen from the rear, with loading tracks and skirting plates removed.

The engine compartment cover was made in three pieces in the last series, and the opening was thus enlarged.

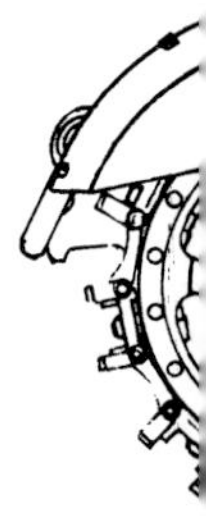

At the front, near the radioman, was an emergency exit hatch. This picture shows the position of the hatch; the one below shows it closed.

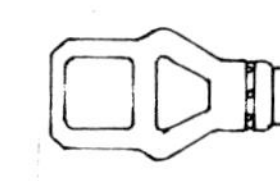

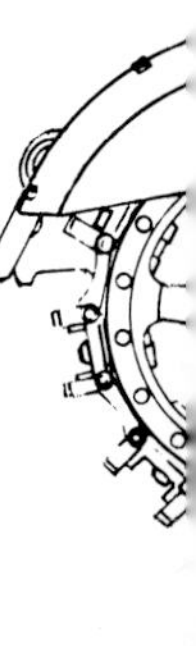

Panzerkampfwagen **Tiger Type B (Sd.Kfz. 182), Porsche turret.**

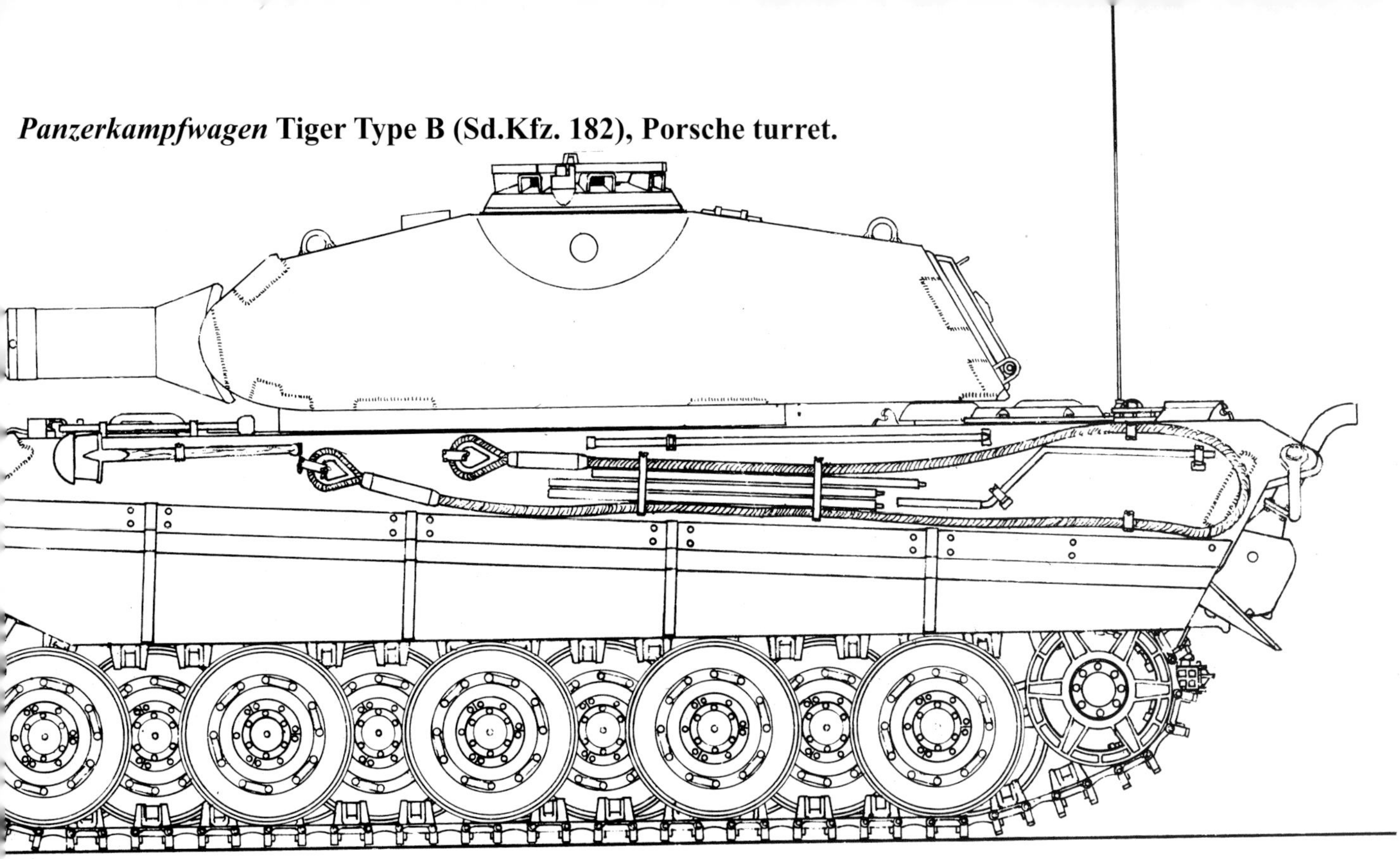

Panzerkampfwagen **Tiger Type B (Sd.Kfz. 182), production turret.**

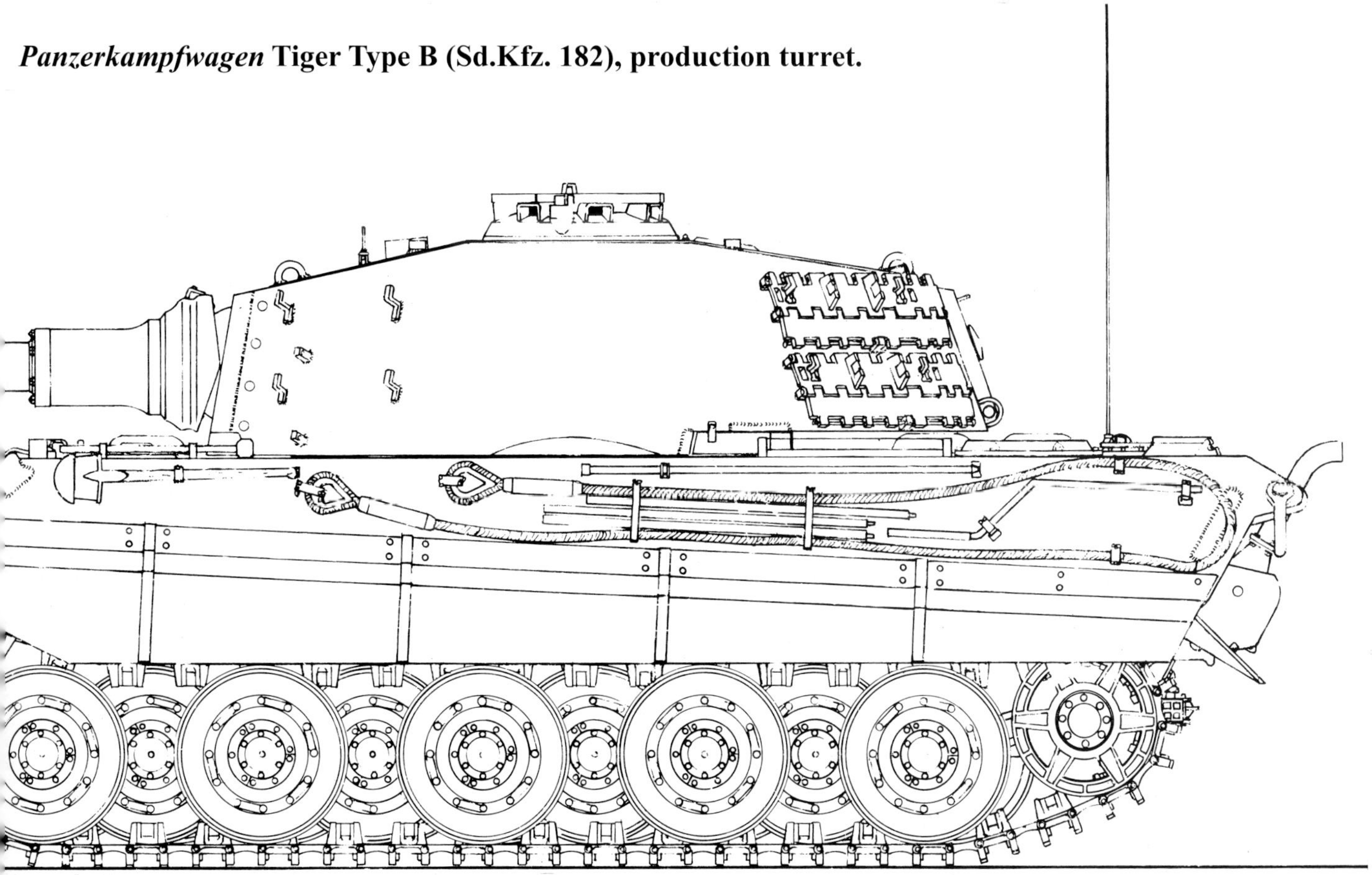

elevation machine (spindle aiming machine). The elevation field extended from -8 to +15 degrees. The turret could be turned by the turning apparatus, either by the vehicle's motor via a fluid drive, or swung by hand by the gunner. The turret was set on its ball bearings. The front wall was arched, while the side and rear walls were tilted 60 degrees out of the vertical, and bent outward on the ball bearings, as well as at the commander's cupola. The turret roof was sloped 12 degrees at the front and back. The turning ring had inner gearing with 208 teeth, and the carrying balls of the ball bearings had a diameter of 45 mm. The separating balls located between the carrying balls measured about 43 mm. In the ring nut of the outer ball-bearing ring, a sealing hose was laid; it sealed the turret attachment when fording. On the handwheel of the elevating machine was the firing lever for the gun, and by stepping on a foot pedal, the MG firing apparatus was worked. The commander's cupola was in the left center of the turret roof. It served as an entry for the tank commander, and allowed a view. The hatch in the turret roof was the entrance and exit for the rest of the tank's crew. In the rear wall of the turret was a hatch that allowed the installation and removal of the gun. There was also a machine-pistol port in the back wall, with a plug to close it. The close-in defense weapon mounted in the turret roof fired the Fast Smoke Cartridge 39, grenades, *Rauchsichtzeichen* 160 orange smoke plumes, and *Leuchtgeschosse* R tracers.

Since the Porsche firm's "VK 4502"—which was being developed at the same time—never went beyond the planning stage, the turrets planned for it (described above), 50 of which were built, were used on the Henschel "VK 4503." The following

The heavy wear on the teeth of the drive sprocket can be seen clearly in this picture. But only every other tooth shows this wear. The reason was an uneven division of the tracks.

The Dräger protective ventilation system was also supposed to be installed in the Tiger B, but remained at the test stage. The pictures show the extent of this equipment.

The functioning of the protective ventilation system was tested by setting off smoke around the vehicle. The device produced a maximum air pressure of 7.4 mm WS at 2500 rpm. The test length was about 40 minutes. The device prevented any smoke from entering the vehicle.

numbers were contracted for:

Number Made	**Purchase contract**	**Army contract**	**Chassis Numbers**
Test 3	424 056	SS 006-6362/42	
Series 176	420 500	SS 4911-210-5910/42	280001-280176
Series 350	420 530	SS "	280177-280526
Series 379	420 590	SS "	280527-280905
Series 329	420 680	SS "	280906-281234

The whole contract thus covered 1237 units, three of which were test models. The showing of the wooden model took place on

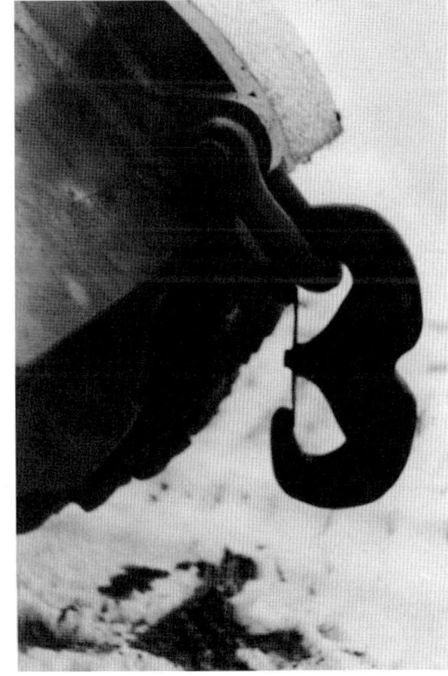

In tests, 3-shaped hooks were made for towing heavy vehicles. They were fitted with a safety latch.

The pictures show tests in which a *Jagdtiger* towed a braked Tiger B.

A bow towing eye was created to allow a vehicle to be turned sideways while towing.

On this Tiger B, chassis no. 280009, the left forward running-gear crank broke after running 1400 kilometers in testing.

On October 7, 1944, there was a severe air raid on the Henschel works in Kassel. This picture shows destroyed railroad cars loaded with tank tracks.

A Tiger B chassis near the destroyed buildings.

To eliminate ventilation damage from fighter-bombers, the front and rear ventilator gratings were covered with steel plates.

Destroyed vehicles were in the last stages of equipping. The damage to the vehicles was considerable.

Already prepared hulls for the Tiger B, among other things, are seen in front of the destroyed building.

The Henschel firm's assembly line after the air raid.

Fifty of the Tiger II had to be fitted with the turret built for the Porsche Tiger II.

October 20, 1943. Hitler had already ordered in January 1943 that new developments not be made known to the enemy by too early combat use.

Superiority could be maintained only for one period of combat (at most a year). Therefore, superiority for 1944 had to be planned. Tiger I and Panther would preserve it for 1943. It would be assured for 1944 by the *Mäuschen* (Little Mouse) tank and the new Tiger with the 8.8 cm L/71 gun.

Despite the greatest pressure, especially from the Ammunition Ministry, which absolutely insisted on bringing out the first production Tiger 3 (Type B) in July 1943, the beginning of the new series was scheduled for September. In February 1943, Speer's decision that the unification of Panther II and Tiger II components had to be introduced was already known. On May 3, 1943, Henschel declared that it could not reckon on beginning Tiger 3 production before January or February 1944. In these discussions, a Tiger assault gun on the second chassis was always talked about, but it would have been so heavy that Henschel cranes would no longer be sufficient to move it. The Tiger 2 assault gun, unlike Assault Gun 1, would have a loose body. The Henschel firm explained that it had no lathe of 4000 to 4500 mm diameter.

On July 5, 1943, regulations stated that foreign workers could not be employed without permission. On November 18, 1943, the first production turret for the Tiger II* was examined at Wegmann. A number of faults were found, most of which could only be rectified in later production. The first prototype of the new Tiger ran in October 1943. Two more vehicles were delivered in December of the same year. Series production began hesitantly in January 1944; larger numbers were not produced until May 1944.

After Type E went out of production in August 1944, a monthly production of 100 Type B vehicles (Tiger B) was foreseen. The following numbers were actually produced by Henschel in Kassel:

Month	**1943**	**1944**	**1945**
January	--	3	40
February	--	5	42
March	--	6	18
April	--	6	--
May	--	15	--
June	--	32	--
July	--	45	--
August	--	84	--
September	--	73	--
October	1	26	--
November	--	22	--
December	2	60	--
Total	3	377	100

The new vehicle was designated "*Panzerkampfwagen* Tiger, *Ausführung* B (Sd.Kfz. 182)."

In December 1943 Hitler considered it necessary that the shell catcher, which had been built under the lower wall of the turret on both sides of the gun, should be eliminated no matter what. Tests must be made at once to determine to what extent an improvement could be made by welding on a deflector. The turret taken over from Porsche design no. 180 also needed an increased amount of work, especially as to the use of curved plates of great strength. In May 1944 the first production turret developed by Krupp for the Tiger II was exhibited by Wegmann; it was installed as of vehicle no. 51. It had a smaller frontal area, with a considerably increased armor thickness. The ammunition supply carried in the vehicle could also be increased from 72 to 84 rounds. The rear part of the turret sidewalls was approved by WaPrüf 6 for carrying spare track links.

On June 5, 1944, the OKH WaPrüf 6 Pz IIIc notified Dipl.-Ing. Stollberg of Henschel that no permission existed to change from the present lubrication of the Tiger tank to a central lubrication system. Central lubrication had been installed for testing at Haustenbeck. The Gebr. Böhringer firm of Göppingen had problems with the turret-turning system Types L3S1 and L4S1. There were constant problems with oil leaks, and the housings also showed porous spots.

The original turrets for the Tiger II were also made by the Skoda works in Königgrätz, which had delivered eleven of them to Wegmann by August 1944.

In 1944 the Ordnance Office required the installation of a gas protection system in the Tiger B and Panther tanks. It took up a lot of space, and was thus hard to house, with many filters. It consisted of a switching apparatus, and a centrifugal blower to produce high pressure in the fighting compartment. The blower was driven by the gearbox through a special shaft. The system, made by the Drägerwerk in Lübeck, was only installed for testing.

As of August 1944, a change from roller to journal bearings was called for. The PAN-Metallgesellschaft of Mannheim offered Henschel Radiax journal bearings made of a tin-free special brass alloy (PAN-So-Ms 3a) of metal class 355. Their extra-finely porous, lubricant saving structure was to offer better lubricating conditions than the homogeneous type.

* Type 180, Porsche design.

Four-side views of the Tiger Type B tank (Sd.Kfz. 182) with production turret.

© H.L.Doyle'76

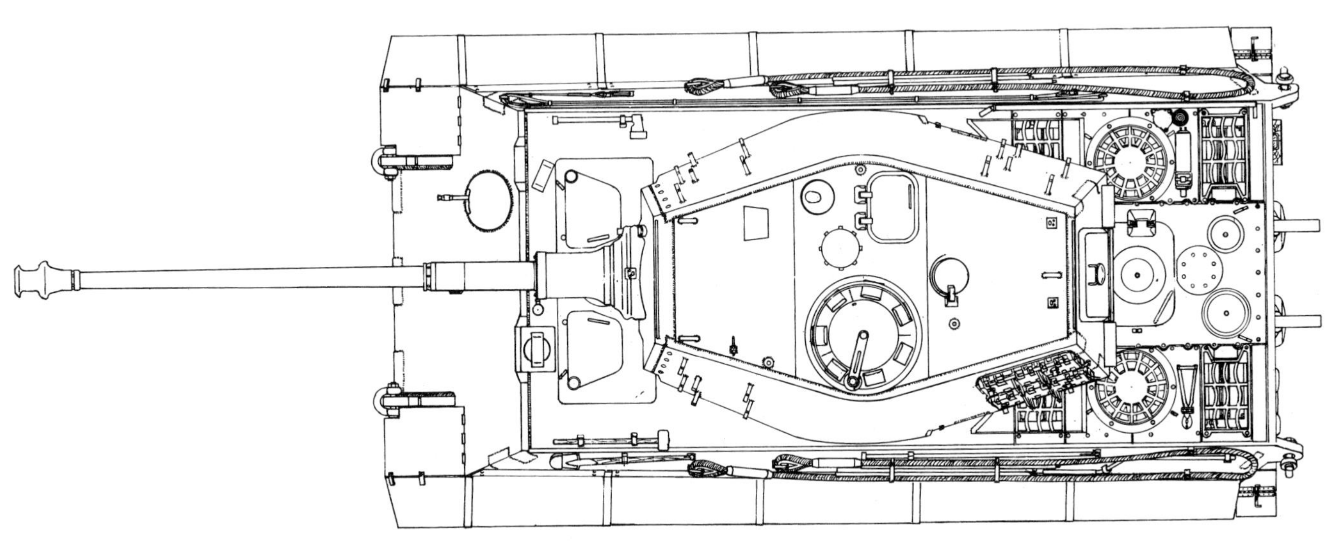

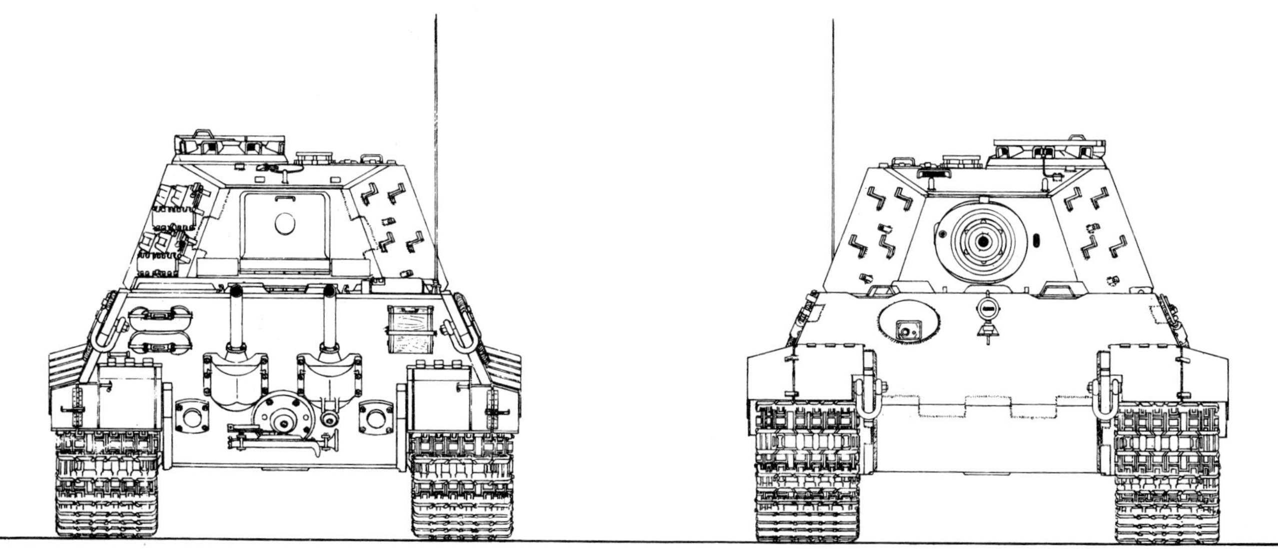

Longitudinal and transverse views of the Tiger Type B tank with production turret.

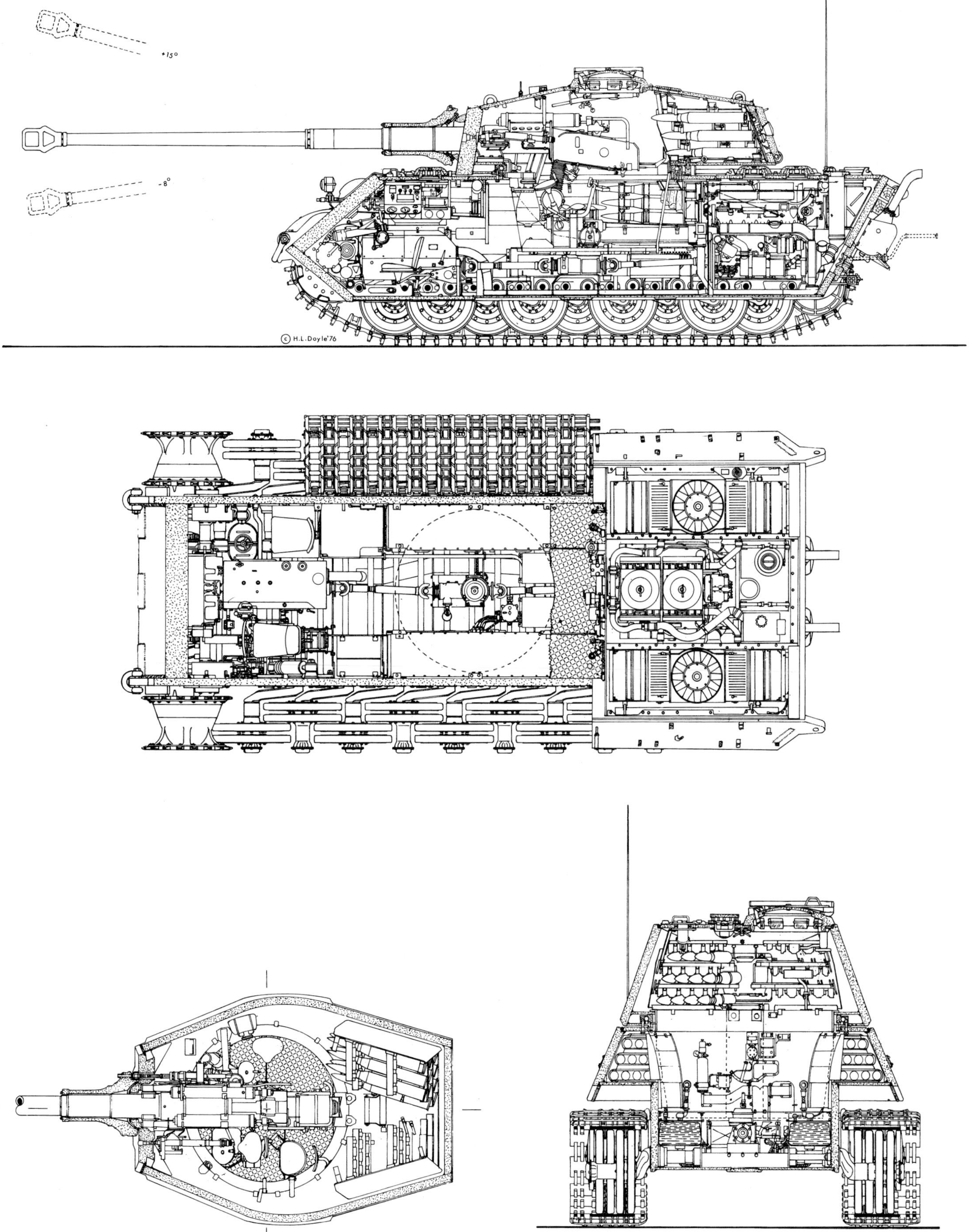

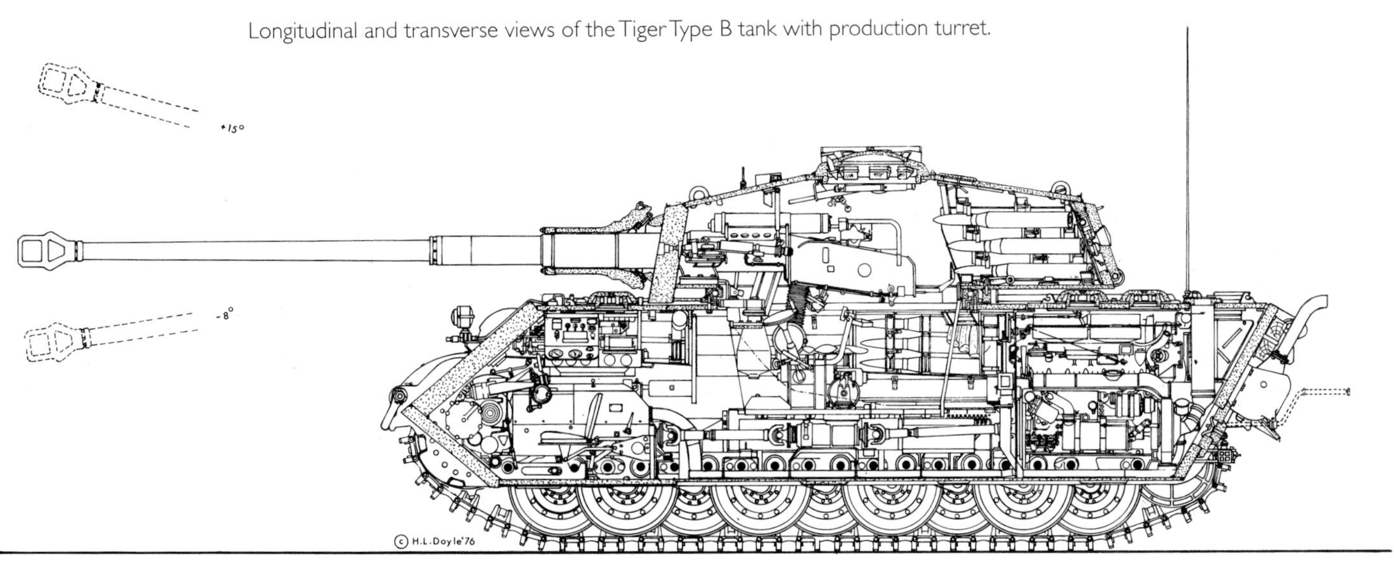

This comparison shows the old (left) and final production turrets of the Tiger II.

On July 28, 1944, it was decided that the Tiger E test model no. 250 018 would be sent back to Kummersdorf in mid-August, and a redesigning of the Tiger B road wheel mounts would be undertaken, concerning the series production of the roller bearings. Henschel announced on August 28, 1944, that journal bearings with grease lubrication were already being tested. A journal bearing version for production hubs and cranks was ready by the end of August. In the end, these tests brought no usable results.

On August 19, 1944, the OKH WA J Rü 6/VIII ordered an additional camouflage painting for all armored vehicles, effective immediately. Besides the basic yellow color, spots of olive green paint (RAL* 6003) and red-brown (RAL 8017) had to be applied. This was of great importance to the troops; every effort was to be made to apply the new camouflage colors to part of the August production. The vehicle, also known to the enemy as "King Tiger," was in action as of August 1944.

*RAL = *Reichsausschuss für Lieferbedingungen und Gütesicherung beim* DIN.

The first showing of the Tiger B with production turret (chassis no. 280 100), with a full-size wooden dummy of the Panther II behind it.

In September 1944 there came further regulations about the replacement of ball bearings. The MIAG firm made the suggestion to replace the central roller bearing in the planetary gear of the steering gear and the final drives of the Tiger. Similar tests in the Panzer III had been successful. In order to lower the stress on the Tiger B steering gear, another test was begun with a small radius in first gear enlarged from 1.78 to 2.5 meters. Corresponding results on the required numbers of teeth on wheels 12 and 13 (instead of 45/50 teeth with 2.5 meter radius 40/60 teeth) had already been provided in May 1944. The suggestion was made to build two or three production Tiger B tanks with the changed small radius. But as the large sun drive wheel was located right next to the sun wheel in the steering gear, the central roller bearing in the planetary gear had to take up about half of the pressure of this wheel, and thus this bearing position could not be done without. Journal bearings were made standard in the hand and foot levers. Interestingly, a message of September 23, 1944, spoke of a two-ton crane attached to a Tiger B by "mushrooms"; no other information exists.* In November 1944, attempts were begun to accomplish a weight reduction in the Tiger B. The result was a loss of about ten tons, to be accomplished chiefly by reducing the side armor to the thickness of the Tiger E.

On November 18, 1944, the installation of simulated fire cartridges was called for. They made it possible for the crews to pretend their vehicle was on fire in case of enemy fire. The up-and-down adjustment of the driver's seat urgently needed improvement. At the end of November 1944 the new track (Type Kgs 73/800/152) for the Tiger B was introduced. Five camouflage attachments were welded onto each side of the turret. As of March-April 1945, a compressorless barrel blow-off, using an air cylinder activated by the recoil of the gun, was to be introduced.

*For installing and removing motors, gearboxes, and parts of the running gear, this crane, which was to be mounted on the turret, had been developed. The attachments for it were supposed to be provided on all turrets, to make removing or installing the components easier for the troops.

The details of the turret are seen in the smaller but stronger front plate and the long gun mounted in a "boar's head" mantlet.

This version of the Tiger B was built until the war's end.

The last type of Tiger B seen in action in Budapest.

At the same time, the MG 34 was to be replaced by the MG 42. For this, a completely new machine-gun mount had to be created. The machine-gun ball mantlet by the radioman was to be replaced by a machine-pistol mount. The armor protection caps for the torsion-bar springs were eliminated. After supplies were used up, the inner paint was also eliminated. At the end of November 1944 there were further instructions as to the paint. The colored outer paint was kept, but all tank body parts were to be given one coat of dark green (RAL 6003), and be delivered thus to the assembly firms. They were to add the bright colors—red-brown or dark yellow—according to the prescribed camouflage appearance. Three different camouflage patterns were planned for every vehicle, and made known by WuG 5. The colors were sprayed on, and with as sharp contours as possible.

While vehicles were being transported to the front, there was an extraordinarily high loss through weapon fire from Allied fighter-bombers. In particular, ventilation openings were damaged by bullets and splinters. Shields that did not interfere with the streams of fresh and hot air were created for the inlet and outlet openings of the engine compartment cover. Because of the shortage of natural leather, canvas or paper covered canvas were prescribed for the seats in tanks. The attachable aircraft protection device on the commander's cupola was dropped in March 1945 in favor of a two-armed version.

By the end of January 1945, 417 Tiger II had been delivered. The schedule for this vehicle was as follows: February 45, March 50, April 50, May 60, June 60, July 60, August 60, and September 45.

Major problems resulted again in the final drives of the Tiger II. In November 1944, Hitler had ordered the use of force to assure the production of improved final drives.

In and of itself, the formation of the final drives was technically successful. With the given weight of the vehicle, the high torque of the track drive could be taken up only by a planetary gear. For the Panther—to expedite production—a crown-wheel drive, still with a highly stressed intermediate gear in the mounting, had been provided, which led to frequent breakdowns. Even in the securely proportioned final drive of the Tiger, there were more breakdowns than expected. They were found even more frequently in the *Jagdtiger*. The latter's limited traversing field of the gun made more frequent turning of the vehicle while firing necessary than in the tank. The problems were, though, considerably eliminated.

The guiding teeth of the tracks had only two millimeters of play on each side, whereas the Tiger E had had four mm. The lack of precision in the production of the rubber-sprung road wheels and their attachment to the hubs was too great to get by with so little play. There was also the introduction of "staggering" instead of "boxing" the road wheels. The cranks were not evenly stressed, and thus had different shapes and settings. With the one-sided stress on the inside, the track bolts bent and could no longer turn. Thus, the track's resistance to bending was much increased. The rubber-sprung road wheels were pushed off their axis, and thus were located wrongly, which made the discs "stagger." A final elimination of this problem had not been achieved by war's end. Henschel used the stage process in building the Tiger B, as already for Type E, and had its assembly line divided into nine stages of six hours each. The average time needed to finish a vehicle was 14 days. There were 18 to 2 tanks on the hull production line, while ten were on the assembly line. In terms of raw material need (without weapons), the following differences from the "Panther I" existed:

	Panther I	**Tiger II**
Iron unalloyed (kg)	33,409	44,009
Iron alloyed (kg)	44,060	75,789

Iron total (kg)	77,469	119,798
Coarse & medium plates (kg)	30,735	62,976
Fine plates (kg)	1,888	2,248

Only a few of the "Tiger II" tanks were still fitted with fording apparatus. These vehicles—the heaviest tanks used by German *Wehrmacht* troops until the war's end—were used by eleven independent Heavy Army Tank *Abteilungen*, and also by four Armored Regiments. Their size and light performance weight did not always let their excellent armament and armor be utilized, and yet they constituted a significant focal point weapon. As for maintenance, they were almost always a problem.

While the tanks were in action, serious damage constantly occurred in the Maybach powerplants, leading in many cases to the total breakdown of the tanks. An investigation branch of the Panzer Commission, created especially for this purpose, visited the Maybach works on November 23 and 24, 1943, in order to become familiar with the problem on the spot. There was, in particular, big-end bearing damage, which led to engine failure. The Commission was instructed to set up a program to eliminate these problems immediately, in order to give the motor an assured life of at least 2000 km (equal to about 100 hours of use). Suggestions for redesigning the "HL 230" motor, and for creating a new tank motor were also made.

Dr. Maybach announced that the first test motor had reached the test bench at the same time that the series production had begun in April 1943. The motor was a further development of the "HL 210" model, which had already proven itself to a certain degree. The tests of the new motor on the test bench already showed leaking cylinder head seals, which led to water damage, plus the failure of big-end bearings. The oil level was hard to check, and the cooling water was hard to fill. Carburetor backfires caused fires in the engine compartment.

The connecting-rod bearings had buildups of carbon and iron oxide, plus lens and pipe buildups. The blend of lead and bronze also had been made with too little lead and too much phosphorus. The introduction of "Glyco" bearing shells as of November 1, 1943, in place of the earlier journal bearings had brought no improvement. Too great bending and swinging on the rear end of the shaft was thought to be the cause, and adding an eighth main bearing after the vibration damper was foreseen. Five of these motors were already running at Kummersdorf at that time, and one of them had suffered bearing damage after 1576 km, while another had shown light signs of wear on the sixth bearing after 2647 km. The other three motors had run more than 2000 km without damage.

At another showing, 28 Type "HL 230" motors were shown, 26 of them dismantled. It was found that insufficient ventilation had been provided for the cooling system, which led to air bubbles. Of the 26 dismantled motors, 23 showed damage to the big-end bearings. Above all, crankcase bearings 5 and 6 were affected. It was noted that the distance from the shell bearings to the connecting rods from split joint to split joint was only about 1.5 mm. Thus, the rising flange of the half of the shell on the right side, which was bent inward by the pressure of combustion, scraped the oil film off. There were almost always signs of wear at this point.

In addition, insufficient hardening of the bearing journals of the crankshaft was found. The suggested changes to the cylinder head seals with copper rings and a Reinz gasket were also criticized. In the long run, such a combination promised no lasting improvement. The following suggestions were set forth:

- Moving the rising big-end shell flange by 0.02 to 0.03 mm.
- A later exchange of main and auxiliary connecting rods, so that the flange on the falling half of the shell, stressed by the pressure of combustion on the auxiliary rod, came to a stop.
- A suggested oil equalization like that of the Daimler-Benz model.
- An immediate test with an oil additive like IG 891 or the like, all the more so as the total running of the engine at the factory

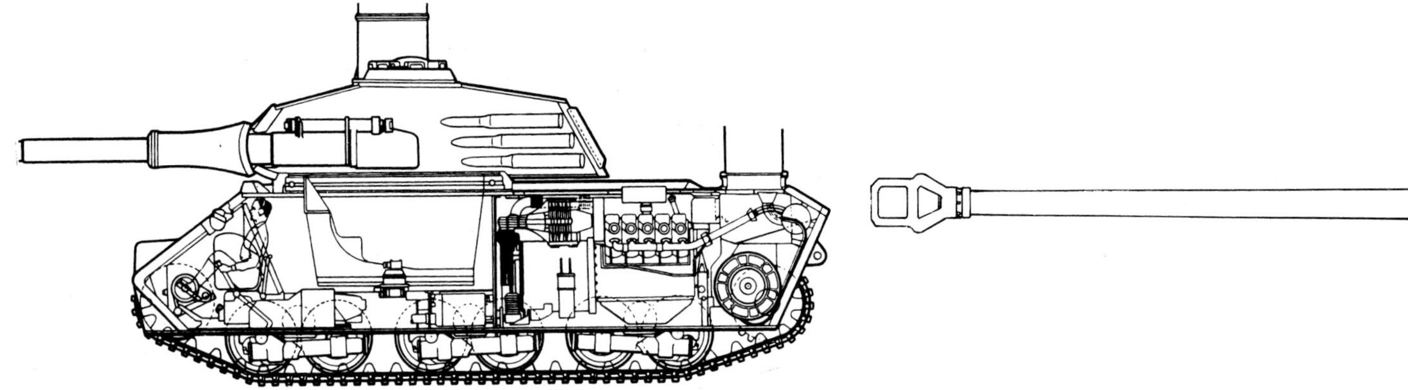

A comparison of the Porsche designs 180/181 with front and rear turrets. This model existed only on paper.

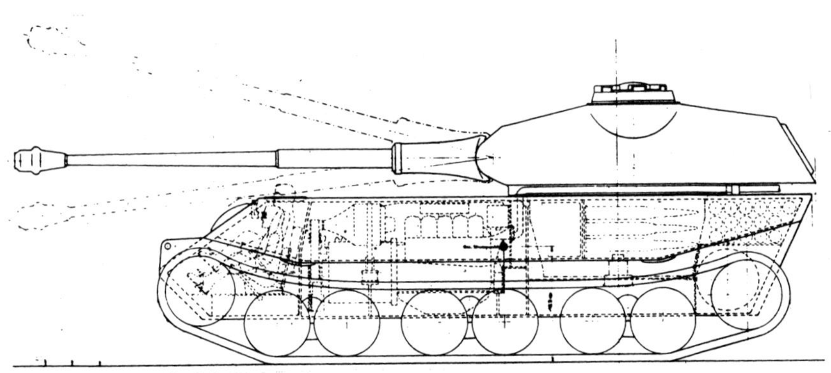

A three-side view of VK 4502 (P) with the fighting compartment to the rear.

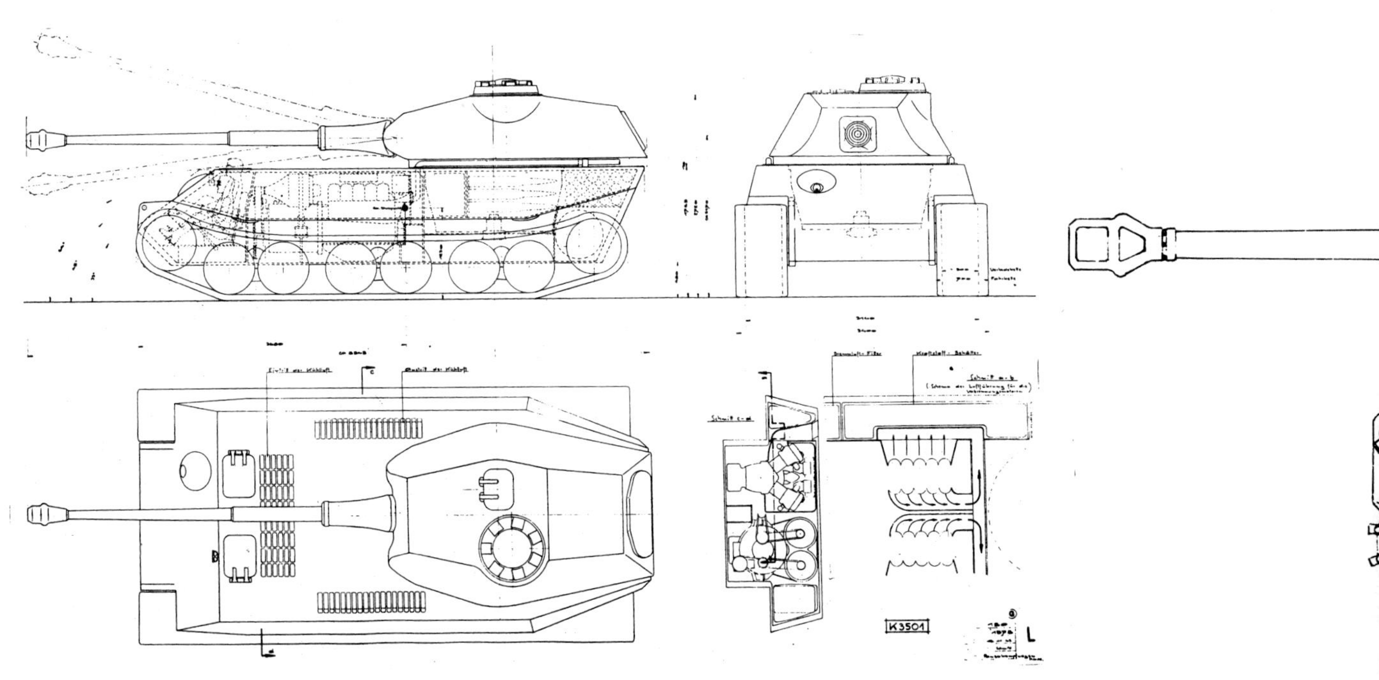

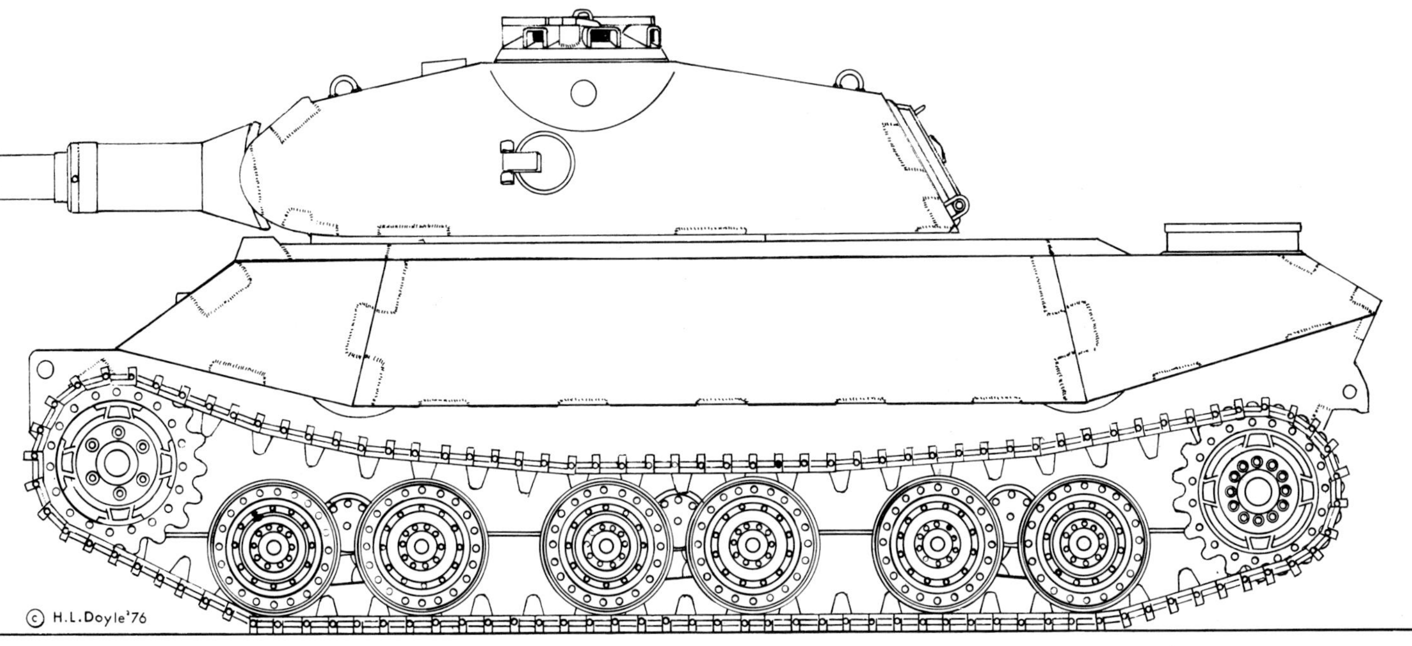

***Panzerkampfwagen* VK 4502 (P), turret to the front (suggestion)**
Porsche suggestion for the Tiger II (Porsche type 180/181).

***Panzerkampfwagen* VK 4502 (P), turret to the rear (suggestion).**

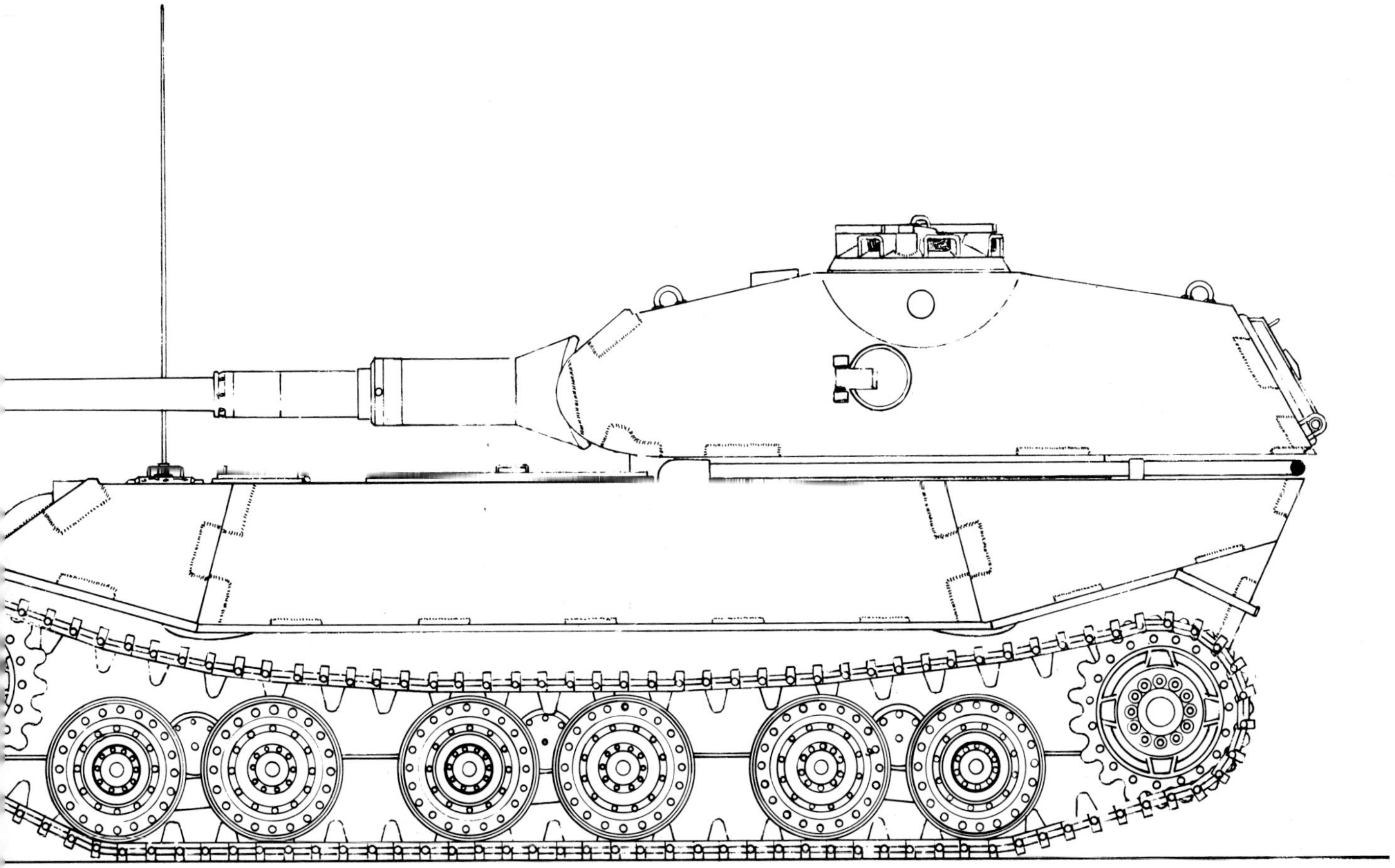

only lasted two or three hours, and thus created no danger of piston ring sticking for Maybach. In addition, the uniform oil of the *Wehrmacht* was said to have very bad qualities.

- Improving the dirt filtering during running-in, since many bearing shells were fluted. Changing the filter so that not all the dirt was taken out of the filter by the working of the pressure adjusting valve.
- Changing of the lubricating channels of the crankshaft to 90 degrees before and after. This had already been done to four Maybach test motors, and had proven itself to date.
- Checking screws for length (a check had found only 0.13 to 0.16 instead of 0.17), on account of the insufficiency of the torque key.
- Special testing of the shell strength. A check of a shell half found fluctuations of up to 0.07.
- Since it was to be assumed that the constant wear on big-end bearings 5 and 6 was caused not only by the bending of the shaft end, but also by insufficient oil supply as a result of foam buildup (the oil entered the crankcase from the rear), a measurement of the foam by a parallel pipe with a measuring glass appeared to be urgently needed.

In addition, it was found that the oil supply was completely insufficient for a total circulation of 96 liters per minute, since foam tests had shown that it took minutes until the foam had broken up. A considerable enlargement of the oil tank was thus necessary. Even by war's end not all of the problems had been solved.

Only the basic types developed for the French Army attained the otherwise comparatively high level of stability of the Maybach motors.

In 1961 a "Tiger B" came back to Germany as a gift of the U.S. Army to the *Bundeswehr*, and was put on display at the Combat Troop School 2 in Munster. The "VK 4502"* planned on paper by the Dr.-Ing. h. c. F. Porsche KG also had a newly developed hull with angled walls. The Porsche Type "180" had running gear similar to those of Type "101" but strengthened, which now had a wheel load of 4650 kg. The total weight was estimated as some 64 tons. The twin-engine system of Type "101/3" was planned, but the motors were to be fitted with a new cylinder head. As usual, they drove two generators, which ran two electric motors. The tracks, made of 130 mm links, were 640 mm wide as before; the ground pressure had risen to 1.15 kg/cm². Of the ammunition for the 8.8 cm KwK L/71, 16 shells were carried in the turret, 42 in the hull, and about ten over the hull floor. A second suggestion for the Type "180" concerned the use of two "101/4" motors. There were only minor differences. While the Type "180" had gasoline-electric drive, Type "181" was designed for hydraulic drive. Now 700 mm wide tracks were suggested, lowering the ground pressure to 1.06 kp/ cm², and reducing the wheel load to 4620 kg. The gear ratio was changed, although the running gear was not changed otherwise. The first "181" design was still projected with two Type "101/4" engines; the second was to have two 16-cylinder Porsche-Deutz Diesel engines with 110 mm bore and 130 mm stroke, giving a displacement of 19.6 liters. The maximum power of each engine was to be circa 370 HP as 2000 rpm. The power-to-weight ratio of the vehicle was raised from 8.5 to 10.4 HP/ton. In the third design of the Type "181" a Porsche diesel engine was to be used, an X-16 that was supposed to produce 700 HP at 2000 rpm. With a bore of 135 mm and a stroke of 160 mm, the displacement was 37 liters. Only one motor was to be installed, but the motor never went into production. The Porsche Types "180" and "181," also called "Special Vehicle III," were also designed with a rear fighting compartment, with the powerplant in the middle. Other than the turrets, which were later used on the first production "VK 4503" vehicles made by Henschel, these vehicles were not built.

Variants

The rebuilding of the Porsche 'Tiger" as an assault gun with no turret, ordered on September 26, 1942, had meanwhile been directed in collaboration with the Altmärkisches Kettenwerk GmbH (ALKETT). On February 7, 1943, despite being advised of the prevailing weaknesses of the running gear and the resulting insufficient road tests, Hitler ordered the production of 90 tank destroyers on the Porsche "Tiger" chassis, with the long 8.8 cm gun and 200 mm front armor (Ferdinand), by all available means. The still needed testing and the production were to be supported so that vehicle after vehicle could be brought to the front in the shortest time. Since the creation of the air-cooled motors originally planned for these vehicles had not yet begun, the chassis were fitted with two water-cooled Maybach Type "HL 120" motors. The engine compartment was moved to the middle of the vehicle. The electric power lines were produced by Siemens-Schuckert. The front armor of the hull was increased to 200 mm by adding 100 mm plates. The fixed armored body had 200 mm armor in front, and 80 mm on the sides and rear. The traversing range of

*As counterparts to the Henschel Tiger II
VK 4501 (P) Porsche Type 101 Porsche Tiger I**
VK 4502 (P) Porsche Type 180 Porsche Tiger II
**also *Panzerjäger* (P) *Elefant*, formerly Ferdinand
***also *Panzerjäger* Tiger "*Jagdtiger*"

The ordered rebuilding of the Porsche Tiger as a tank destroyer required partly extensive hull modifications. The pictures show the hull at left with the engine compartment in back. At right is the rebuilt hull, with the engine compartment in the middle. This was separated from the fighting compartment by a firewall at the back.

The last chassis of the Porsche Tiger series is shown at the Nibelungenwerk.

These pictures show the assembly of the Tiger (P) tank destroyer in different stages.

After being finished, the vehicles were driven in.

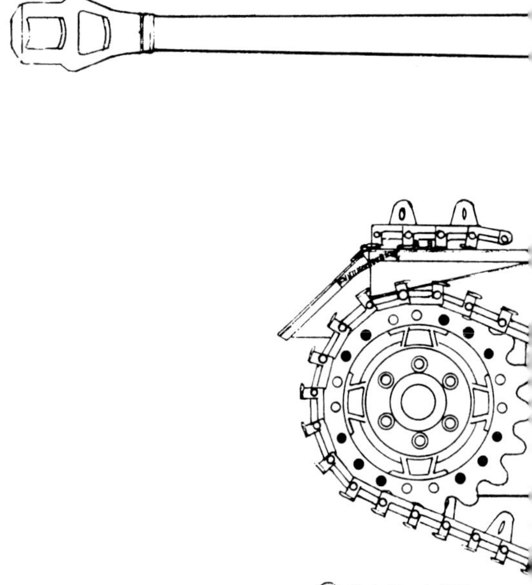

On May 8, 1943, the last vehicle, with chassis no. 150100, was finished. (Note the toothed leading wheels at the front.)

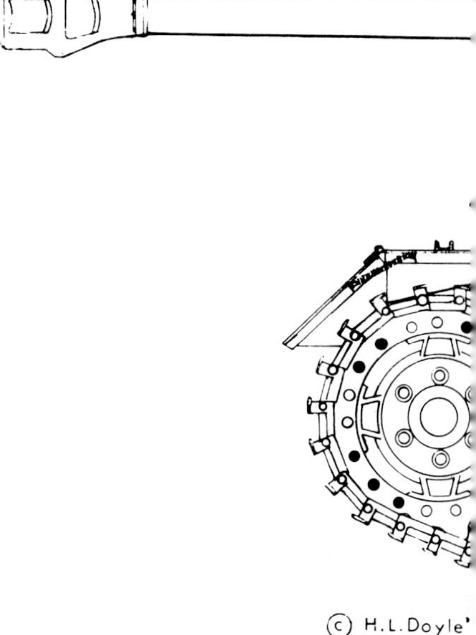

Panzerjäger **Tiger (P) for 8.8 cm Pak 43 L/71 (Sd.Kfz. 184) "*Elefant.*"**

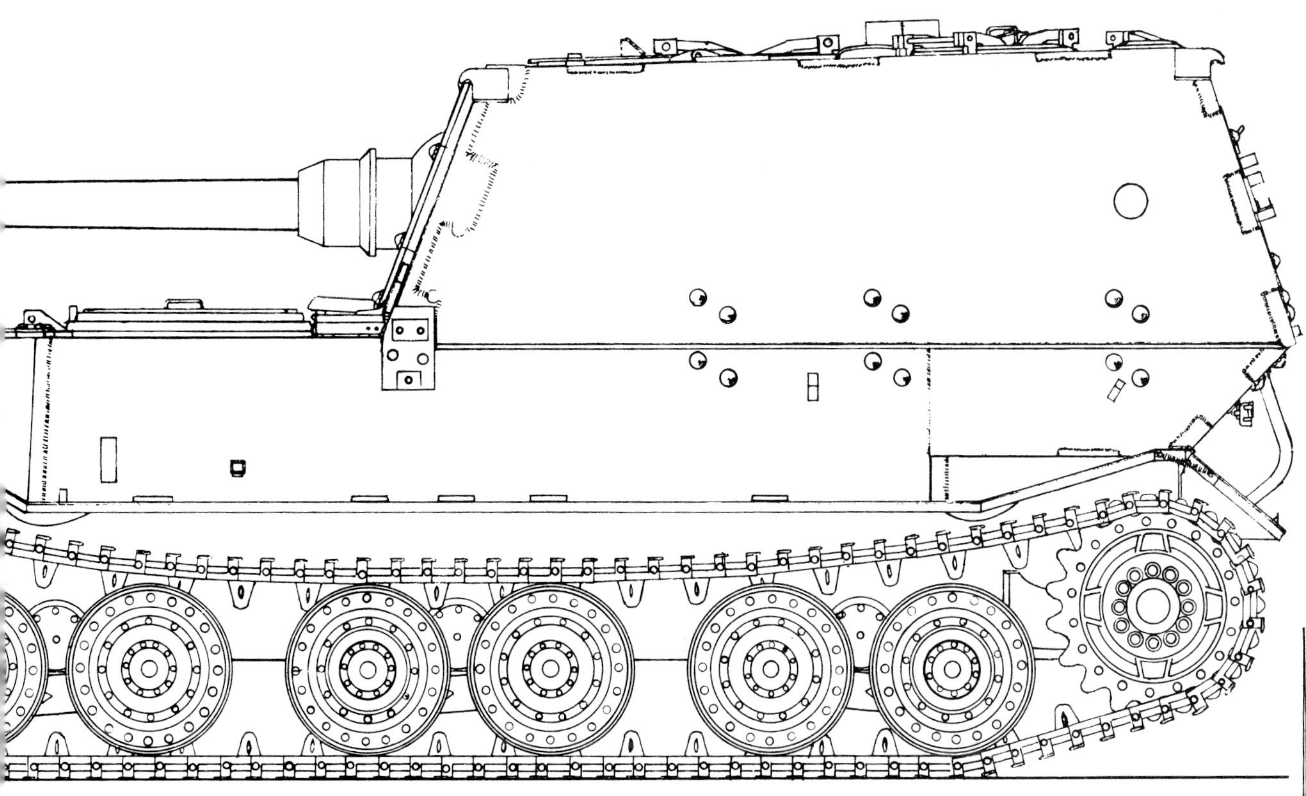

Panzerjäger **Tiger (P) for 8.8 cm Pak 43 L/71 (Sd.Kfz. 184) "*Elefant*" after general overhauling.**

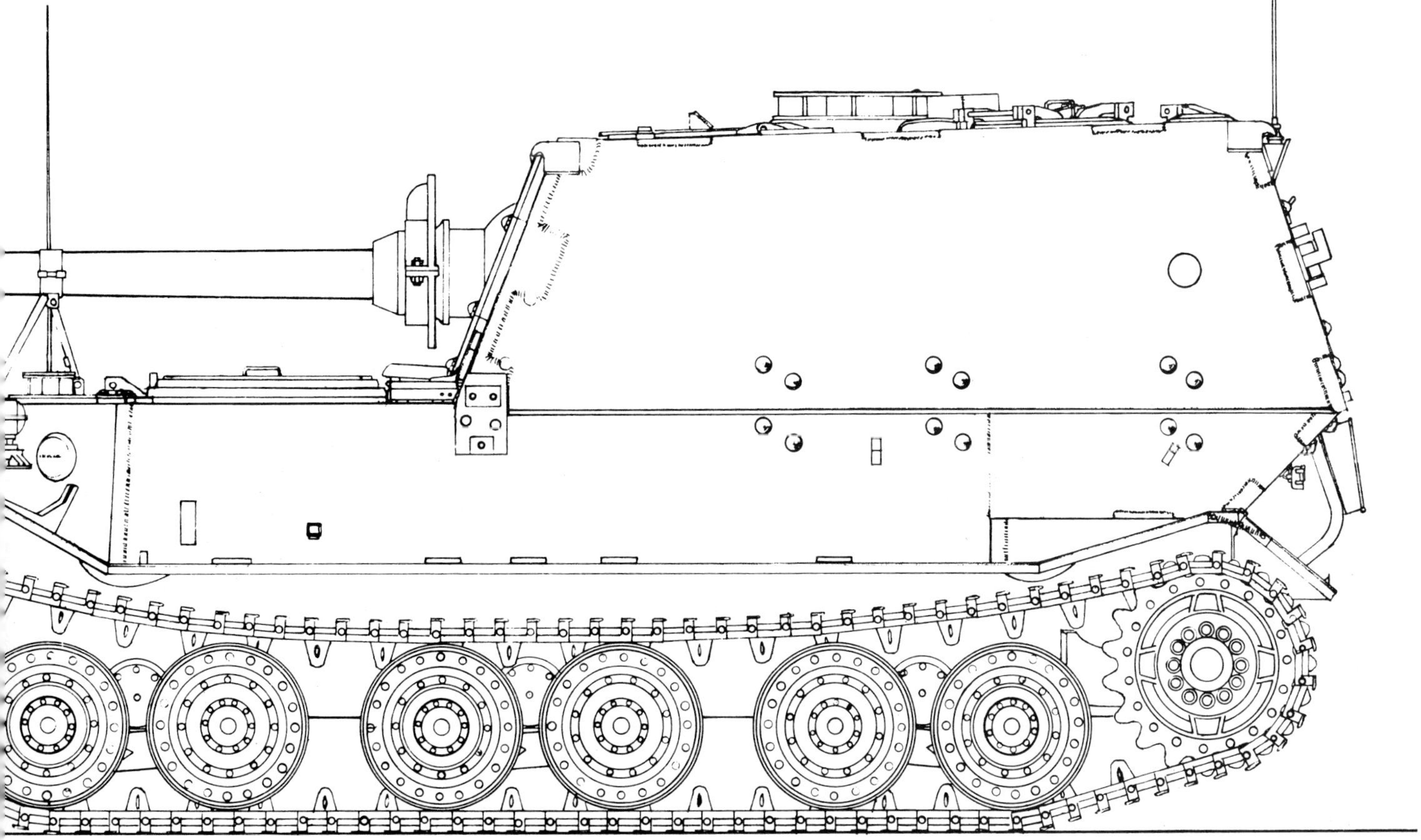

Four sides of the Sd.Kfz. 184 in the original production version.

Covered with tarpaulins, the "Ferdinand" vehicle, later "*Elefant*," went to the front.

the 8.8 cm Pak 43/2 L/71 (made by Dortmund-Hoerder Hüttenverein in Lippstadt) was 28 degrees, and the elevation range went from –8 to +14 degrees. The firing height was 2310 mm. The crew consisted of six men. With a fighting weight of 65 tons, a top speed of 20 km/h was possible. The fuel supply of 950 liters allowed a range of 150 km on the road. Fifty rounds of ammunition were carried. The rebuilding of the chassis and installation of the armored body at the Nibelungenwerk was finished on May 8, 1943. The vehicles first saw action in two *Abteilungen* of a *Panzerregiment* during Operation :Citadel" in July 1943. Their official designation was "*Panzerjäger* Tiger (P) - *Elefant* - for 8.8 cm Pak 43 L/71" (Sd.Kfz. 184) (chassis no. 150 001 to 150 100). The technical failures were high, and the meager supply of ammunition and lack of any close-in defensive weapon (only a machine gun carried loose was on hand) were also noticeable weaknesses. The vehicles were either lost to enemy action, or were worn out quickly because of their technically complex gasoline-electric drive. The remaining fifty vehicles were fitted with an MG 34 installed in a ball mantlet near the radioman while being overhauled in Germany. Also, the hitherto unprotected gun mount was protected by an armor plate attached to the barrel. The gun commander was also given the necessary commander's cupola. Some of the vehicles saw action in Italy.

Five Porsche "Tiger" chassis were built and used as recovery and towing vehicles. They were not fitted with extra armor, and in the rear of their low armored bodies they had a ball mantlet for an MG 34 for self defense.

In the Kursk offensive (Operation "Citadel") in early July 1943, the ninety Ferdinands gathered in *Jagdpanzer* Regiment 656 suffered heavy loses. Here are two vehicles that fell into Russian hands.

Details of the Porsche running gear with clearly visible road wheels.

The remaining vehicles went back to the Nibelungenwerk, and were generally overhauled there. They now had a machine gun mounted near the radioman, a shield for the gun, and a commander's cupola.

Front and rear views of the "*Elefant*" in its final form.

Above and left: The two Tiger (P) tank-destroyer *Abteilungen* received towing vehicles of the same type, but with no heavy armor plate. They had an MG 34 for close-in defense.

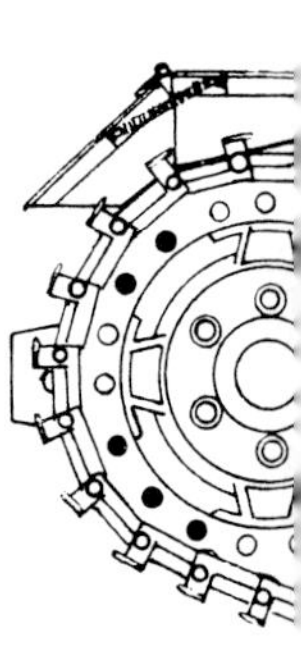

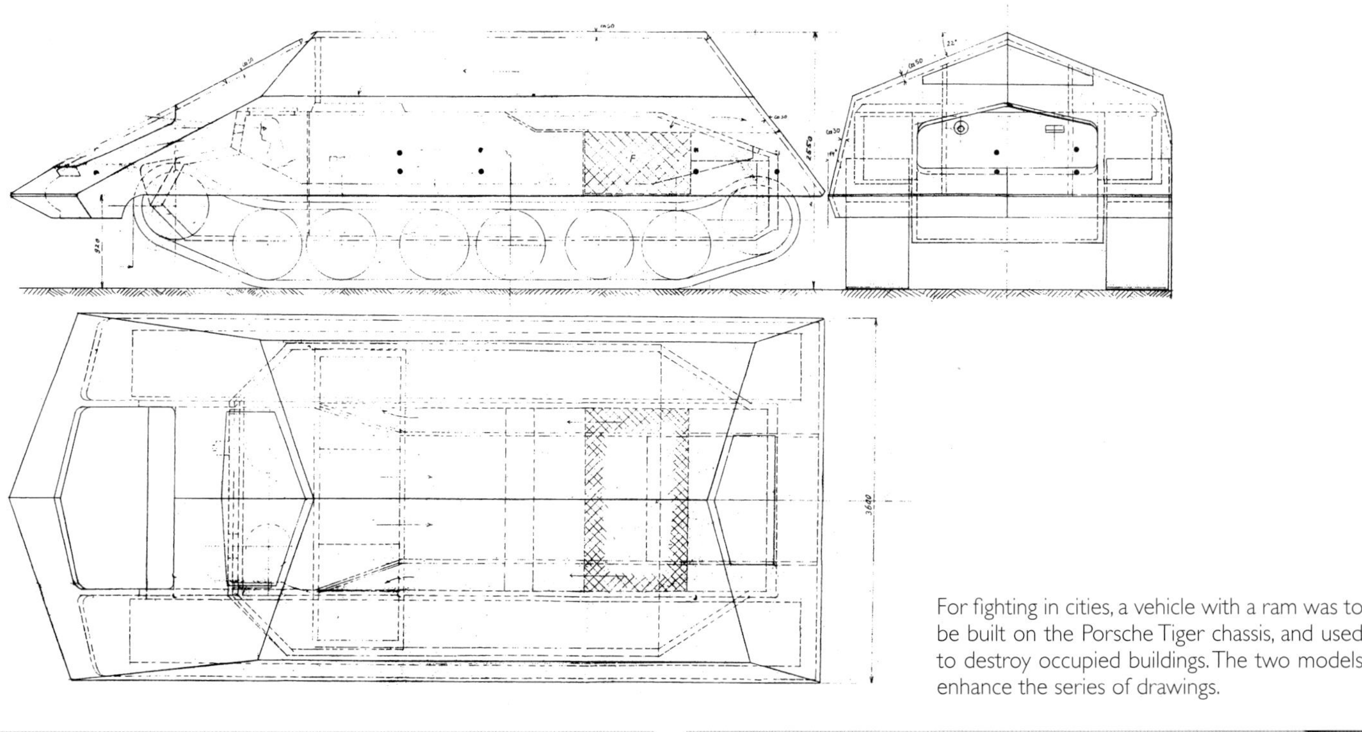

For fighting in cities, a vehicle with a ram was to be built on the Porsche Tiger chassis, and used to destroy occupied buildings. The two models enhance the series of drawings.

Ppanzerbergewagen Tiger (P)

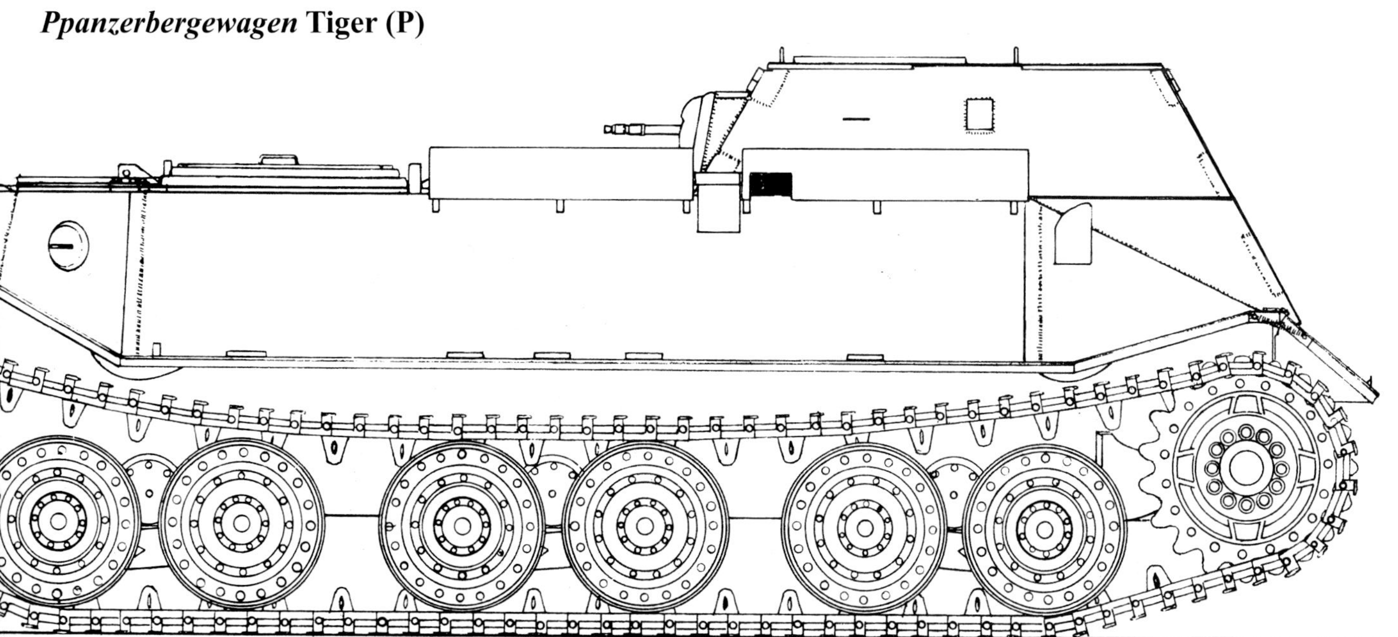

Rammpanzer Tiger (P) (suggestion).

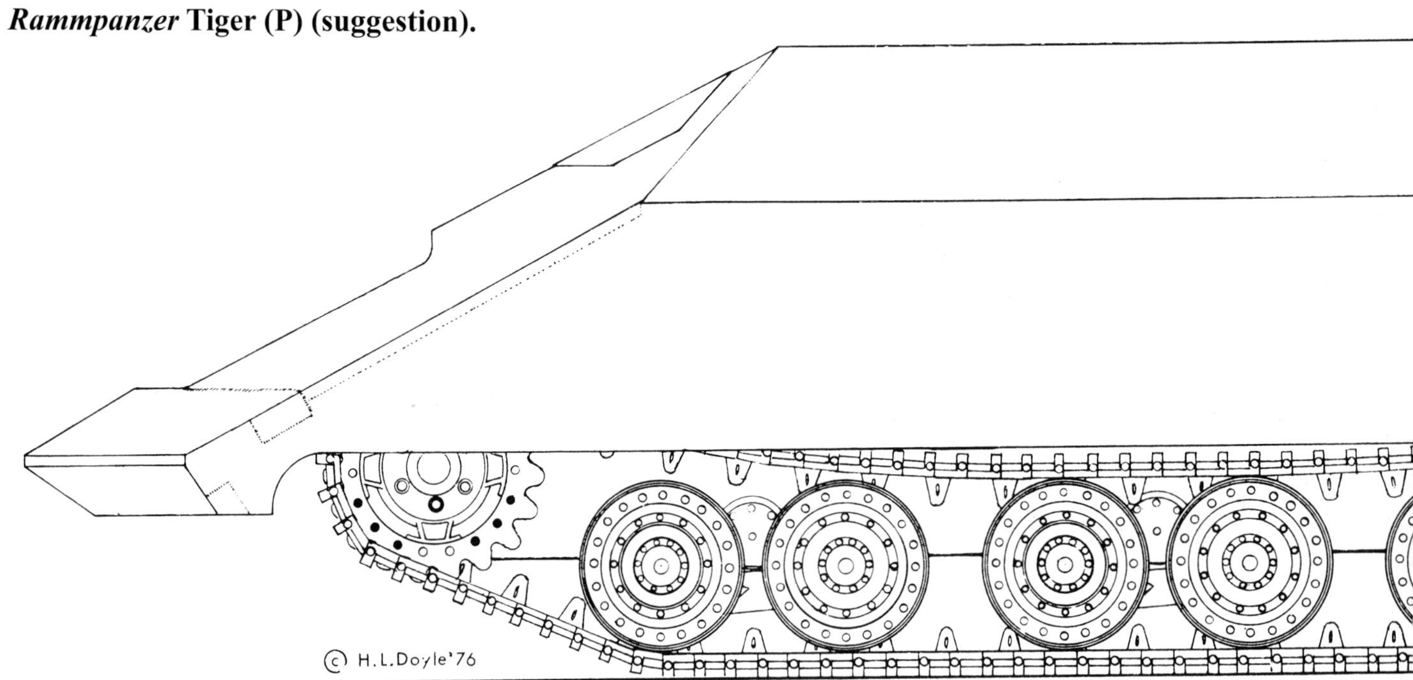

On January 5, 1943, Hitler expressed his agreement with the suggestion to build three "Ram-Tigers" on Porsche chassis. The concept had arisen through the experience of street fighting in Stalingrad. The chassis were to have a ram hood for breaking into buildings of all kinds, and to carry fuel in trailers. These designs were never realized.

The "Adolf Hitler" Tank Program also called for the building of an assault gun with the 8.8 cm KwK L/71 on the Tiger I chassis. The vehicle was known as a "super heavy self-propelled mount" (ss.Sfl), and planning was begun early in 1943. It was thought that it might later be armed with the 12.8 cm Pak L/61. Production was to begin in October 1943, and 50 were to be built by December. In August, though, the decision was made in favor of building normal Tigers instead of the ss.Sfl.

Jagdtiger

During the design work on the "Tiger B" at Henschel, the designing of an assault gun based on the "Tiger B" had to be started. In cooperation with Krupp, this vehicle was to carry a 12.8 cm

The showing of the full-size wooden model of the *Jagdtiger* to Hitler took place on October 20, 1943. In the background are a Tiger B and a *Jagdpanther*, in the foreground is an Italian Type P 40 tank.

The first dummy of the *Jagdtiger* under construction.

gun in a fixed body. The chassis had to be lengthened some 260 mm at the rear, and the two-piece hatch at the end of the body had to be made gas-tight and secure from shots. A new ammunition storage was designed, since the 12,8 cm gun used separated ammunition. For the gun barrel, which projected far to the front, a barrel brace later proved to be necessary. The wooden model of the "*Jagdtiger*" was shown to the *Führer* at Arys* on October 20, 1943. On April 7, 1944, Hitler could be given the first photos of the "*Panzerjäger* Tiger" Type B (Sd.Kfz. 186). The showing of the first production model took place on April 20, 1944. The fighting weight with a six-man crew, 40 rounds of ammunition, and 860 liters of fuel was 75.2 tons. It was thus the heaviest armored vehicle used by any nation in its day. The fixed armored body had 250 mm front armor inclined at 75 degrees. The sides and rear had 80 mm armor. The primary armament, made at the

* The Arys Troop Training Center in East Prussia.

A comparison of the Tiger B and *Jagdtiger* shows the tank above, with turning turret and 8.8 cm KwK 43 L/71, and below, the *Jagdpanzer* with 12.8 cm Pak 44 L/55.

A *Jagdtiger* body damaged by bombs at the Nibelungenwerk.

The pictures show part of the *Jagdtiger* production at the Nibelungenwerk.

Krupp-Bertha-Werk in Breslau, was mounted in a "boar's head" mantlet. This 12.8 cm Pak 44 (also Pak 80) L/55, with a muzzle velocity of 920 m/sec, was the most powerful antitank weapon of World War II. The firing height was 2165 mm. An MG 34 was mounted in a ball mantlet in the bow near the radioman.

On September 12, 1944, Henschel suggested a price of ca. RM 140,000 for the first 100 "Tiger-*Jäger*," which was considerably below the known prices of armored vehicles. On October 12, 1944, the suggestion was given to Hitler to produce the "*Jagdtiger*" at first in a single series of 150 models, so that these vehicles would be available to the Inspector-General of the Panzer Troops for special purposes. The foreseen running production of 50 "*Jagdtiger*" per month was then supposed to run out, in order to use the capacities and production materials to build more numerous "Panthers," because of the greater combat

The *Panzerjäger* Tiger type B "*Jagdtiger*" (Sd.Kfz. 186).

A look at the roof of the *Jagdtiger* with the entry hatch, and the kidney shaped lid where the optics were housed.

The picture shows the opened driver's visor with the periscope before it.

A look from above shows the open radioman's hatch, the air intake before it, and the periscope with its curved steel shield at the left.

This picture shows the radioman's hatch when closed.

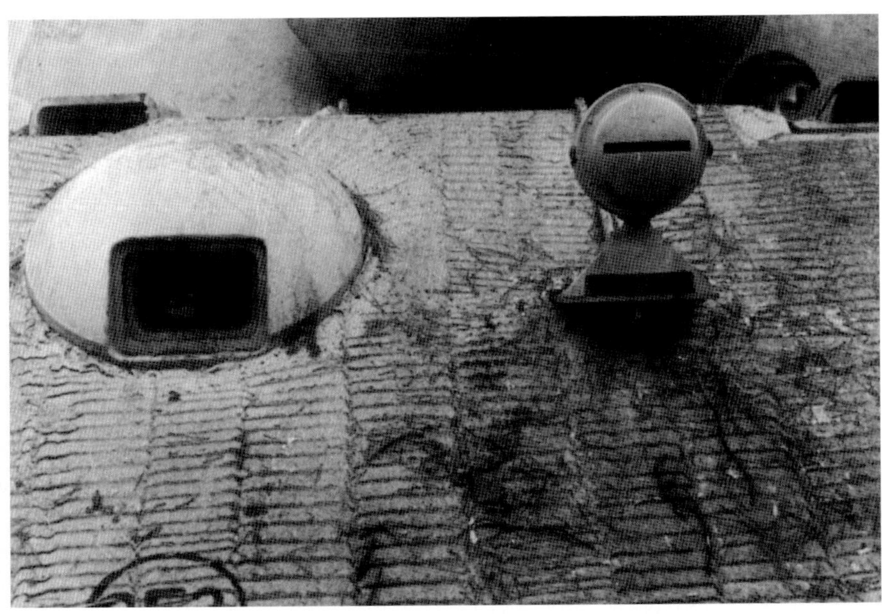

Above: The bow of the *Jagdtiger* and the MG mount and main headlight. Right: The right side of the rear, with the starting crank and the right muffler.

The "boar's head" mantlet with its lifting apparatus.

The engine compartment cover with inlet and outlet gratings. The fuel filler is at the left, the cooling-water filler at the right. At the lower right on the roof is the shield for the loader's periscope.

Here the top of the body is removed.

The inside of the fighting compartment, with the gun and gun shield.

At the top of the picture is the rubber-like mount cover that sealed the fighting compartment from the front.

To the left of the gun is the gunner's seat, to the right, the commander's.

The gunner's seat, seen close-up, with cartridge racks at the left.

The breech of the 12.8 cm gun, with recoil apparatus and protective frame, plus the counterweights at the left.

A look at the left side of the body, with the traversing and elevating machines.

A look through the double doors of the rear hatch shows ammunition racks at right.

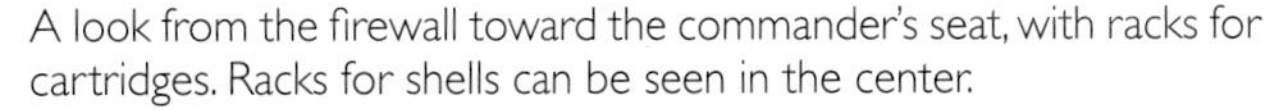

A look from the firewall toward the commander's seat, with racks for cartridges. Racks for shells can be seen in the center.

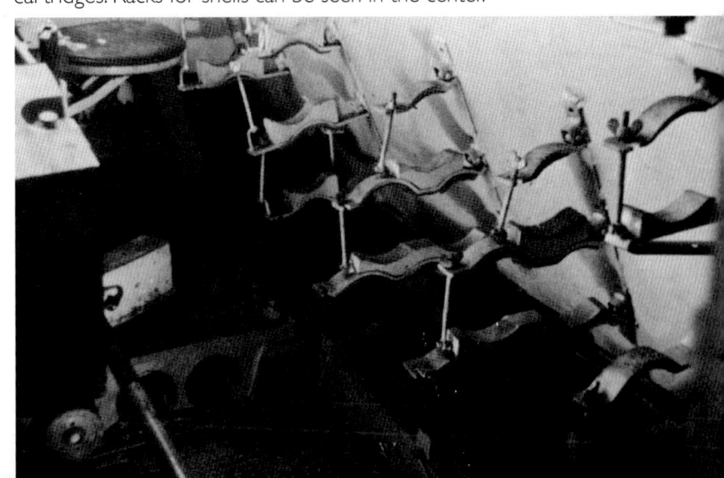

This view of the firewall shows details of the automatic fire extinguishing system. At the upper right is the fuel injection pump.

Shells and cartridges were stored separately.

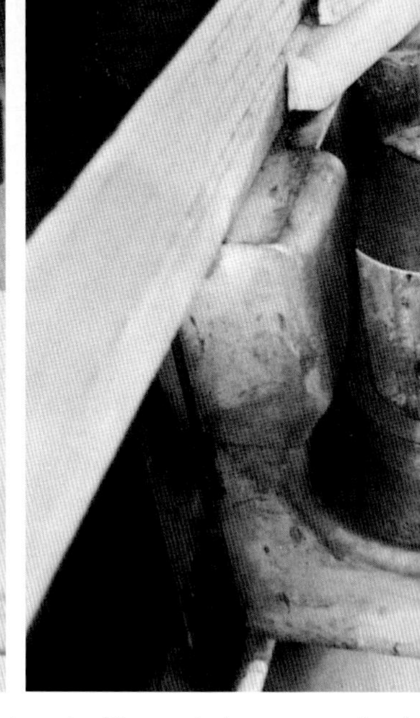

Shells and cartridges were stored separately. The breech of the gun is shown opened and closed. The counterweights are attached at the left.

Panzerjäger Tiger Type B (Sd.Kfz. 186) "*Jagdtiger.*"

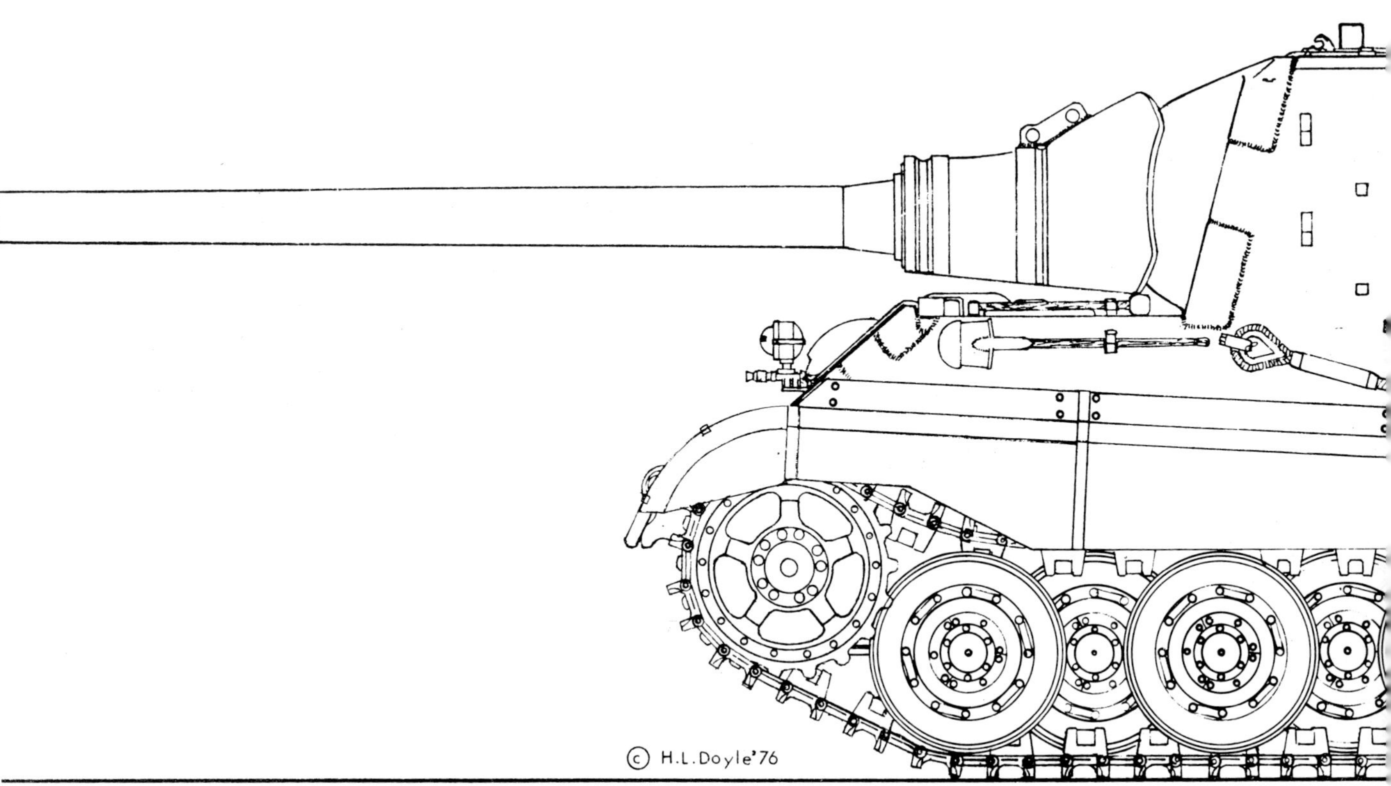

Details of the shell storage are shown here.

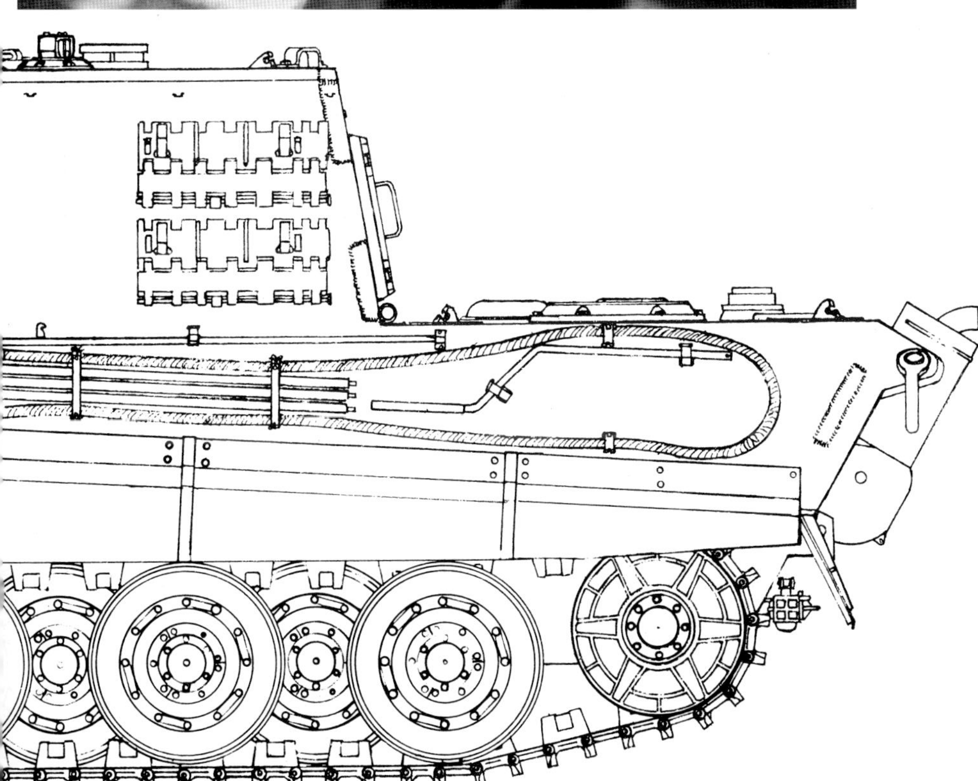

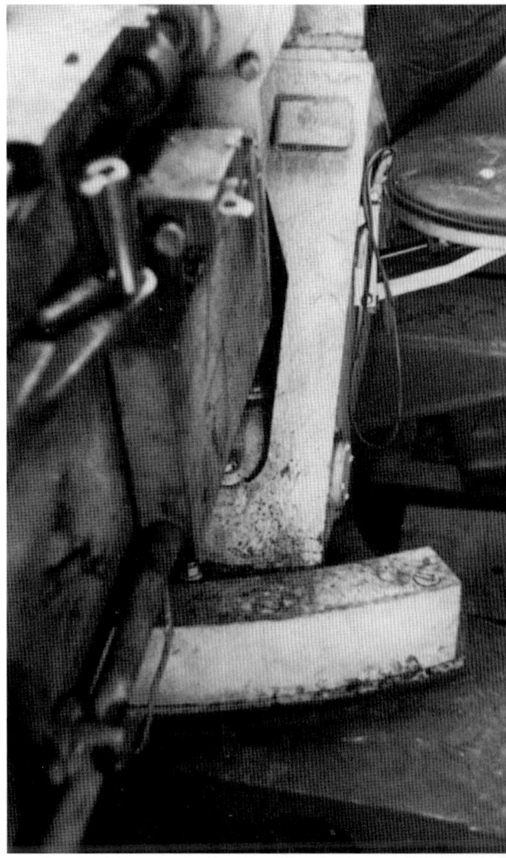

Above: At left is the handle that opened the breech of the gun. At the upper right is the commander's seat. Below: A look from above at the gunner's seat with the traversing machine.

The left wall with racks for shells and cartridges.

This picture through the radioman's hatch shows the racks for the radio equipment.

weight. Hitler wanted to confer with Guderian and Buhle about this again before making a final decision. On December 5, 1944, Hitler ordered that, along with the ongoing attempts to design a flamethrowing tank, two other developments were in urgent need of solutions:

- A heavy tank, most practically the "Tiger," should have a long range flamethrower behind heavy armor, for use as a spearhead vehicle.
- On December 29, 1944, Hitler thought of the use of a new "*Jagdtiger*," especially if one "could create a flame 200 meters long."

On January 5, 1945, Hitler stressed that under no circumstances could the production of the "*Jagdtiger*" end after the first 150 of them were built. Everything had to be done, naturally considering the capacities of the heavy steel rolling mills, to produce as many as possible per month.

On February 26, 1945, Hitler ordered the immediate introduction of forced measures to increase "*Jagdtiger*"* production to the greatest numbers in the shortest time. When a problem

* First used by *Jagdtiger Abteilung* 512 at the Remagen bridgehead on March 10, 1945.

Under the radioman's seat there was an exit hatch in the floor of the hull.

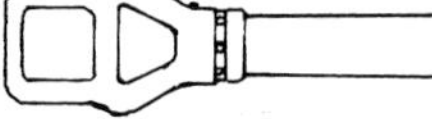

The radioman's seat, seen from the back. At left is the sheet metal cover of the gearbox.

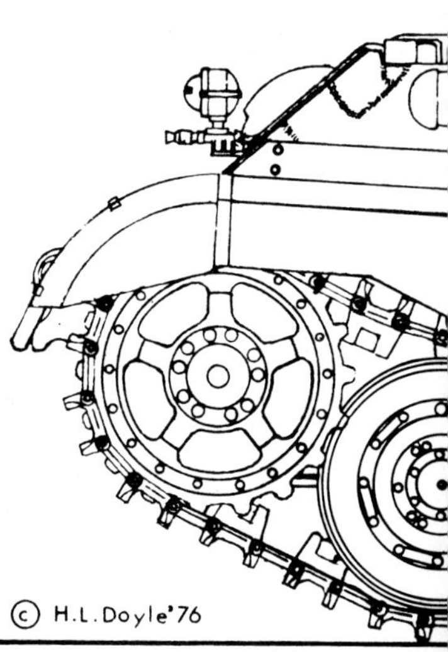

The MG 34 was mounted in a ball mantlet ahead of the radioman's seat.

The driver's seat, with steering wheel and control levers.

Tiger *Panzerjäger* for 8.8 cm Pak 43/3 (Sf) (Sd.Kfz. 185).

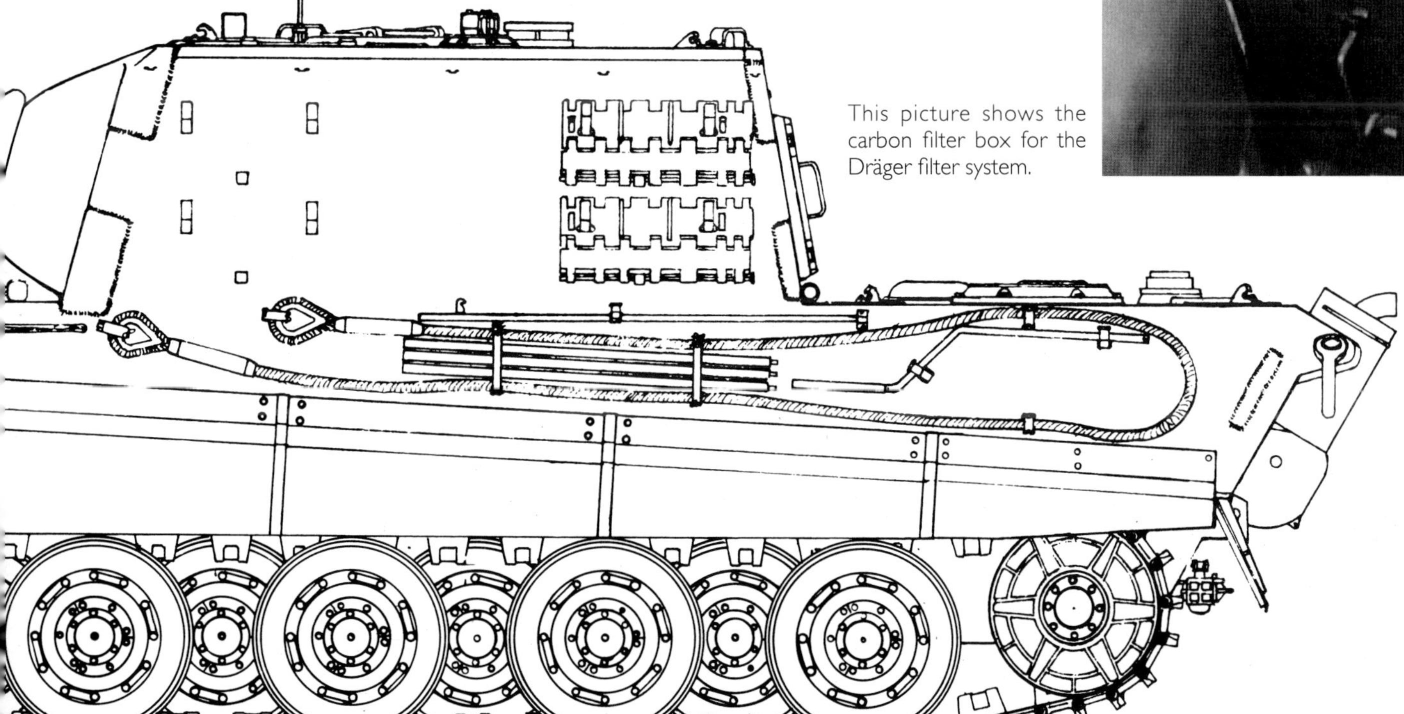

This picture shows the carbon filter box for the Dräger filter system.

with the supplying of 12.8 cm guns occurred as of that March, he ordered an immediate search for the guns wherever they were, and if necessary, taking those 12.8 cm guns mounted in captured mounts. If this should prove to be impossible, the *Jagdtiger* should be armed with the 8.8 cm Pak 43/3 as an interim solution. A series of at least 25, and at most 50 vehicles was foreseen.

The Halle'sche Maschinenfabrik was supposed to rebuild the *Jagdpanther* gun for use in the *Jagdtiger*. It was designated "Pak 43/3 Type D." The weapon was to be fired-in, ready for installation, and delivered from Lippstadt. The cutout on the front wall of the body was modified by the Eisenwerke Oberdonau. The vehicle armed with the 8.8 cm Pak was designated "*Panzerjäger* Tiger for 8.8 cm Pak 43/3 (Sf) (Sd. Kfz. 185)."

In fact, 48 *Jagdtiger* were built in 1944 by the Steyr-Daimler-Puch AG, Werk Nibelungen GmbH. By the end of January 1945, 60 of these vehicles had been delivered.

The schedule for *Jagdtiger* production in 1945 called for the following quantities:

Jan.	Feb.	March	April	May	June	July	August
	13	40	37	25	25	25	25

Vehicles of the E series were planned as replacements.

Since Henschel had to finish these vehicles at the Nibelungenwerk, great efforts were made by interested parties to fit them with the Porsche running gear, and also equip the tank with it. The result was war contract "258" to the Porsche

Since the *Jagdtiger* was built at the Nibelungenwerk, efforts were made to fit it with simplified running gear. This new system had been developed by Porsche. This comparison shows the original running gear at the top and the Porsche type below.

***Panzerjäger* Tiger Type B (Sd.Kfz. 186) "*Jagdtiger*" test vehicle with Porsche running gear.**

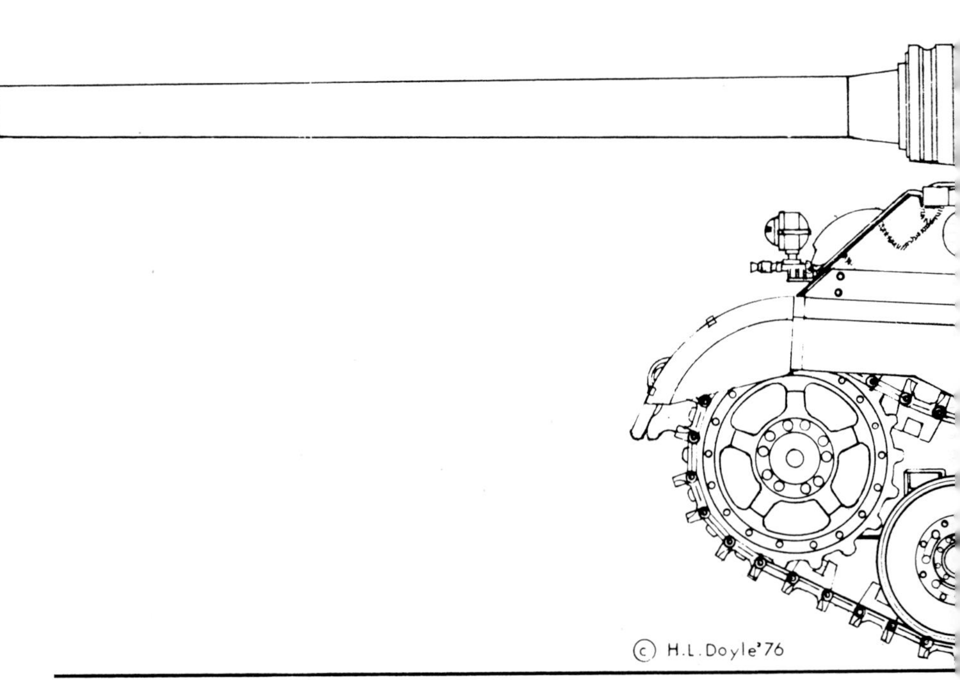

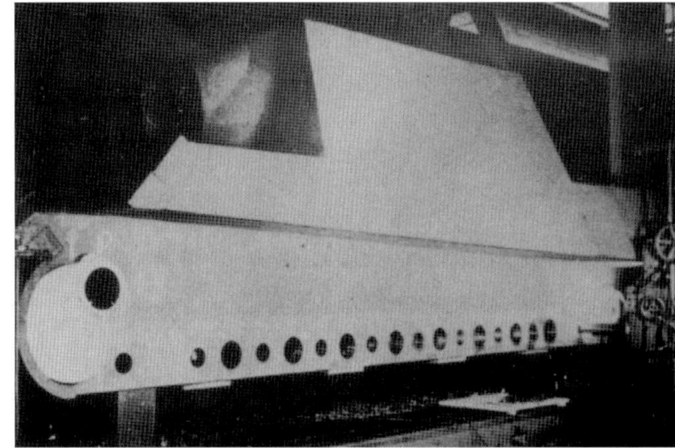

The Henschel suspension demanded precisely opposite boreholes, which cost a lot of time during manufacturing.

The Porsche suspension lacked the time consuming, precise boring of the holes in the hull. Nor did the structures attached on the two sides have to be exactly in line.*

* The suspension characteristics had grown worse.

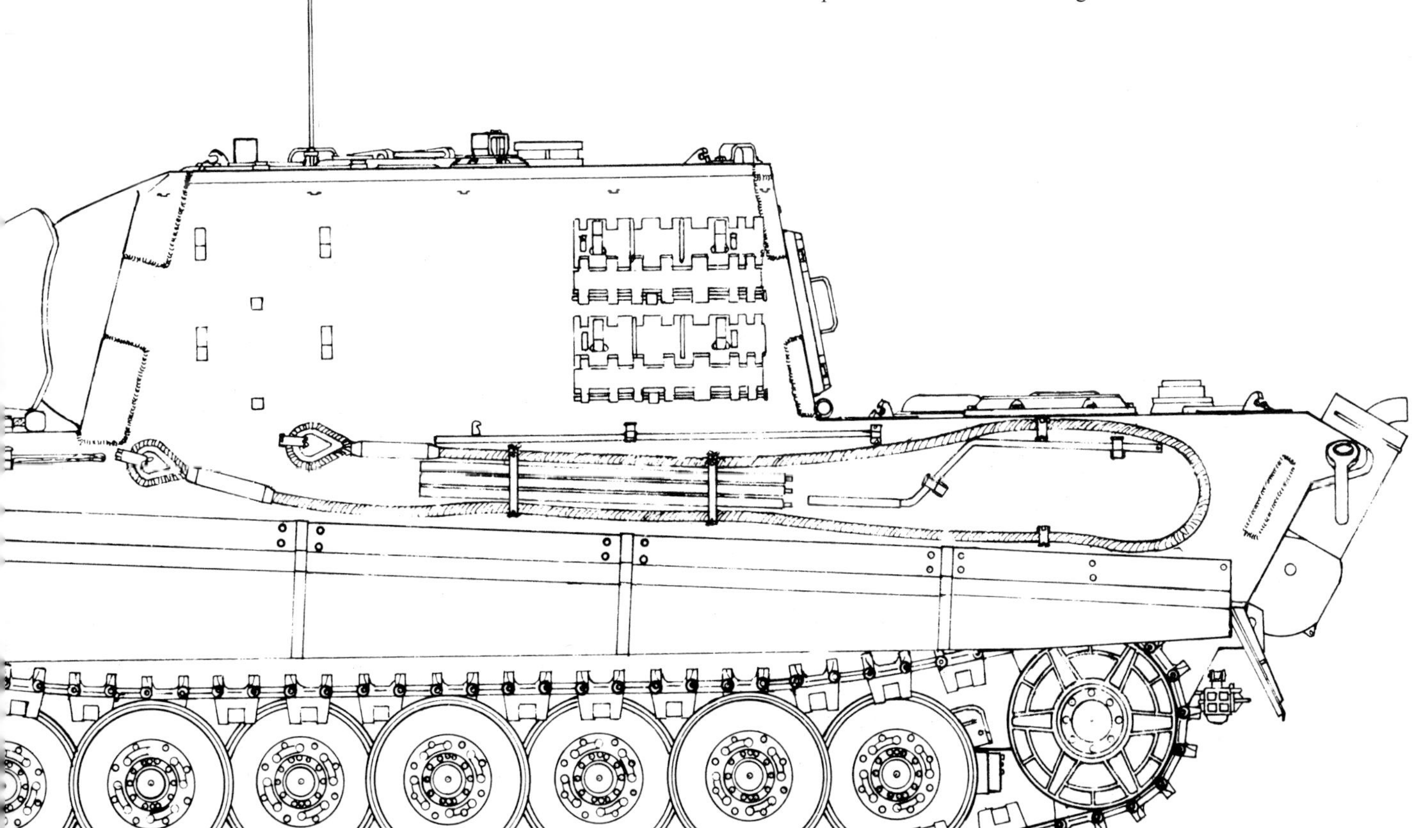

The Porsche running gear with longitudinal torsion-bar suspension, seen from inside.

The *Jagdtiger* with chassis no. 305 001 and 305 004 were rebuilt with Porsche running gear. This picture shows one of them with its gun barrel lashed down.

The drive sprocket and front road wheels of the Porsche running gear.

The left side of the vehicle, looking to the front.

The leading wheel of the Porsche running gear.

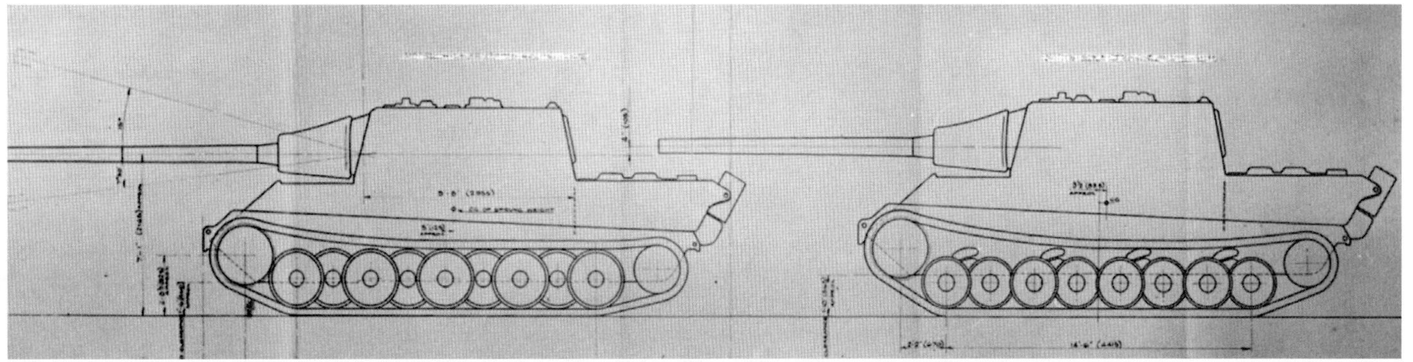

The drawings show a comparison of the two chassis types, with the Henschel on the left, the Porsche running gear on the right.

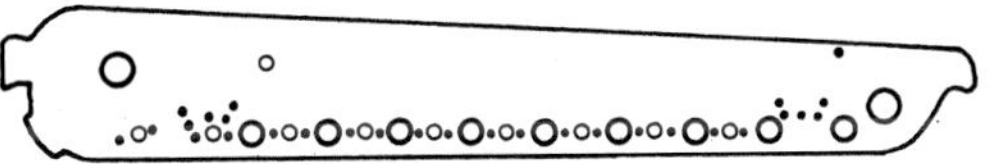

HENSCHEL

Hull work time	360 hours
Cost of necessary tools	RM 866,000
Raw material weight of suspension, including Shock absorbers	17,200 kg
Weight of parts, worked	9,480 kg
Machine-work time for suspension parts Including shock absorbers	460 hours

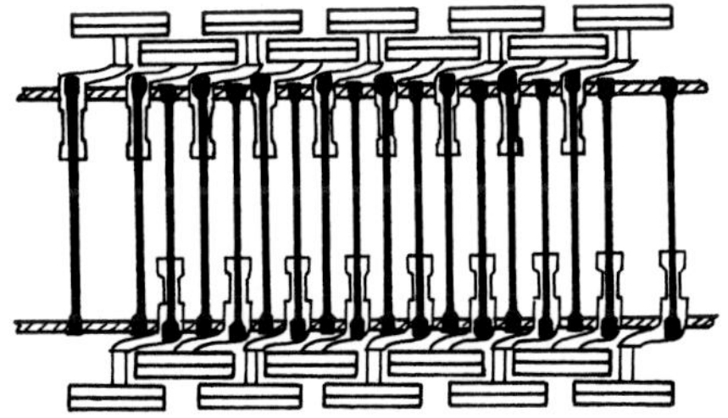

To remove a crank arm, it is necessary to remove the wheels next to it. 18 torsion bars, each 1960 mm long, with a complete weight of 887 kg.
Central lubrication for 36 suspension-arm bearings.
Heaviest forged piece (arm) 200 kg.

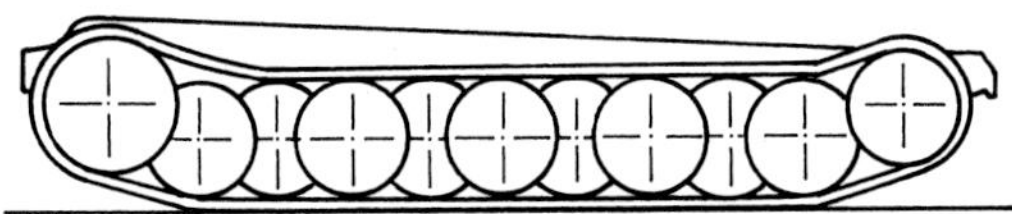

PORSCHE

Hull work time	140 hours
Cost of necessary tools	RM 462,000
Raw material weight of suspension, including Shock absorbers	12,000 kg
Weight of parts, worked	6,800 kg
Machine-work time for suspension parts, Including shock absorbers	230 hours
Cost savings for machines	RM 404,000

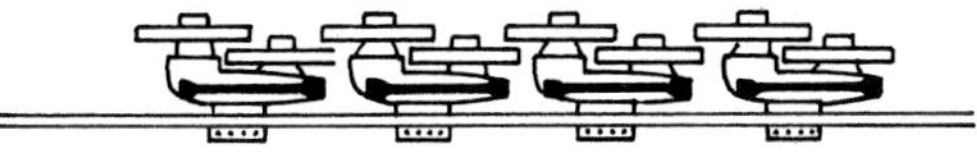

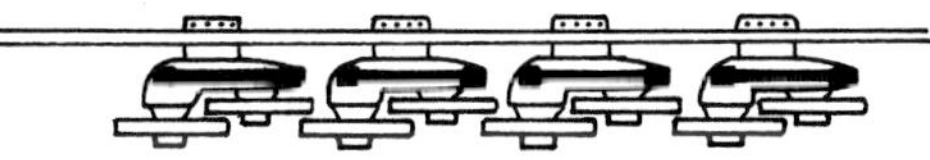

It is possible to remove a wheel truck without removing other parts. No winch is needed. All screwed connections can be reached from outside.

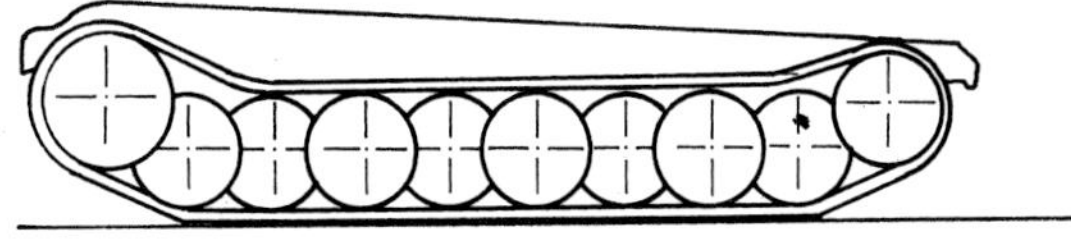

Schematic comparison of the two suspension systems.

firm, which was supposed to create uniform running gear for the "Tiger" and "Panther" with the least use of cheap materials. Thus, a running gear aggregate was created that was attached to the hull of the tank from outside, and turned by means of a gudgeon. For suspension, each pair of road wheels with rubber saving steel rims had a torsion bar. The scissor-like movement of the two carrying tubes was turned into rotating movement by a lever. One tube was mounted flexibly with its end at the trunnion on the hull, and was flexibly connected with the other tube at its other end. This design resulted in considerable material and work saving, compared to the usual staggered running gear. The hull work time apparently was reduced from 360 to 140 hours. Repairs to the tanks could also be done quickly by simply changing the whole aggregate without removing the parts inside the tank. Ten vehicles were built with this running gear for testing. The tests were satisfactory, but afterward the war situation prevented any thought of series production. The studies undertaken by Krupp toward the end of 1944 for rearming all German armored vehicles resulted in the suggestion to install a 10.5 cm KwK L/68 in the "Tiger II" tank. As with the tests of the "Panther" made in March 1945, to devise a more stable attachment of the optics, the installation of "view stabilized optics with advanced ignition gyroscope" was planned. This was the invention of one Ernst Haas of the Kreiselgeräte firm in Berlin. It may be assumed that the wish for this device was inspired by the stabilized type already used in the American "M 3" since 1941. While Krupp drawing Hln-E 151 concerned the installation of a 10.5 cm KwK in the "Tiger II," drawing Hln-E 150 showed the installation of a 12.8 cm L/66 gun in the "Tiger" tank destroyer. The traversing field was 10+10=20 degrees. Neither rearming took place.

This picture shows details of the rear of the vehicle.

The vehicle from the front.

The *Jagdtiger* seen from the right rear, with the towing shackles attached.

The two sides of the *Jagdtiger* with the barrel braced and spare track links.

During tests of the ventilation system, a road wheel broke off the ***Jagdtiger*** with Porsche running gear. The pictures show the wheel truck with the broken flange.

These two pictures show details of the broken flange and the attachment place.

The *Jagdtiger* with Porsche running gear.

A suggestion from the Krupp firm for rearming all existing armored vehicles advocated the installation of a 10.5 cm KwK L/68 in the Tiger II.

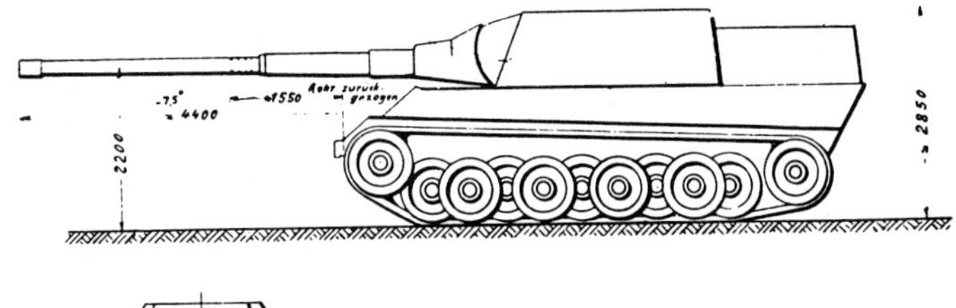

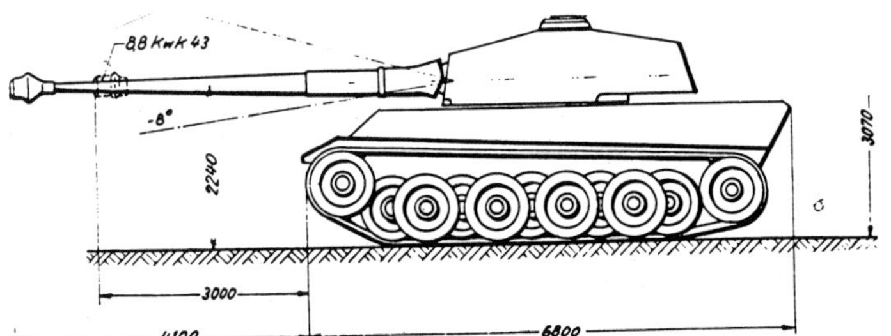

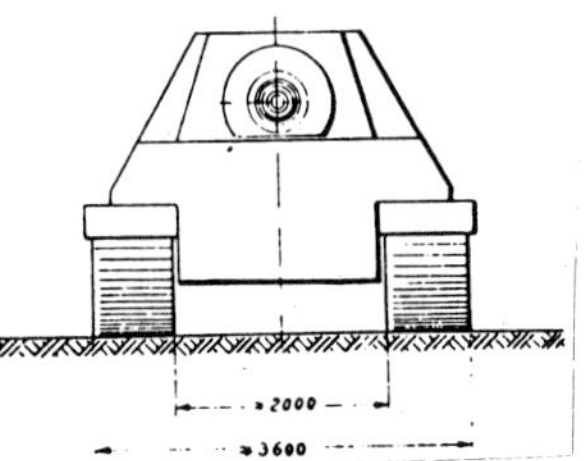

The *Jagdtiger* was also to be rearmed with the longer 12.8 cm L/66 gun.

The first prototype of the Armored Mortar 38 still had the rubber tired running gear of the Tiger E.

The Tiger Assault Mortar with 38 cm gun was shown to Hitler.

Sturmtiger (also called *Sturmmörser*)

On August 5, 1943, it was suggested to Hitler that the production of a "Tiger Mortar" be started, using a 38 cm Navy mortar (Device 562—*Sturmmörserwagen* 606/4). Hitler agreed with Guderian's suggestion of making just one test piece at first. The planned goal was to be ten per month. On October 20, 1943, the iron model of the "*Panzermörser* 38 cm" on "Tiger I" chassis was exhibited at Arys.* On April 19, 1944, Hitler ordered, within the limits of production possibility, up to a total of twelve bodies and barrels for assault mortars to be built and mounted on repaired "Tiger I" chassis. A production of seven more "*Panzermörser* 38 cm" was prepared, and the first vehicle was supposed to be finished on 15 September, each the rest a day later, so that the 7th vehicle could be delivered on 21 September. Hitler attributed great significance to this weapon for special action purposes, and temporarily considered a monthly output of at least 300 shells advisable. The first showpiece with an iron body, after doing its job in the east, was supposed to be fitted with a steel body by Alkett, and be sent to its scene of operations in the west. The necessary preparations

* A troop training camp in East Prussia.

38 cm *Sturmmörserwagen* "*Sturmtiger.*"

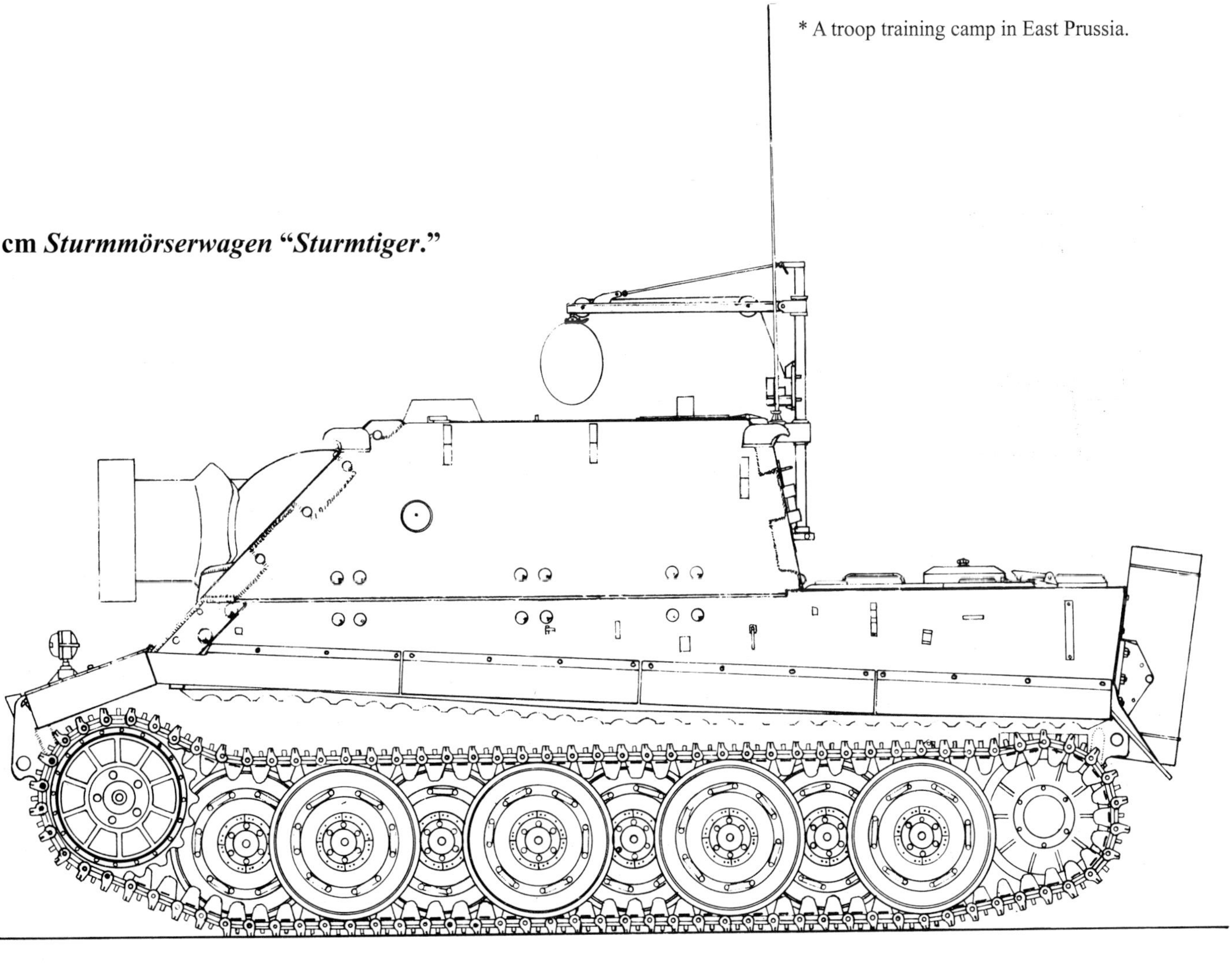

Panzermörser 38 cm, right side, with loading crane.

A shell is seen in the loading hatch.

A Rocket Explosive Shell 4581 is seen before loading.

Stowing the shell in the loading area.

A crane is used to load the shell into the vehicle.

The Rocket Explosive Shell is placed in the barrel by means of a rammer.

The breech could simply be held, as the gases of the propellant charge were led out to the front.

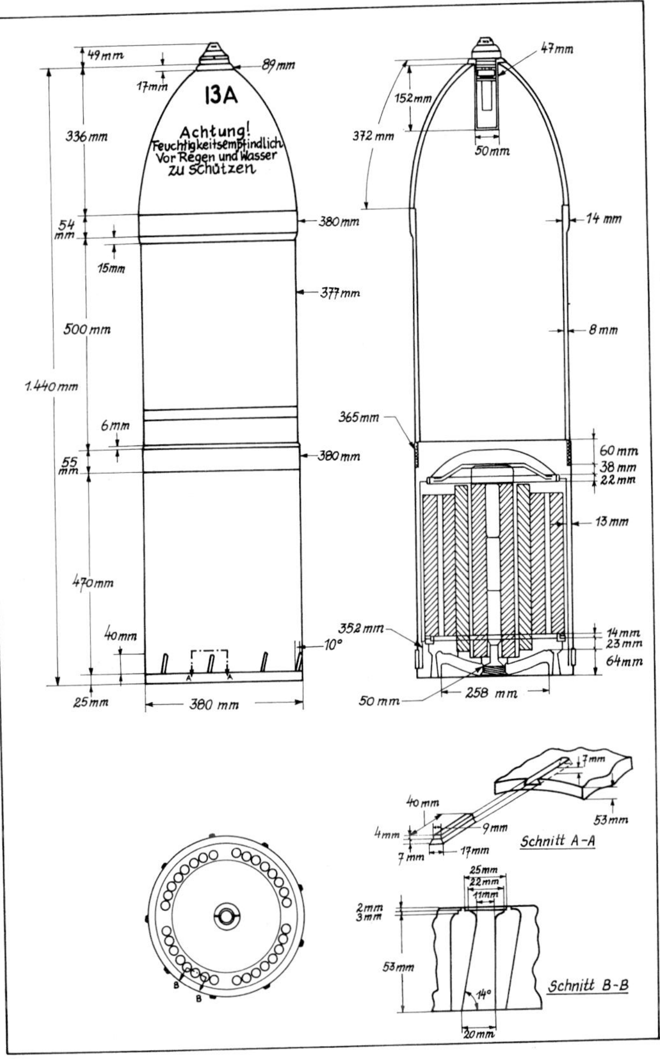

Design of the 38 cm Rocket Explosive Shell 4581.

A *Sturmmörser* 36 cm in action (1944).

The Rocket Explosive Shell is fired. Its range was up to 6 kilometers.

were to be made so that this rebuilding could be carried out in three days at most. On September 23, 1944, the result of Alkett's special action of producing ten assault mortars under the direction of *Obermeister* Hahne could be announced to Hitler. Hitler expressed his recognition to the involved parties, and ordered that, on the basis of making use of these vehicles, five chassis of the Tiger I coming out of repairs should for the time being be converted to "Tiger Mortars." Alkett produced 18 of these vehicles in 1944.

On January 5, 1945, Hitler declared that the "Tiger Mortar" should go on being built on repaired "Tiger I" chassis until the gun could be used on a lighter self-propelled mount. All the repaired chassis were fitted with rubber-sprung steel road wheels. The total weight was 65 tons. The fixed armored body, with 150 mm front armor, was made by the Brandenburgische Eisenwerke of Kirchmöser. The crew consisted of five men. Fourteen rounds of ammunition could be fired. The Rocket Launcher 61, 38 cm L/5.4 fired the 350 kg Heavy Rocket Explosive Shell 4581 at ranges up to 6 kilometers. An onboard crane eased the loading of the vehicle. The breech could be held easily, as the combustion gases were ducted and ejected out the front. An MG 34 was mounted in a ball mantlet near the driver. The vehicle itself grew out of the urge to create a self-propelled heavy artillery that, under armor protection, could give support to the infantry. In February 1945 there were 16 of these guns on hand. The first Assault Tigers were used in Warsaw in the late summer of 1944.

Self-propelled Mounts

In the spring of 1942, the HWA issued a contract for the creation of a "17 cm cannon as armored self-propelled mount." This Device (5-1702 (17 cm K 43) (Sfl)) was supposed to use the barrel, cradle, barrel brake, recuperator, equalizer, and upper mount of the 17 cm cannon in a mortar mount. The weight when ready to drive was 53 tons, plus 13 tons when loaded. One vehicle, on parts of "Tiger" chassis, was contracted for. The presumed delivery date

Tiger chassis were to be used to create heavy self-propelled mounts. To lay out the components, wooden dummies in the form of the later steel bodies were built at first. Thus, the space relationships were determined. The pictures show the first tests of the Grille 17 vehicle built by the Krupp firm.

The full size wooden model of the *Geschützwagen* VI with the 17 cm gun.

The vehicle was found by the Allies in a half finished condition in 1945. The upper sidewalls could be folded inward for rail transport.

was the autumn of 1943. Only the Krupp firm had worked with the development of the 17 cm and 21 cm self-propelled mounts, and had solved the request for all-around fire, as well as the removability of masses and weights. Krupp placed the vehicle with its tracks on a turntable and let it drive until its center of gravity was over its turning point, thus attaining all-around fire. By moving the gun backward from the chassis and setting it on the turntable and tailplate, its dismountability was also accomplished. For railroad

Four views of the *Geschützwagen* VI, which used a lengthened Tiger B chassis.

17 cm K 44 (Sf) *Geschützwagen* VI

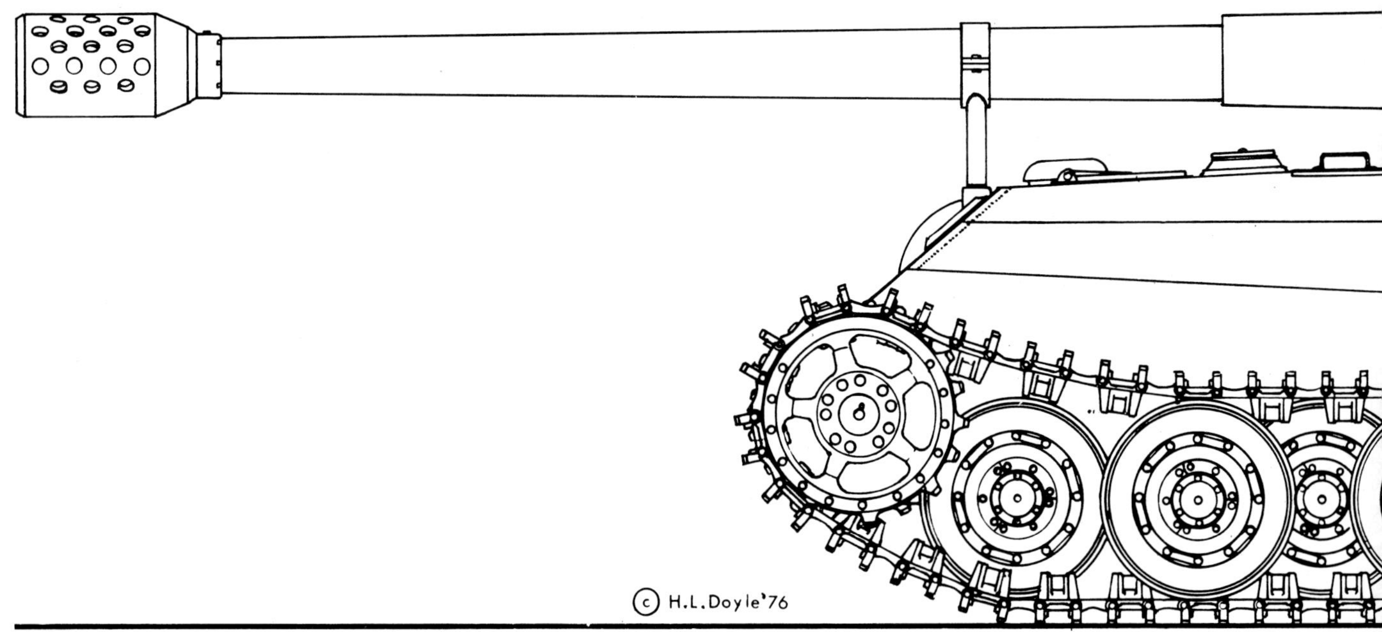

loading, a special low-loader car designed for the "Tiger" was planned. To keep inside the profile borders, the sidewalls of the fighting compartment armor folded inward.

The dismountability of the vehicle was given up as of 1944, and the new design requirements called for a self-propelled mount of conventional type. One version of this "17 cm K 44 (Sf)/Gw VI" was under construction in Sennelager* in 1945, but was never finished. With an eight-man crew, five rounds of ammunition, and 30 mm front armor, its fighting weight was 58 tons. The side armor was made of 16 mm plates. The powerplant and running gear were those of the "Tiger II," but eleven road wheels per side were planned. A similar layout was that of "Device 5-2107 (21 cm Mrs. 18/43) (Sfl)." This armored self-propelled mount with a 21 cm Mortar 18 L/31 was supposed to be finished in the autumn of 1943. The weight in driveable condition was calculated at 52.7 tons, while that of the unloaded gun was 12.7 tons. The "21 cm

* An outdoor facility of the Henschel firm.

21 cm Mrs. 18/43 (Sf) *Geschützwagen* VI

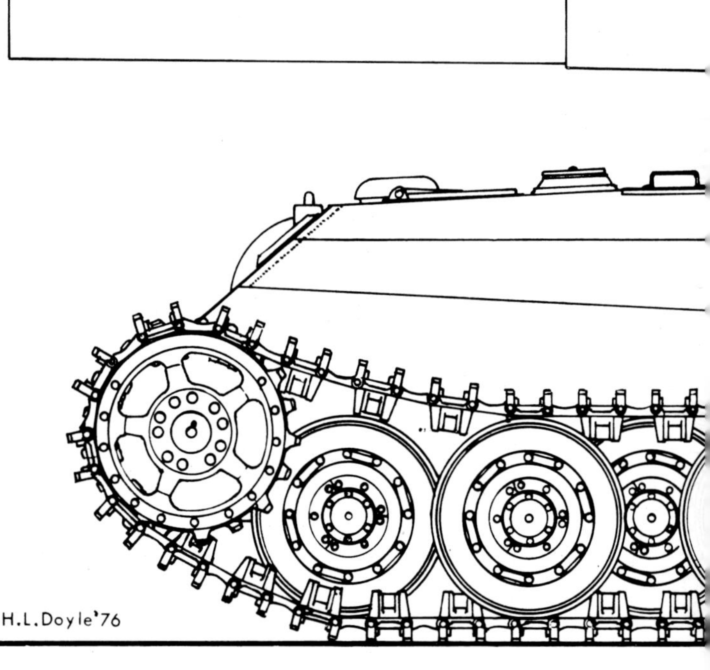

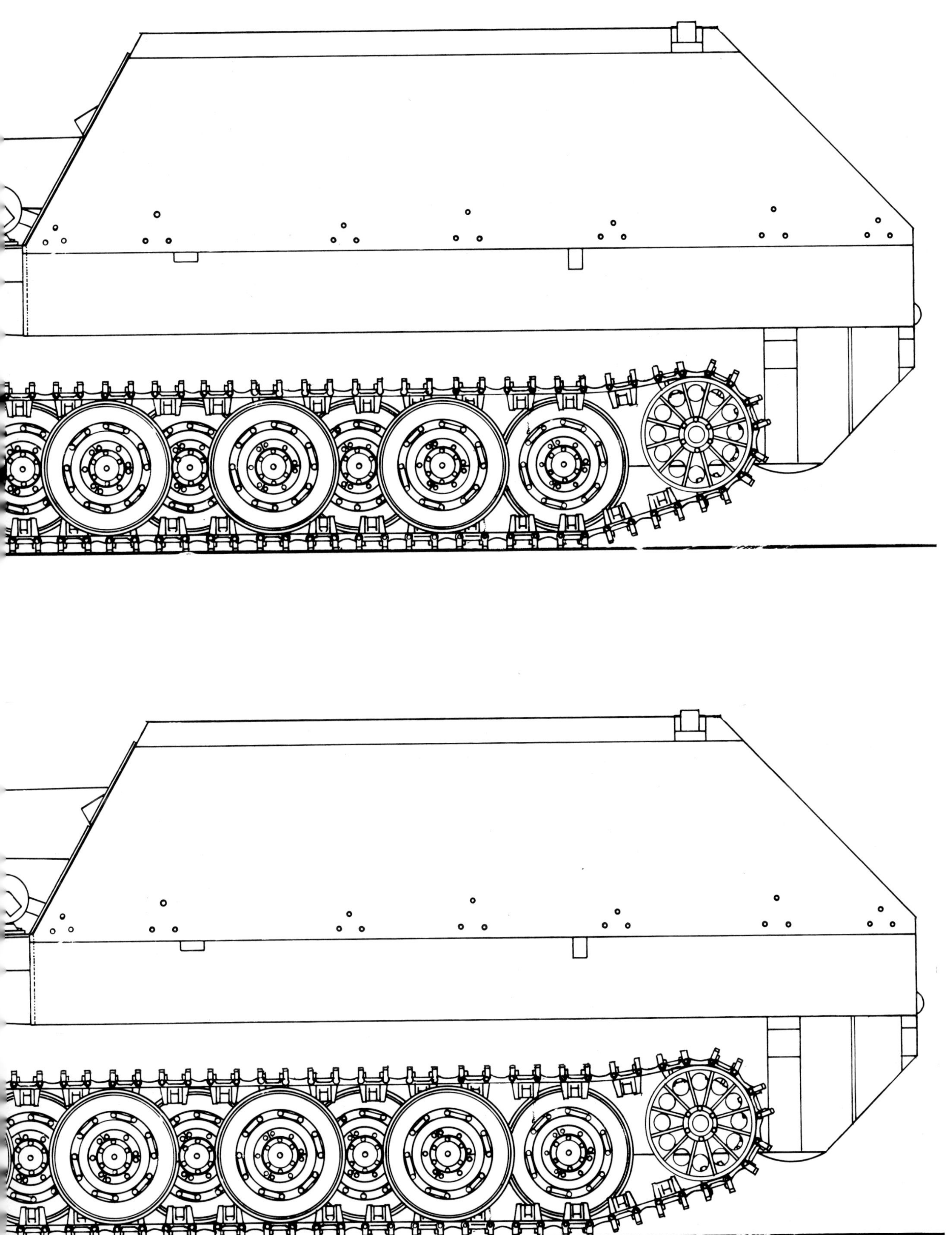

Mrs. 18 (Sf)/Gw VI" that was requested later was identical to the 17 cm vehicle in appearance and weight, but could carry only three shells. This vehicle was never built.

The task imposed by the Ordnance Office in January 1941 of making the 24 cm Kanone 4 mobile was solved by Krupp by having it carried between two unarmored "Tiger 1" chassis. The Henschel firm was empowered by OKH WaJRü (WuG 6) VIIIA2 No. 9846/42 to prepare all the components needed for the chassis. The construction was to be done by Krupp. The contract was issued under the name "Tiger H as carrier vehicle for heaviest guns."

The originally planned mounting on the Device 040/041 mount left much to be desired in terms of mobility and marching speed. Then the barrel and mount, along with the bottom plate and four spars, were to be suspended between two Tiger chassis. The unarmored chassis weighed about 25 tons. Hydraulic lifts built into the chassis allowed a quick lowering of the entire gun, so that both vehicles could be removed without problems. In marching trim the weight per unit was some sixty tons, thus not exceeding the normal fighting weight of the Tiger tank.

To assure an even towing performance, a hydraulic synchronization of the two powerplants was planned. On roads the gun was supposed to reach a speed of 30 to 35 km/h. So that road bridges would always be burdened with just one vehicle, and the other would be on solid ground before and after the crossing, the distance from one vehicle's center to the other was set at 20 to 22 meters.

Henschel reported that contributing additional chassis components besides series production and spare parts delivery was unfortunately not possible, since their production capacity was spoken for to the limit.

A similar type of transport was planned by the Friedrich Krupp AG in Essen to transport the 28 cm K 5 Railroad Cannon. Here two towing machines with "Tiger B" chassis (Device 566 Load Carrier 606/5 for K 5/3 (Tiger)) were to carry either the barrel, mount, or bottom plate between them. A further "Tiger" load carrier moved the breechblock and breech.

For the 30.5 cm grenade launcher going into production in 1945, the Device 817—the *Geschützwagen* für 30.5 cm GrW Sfl

24 cm Kanone 4 with Tiger I load carriers.

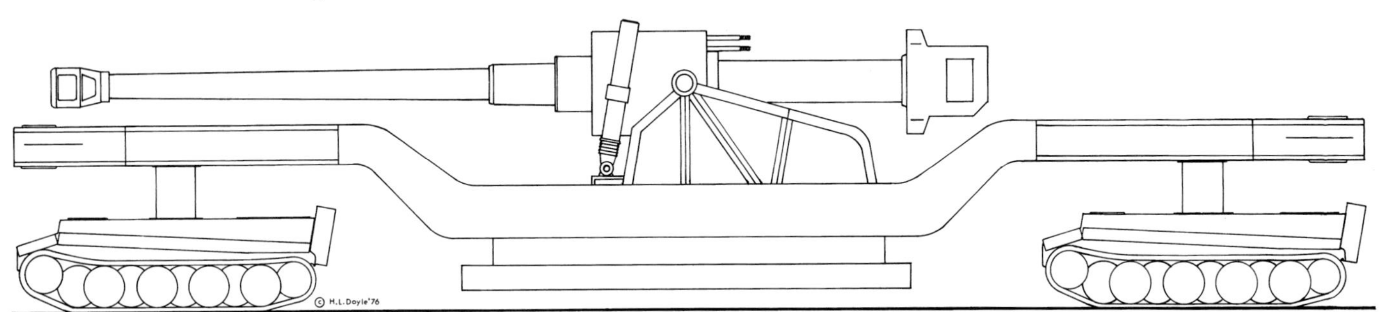

28 cm Kanone 5 with Tiger II load carriers.

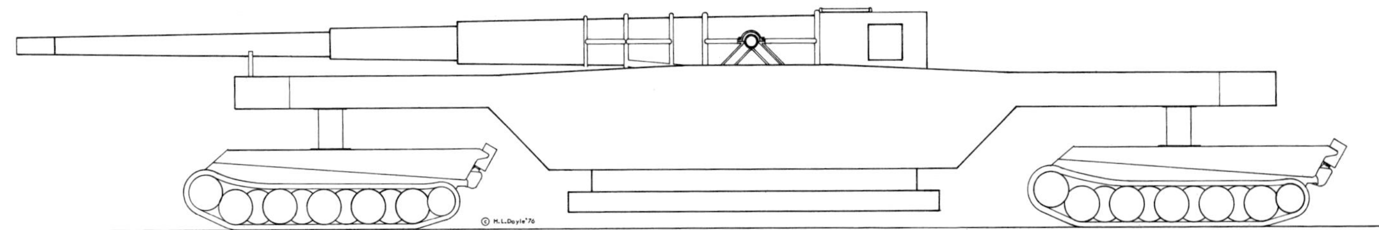

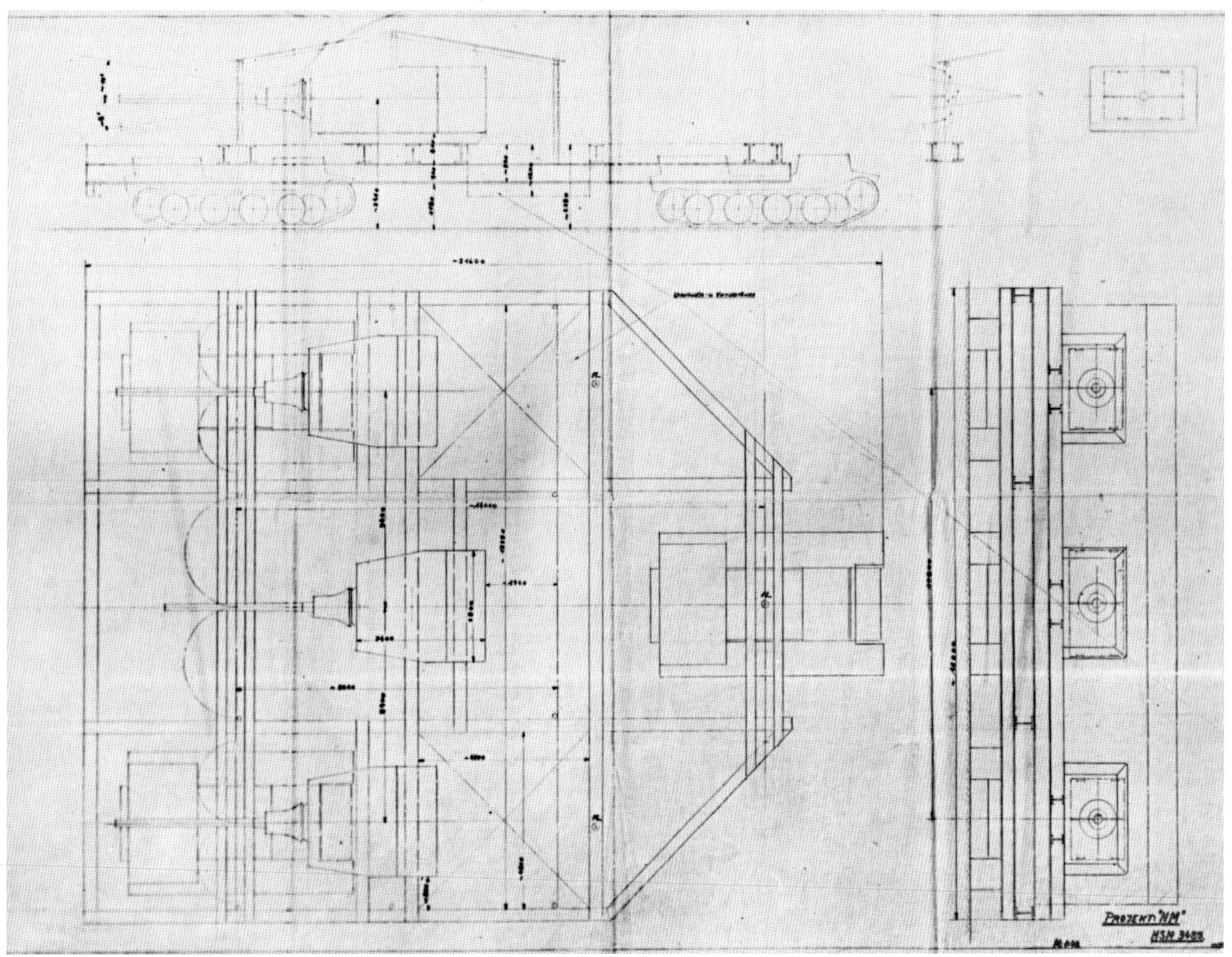

A mystery to this day is this Project "NM" of 1943. Here three turrets with canons of 12.8 cm or larger size and three Tiger E chassis were to be made mobile together.

(606/9) on "Tiger" chassis—was to be built. But like the self-propelled mount for a 42 cm grenade launcher, also to be built of "Tiger" components, it was never built. Here, too, the lengthened Tiger B running gear was to be used. The weight of the launcher was 18 tons, while that of the complete vehicle was 65 tons. Both versions were to allow all-around fire.

Armored Command Tanks

It was planned to produce every tenth Tiger tank with special radio equipment as an armored command tank. The added radios gave the outside sign of a star antenna, its quiver fastened to the rear wall of the first vehicles. In the second one it was seen that in that spot it was crushed by the shackle when the vehicle was lifted. Thus, it was moved back to its originally planned place on the turret roof. On October 11, 1943, it was determined that only every 20th Tiger E turret should be set up for a command tank. Equipped with the Fu 5 and Fu 8 radio sets, the Tiger Armored Command Tank was given the special vehicle number 268.

After the B version was introduced, the question was raised on June 9, 1944, as to how many command tanks of this type should be built. In principle, command tanks were ordered only after the new production turret was introduced (as of no. 51). WaPrüf 7, in cooperation with paint manufacturers, had developed a contact paint color that, once motor vehicles had been desensitized, was used successfully as a replacement for tinning on contact-blank spots. As of June 1944 it was also insisted on for tanks and armored command vehicles. As of August 1944 the 30-watt system was moved to the turrets of command tanks. The antenna port in the turret roof was simplified; only minor changes were made to the hulls of the command tanks.

A conference of July 17, 1944, decided that in the future all combat vehicles should be set up so that they—whether with the troops or in the arsenals—could have additional equipment added to turn them into command vehicles. The building of special command vehicles at the factories could then be dropped. Chassis no. 284 was chosen by WaPrüf 6 for this test. The Wegmann firm hoped to have the finished turret ready by September 12, 1944. This version differed from the tank only slightly in the case of the radio sets. Only the Pz 20 box disappeared from the hull. In its place, the HSK 4218 component was used. A loading connection was to be made. In the fighting compartment, the machine set GG 400, an equipment box for radio parts, a support basket, and six lengthening rods were kept. The equipment box became smaller, and found a place in the radio niche, along with the machine set. The ammunition kept there was not included in the command tank. Yet the new command tank carried more ammunition than the previous one. The exhaust attachment for the GG 400 machine set was dropped, because the latter was to be operated outside the vehicle.

At the beginning of February 1945, the Inspector-General of the Panzer Troops ordered the previous radio equipment for the Tiger command tank to be further simplified:

- In principle, the radio and speaker equipment of the tank was kept in the rebuilding of the command tank.
- Of the formerly used components, boxes 4, 6, 9, and 10 in the chassis, boxes 3, 7, and 8 in the turret, and the box for the radio equipment were dropped.
- As already planned, though, the following changes were made from the current series:
  a) Installation of Antenna Foot no. 2 in the tank instead of no. 1
  b) Installation of cable distributor no. 1 in the chassis, instead of the B 23 Distributor Box.

A Tiger B command tank. Externally, they could be recognized only by the extra antennae.

c) Installation of the Pz container lock in the command car.
- For every tank, the Pz 30 Type a box was to be used instead of the Pz 21 as a connection box.
- The Pz 21 Type B (instead of no. 22 in the series) near the gunner had to be interchangeable with the Pz 30 box in the command tank.

The omitted boxes no, 3, 7, and 8 from the turret were replaced by the Pz 21 box (Type C).

By February 3, 1945, the new turret was brought to Henschel by Wegmann for shipping.

After the test vehicle was examined it was decided, among other things, that the protector for the antenna connection should be provided in every vehicle. At the beginning of the new series, Antenna Foot no. 2 was installed instead of no. 1. The set of devices needed for installation in a command tank were designated "Satz *Funkbauteile* Fu 8 *für Panzerkampfwagen Tiger*." The displayed model was set up again as a normal tank and delivered.

Recovery Tanks

In single examples a "Tiger" recovery tank also appeared, in which a "Tiger I" chassis was modified for this purpose, probably by the troops themselves. The turret was kept, but the gun was removed. Over the opening in the roller mount a covering plate was screwed on. On the turret roof was a holder for a loading boom, which was obviously linked by a welded on bracket with the elevation machine. Thus, if need be, loads could be raised and lowered. In single cases, "Tiger" chassis without turrets were also used as socalled towing hulls for use in recovery work.

To lift heavy turrets off or remove the motors of "Panther" and "Tiger" vehicles, a mobile portal crane with 15 tons of lifting power was created by the firm J. S. Fries & Sohn in Frankfurt on the Main. This device was loaded onto two single-axle chassis (tire size 8.00-20), and despite its size it was fairly mobile. Four road wheels of 150 x 410 mm size allowed the device to be moved with the load. Eight men were able to make the device ready for use within twenty minutes. It was a valuable help in field repairs.

Other sources call this vehicle a charge layer.

A Tiger Type E tank rebuilt by the troops as an armored recovery vehicle. The cannon was removed, and the opening closed with an armor plate. A rack for a crane was added on the turret roof.

At the end of 1943 the District Combat Staff in Magdeburg, in cooperation with the Krupp-Gruson firm, had developed a plowing device in the form of a much strengthened V plow, which was used to clean up debris after air raids. In a short time this plow could be attached to an available tank. This apparatus weighed 1580 kg, and cost about 1200-1500 RM. Masses of rubble up to 80 cm could be plowed effortlessly. The plow projected some 25 cm beyond the tank's tracks on either side. The Magdeburg street plowing device had a blade width of 3.4 meters. The police chief in Kassel requested a similar device, which could be attached to a Tiger B, in August 1944. The work was done by the locomotive works, mainly by blacksmiths and boilermakers from the Henschel firm.

In view of the fuel shortage, Henschel also looked into the development of a steam powered towing tractor. This project was originally intended for a tank, but the size of the boiler and condenser did not leave enough space for the fighting compartment. The development was stopped toward the end of the war. The Ordnance Office was no longer interested in a steam powered tractor at that time.

As of 1942 the fuel shortage in Germany demanded drastic solutions. Among the replacement and training troops in particular, the very small fuel allotments inspired the use of "home made" fuels. With all the vehicles of these units, including the tiger tank, attempts and rebuildings were made for the use of bottled gas. Even the armored vehicles were not spared the installation of wood-gas generators. Although the armored vehicles could scarcely be shifted above second gear, wood-gas generators were installed in a "Tiger II" tank at Fallingbostel in 1944. Really a sad scene.

Otherwise

Out of the need to improve the power-to-weight ratio of heavy vehicles, interesting motor developments took place during the war. Now we can have a closer look at them. The low-powered engine of the Maybach Type "HL 230" was to be improved. The powerplant listed as model "HL 234" was envisioned in two steps as a further development of the "HL 230." First, the power was increased from 700 to 800 HP by direct fuel injection. At the same time the compression ratio was raised, and a second cooling-water pump was added. Value was placed on a better division of the cooling liquid. The normal valve springs were replaced by cup springs. The big-end bearings and cylinder head gaskets were improved. Prototypes were built and tested on the test bench. Series production was planned for mid-1945. As a further development, a powerplant with a supercharger was foreseen, which would bring the power to almost 1000 HP. The highest engine speed was 3000 rpm. The supercharger was driven by a one-liter, two-cylinder four-stroke motor, which was to produce some 50 HP. This component was to be placed in the V of the main motor. One of these motors was installed in a "Tiger," but the servicing hatch was not closed off. The fuel consumption was about 225 g/HP/hr at 2000 rpm, and 235 g/HP/hr at 3000 rpm. An in-line 12-cylinder motor was also developed by Maybach. This motor weighed 600 kg, and produced 500 HP normally and 700 HP supercharged. At the same time tests were made on a Diesel version of the "HL 234," but they showed no usable results. The injectors for it were made by Bosch. All these powerplants used water-cooling, as Dr. Maybach insisted on this cooling on principle. His saying that "he had come into this world water-cooled" ended any further discussion of the subject.

Since the installation details of the HL 234 motor differed from those of the HL 230, it became necessary to deliver the link between the dust removal box and elastic connector and the ventilator along with the motor in the future. Since the exhaust pipes also had to be changed, it became necessary to locate the manifolds, formerly supplied by Henschel when delivering the motors, at the rear. Because of the different location of certain components in the engine compartments of the Panther and Tiger tanks, it was necessary to create slightly modified versions for the HL 234. The further development of the HL 234 motor was continued after the war by Maybach engineers in France.* It was later installed in prototypes of the French "AMX 50" tank.

The German Army leadership wanted only carburetor engines for armored vehicles, since the involved German industry had found that synthetic Diesel fuel could not be made practically. These views became irrelevant only in 1942, as synthetic Diesel fuel could be produced in sufficient quantities from then on. From that time on the development of Diesel tank motors was forced. The Army Ordnance Office (WaPrüf 6) had pushed the Ruhrbenzin AG and I. G. Farbenindustrie AG to develop a shot-safe fuel, especially for armored vehicles. Its introduction depended on the use of Diesel engines in these vehicles. At the same time, lubricating oils and fuels for the tropics and uniform motor oils for the *Wehrmacht* were required on the basis of German raw materials. The attempts of the Daimler-Benz AG to have their "MB 507" Diesel engine used instead of the Maybach "HL 230" motor had finally failed toward the end of 1943. On December 23, 1943, Lieutenant Colonel Schaede, head of the "Production" Group at the Ministry of Armament and War Production, explained that the "MB 507" was not considered as a tank motor because of lacking capacity for production. If a Diesel engine was going to be accepted, then it would be one of the air-cooled motors developed on orders from the *Führer*.

In spite of that, the experiments that were underway with the "MB 507" were to be completed, so as to have suitable suggestions available for all cases.

As of 1942, Porsche had been developing an air-cooled Diesel engine that was to be interchangeable with the available Maybach "HL 230" for installation in existing armored vehicles. At the Simmering-Graz-Pauker AG in Vienna two test motors were built. This firm had also developed test benches for these large engines, and taken over the whole experimental development. Among others, the following Porsche one-cylinder test motors were being tested for use in armored vehicles:

Type	for Motor	Bore mm	Stroke mm	Displ. liters	Fuel	System	Note
117	101	115	145	1.5	gasoline	carburetor	cylinder head A
119	101	115	145	1.5	gasoline	carburetor	cylinder head B
158	101	115	145	1.5	Diesel	fuel injection	
159	101	115	145	1.5	Diesel	Simmering pre-ignition	
191	190	120	145	1.64	Diesel	Simmering pre-ignition	
192	203	135	160	2.3	Diesel	18-cyl. project	
193	101/93	120	145	1.64	gasoline	fuel injection	
213	212	150	170	3.0	Diesel		

From the two-liter unit (Porsche Type 192) an X-16-cylinder motor was developed and equipped with two exhaust turbochargers made by BBC-Mannheim. The burning system was the pre-ignition chamber type of the Simmering-Graz-Pauker AG. This was particularly suited for supercharging, and for the related flushing for inner cooling of the combustion chamber. The cooling fan and oil cooler were built along with the motor. Porsche's earlier experience with the formation of cylinders and cooling fins were greatly relied on. Professor Kamm of Stuttgart calculated the turbochargers. The pressure had been kept at the lowest possible level of 0.5 atmospheres, so as to maintain the long engine life

The engine test bench at Simmering-Graz-Pauker in Vienna, on which large motors of up to 1500 HP could be tested.

required by the Ordnance Office. The motor had a dry weight of about 2000 kg; its outer dimensions were 1680 x 2500 x 1150 mm. It was planned to increase the drive to 3000 rpm from a crankshaft speed of 2000 rpm. The one-cylinder unit of this motor had run for 100 hours on the test bench in Vienna and produced 47 HP at 2100 rpm. The compression was between 13.8 and 14 : 1. To be able to calculate the performance of the entire engine, it had to be kept in mind that in these tests nothing had been taken off for the power of the cooling fan.

On January 5, 1945, Hitler was advised, through a talk by Colonel Holzhäuer, on the state of development of the 16-cylinder air-cooled Porsche-Simmering engine. At this time Hitler emphasized again the importance of this work. He constantly awaited further reports on the test results of the experimental motors and vehicles.

The X-16-cylinder engine developed by Porsche was air-cooled. At left is the opened camshaft drive, and in the middle the flywheel end. Two of the four injection pumps can be seen at left. At right the cylinder head is removed, and the rocker arms that operated the valves can be seen.

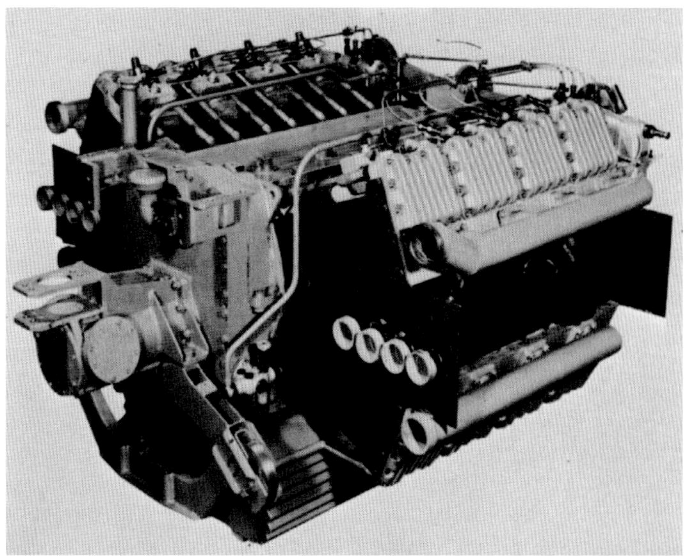

The Type Sla 16 motor, assembled but without cooling fans.

One of these motors was built into a "Tiger B" chassis at the Nibelungenwerk, resulting in a fully new type of engine compartment. Major modifications had to be made to the hull and the track positions. In the process of increasing the engine's performance, the use of the 3-liter cylinder unit (Porsche Type 213) was tried. With 48 liters of total displacement, a performance of 1500 HP at 2500 was expected. The Simmering-Graz-Pauker AG called this motor Type "Sla 16"; Porsche called it Type "212."

The Type "V 6 11.5/16" V-12-cylinder, two-stroke, supercharged Diesel engine made by MAN was supposed to be ready for production by 1941. This 400 HP engine was not yet ready by 1943, and was then dropped because of its too meager power.

An air-cooled 12- or 16-cylinder Diesel engine made in cooperation with Argus, with a power of 800 HP, never went beyond project status. It would also have caused major changes to the tank hull.

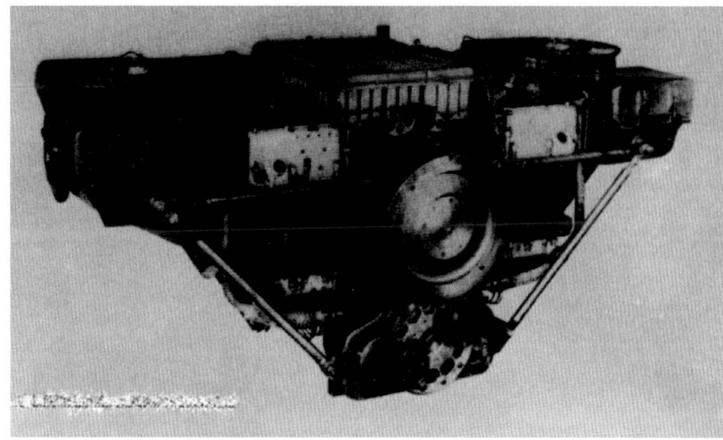

The motor with the cooling fans, ready for installation, could be fitted into the engine compartment of the Tiger B with minor alterations.

A 12-cylinder, 30-liter carburetor engine with rotary valves was planned by Auto-Union. It was to produce 900 HP. A one-cylinder experimental motor formed the research basis for a tank engine from the Adler-Werke. This 2.5-liter unit produced 87.5 HP at 3000 rpm. A performance of 1050 HP was expected from the 12-cylinder motor. A test motor was supposed to be ready by July 1945. The OKH had given a contract to the Klöckner-Humboldt-Deutz AG late in 1943 to develop a Diesel motor that was to produce a maximum of 700 HP at 2000 rpm. The condition had been set that the motor to be developed had to fit into the engine compartments of existing tanks without significant changes to the vehicles.

The installation tests showed that this condition was fulfilled only by a V-8-cylinder, two-stroke Diesel engine with a bore of 170 mm and a stroke of 180 mm.

To clear up basic questions, such as flushing, combustion, mounting, lubrication, and pistons, two one-cylinder engines were first built and run. The maximum production of 86.5 HP at 2000 rpm represented a medium piston pressure of 4.8 kg/cm^2. The compression ratio was 15 : 1. The very first tests showed that the targeted performance was attainable without great difficulties.

After the first satisfactory one-cylinder tests, three 8-cylinder motors of Type "TM 118" in 90-degree V-form were contracted for. Of these, one motor was chosen for production. When the development department was moved to Altmorschen in February 1945, and then to Ulm at the end of March, many of the parts prepared for the motor were lost.

Even a BMW aircraft motor* in radial form was to be modified for use in the "Tiger B" chassis. The required hull changes proved to be too excessive, so this development was not continued. Porsche was given the task of developing a turbine engine producing 1000 HP. Its installation in a tank was to be studied to find out whether radial engines used by the *Luftwaffe* could be used for this purpose.

An exact calculation of fuel consumption and torque showed the impossibility of using available turbines or parts of them. For use in a vehicle the torque was unsuitable, and the consumption at full throttle was between 600 and 700 g/HP/hr. At slower speeds the power declined quickly.

Thus, a new motor was projected (Porsche Type 305) that had the following essential characteristics:

An axial compressor with combustion chamber and turbine that served solely to operate the axial compressor. Between the axial compressor and the combustion chamber, part of the compressed air was ducted off and led to a second combustion chamber. The exhaust gases of the second chamber drove a special drive turbine, which was to power the vehicle through a gearbox. This arrangement assured a torque course that gave a fivefold increase of the torque, as opposed to the maximum engine speed. The fuel consumption was lower than in the project without a particular drive turbine, but it always attained insufficient power. To improve the degree of performance a heat exchanger was considered. Through the project with the separated drive turbine it would have been possible to succeed with a two-stage gearbox.

Porsche was able to confirm various results through testing, but the project did not go beyond the testing stage because of the war. The work itself was largely carried out by the *Waffen*-SS test center in Vienna.

Of all the new powerplant developments, those of the Maybach firm were the most advanced. The need for increased engine power, and the resulting improvement of the power-to-weight ratio of the heavy armored vehicles overshadowed all other considerations. To save space in the limited engine compartments, it was necessary

* Type 132 Dc radial engine, 880 HP, 27.7-liter displacement.

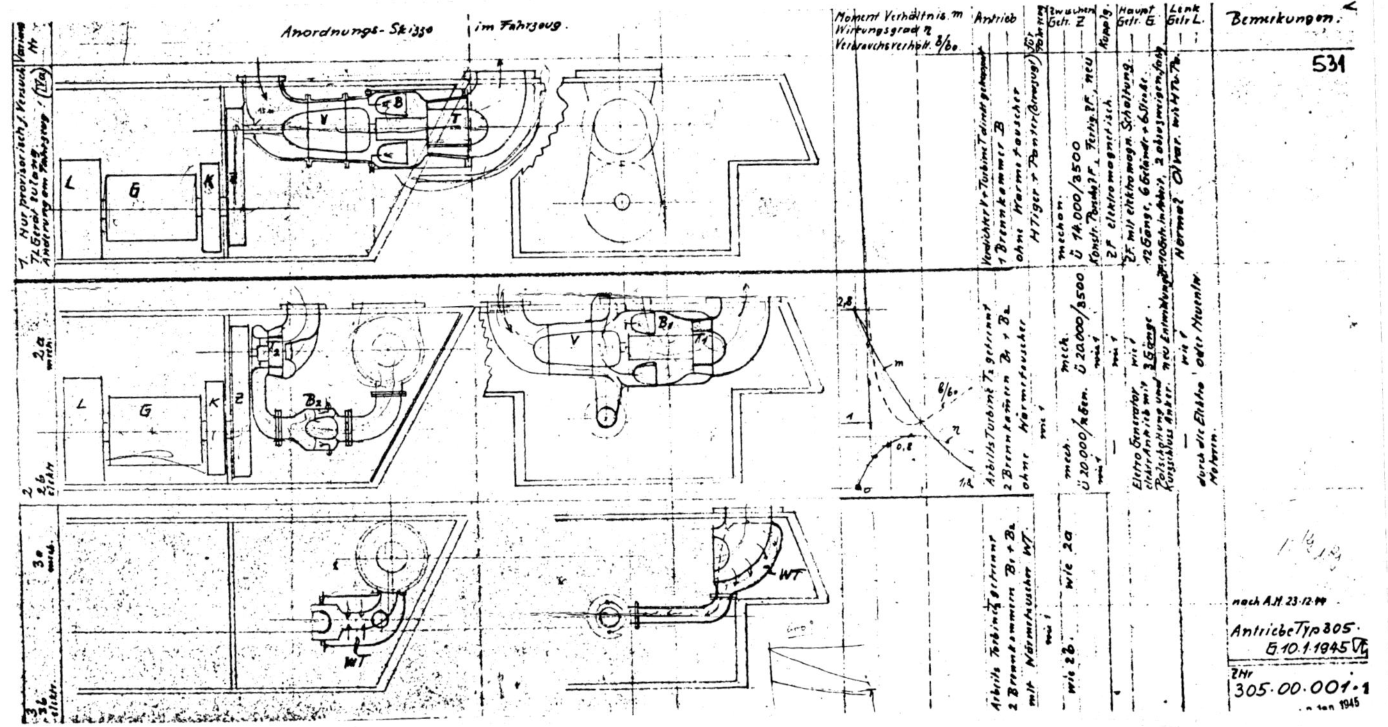

These drawings show Porsche attempts to house a turbine in the engine compartment of the Tiger. These tests had not been completed when the war ended.

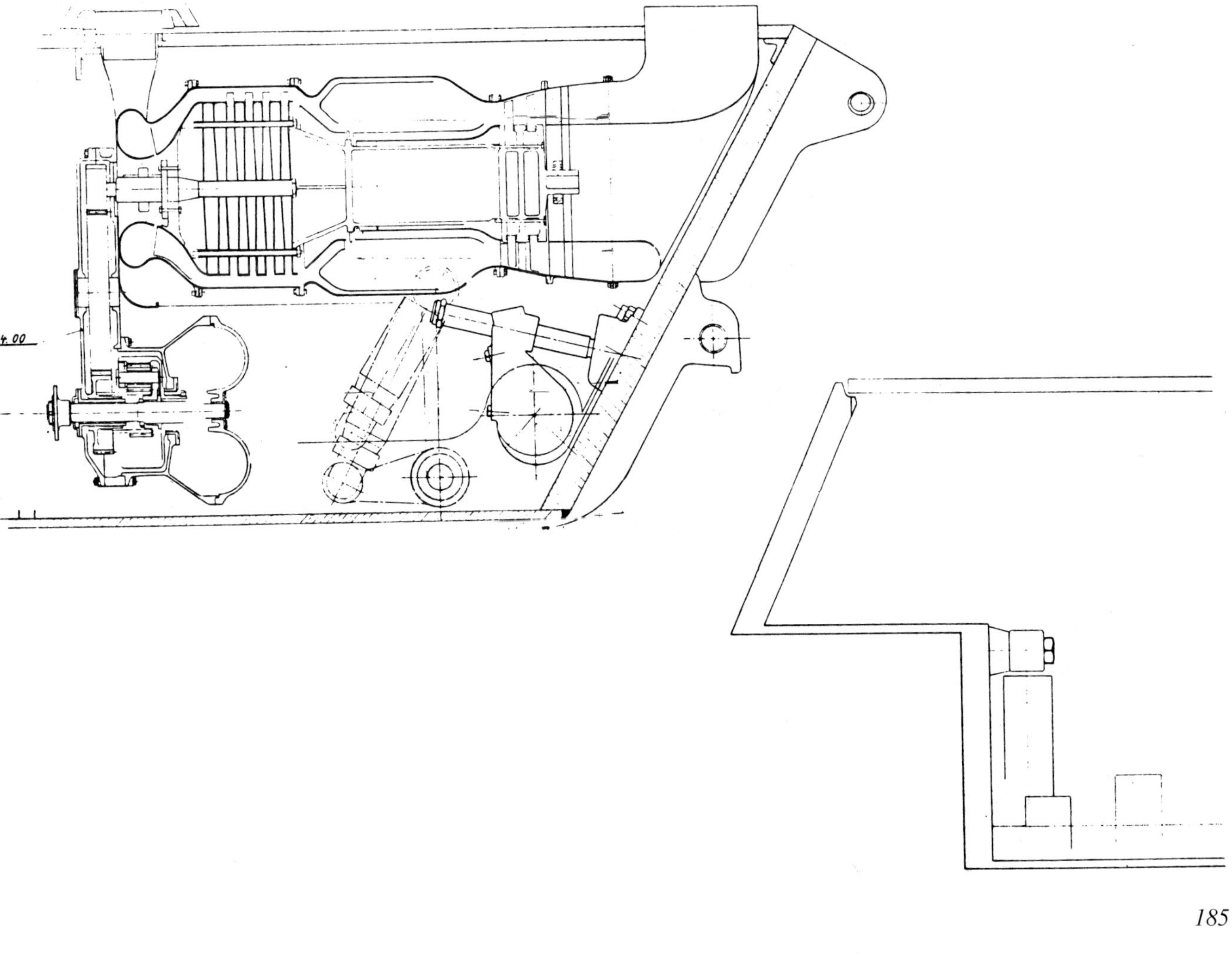

to put less emphasis on accessibility for servicing. Despite all efforts in the field of engine development, the Maybach "HL 230" carburetor motor was still in use in "Tiger" and "Panther" tanks at war's end.

A better degree of effectiveness in gearboxes was also sought. Easier shifting and simpler design were sought. So the J. M. Voith firm of Heidenheim built a socalled "PANTA" flow gearbox, which was to be installed in the "Tiger B." Testing was halted on November 15, 1944. The AEG railroad department also worked on the concept of a torque converter (centrifugal pumps and turbines, three-step shifting) in 1943-44. The AEG had already developed a torque converter for Henschel in 1939, but it could not be installed in tanks because of its size and weight. A gearbox for the "Tiger B" was being built, but was never installed.

The Pulsgetriebe GmbH in Leipzig had created an eight-speed gearbox, Type PP 33, in 1944. It was capable of transmitting a maximum of 1000 HP at 3000 rpm with a total ratio of 1 : 18.7, and a middle-stage factor of 1.5. With an aluminum housing it weighed 850 kg. The eight forward speeds were derived from three sets of planetary crown wheels in a row. The fourth set shifted all eight forward speeds to reverse at half speed by means of a clutch. The gearbox maintained power and did not run free, and in fact

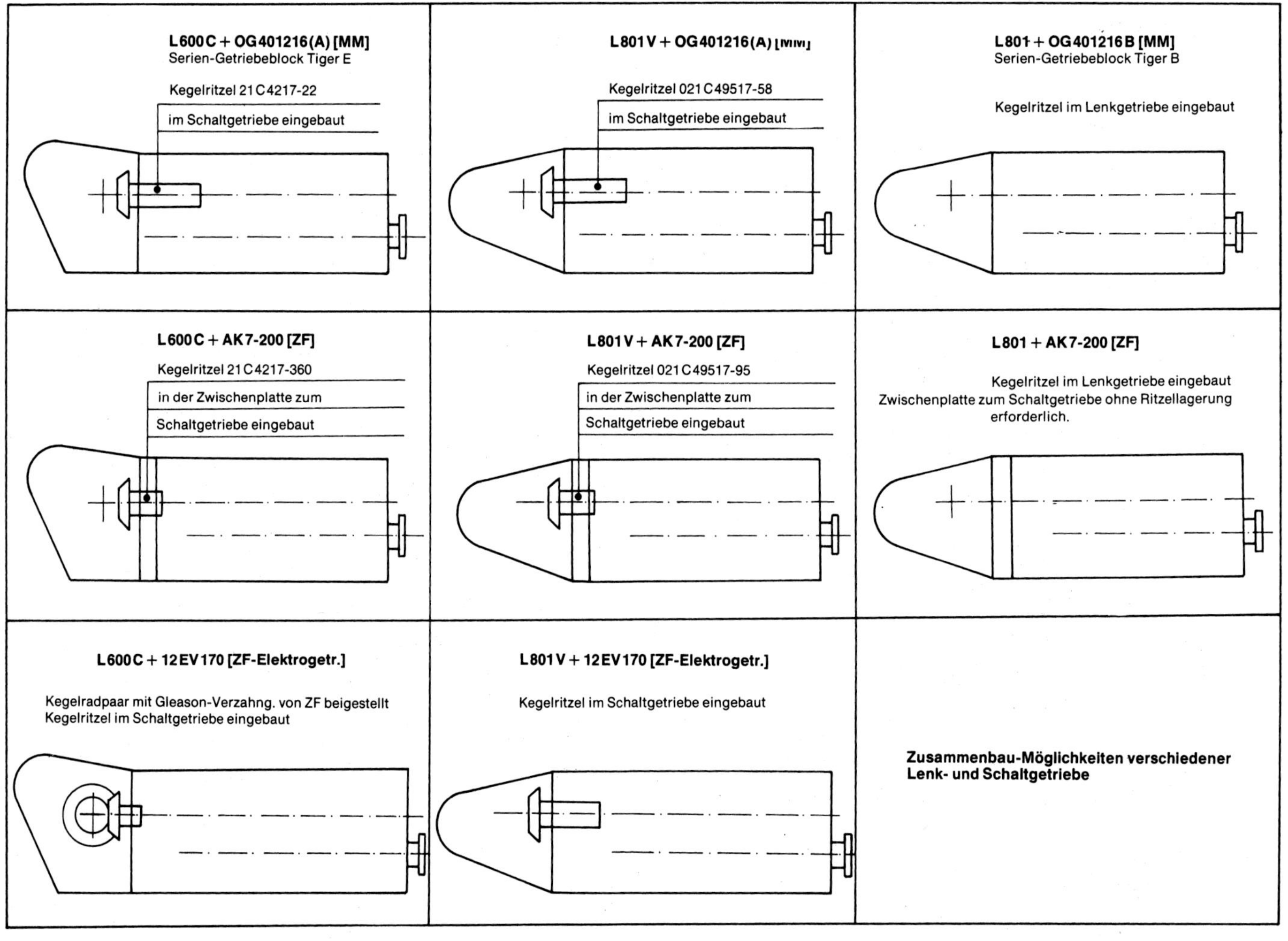

would transmit the full torque of the motor smoothly, even during shifting up or down. The clutch was used only for starting. Only unground, hardened gears with remarkably small intervals were used in the gearbox. Although Henschel was not convinced of its effectiveness, one of these gearboxes was sent to Sennelager to be installed in a Tiger chassis.

As already in the Panzer IV tank, the OKH empowered the Zahnräderfabrik Augsburg (formerly Joh. Renk AG) in contract no. SS 4912,0006,4819,42 to develop new hydrostatic fluid steering gears as quickly as possible. They were intended for the "Kätzchen"* (Kitten) armored vehicle, while at the urgency level of DE 504, by RM BuM ruling of February 25, 1943, No. 5872/43, similar steering gears were required for the "E 10," "Tiger II," and "Panther II" vehicles. The firm also worked on a newly developed OLVAR gearbox. The use of a hydrostatic steering gear (stepless, with constant radial changes) in the "Tiger II" was prepared for but never carried out.

The Zahnradfabrik Friedrichshafen had developed a socalled "Electro-gearbox" at this time, but it was plagued by chronic clutch problems. An electric clutch was planned for every pair of gears. In case of a production end at Maybach, it was foreseen that, under certain conditions, the "all-claw" gearbox Type "AK 7-200," used in the "Panther," could also be used in the "Tiger B." A v-n diagram made by the author at Sennelager in 1944 gave a maximum velocity for the vehicle of 46 km/h in 7th gear at 3000 rpm. The tests were not too successful, especially because of the too-meager gear reduction. The tests were finished so as to have a substitute gearbox available for the "Tiger."**

In the meantime, Henschel worked on an improved steering gear for the "Tiger." This Type "L 1201" was simpler in its basic design, and could transmit more power. About 80% of the detailed drawings were already made, and it was expected that fewer gears and 25% fewer ball bearings would be needed for this new steering gear, with performance increased by 50%.

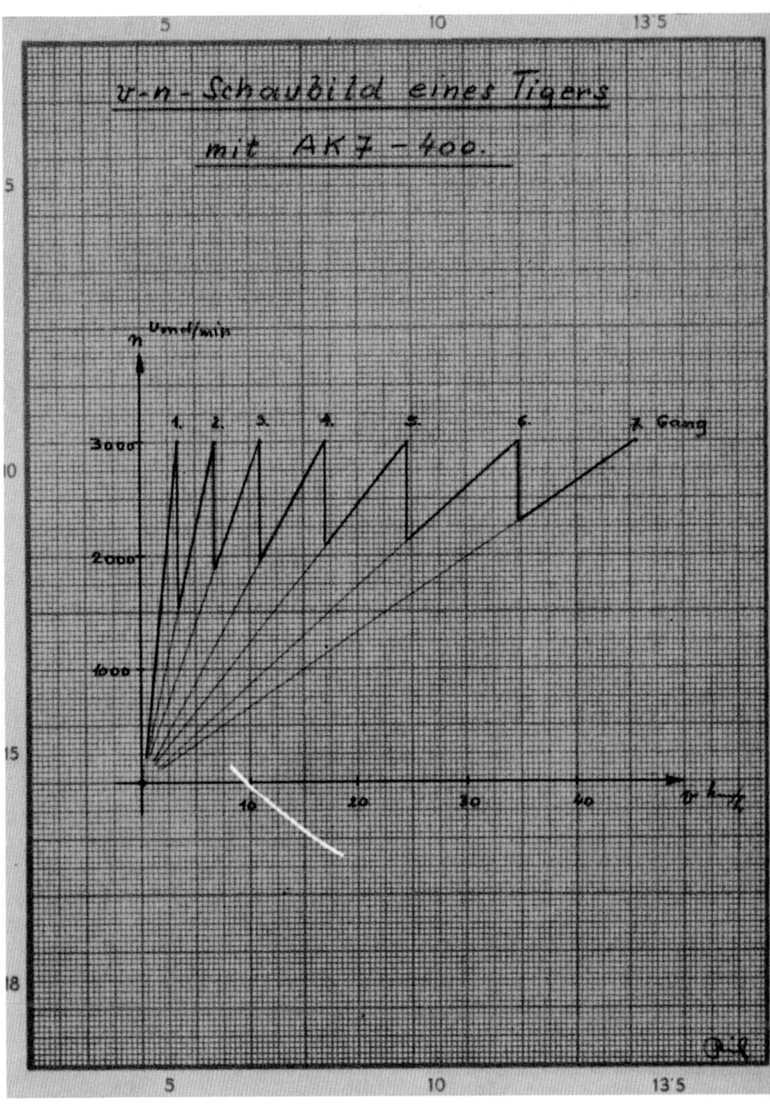

The n-v diagram for a Tiger B with ZF AK-7-200 gearbox.

*The "Kätzchen," a fully tracked multipurpose vehicle built under Contract SS 006-6032/42 to Auto-Union. Maybach HL 50 Z motor, ZFAK 8-45 gearbox.

**ZF also built two "Mekydro" gearboxes for testing by Contract SS 0006-6423/42 for use in the Tiger.

As for the running gear design and the choice of suspension, it may be assumed that toward the end of the war the tendency toward dropping torsion-bar suspension became clear. It turned out that the main reason was the fact that the torsion-bar suspension took up too much room inside, and was too expensive to produce. The Adler firm delivered drawings for independent suspension for the "Panther" and "Tiger," which included disc-spring packets mounted outside. These "spring units" were maintenance free, and could easily be changed and installed in the "Tiger."

The systematic destruction of the factories where ball bearings were made was the reason for the request to replace as many roller bearings as possible with journal bearings. The impossibility of such a change in terms of production technology soon became evident. Yet replacement designs for the Tiger E and B were worked out and tested.

It is obvious that attempts were made to improve the two tanks still in production (the "Panther II" and "Tiger II") as much as possible, and unify their maintenance. With the planned changes, they undoubtedly would have been the most modern tanks of World War II. Yet toward the end of 1944, serious doubts surfaced as to whether tanks of the "Tiger" class were not already too heavy and ponderous for tactical action. Even Henschel engineers were of the opinion that the "Panther" was suited for mass production, and had certain tactical advantages. In view of the industry's efforts to save money, in terms of work hours needed per tank, and of production problems because of raw material shortages and air raids, a smaller, more quickly built vehicle was preferred.

In February 1945 front officers urgently requested that the Henschel research department produce a 35-ton tank that could be made quickly out of already tested parts. On the other hand, after the Allied landing in France the industry no longer had any hope, and all socalled "tank building programs" were no longer worked on very seriously.

There was no doubt that vehicles of the "Tiger" class had reached boundaries that had to be accepted, in terms of size and weight, for usable tanks.

But there is also no doubt that the survivability of the "Tiger" was raised in two senses: for one thing, by the heavy armor protection in itself, and for another, by the resulting combat morale of the crews. In addition, the superiority of its primary armament in tank combat was obvious.

On the other hand, there were the sensitivity and weakness of the powerplant and running gear, the too-high specific ground pressure, and a too-low power-to-weight ratio.

As much as the "Tiger" tank became a legend, the troops themselves would have been better served by greater numbers of lighter, more mobile, and reliable tanks.

The only Tiger tank remaining in Germany is this Type B at combat School 2 in Munster.

Appendix A: Technical Data of Tiger E (old turret)

General Vehicle Data

Fighting weight	57,000 kg
Loaded weight (with loading tracks)	52,500 kg

Speeds

Sustained road speed (Autobahn)	40 km/h
Sustained moderate off-road speed	20-25 km/h
Range on road (Autobahn)	195 km
Range off road (moderate terrain)	110 km

Performance

Trench crossing ability	2.50 meters
Step-climbing ability	0.790 meter
Grade-climbing ability	upgrade or downgrade 35%
Fording ability	4 meters
Crew	5 men

Weights and measures

Overall length, barrel forward	8450 mm
Overall length, barrel backward	8434 mm
Overall length minus barrel overhang	6316 mm
Barrel overhang, barrel forward	2116 mm
Overall width, combat tracks plus skirting	3705 mm
Overall height	3000 mm
Length over tracks	5850 mm
Width over combat tracks	3547 mm
Width over loading tracks	3142 mm
Track ground contact	3605 mm
Track ground contact at 20 cm sinking depth (Horizontal projection)	5150 mm
Track with combat tracks	2822 mm
Track with loading tracks	2622 mm
Height from road to skirting plates	1800 mm
Firing height	2195 mm
Ground clearance, front and rear	470 mm

Hull and Body

Greatest hull length		5965 mm
Hull width outside at running-gear level		1920 mm
Hull width at center, with extensions		3140 mm
Light hull width at running-gear level		1800 mm
Light hull width at center, with extensions		2980 mm
Hull height to top of armor		1335 mm
Hull armor	Thickness	Angle of tilt
Front by driver	100 mm	81 degrees
Bow	100 mm	10 degrees
Sides	60 mm	90 degrees
Rear	80 mm	81 degrees
Roof	25 mm	
Bottom	25 mm	
Weight of hull with roof, ready to install		20,800 kg

Drive Assembly

Running Gear	combat tracks	loading tracks
Guiding teeth per link	2	2
Bolt length	716 mm	658.5 mm
Bolt diameter	28 mm	28 mm

Specific ground pressure on hard ground (weight/2 x ground - contact x track width	1.05 kg/sq.cm	1.46 kg/sq.cm
Sinking-in depth	0.735 kg/sq.cm	1.02 kg/sq.cm
Track /ground contact	1:1.278	1:1.384

Road Wheels

Type of running gear	staggered
Type of road wheels	steel with rubber pads
Number of road wheels per side	8
Road wheel diameter	800 mm
Load per road wheel	3440 kg
Distance between road-wheel axles	515 mm
Play between road wheel and track	2 mm

Cranks and suspension

Material of bearing boxes	Novotext
Type of springs	torsion bars
Number of springs	16
Torsion-bar diameter	first + last 58 mm, middle 55 mm
Head diameter	80/85 mm
Sprung length of torsion bar	1730 mm
Overall length of torsion bar	1890 mm
Distance from ground to center of torsion bar	95 mm

Drive Sprockets, Leading Wheels, Shock Absorbers

Drive sprocket part diameter	841.37 mm
Division of drive sprocket	131 mm
Leading wheel diameter	600 mm
Greatest track-tension distance	115 mm
Number of shock absorbers	4

Machinery

Motor	Maybach Motorenbau G.m.b.H.
Type	HL 230 P 45
Performance at 3000 rpm, 20° C air temperature and 760 Torr	700 HP
Weight of motor	1300 kg
Number of cylinders	12
Stroke	145 mm
Bore	130 mm
Displacement	23,000 cc
Compression ratio	6.8 : 1
Ignition:	2 magnetos with built-in spark-snapper
Fuel consumption per HP and hour	1/PS/hr
Fuel consumption, 100 km on road	270 liters
Fuel consumption, 100 km off road	480 liters

Cooling System

Type of cooling	water
Number of radiators	2
Height of radiator	490 mm
Width of radiator, block	892 mm
Depth of radiator	200 mm
Front surface of radiator	0.437 sq.m.
Number of double cooling fans	2
Diameter of cooling fan	437 mm
Speed of fan at top engine speed, summer/tropics	4150 rpm
Speed of fan at top engine speed, winter	2950 rpm
Type of cooling fan drive	gears and shafts
Maximum power	50 HP
Number of air filters	2
Maker and type of air filters	Mann and Hummel

Gears and Steering Gears

Greatest angle of intermediate shafts	front 1, bottom 2 degrees
Length of intermediate shaft	front 885, bottom 840 mm
Gearbox made by	MM/Adler
Gearbox type	OG 40 12 16 A
Number of forward gears	8
Number of reverse gears	4
Space between main shafts	181.5 mm
Overall length of gearbox	1372 mm
Overall width of gearbox	556 mm
Overall height of gearbox	591 mm
Gear reduction ratio	1 : 11
Speeds at 3000 rpm:	
1st gear	2.84 km/h
2nd gear	4.24 km/h
3rd gear	6.18 km/h
4th gear	9.17 mph
5th gear	14.1 km/h
6th gear	20.9 km/h
7th gear	30.5 km/h
8th gear	45.4 km/h

Reverse gear	3.75 km/h
Total spring of gearbox	1 : 16
Type of bevel gearing	Klingelnberg palloid spiral
Bevel-gear reduction	1 : 1/06
Steering gear type	two-radii, L 600 C
Steering gear reduction	1 : 1.333
Number of steering steps	2
Number of clutches in step gears	4
Material of lamella coating	Jurid or Emero
Number of gears	29
Smallest turning circle	3.44 m
Largest turning circle	165 m
Steering activation (oil pressure 6.5 atu")	Argus apparatus
Length of gearbox and steering gear	1812 mm
Weight of gearbox and steering gear	1345 kg

Final Drive and Brakes

Final drive reduction	1 : 10.7
Type of brakes	Argus claw-disc
Brake location	between steering gear and track drive
Foot brake works on	2 steering-gear shafts (2 brakes)
Brake drum diameter	550 mm outside
Brake material	Emero coating
Brake cooling	fins on housing
Brake activation	mechanical, foot pedal & hand lever

Capacities

Fuel capacity in four tanks	540 liters minus reserve
Fuel capacity in 20-liter canisters	__ liters
Water capacity in radiator and motor	__ liters
Water capacity in containers	__ liters

Turret

Turret weight	11,000 kg
Turret height with commander's cupola	1200 mm
Diameter of turning circle	1830 mm

Armament

Primary armament	KwK 36, 8.8 cm, L./56
Ammunition carried	92 rounds
MG 42 (or MG 34) carried	2
39 belt bags of 150 rounds each	5850 rounds
Machine pistols carried	1
6 magazines of 32 rounds each	192 rounds
Explosive shells	2

The following data changed with the use of the new turret (with swinging-out commander's hatch)

Overall length with barrel forward	8455 mm
Overall length with barrel backward	841 mm
Overall length minus barrel overhang	6335 mm
Barrel overhang with barrel forward	212 mm
Overall height	2885 mm

State of change "a" as of May 10, 1944

Appendix B: Technical Data of Tiger B (as of 51st vehicle)

General Vehicle Data

Fighting weight 69,800 kg*
Loading weight 66,300 kg*

Speeds
Sustained road speed (Autobahn) 38 km/h
Sustained moderate off-road speed 15-20 km/h
Range on road (Autobahn) 170 km
Range off road (moderate terrain) 120 km

Performance
Trench crossing ability 2.50 meters
Step climbing ability 0.85 meter
Grande climbing ability upgrade or downgrade 35 degrees
Fording ability 1.60 meters
Crew 5 men

Weights and Measures
Overall length, barrel forward 10,206 mm*
Overall length, barrel backward 9966 mm*
Overall length minus barrel overhang 7380 mm
Barrel overhang, barrel forward 2906 mm*
Overall width, combat tracks plus skirting 3755 mm
Overall height 3090 mm
Length over tracks 6400 mm
Width over combat tracks plus bolt overhang 3625 mm
Width with loading tracks 3270 mm
Track contact length 4120 mm
Track contact length at 20 cm sinking depth 5400 mm (horizontal projection)
Track with combat tracks 2790 mm
Track with loading tracks 2610 mm
Height from road to skirting plates 1860 mm
Firing height 2260 mm
Ground clearance front 495 mm, rear 510 mm

Weight and Volumes
Weight of chassis ready to run, minus turret, Armament, ammunition, equipment, etc. ca. 52,000 kg
Total volume 17.4 cub.m
Volume of fighting compartment ca. 11 cub.m
Volume of engine compartment ca. 2.2 cub.m
Volume of turret above upper hull rim ca. 4.2 cub.m
Remaining volume minus engine + fighting com. ca 2 cub.m

Hull
Weight of gun barrel 28,000 kg
Empty weight after working 27,700 kg
Maximum outer hull length 7134 mm
Hull width outside, at running-gear height 1928 mm
Hull width outside, center, with extensions 2938 mm
Light hull width, running-gear height 1768 mm
Light hull width, center, with extensions 2778 mm
Hull height from bottom to top of armor front 1365, rear 1350

* See page 195.

mm
Hull armor plate thickness tilted from horizontal
Front by driver 150 mm 40 degrees
Bow 100 mm 40 degrees
Sides 80 mm below 90, above 65 deg.
Rear 80 mm 60 degrees
Roof 40 mm
Bottom front 40, rear 25 mm

Drive Assembly
Running GearCombat track loading track
Guiding teeth per link 2 2
Bolt length 818 mm 658.5 mm
Bolt diameter 24 mm 24 mm
Specific ground pressure on firm ground:
weight/2 x ground contact
length x track width 1.02 kg/sq.cm 1.23 kg/sq.cm
Sinking depth 0.777 kg/sq.cm 0.943 kg/sq.cm
Track/ground contact length 1 " 1.475 1 : 1.1578

Road Wheels
Type of running gear staggered
Type of road wheels steel with rubber pads
Number of road wheels per side 9
Road wheel diameter 800 mm
Weight on each road wheel 3610 kg
Distance between axles 515 mm
Play between road wheel and track 2-4 mm

Cranks and Suspension
Material of bearing boxes Novotext
Type of springs torsion bars
Number of springs 18
Torsion bar diameter 60-63 mm
Head diameter 90 mm
Sprung length of torsion bar 1800 mm
Total length of torsion bar 1960 mm
Distance from hull bottom to torsion bar 95 mm

Drive sprocket, leading wheel, shock absorber
Drive sprocket part diameter 870 mm
Division of drive sprocket 151 mm
Leading wheel diameter 650 mm
Greatest track tension distance 210 mm
Number of shock absorbers 4

Machinery
Motor made by Maybach Motorenbau G.m.b.H.
Type HL 230 P 30
Performance at 3000 rpm, 20° C air temperature,
and 760 Torr. 700 HP
Weight of the motor 1300 kg
Cylinders 12
Stroke 145 mm
Bore 130 mm
Displacement 23,000 cc
Compression ratio 6.8 : 1
Ignition two magnetos with built in-spark-snappers
Fuel consumption per HP and hour __l/HP/hr
Fuel consumption per 100 km on road 500 liters
Fuel consumption in moderate terrain 700 liters

Cooling System
Type of cooling water
Number of radiators 4
Height of radiator324 mm
Width of radiator 522 mm
Depth of radiator 200 mm
Front surface of radiator 0.169 sq.m
Number of cooling fans 2 double
Diameter of cooling fan 520 mm
Cooling fan speed at top rpm, summer/tropics 3765 rpm
Cooling fan speed, winter 2680 rpm
Type of cooler drive crown wheels and shafts
Maximum cooling power needed 40 HP
Number of air filters 2
Maker and type of air filter Mann & Hummel

Gearbox and Steering Gear
Greatest angle of intermediate shafts front 2 deg. 25', rear 2 deg.
Length of intermediate shaft front 993 mm, rear 1187 mm

Gearbox
Gearbox made by MM/ZF
Gearbox type OG 40 12 16 B
Number of forward speeds 8
Number of reverse speeds 4
Distance between main shafts 181.5 mm
Overall length of gearbox 1266 mm
Overall width of gearbox 600 mm
Overall height of gearbox 620 mm
Gear reduction ratio 1 : 11
Speed at 3000 rpm, 1st gear 2.57 km/h
2nd gear 3.83 km/h
3rd gear 5.62 km/h
4th gear 8.33 km/h
5th gear 12.75 km/h
6th gear 18.95 km/h
7th gear 27.32 km/h
8th gear 41.5 km/h
Reverse gear 3.39 km/h
Total spring of gearbox 1 : 16
Type of bevel gearing Klingelnberg-Palloid spiral
Bevel gear reduction 1 : 1.05
Steering gear manufacturer H & S
Type two radial link L 801
Reduction of steering gear 1 : 1.2955
Number of steering stages 2
Number of clutches in step links 4
Material of lamellar coating Jurid or Emero
Number of gears 25
Smallest turning circle 2.08 m
Largest turning circle 114 m
Steering activation Argus apparatus
Total length, gearbox and steering gear 1690 mm**
Total weight, gearbox and steering gear 1200 kg

Final Drive and Brakes
Final drive reduction ratio 1 : 12.56
Type of brakes Argus claw-disc LB 900.4
Position of brakes between steering gear and track drive
Foot brake works on steering driveshaft
Outer diameter of brake drums 565 mm
Material of brakes Ge. [?]
Brake cooling cooling fins on brake housing
Brake activation mechanical foot pedal and hand lever

Capacities
Fuel capacity in 7 tanks, without reserve 860 liters
Fuel capacity in 20-liter canisters __ liters
Water capacity of radiators and motor ca. __ liters

Turret
Turret weight 13,500 kg
Empty weight without weapon ca. 8000 kg
Turret height with commander's cupola 1217 mm
Diameter of turning circle 1850 mm

Armament
Primary armament KwK 43, 8.8 cm (L/71)
Ammunition 68 in racks, 16 loose on platform 84 rounds*
Machine guns 2 MG 42 (or MG 43), 1 AA gun 3
32 belt bags of 150 rounds 4800 rounds
Machine pistols 1
6 magazines of 32 rounds each 192 rounds
Explosive shells 3
To be noted:

* Data so marked vary from no. 1-50 with old (Porsche) turret type, as follows:

Fighting weight	68,500 kg
Loading weight	65,000 kg
Overall length with barrel forward	10,280 mm
Overall length with barrel backward	9,960 mm
Barrel overhang with barrel forward	2900 mm

** In L 8021 test version (12 x) with OG 40 12 16 1790 mm

HENSCHEL & SOHN
G. M. B. H.
KASSEL

LOKOMOTIVE, KASSEL
KASSEL 241 51
FERNSCHREIBER 03 234
RB-NR. 0/0591/0013

BANKVERBINDUNGEN:
REICHSBANK, KASSEL, KONTO-NR. 42/83
DEUTSCHE BANK, FILIALE KASSEL
DRESDNER BANK, FILIALE KASSEL
COMMERZBANK, FILIALE KASSEL
BERLINER HANDELSGESELLSCHAFT, BERLIN
REICHS-KREDIT-GESELLSCHAFT, BERLIN
POSTSCHECKKONTO: FRANKFURT AM MAIN NR. 384 60

Maschinenbau
422 878 Auftrag-Nr.

Fi
Sh Tsusho Kaisha, Ltd., T o k y o ,
übe a. Showa Tsusho Kaisha, Ltd.,
B l i n .

Rechnung Nr. 10047

KASSEL, den 23.November 1943

~~XXXXXXXXXXXXXXXXXXXXXXXXXXXXX~~ Wir sandten für Ihre Rechnung und Gefahr a ~~XXXXXXXX~~ Lieferung

~~XXX~~ als Wir führten die untenverzeic e Lieferung aus.

Vorg.:

Lfd. Nr.	Stück	Gegenstand	ungs-Nr.	Stück-Preis RM	Gesamt-Preis RM
	1	Panzerkampfwagen Tiger A führung E gemäss Angebot der Firma lies & Co. Berlin, vom ~~17.10.1943~~ 0.1943 nebst Ergänzung vom 11.10.194		645.000,-	645.000,-

Die Zahlung hat zu 100% freien Reichsmark gemäss dem d ch-japanischen Zahlungsabkomme erfolgen, und zwar bei Versandber chaft, spätestens innerhalb vo Wochen nach gemeldeter Versandberei aft.

MB Verk. Nr. 4 1000 S. 9. 43. K/0471

Appendix C: Bill for the Tiger E sold to Japan.

Appendix D:

Temporary technical delivery conditions for chassis of *Panzerkampfwagen* VI

(Sd.Kfz. …)
Delivery conditions and norm pages to be noted:
See page no. 1

TL 21/2014	Technical delivery conditions for armored full-track chassis without additions
TL 21/6005	Technical delivery conditions for water-tube radiators without additions
TL 21/6009	Technical delivery conditions for brake parts of special cast iron, built by Goetze, Burscheid, without additions
TL 21/6014	Technical delivery conditions for shock absorbers for half- and full-track vehicles, without additions
TL 21/7007	Technical delivery conditions for dimmer caps, without additions
TL 21/9002	Conditions for sending motor vehicles (parts and tools)
TL 21/900	Technical delivery conditions for installation and removal of desensitizing and screening to full desensitizing of chassis and bodies for radios
TL 21/9007	Technical delivery conditions for special screws for armored vehicles, without additions
TL 21/....	Technical delivery conditions for torsion bar springs for tracked vehicles (still in the works)
TL 1003	Technical delivery conditions for purses (containers) of leather and weave, without additions
TL 1006	Technical delivery conditions for wooden boxes, Type II, without additions
TL 4001	Technical delivery conditions for steel sheet, without additions
TL 4003	Technical delivery conditions for raw and pre-worked cast steel, without additions
TL 5000	Technical delivery conditions for fawn leather
TL 5005	Technical delivery conditions for chrome leather
TO 5006	Technical delivery conditions for [kernsohl] leather
TL 5008	Technical delivery conditions for white leather
TL 5110	Technical Delivery Conditions for undyed cotton tent fabric
TL 5118	Technical delivery conditions for raw field-gray canvas, impregnated and not impregnated
TL 5200	Conditions for wood
TL 5901	Technical delivery conditions for felt according to HgN 126 21
TL 6303	Conditions for paint
TL 6311	Conditions for phosphate rust-protection processes
TL 9001	Conditions for welded connections
TLM 0101	Conditions for highly stressed welded connections made of steel
TL 9900	Material testing: Chemical and mechanical testing
TL 9901	Material testing: Steel and non-ferrous metals
HgN 107 10	General finishing instructions I
HgN 107 40	Tearing rods
HgN 107 41	Seams in leather, fabric, Zellon, etc.
HgN 113 29	Allowable deviations for masses without stated tolerances

Defining the object to be delivered

Technical Requirements

1. Chassis of the Pz.Kpfw. VI by Group List 021 Gr 39000, and accompanying drawings and lists.
2. The chassis must fulfill the following conditions:
   a)Highest speed of the total weight of 32,000 kg burdened by weights, factory-finished chassis on straight roads of medium structure with an upgrade of 3 degrees and engine speed of 3000 rpm: 24 km/h
   b)Grade climbing ability: upwards 30 degrees, downwards 45 degrees
   c)trench crossing ability [nothing stated; page 199]
   d)Fording height 1.20 m
   e)Ground clearance 0.450 m
   f)Weight of the factory-finished chassis including fuel and oil, but not tools or equipment
3. For welding of all parts, TLM 0101 is to be taken as the basis

Acceptance

4. Carry out all applicable tests on chassis.
Check central lubrication, to see if all lubrication points are supplied with lubricant.
Check the play of the road wheels.
Check settings of lights.
Send back insufficient chassis or components or parts.

Material Tests

5. Carry out material testing according to Appendix 1.
Measure and Weight Testing
6. Check measurements particularly according to Appendix 3.
7. Check weights of samples (see No. 2 f) and note in acceptance report.

Performance Testing

8. The chassis are to be tested for attaining the requirements listed in No. 1 a) through c).

Appendix D: Technical Data

see following

Vehicle	**Panzer VK 3001 (P) (Pz. Sfl. V)**	**12.8 cm Sfl L/61 (VK 6501)**	**Panzer VII**
Type	100	VK 3001 (H)	SW
Made by	Nibelungenwerk	Henschel/Rheinmetall	Henschel
Years built	1939-1941	1939-1942	1940-1941
Data source	Porsche drawing	various	Handbuch WaA, #42
Motor	Porsche 100 (2)	Maybach HL 116 S	Maybach HL 224
Cylinders	V-10, 72 degrees	6 in-line	V-12, 60 degrees
Bore x stroke mm	105 x 115	125 x 150	125 x 145
Displacement cc	10,000	11,048	21,353
Compression ratio	5.9 : 1	6.5 : 1	6.5 : 1
RPM normal/max.	2500	2600/3300	3000
Engine power	210 x 2, 410	265/300	600
Valves	drop	drop	drop
Crankshaft bearings	6 journal	8 journal	7 roller
Carburetor	1 Solex 40 JFF II	2 Solex 40 JFF II	2 Solex downdraft
Firing order	1-8-3-10-5-9-4-7-2-6	1-5-3-6-2-4	1-12-5-8-3-10-6-7-2-11-4-9
Starter	Bosch AL 24 V	Bosch BNG 4/24	Bosch 24 V
Generator	Bosch GQL 300/12	Bosch GQL 300/12	Bosch GULN 700/12
Batteries/volts/Ah	2/12/120	2/12/105	4/6/105
Fuel supply	pumps	pumps	pumps
Cooling	air, fans	water	water
Clutch	none, gas-electric	3-plate dry	multi-plate
Gearbox	Porsche-Siemens	ZF SSF 77 Aphon	Maybach
Speeds fwd/rev	2/2	6/1	5/1
Drive sprockets	front	front	front
Final drive ratio	1 :	1 :	1 :
Top speed km/h	60	19.6	26
Range on/off road			
Steering	Porsche-Siemens	DB-Wilson clutch	3-radius
Turning circle			
Suspension	torsion bars, longit.	torsion bars, transv.	torsion bars, transv.
Lubrication	central + high-pres.	high-pressure	high-pressure
Brakes made by	Porsche-Siemens	DB-Henschel	Perrot
Brake activation	electric	mechanical	mechanical
Brake type	disc	inner shoe	inner shoe
Brakes act on	drive	drive	drive
Running gear	road wheels + rollers	road wheels + rollers	road wheels + rollers
Road wheel size	600 mm	700/98-550	
Track of vehicle mm	2600	2100	
Track ground contact	3225 mm	4750 mm	
Track width	600 mm	520 mm	800 mm
Links per track	88	85	
Track type			
Ground clearance	490 mm	280 mm	
Overall length mm	6600 (minus gun)	9800 (7200 – gun)	
Overall width mm	3200	3170	
Overall height mm	3030	2670	
Ground pressure	0.9 kp/sq.cm	0.8 kp/sq.cm	
Fighting weight kp	30,000	35,000	65,000
Crew	4	5	5
Fuel consumption	230-250 g/HP/hr		
Fuel capacity	450 liters		
Armor, hull front mm	50	40	100
Armor, hull sides mm	40	30	
Armor, hull rear mm	30	20	
Armor, turret front mm	30		
Armor, turret sides mm	15		
Armor, turret rear mm	15		
Grade climbing	24 degrees		
Step climbing			
Fording			
Trench crossing			
Primary weapon	7.5 cm KwK L/24 or 10.5 cm	12.8 cm K 40 (18)	7.5 cm KwK L/24
Other weapons			
Notes			

Vehicle	**Panzer VI VK 3601 ***)**	**Panzer Tiger I (Sd.Kfz. 181) E**	**38 cm Sturmmörser Tiger**
Type	VK 3601	VK 4501 (H)	VK 4501 (H)
Made by	Henschel	Henschel	Alkett (rebuilt)
Years built	1942	1942-1944	1944-1945
Data source	Handbuch WaA D 36	D 656/23. 5/10/1944	Handbuch WaA G369
Motor	Maybach HL 174 *)	Maybach HL 210 **)	Maybach HL 210 **)
Cylinders	V-12, 60 degrees	V-12, 60 degrees	V-12, 60 degrees
Bore x stroke mm	125 x 130	125 x 145	125 x 145
Displacement cc	19,144	21,353	21,353
Compression ratio	6.5 : 1	7 : 1	7 : 1
RPM normal/max.	3000	2500/3000	2500/3000
Engine power	550 HP	650 HP	650 HP
Valves	drop	drop	drop
Crankshaft bearings	7 roller	7 roller	7 roller
Carburetor	2 Solex 40 JFF II	4 Solex 52 JFF II D	
Firing order	1-12-5-8-3-10-6-7-2-11-4-9	12-1-8-5-10-3-7-6-1-2-9-4	
Starter	Bosch BNG 4/24	Bosch BPD 6/24	Bosch BPD 6/24
Generator	Bosch GQL 300/12-900	Bosch GULN 1000/12 or 700 W	
Batteries/Volts/Ah	2/12/105	2/12/120 or 150	2/12/120 or 150
Fuel supply	pumps	2 Solex pumps	2 Solex pumps
Cooling	water	water	water
Clutch	multiplate wet	multiplate wet	multiplate wet
Gearbox	Maybach OLVAR 401216	Maybach OLVAR OG 401216 A	
Speeds fwd/reverse	8/1	8/4	8/4
Drive sprockets	front	front	front
Final drive ratio	1 : 10.75	1 : 10.75	1 : 10.75
Top speed km/h	40	45.4	45.4
Range on/off road	100/60	100/60	
Steering	Henschel 2-radius	HS L 600 C 2-radius	
Turning circle m	7.0	7.0	7.0
Suspension	torsion bars, transverse	torsion bars, transverse	
Lubrication	central + high-pressure	battery + high-pressure	
Brakes made by	Südd. Arguswerke	Südd. Arguswerke	
Brake activation	mechanical	mechanical	mechanical
Brake type	disc	disc	disc
Brakes act on	drive	steering gear shaft	
Running gear	stepped	box	box
Road wheel size	800 x 95 E		
Track of vehicle mm	2620	2822, 2622 (loading tracks)	
Track ground contact	3640 mm	3605 mm	3605 mm
Track width mm	520	725, 520 (loading tracks)	
Links per track	96	96	
Track type	Kgs 63/725/130, Kgs 63/520/130 (load.)		
Ground clearance mm	450	470	470
Overall length mm	6050	8450/8434/6316	6280
Overall width mm	3140	3705	3570
Overall height mm	2700	3000	2850
Ground pressure	1.04 kp/sq.cm	1.5 kp/sq.cm	
Fighting weight kp	36,000-40,000	56,900	65,000
Crew	5	5	5
Fuel consumption	535/935 l/100 km	535/935 l/100 km	
Fuel capacity	534 in 4 tanks	534 in 4 tanks	
Armor, hull front	100 mm	100 mm	150 mm
Armor, hull sides	60 mm	80/60 mm	80/60 mm
Armor, hull rear	60 mm	80 mm	80 mm
Armor, turret front	80 mm	100 mm	150 mm
Armor, turret sides	60 mm	80 mm	80 mm
Armor, turret rear	60 mm	80 mm	80 mm
Grade climbing	35 degrees	35 degrees	35 degrees
Step climbing	790 mm	790 mm	790 mm
Fording	1200 mm	1200 mm	
Trench crossing	2300 mm	2300 mm	2300 mm
Primary armament	Weapon 0725	8.8 cm KwK 36 L/56	38 cm StuM 61 L/54
Other armament	2 MG 34	2 MG 34 (3920)	1 MG 34
Notes	*) later HL 210 P 45 ***) interim stage	**) P 45; as of #251, HL 230 P 45	

Vehicle	Panzer VI Tiger (P) VK 4501	Tiger 9P) design with ram	Panzerjäger Tiger P Ferdinand/Elefant
Type	101	101	101
Made by	Nibelungenwerk	not built	Nibelungenwerk
Years made	194101942	not built	1942-1943
Data source	Handbuch WaA D 41	Porsche drawing	D 656/1. 5/1/1943
Motor	Porsche 101/1 x 2	Porsche 101/1 x 2	Maybach HL 120 TRM x 2
Cylinders	V-10, 72 degrees	V-10, 72 degrees	V-12, 60 degrees
Bore x stroke mm	115 x 145	115 x 145	105 x 15
Displacement cc	15,060	15,060	11,867
Compression ratio	5.9 : 1	5.9 : 1	6.2-6.5 : 1
RPM normal/max	2000/2500	2000/2500	2600
Engine power	320 x 2 = 640 HP	320 x 2 = 640 HP	265, 530 HP
Valves	drop	drop	drop
Crankshaft bearings	6 journal	6 journal	7 roller
Carburetor	Solex 50 JFF II	Solex 50 JFF II	2 Solex 40 JFF II
Firing order	1-8-3-10-5-9-4-7-2-6	1-12-5-8-3-10-6-7-2-11-4-9	
Starter	Bosch AL/SED	Bosch AL/SED	Bosch BNG 4/24
Generator	Bosch LQ 3000/24	Bosch LQ 3000/24	Bosch GQL 300/12
Batteries/Volts/Ah	2/12/150	2/12/150	4/12/120
Fuel supply	pumps	pumps	pumps
Cooling	air, fans	air, fans	water
Clutch	none, gas-electric	none, gas-electric	none, gas-electric
Gearbox	Porsche-Siemens rpm shifter	Porsche-Siemens	
Speeds fwd/reverse	3/3	3/3	3/3
Drive sprockets	rear	rear	rear
Final drive ratio	1 : 15	1 : 15	1 : 16.75
Top speed km/h	35	35	20
Range on/off road	80 km	80 km	150/90 km
Steering	Porsche-Siemens	Porsche-Siemens	Porsche-Siemens
Turning circle m	2.15	2.15	2.15
Suspension	torsion bars, longitudinal	torsion bars, longitudinal	
Lubrication	battery + high-pressure	battery + high-pressure	
Brakes made by	Porsche-Siemens	Porsche-Siemens	Porsche-Siemens
Brake activation	hydraulic/mechanical	comp. air/electrical	
Brake type	disc	disc	inner shoe
Brakes act on	drive	drive	drive
Running gear	steel road wheels	steel road wheels	steel road wheels
Road wheel size	794 mm	794 mm	794 mm
Track of vehicle	2640 mm	2640 mm	2640 mm
Track ground contact	4175 mm	4175 mm	4175 mm
Track width	640 mm	640 mm	640 mm
Links per track	109	109	109
Track type	Kgs 62/640/130	Kgs 62/640/130	Kgs 62/640/130
Ground clearance	480 mm	480 mm	480 mm
Overall length mm	9340/6700	8430	8140
Overall width mm	3140	3600	3380
Overall height mm	2800	2550	2970
Ground pressure	1.06 kp/sq.cm	1.14 kp/sq.cm	1.23 kp/sq.cm
Fighting weight kp	57,000-59,000	60,170	65,000
Crew	5	1	6
Fuel consumption	250-270 g/HP/hr	250-270 g/HP/hr	1200 g/HP/hr
Fuel capacity	520 liters	520 liters	540 + 540 = 1080 l
Armor, hull front	100 mm	100 mm	100 + 100 mm
Armor, hull sides	80 mm	80 mm	80 mm
Armor, hull rear	80 mm	80 mm	80 mm
Armor, turret front	100 mm	30 mm	200 mm
Armor, turret sides	80 mm	30-50 mm	80 mm
Armor, turret rear	80 mm	30 mm	80 mm
Grade climbing	30 degrees	30 degrees	22 degrees
Step climbing mm	780	780	780
Fording mm	1000	1000	1000
Trench crossing mm	2640	2640	2640
Primary armament	8.8 cm KwK 36 L/56	none	8.8cm StuK 43/1 L/71
Other armament	2 MG 34	none	1 MG 34 loose
Notes	70 rounds	55/600 rounds	

Vehicle	***Bergepanzer* Tiger (P) VK 4501 P**	***Panzer* VK 4501 (P) HA**	***Panzer* VK 4502 (P) (design)**
Type	101	102	180/181*)
Made by	Nibelungenwerk	Nibelungenwerk	not built
Years built	1943	1943	(1943-1944)
Data source	D 656/1, 5/1/1943	Porsche archives	Porsche drawing
Motor	Maybach HL 120 TRM x 2	Porsche 101/1 x 2	Porsche 101/4 x 2
Cylinders	V-12, 60 degrees	V 10, 72 degrees	V 10, 72 degrees
Bore x stroke mm	105 x 115	115 x 145	115 x 145
Displacement cc	11,867	15,060	15,060
Compression ratio	6.2-6.5 : 1	5.9 : 1	6.4 : 1
RPM, normal/max.	2600	2000/2500	3200
Engine power	265 x 2 = 530 HP	320 x 2 = 640 HP	350, total 670 HP
Valves	drop	drop	drop
Crankshaft bearings	7 roller	6 journal	6 journal
Carburetor	2 Solex 40 JFF II	1 Solex 50 JFF II	1 Solex 50 JFF II
Firing order	1-12-5-8-3-10-6-7-2-11-4-9	1-8-3-10-5-9-4-7-2-6	
Starter	Bosch BNG 4/24	T 141 9 HP aux.motor	Bosch AL/SED
Generator	Bosch GQL 300/12-900	Bosch LW 3000/24	
Batteries/Volts/Ah	4/12/120	2/12/120	4/12/120
Fuel supply	pumps	pumps	pumps
Cooling	water	air, fans	air, fans
Clutch	none, gas-electric	hydraulic	none, gas-electric
Gearbox	Porsche-Siemens	Voith NITA torq. cv.	Porsche-Siemens
Speeds fwd/reverse	3/3	2/1	2/1
Drive sprockets	rear	rear	rear
Final drive ratio	1 : 16.75	1 : 15	1 :
Top speed km/h	25	35	35
Range on/off road	160/100 km	80 km	
Steering	Porsche-Siemens	Porsche-Siemens	Porsche-Siemens
Turning circle m	2.15	2.15	2.15
Suspension	torsion bars, longit.	Torsion bars, longit.	Torsion bars, longit.
Lubrication	battery+high-pressure	battery+high-pressure	battery+high-pressure
Brakes made by	Porsche-Siemens	Su"dd. Arguswerke	Porsche-Siemens
Brake activation	compr.air, electric	hydraulic	hydraul., mechanical
Brake type	inner shoe	disc	disc
Brakes act on	drive	drive	drive
Running gear	steel road wheels	steel road wheels	steel road wheels
Road wheel size	794 mm	794 mm	794 mm
Vehicle track mm	2680	2640	2700
Track ground contact	4175 mm	4115 mm	4115 mm
Track width mm	640	640	700/500 (loading)
Links per track	109	109	109
Track type	Kgs 62/640/130	Kgs 62/640/130	
Ground clearance	480 mm	480 mm	480 mm
Overall length	6700 mm	6700 mm	8345 mm
Overall width	3380 mm	3140 mm	3400/3140 (loading)
Overall height	2800 mm	2740 mm	
Ground pressure	0.9 kp/sq.cm	1.06 kp/sq.cm	1.15 kp/sq.cm
Fighting weight kp	47,200	59,000	64,000
Crew	4	5	5
Fuel consumption	1200 ltr./100 km	250-270 g/HP/hr	270 g/HP/hr
Fuel capacity	540 + 540 = 1080 l	520 liters	
Armor, hull front	100 mm	100 mm	100 mm
Armor, hull sides	80 mm	80 mm	80 mm
Armor, hull rear	80 mm	80 mm	80 mm
Armor, turret front	100 mm		
Armor, turret sides	80 mm		
Armor, turret rear	80 mm		
Grade climbing	2 degrees	30 degrees	30 degrees
Step climbing	780 mm	780 mm	
Fording	1000 mm	1000 mm	
Trench crossing	2640 mm	2640 mm	
Primary armament	8.8 cm KwK43 L/71		
Other armament	1 MG 34	2 MG 34	
Notes	hydraulic drive hydraulic drive	*) 181 designed for	

Vehicle	*Panzer* Tiger II (Sd.Kfz. 182)	*Panzer* Tiger II *) (Sd.Kfz. 182)	*Panzerjäger* Tiger *Jagdtiger* (Sd.Kfz.186)
Type	B, VK 4503	B, VK 4503	B, VK 4503
Made by	Henschel	Henschel	Nibelungenwerk
Years built	1943-1944	1944-1945	1944-1945
Data source	D 656/43, 9/1/1944	D 656/43, 9/1/1944	Handbuch WaA,G360
Motor	Maybach HL 230 P 30		
Cylinders	V-12, 60 degrees		
Bore x stroke mm	130 x 145		
Displacement cc	23,095		
Compression ratio	6.8 : 1		
RPM normal/max.	2600/3000		
Engine power	600-700 HP		
Valves	drop		
Crankshaft bearings	7+1 roller		
Carburetor	4 Solex 52 JFF II D		
Firing order	1-8-5-10-3-7-6-11-2-9-4-12		
Starter	Bosch BPD 6/24 ARS 146 + AL/ZMJ/R 12		
Generator	Bosch GTLN 700/12-1500 L 1		
Batteries/Volts/Ah	2/12/150		
Fuel supply	2 Solex double pumps		
Cooling	water		
Clutch	multi-plate wet		
Gearbox	Maybach OLVAR B 401216		
Speeds fwd./reverse	8/4		
Drive sprockets	front		
Final drive ratio	1 : 12/56		
Top speed km/h	41.5		
Range on/off road	170/120 km		
Steering	HS L 801 two-radius		
Turning circle m	4.16		
Suspension	torsion bars, longitudinal		
Lubrication	4 central batteries + high pressure		
Brakes made by	Süddeutsche Arguswerke, Type LB 900-4		
Brake activation	mechanical		
Brake type	disc (565 mm diameter)		
Brakes act on	drive		
Running gear	stepped		
Road wheel size	800 mm		
Vehicle track mm	2790, 2610 with loading tracks		
Track ground contact	4120 mm	4120 mm	4240 mm
Track width mm	800 mm, 660 (loading)		
Links per track	92		
Track type	Kgs 73/800/52		
Ground clearance	485 mm	485 mm	490 mm
Overall length mm	10,280	10,286	10,654
Overall width mm	3625/3755 w/ skirting plates	3625/3755 w/ skirting plates	3625
Overall height mm	3075	3090	2945
Ground pressure	1.02 kp/sq.cm	1.02 (loadg. trk. 1.23)	1.06 kp/sq.cm
Fighting weight kp	68,500	69,800	75,200
Crew	5	5	6
Fuel consumption	750/1000 liters/100 km	750/1000 liters/100 km	800/1100 l/100 km
Fuel capacity	85+145+145+80+65+170=860		
Armor, hull front	150 mm	150 mm	150 mm
Armor, hull sides	80 mm	80 mm	80 mm
Armor, hull rear	80 mm	80 mm	80 mm
Armor, turret front	100 mm	180 mm	250 mm
Armor, turret sides	80 mm	80 mm	80 mm
Armor, turret rear	80 mm	80 mm	80 mm
Grade climbing	35 degrees	35 degrees	35 degrees
Step climbing	850 mm	850 mm	880 mm
Fording	1750 mm	1600 mm	1750 mm
Trench crossing	2500 mm	2500 mm	2500 mm
Primary armament	8.8 cm KwK 43 L/71	8.8 cm KwK 43 L/71	12.8 cm Pak 44 L/56
Other armament	2 MG 34 (5850 rds.)	2 MG 34 (5850 rds.)	1 MG 34 (1500)
Notes	Porsche turret, 72 rounds	*) production turret 84 rounds	40 rounds

<table>
<tr><th>Vehicle</th><th>Panzerjäger Tiger
Test vehicle</th><th>Panzer Tiger II
test vehicle</th></tr>
<tr><td>Type</td><td>B, 212/258</td><td>B, VK 4503</td></tr>
<tr><td>Made by</td><td>Nibelungenwerk</td><td>Henschel</td></tr>
<tr><td>Years built</td><td>1944-1945</td><td>1945</td></tr>
<tr><td>Data source</td><td>FIAT Final Report 593</td><td>Maybach data</td></tr>
<tr><td>Motor</td><td>SGP Sla 16</td><td>Maybach HL 234</td></tr>
<tr><td>Cylinders</td><td>X-16</td><td>V-12, 60 degrees</td></tr>
<tr><td>Bore x stroke mm</td><td>135 x 160</td><td>130 x 145</td></tr>
<tr><td>Displacement cc</td><td>36,800</td><td>23,095</td></tr>
<tr><td>Compression ratio</td><td>14.5 : 1</td><td>7 : 1</td></tr>
<tr><td>RPM normal/max.</td><td>2000</td><td>3000</td></tr>
<tr><td>Engine power</td><td>750 HP</td><td>800 HP</td></tr>
<tr><td>Valves</td><td>drop</td><td>drop</td></tr>
<tr><td>Crankshaft bearings</td><td>5 journal</td><td>7 journal</td></tr>
<tr><td>Carburetor</td><td>4 Bosch PE 4 Diesel injectn.</td><td>1 Bosch gasoline injection, PZ 12</td></tr>
<tr><td>Firing order</td><td>1-13-12-15-9-14-11-16-10-6-3-8-2-5-4-7</td><td>12-1-8-5-10-3-7-6-11-2-9-4</td></tr>
<tr><td>Starter</td><td>Bosch 10/24</td><td>Bosch BPD 6/24</td></tr>
<tr><td>Generator</td><td>Bosch GULN 1000/24</td><td>Bosch GULN 1000/24-1000</td></tr>
<tr><td>Batteries/Volts/Ah</td><td>2/12/150</td><td>2/12/150</td></tr>
<tr><td>Fuel supply</td><td>pumps</td><td>pumps</td></tr>
<tr><td>Cooling</td><td>air, fans</td><td>water</td></tr>
<tr><td>Clutch</td><td colspan="2">multi-plate, wet</td></tr>
<tr><td>Gearbox</td><td colspan="2">Maybach LVAR B 401216</td></tr>
<tr><td>Speeds fwd./reverse</td><td colspan="2">8/4</td></tr>
<tr><td>Drive sprockets</td><td colspan="2">front</td></tr>
<tr><td>Final drive ratio</td><td colspan="2">1 :</td></tr>
<tr><td>Top speed km/h</td><td colspan="2">41.5</td></tr>
<tr><td>Range on/off road</td><td colspan="2">170/120 km</td></tr>
<tr><td>Steering</td><td colspan="2">HS L 801 two-radius</td></tr>
<tr><td>Turning circle</td><td colspan="2">4.8 meters</td></tr>
<tr><td>Suspension</td><td>torsion bars, longitudinal</td><td>torsion bars, transverse</td></tr>
<tr><td>Lubrication</td><td colspan="2">4 central batteries + high pressure</td></tr>
<tr><td>Brakes made by</td><td colspan="2">Süddeutsche Arguswerke</td></tr>
<tr><td>Brake activation</td><td colspan="2">mechanical</td></tr>
<tr><td>Brake type</td><td colspan="2">disc</td></tr>
<tr><td>Brakes act on</td><td colspan="2">drive</td></tr>
<tr><td>Running gear</td><td>steel road wheels</td><td>stepped road wheels</td></tr>
<tr><td>Road wheel size</td><td>800 mm</td><td></td></tr>
<tr><td>Vehicle track mm</td><td>2790</td><td>2790</td></tr>
<tr><td>Track ground contact</td><td>4415 mm</td><td>4100 mm</td></tr>
<tr><td>Track width mm</td><td>800</td><td>800</td></tr>
<tr><td>Links per track</td><td></td><td></td></tr>
<tr><td>Track type</td><td></td><td></td></tr>
<tr><td>Ground clearance</td><td>565 mm</td><td>485 mm</td></tr>
<tr><td>Overall length</td><td>10,370 mm</td><td>7260 mm</td></tr>
<tr><td>Overall width</td><td>3590 mm</td><td>3625 mm</td></tr>
<tr><td>Overall height</td><td>3050 mm</td><td></td></tr>
<tr><td>Ground pressure</td><td>1.05 kp/sq.cm</td><td>1.03 kp/sq.cm</td></tr>
<tr><td>Fighting weight</td><td>74,000 kp</td><td>68,000 kp</td></tr>
<tr><td>Crew</td><td>6</td><td>5</td></tr>
<tr><td>Fuel consumption</td><td>800/1100 liters/100 km</td><td>235 g/HP/hr</td></tr>
<tr><td>Fuel capacity</td><td>860 liters (7 tanks)</td><td></td></tr>
<tr><td>Armor, hull front</td><td>150 mm</td><td>150 mm</td></tr>
<tr><td>Armor,hull sides</td><td>80 mm</td><td>80 mm</td></tr>
<tr><td>Armor, hull rear</td><td>80 mm</td><td>80 mm</td></tr>
<tr><td>Armor, turret front</td><td>250 mm</td><td></td></tr>
<tr><td>Armor, turret sides</td><td>80 mm</td><td></td></tr>
<tr><td>Armor, turret rear</td><td>80 mm</td><td></td></tr>
<tr><td>Grade climbing</td><td>35 degrees</td><td>35 degrees</td></tr>
<tr><td>Step climbing</td><td>880 mm</td><td>850 mm</td></tr>
<tr><td>Fording</td><td>1750 mm</td><td>1750 mm</td></tr>
<tr><td>Trench crossing</td><td>2500 mm</td><td>2500 mm</td></tr>
<tr><td>Primary armament</td><td>12.8 cm Pak 44</td><td>8.8 or 10.5 cm KwK</td></tr>
<tr><td>Other armament</td><td>1 MG 42</td><td>2 MG 42</td></tr>
<tr><td>Notes</td><td></td><td></td></tr>
</table>

Appendix F:
Firms that Supplied the Tiger B Building Program

Hulls	Dortmund-Hoerder Hüttenverein, Dortmund Friedrich Krupp, Essen Skoda-Werke Pilsen, Königgrätz Works
Gearboxes	Zahnradfabrik Friedrichshafen, Waldwerke, Passau
Motors	Maybach, Friedrichshafen Auto-Union, Chemnitz
Tracks	August Engels, Velbert
Turrets	Wegmann & Co., Kassel
Fuel Tanks	I. Arnold, Friedensdorf on the Lahn
Pedals & levers	Bergische Achsenfabrik, Wiehl
Exhaust systems	Karl Born, Ascherslaben
Periscopes	Dorst AG, Oberlind-Sonneberg Sylbe & Ponndorf, Schmo"lln
Gas & starter rods	Hermann Fesel, Zwiesel
Gearbox suction	Hermann Fesel, Zwiesel
Skirting plates	Gotthardt & Kühne, Lommatzsch Wilhelm Lenze, Neheim-Hüsten
Ventilation systems	Imperial GmbH, Meissen
Ammunition racks	Richard Krahmer, Chemnitz Schneider & Korb, Bernsbach
Driver's seats	Wilhelm Lenze, Neheim-Hüsten
Gun mantlets	Arno Müller, Leipzig
Starters	Josef Münch, Brotterode
Hatch covers	O.D. Werk Willy Ostner, Branderbisdorf
Shock absorbers	Scheidt & Bachmann, Rheydt
Road wheels	Diana Maschinenfabrik
Drive sprockets	Bochumer Verein, Bochum Bergische Stahlindustrie, Remscheid Ruhrstahl AG, Witten-Annen Eisenwerke Oberdonau, Linz
Leading wheels	Dingler, Karcher & Co., Worms Ruhrstahl AG, Witten-Annen von Tongelsche Stahlwerke, Gu"strow Wittmann AG, Hagen-Haspe Knorrbremse AG, Volmarstein Deutsche Eisenwerke, Mülheim on the Ruhr
Road-wheel cranks	Rothe Erde GmbH, Dortmund Stahlwerke Braunschweig GmbH, Watenstedt Skoda-Werke, Pilsen Eisenwerke Krieglach, Niederdonau
Leading-wheel cranks	Rothe Erde GmbH, Dortmund Stahlwerke Braunschweig GmbH, Watenstedt
Track-drive housings	Dingler, Karcher & Co., Worms von Tongelsche Stahlwerke, Güstrow Deutsche Eisenwerke, Mülheim on the Ruhr Lindener Eisen- und Stahlwerke, Hannover Pleissner GmbH, Herzberg in the Harz
Gearbox housings	Dingler, Karcher & Co, Worms Meier & Weichelt, Leipzig Deutsche Eisenwerke, Mülheim on the Ruhr

Bow shields	Ruhrstahl AG, Witten-Annen		Röchling GmbH, Wetzlar
	Oberschlesische Hüttenwerke, Malapane Werk	Cogged arcs	Charlottenhütte, Niederschelden on the Sieg
			Klöckner-Werke AG, Osnabrück
Gutters & caps	Dingler, Kracher & Co., Worms	Steering brakes	Süddeutsche Arguswerke, Karlsruhe
	Meier & Weichelt, Leipzig	Ventilator drives	Ehrlich, Gotha
	Ruhrstahl AG, Witten-Annen	Turret drives	Ehrlich, Gotha
Torsion bar springs	Hösch AG, Hohenlimburg	Electric equipment	Bosch, Stuttgart

Addendum G As of 5/28/1942

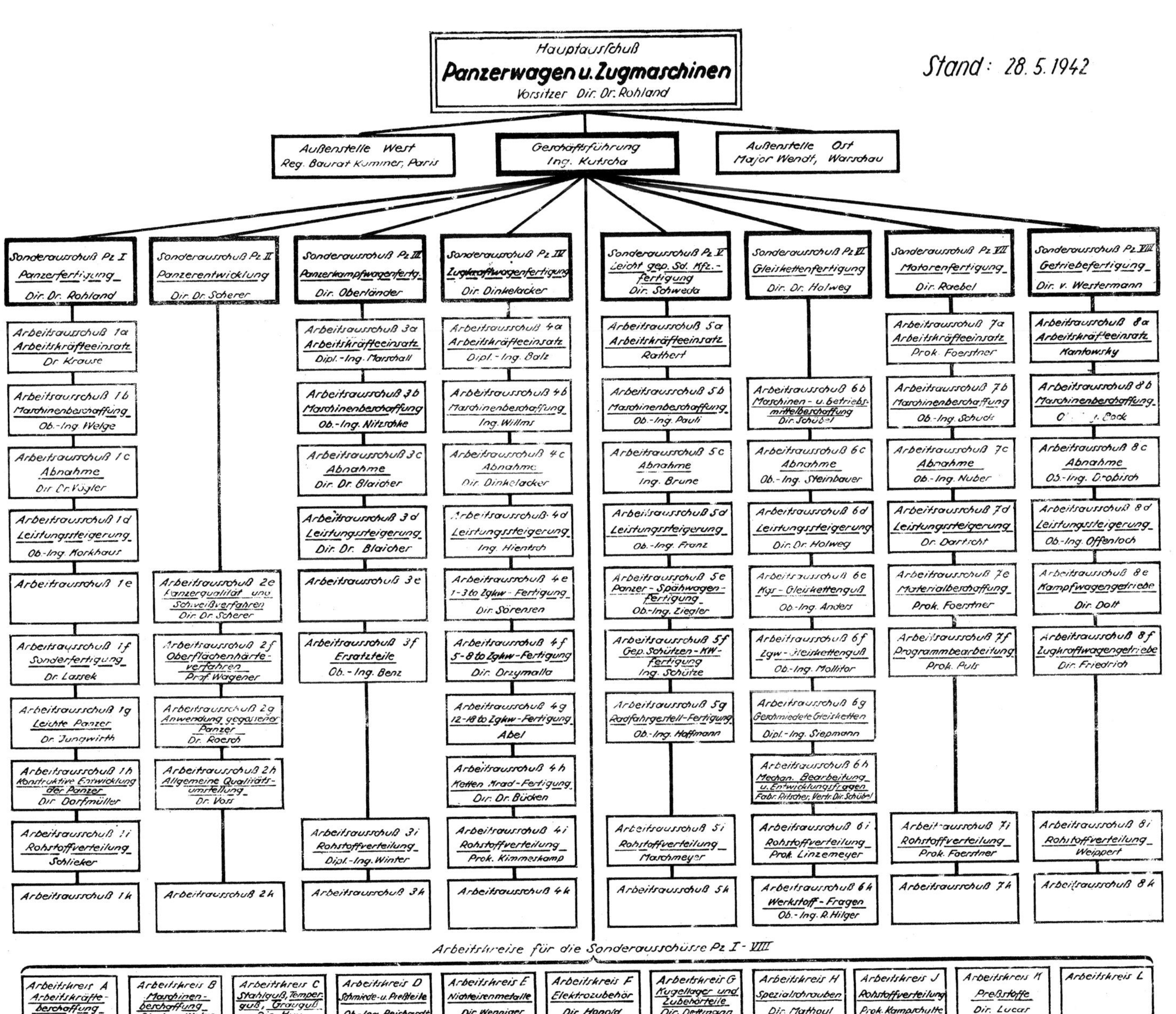

Addendum H

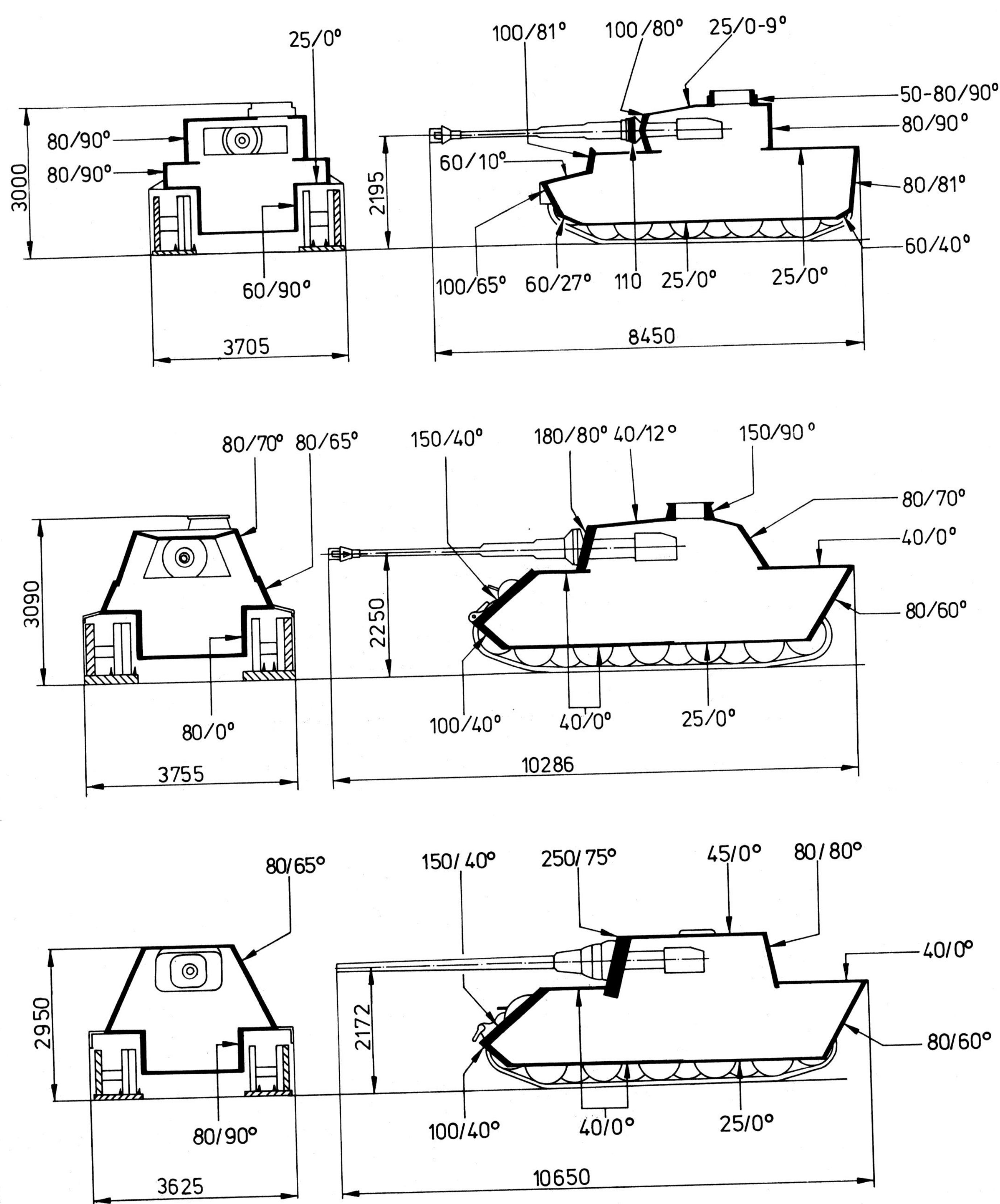

25/0°
80/90°
80/90°
3000
60/90°
3705
100/81°
100/80°
25/0-9°
50-80/90°
80/90°
60/10°
2195
80/81°
60/40°
100/65°
60/27°
110
25/0°
25/0°
8450
80/70°
80/65°
3090
80/0°
3755
150/40°
180/80°
40/12°
150/90°
80/70°
40/0°
2250
80/60°
100/40°
40/0°
25/0°
10286
80/65°
2950
80/90°
3625
150/40°
250/75°
45/0°
80/80°
40/0°
2172
80/60°
100/40°
40/0°
25/0°
10650

Appendix I:
Maybach Motor Data

Model HL	cylinders	Bore mm	Stroke mm	1-cyl. volume l	total volume l	rpm	HP	kp/HP
10	2	100	70	0,5498	1,0996	5000	70	
30	4	95	110	0,780	3,1188	3500	113	2,18
33	4	100	106	0,832	3,3301	4000	120	
42	6	90	110	0,700	4,1987	3000	100	3,8
45	6	95	110	0,780	4,6782	3800	147	2,32
50	6	100	106	0,832	4,9951	4000	180	
54	6	100	115	0,903	5,4193	2600	110	4,13
62	6	105	120	1,039	6,2345	2600	135	3,96
66	6	105	130	1,126	6,7540	3200	180	2,49
SHL 66	6	105	130	1,126	6,7540	2200	125	
85	12	95	100	0,709	8,5068	2600	185	4,21
87	6	125	130	1,595	9,5720	2400	180	
90/100	12	100	106	0,832	9,9903	4000	400	
92	6	120	135	1,527	9,1610	2400	180	
101	12	105	115	0,996	11,9494	3800	510	
116	6	125	150	1,841	11,0447	3000	265	2,52
120	12	105	115	0,996	11,9494	3000	300	2,98
140	6	140	150	2,309	13,8540	2400	250	
148	6	140	160	2,463	14,7780	2400	260	
150G	6	150	160	2,827	16,9646	3400	320	
157	12	115	125	1,298	15,5803	3500	550	
174	12	125	130	1,595	19,1441	3000	450	
210	12	125	145	1,779	21,3530	3000	650	

*) Test motor with fuel injection and supercharging
**) Test motor with fuel injection
***) Test Diesel motor
HL = Hochleistungsmotor (high-performance motor)

Appendix J:
8.8 cm *Kampfwagenkanone* 43 (L/71)

Measurements, weights and performance data

Measurements:	
Caliber	8.8 cm
Barrel length	6300 cm
Barrel length in calibers	71 caliber
Barrel length with muzzle brake	6595 mm
Rear breech surface to front lock surface	290 mm
Bore from front lock surface to muzzle	6010
Length of rifled section	5150.5 mm
Length of rifled section in calibers	58.5 caliber
Number of riflings	32
Depth of riflings	1.2 mm
Width of riflings	5.04 mm
Width of fields	3.6 mm
Breech:	
Diameter of rear wedge in back	132.4 mm
In front	123.9 mm
Diameter of front wedge in back	92.5 mm
In front	88 mm
Length of loading chamber	859.5 mm
Pitch of rifling	6 degrees, 30 minutes (27, 57 caliber)
Firing height	2245 mm
Elevation field	-8 to +15 degrees
Traverse field	360 degrees
Barrel brake:	
Medium braking power	9000 kp
Fluid contents	6 liters
Recoil length, smallest	380 mm
Recoil length, largest	580 mm
Pneumatic recuperator:	
Initial tension	60-5 kp/sq.cm
Fluid contents	5.3 liters
Air equalizer, initial tension	44 kg/sq.cm
Fluid contents (glycerine bath fluid)	1.78 liters
Weights:	
Barrel with breech and muzzle brake	1605 kg
Barrel with breech	1570 kg
Full barrel	1155 kg
Breech without lock	260 kg
Tension screw	26 kg
Breech lock with inner parts	55 kg
Lock mover	13 kg
Muzzle brake	35 kg
Barrel brake	65 kg
Pneumatic recuperator	60 kg

Total weight of gun 2265 kp

Ballistic data:

	8.8 cm PzGr 39/43	8.8 cm PzGr 40/43	8.8 cm SprGr 43	8.8 cm HLGr 39
Shot weight kg	10.16	7.5	9.4	7.65
Explosive charge kg	0.050	--	1.0	0.77
Muzzle velocity m/sec	1000	1130	750	600
Max. range at +15 degrees meters	--	--	10,000	7400
Muzzle power mt	516	480	269	140.4
Muzzle power per kp barrel Weight mkp	311	290	162	88
Designed gas pressure kg/sq.cm	3700	3700	3700	3700
Used gas pressure at 10° C, kg/sq.cm	2900	2900	1450	850

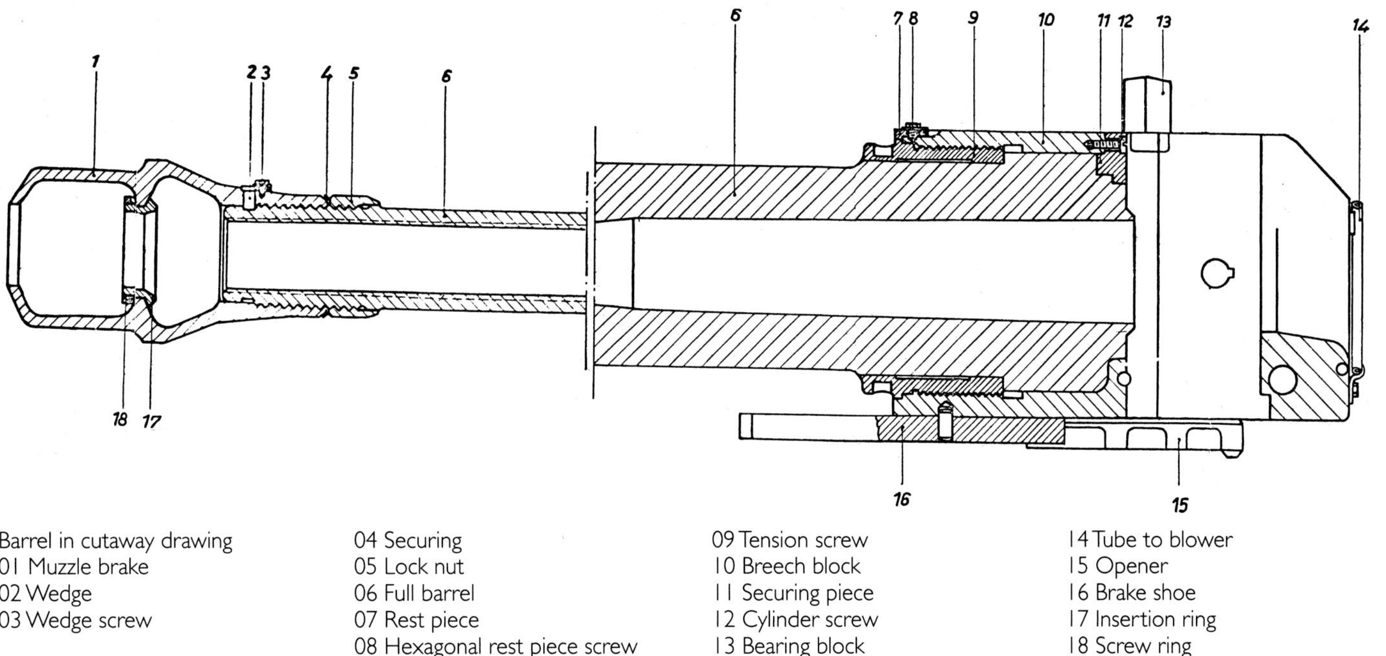

Barrel in cutaway drawing	04 Securing	09 Tension screw	14 Tube to blower
01 Muzzle brake	05 Lock nut	10 Breech block	15 Opener
02 Wedge	06 Full barrel	11 Securing piece	16 Brake shoe
03 Wedge screw	07 Rest piece	12 Cylinder screw	17 Insertion ring
	08 Hexagonal rest piece screw	13 Bearing block	18 Screw ring

Penetrating power	185*	217	90	500 m
At 90-degree angle	(205)**	(270)		
Of striking in mm at	165	193	90	1000 m
Range given in meters	(186)	(233)		
	147	170	90	1500 m
	(170)	(205)		
	132	152	90	2000 m
	(154)	(175)		
Shell weight kg	22.8	19.9	18.6	15.35
Shell length mm	1125.3	1103.1	1167.2	1157.4
Combustion chamber				
Volume liters	9.0	9.14	8.8	9.0
Weight of charge kg	6.8	6.8	3.8	2.0
Casing weight kg	5.8	5.8	5.8	5.8
Casing length mm	82	822	822	82
Casing diameter mm	132	132	132	132

According to training file for senior ensign's training course in 1944 according to Senger and Etterlin (*Kampfpanzer* 1916-1966).

For comparison: results of the 8.8 KwK 36 (L/56)

	8.8 cm	8.8 cm	8.8 cm	
	PzGr 39	PzGr 40	HIGr	
Shot weight kg	10.16	7.5	7.65	
Muzzle velocity	m/sec	810	930	600
Penetrating power	11	156	90	500 m
At 90-degree angle	100	140	90	1000
In mm by statement	92	125	90	1500
Of range in meters	84	110	90	2000

The 8.8 cm KwK 36 (L/56) installed in the Tiger I scarcely differed in penetrating power from the 7.5 cm KwK 43 L/70 of the panther tank. On the other hand, the further development as 8.8 cm KwK 43 L/71 used in the Tiger II showed considerably improved performance from the Panther gun.

Appendix K:
12.8 cm *Panzerjägerkanone* 80

Measurements, weights and performance data	
Barrel caliber	12.8 cm
Barrel length	7020 mm
Barrel length in calibers	55 caliber
Breech from front wedge surface	400 mm
Length of bore	6610 mm
Length of rifled part	5533 mm
Length of rifled part in calibers	43 caliber
Number of riflings	40
Depth of riflings	1.7 mm
Width of riflings	6.05 + 0.6 mm
Width of fields	4.0-0.6 mm
Loading chamber diameters	

Rear wedge part, back	176.4 + 0.2 mm
	Front
162.8 + 0.2 mm	
Front wedge part, back	162.8 + 0.2 mm
	Front
133.5 + 0.2 mm	
Length of loading chamber	1077 mm
Volume of loading chamber	2.88 liters
Pitch of rifling, constant (27 caliber)	6 deg. 38 min. 13 sec.
Center of gravity from rear end of	
	Barrel, with breech lock
1830 mm	
	Without breech lock
1920 mm	

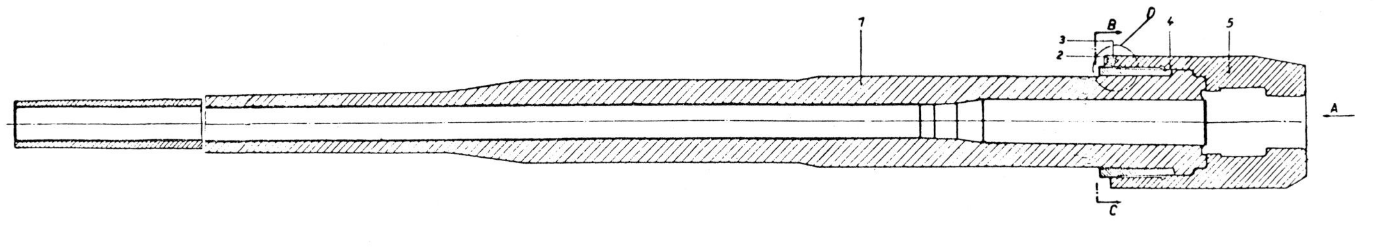

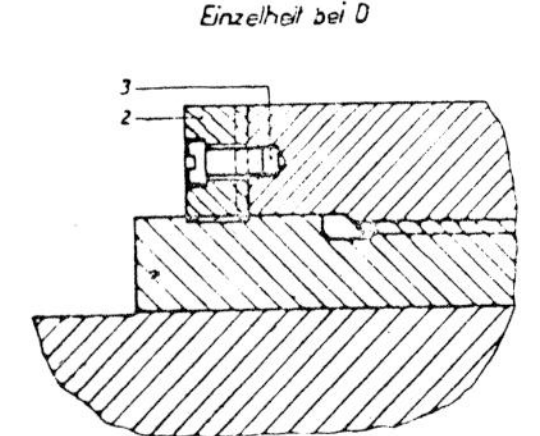

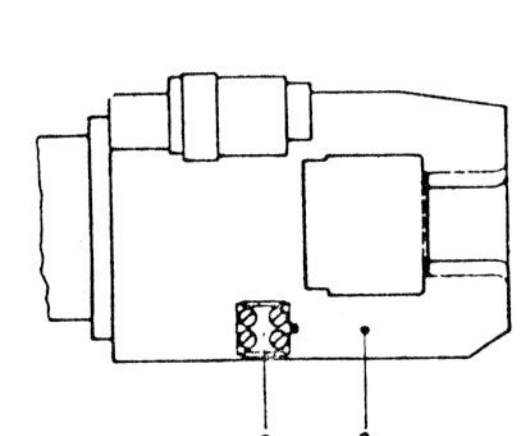

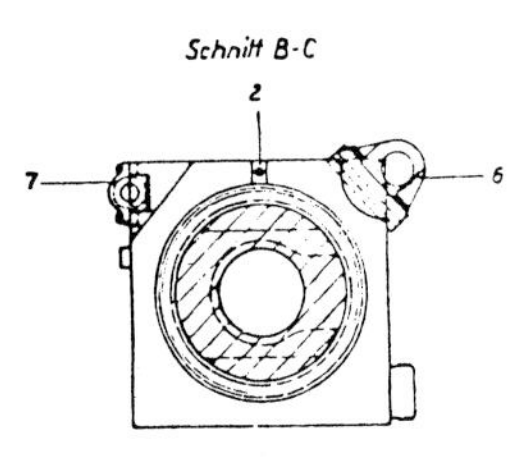

Cutaway view of barrel

1	Full barrel	4	Tension screw	7	Recuperator notch
2	Securing piece	5	Breechblock	8	Pitch notches
3	Cylinder screw	6	Brake notch	9	Cylinder pin

Mount measurements:		
Elevation field		+ 15, - & degrees
Traverse field, left & right, each		10 degrees
Firing height		2150 mm
Barrel brake:		
Median braking power		ca. 33,000 kg
Fluid volume		12.25 liters
Recoil length, normal		870 mm
Recoil, max. (firing pause)		900 mm
Recuperator:		
Initial air pressure		50 kg/sq.cm
Fluid volume		11.6 liters
Periscopic telescope 2/1:		
Setting range for 12.8 cm PzGr 43		from 0 to 4000 meters
Setting range for 12.8 cm SprG L/5.0 from o t0 8000 meters		
Marking divisions		from 0 to 176 lines
Weights:		
Barrel, complete with breech		3300 kg
Full barrel		2200 kg
Breechblock minus lock		810 kg
Tension screw		84 kg
Breech wedge with inner parts		192 kg
Barrel brake		121 kg
Recuperator		121 kg
Total weight of gun		7000 kg
Loading measurements:		
Gun without vehicle,	Length	8000 mm
	Width	1600 mm
	Height	1390 mm

Barrel overhangs front of vehicle by 3050 mm

Ammunition load weight, 12 cm PzGr 43:

Shot with packing 31.8 kg

Cartridge with packing 36.6 kg

12.8 cm SprG L/50 with packing 31.5 kg

Firing performance

	12.8 cm PzGr 43	12.8 cm SprGr
Shot length mm	496.5	623
Shot weight kg	28.3	28.0
Explosive charge kg	0.55	3.60
Muzzle velocity m/sec	920	750
Max. range at 15 deg. elevation m	--	12,200
Muzzle power mt	1270	800
Designed gas pressure kg/sq.cm	3700	3700
Used gas pressure kg/sq.cm	3000	2500
Combustion chamber length mm	967.5	967.5
Combustion chamber volume l	20.4	20.4
Weight of charge kg	15.0	12.2
Casing weight kg	11.6	11.6
Casing length mm	870	870
Casing rim diameter mm	192	192
Casing volume l	18.24	18.24

Appendix L: The "*Tigerfibel* 80"

The "*Tigerfibel*" was approved as a service manual (D 656/27) on August 1, 1943, by the Inspector-General of the Panzer Troops, *Generaloberst* Heinz Guderian. It constituted one of the first, and undoubtedly also one of the best attempts to get away from the dry form of expression, scarcely understandable to the troops, common until then in service manuals. It was created as a pocket sized guide to the operation and combat of the Tiger, using humorous portrayals lightened by—sometimes piquant—caricatures, jokes, morals, and proverbs, and a lot of "soldiers' German," to present all of the technical and tactical knowledge about the Tiger and make it generally understood and practical.

It made the not exactly simple subject matter into an exciting and relaxing reader, awakened joy in learning, and was packed with front-line wisdom. At the same time, it convinced the tiger crews of the superiority of their weapon when used properly, and it contributed much to making the Tiger familiar and popular to the troops.

D 656/27

... Mensch, so'n Schlitten! –

Er fährt sich wie ein Auto

Mit zwei Fingern kannst Du
700 PS schalten,
60 Tonnen lenken,
45 Sachen Straße,
20 Sachen Gelände und
4 m unter Wasser fahren.

The Tiger
Man, such a sled!
It drives like a car.
With two fingers you can
Shift 700 HP
Steer 60 tons
Drive a road at 45,
Drive offroad at 25,
Drive underwater at 4 mph.

Leutnant M. schoß im Nordabschnitt an einem Tage mit seinem Tiger

38 T 34 ab

und erhielt dafür das Ritterkreuz

It shoots everything to bits
Lieutenant M. with his Tiger, in one day in the Northern Sector, shot down 38 T 34 and received the Knight's Cross for it

Er hält alles aus....

It can stand anything...
This Tiger, in the Southern Sector, received in 6 hours:
27 shots from antitank rifles
14 shots of 5.2 cm and
11 shots from 7.62 cm guns.

Dieser Tiger erhielt im Südabschnitt in 6 Stunden:

227 Treffer Panzerbüchse,
14 Treffer 5,2 cm und
11 Treffer 7,62 cm.

Keiner ging durch.

Laufrollen und Verbindungsstücke waren zerschossen,

2 Schwingarme arbeiteten nicht mehr,

mehrere Pak-Treffer saßen genau auf der Kette, und

auf 3 Minen war er gefahren.

Er fuhr mit eigener Kraft noch 60 km Gelände.

Not one penetrated.
Road wheels and connecting pieces were shot up,
2 suspension arms didn't work any more,
Several antitank shells sat right on the tracks, and
It drove onto 3 mines.
It still covered 60 km offroad under its own power.

Er ist von außen nicht kaputt

zu kriegen - aber von innen . . . .

Die Gefahr sitzt in der Wanne!

Darum:

Lies aufmerksam die Tigerfibel,
sonst geht es Deinem Tiger übel.

Motto: Griesgrämig plagt sich nur der Tor
Der Tigermann lernt mit Humor

Moral: Selbst Moralisten und Moral
sind unmoralisch manches Mal!

From the outside there is nothing wrong
To be found—but from inside...
The danger is in the hull!
Therefore:
Read the *Tigerfibel* attentively;
Otherwise it will go badly for your Tiger.
Motto: Only the fool plagues himself grimly
The Tigerman learns with humor
Moral: Even moralists and morals
Are immoral sometimes!
The *Tiger-Fibel*
Issued on August 1, 1943, by
The Inspector-General of the Panzer Troops

Die Tiger-Fibel

HERAUSGEGEBEN AM 1. 8. 1943 VOM

GENERALINSPEKTEUR DER PANZERTRUPPEN

Generalinspekteur
der Panzertruppen

H. Qu., den 1. 8. 43

Ich genehmige die Tigerfibel

Guderian

CONTENTS

BÜCHER, BLÄTTER, BILDER UND BERICHTE ÜBER DEN TIGER

Buch

- D 656/21+ Pz.Kpfwg.Tiger, Ausf. E, Firmen-Gerätbeschreibung und Bedienungsanweisung zum Fahrgestell
- D 656/22+ Pz.Kpfwg. Tiger, Ausf. E und Pz.Bef.Wg. Tiger, Ausf. E, Gerätbeschreibung und Bedienungsanweisung zum Turm
- D 656/23 Pz.Kpfwg. Tiger, Ausf. E, Pflegeheft
- D 656/24 Pz.Kpfwg. Tiger, Ausf. E, Fristenheft
- D 214 8,8 cm KwK 36
- D 635/5 Kraftfahrzeuge im Winter
- D 635/50 Kraftfahrzeuge in Staub, Hitze und Schlamm
- D 659/4 Bergen von Pz.Kpfwg.
- D 659/2 Verladen auf der Eisenbahn
- D 659/2a Pz.Kpfwg. Tiger und Panther, Verladen auf der Eisenbahn
- D 949/2 Der 10-Wattsender UKWc
- D 988/2 Der UKW-Empfänger e
- D 1008/1 Die Funk- und Bordsprechanlage im Pz.Kpfwg. VI
- D 656/23 Handbuch für den Tigerfahrer
- D 656/27 Die Tigerfibel
- HdV 469/IIa Pz.Erkennungsdienst Rußland
- HdV 469/IIb Pz.Erkennungsdienst England-Amerika
- HdV 469/IIIb Pz.Beschußtafel Panzer
- HdV 305 Mun.Behandlung

Es bestellen: Feldeinheiten bei Feldvorschriftenstellen
Ersatzeinheiten und Schulen über Stellv. Gen. Kdo.

Blätter Paderborn:

- 1 Allgemeine Angaben über den Pz.Kpfwg. Tiger
- 2 Das Turmzielfernrohr (T. Z. F. 9 c)
- 3 Munitionsunterbringung im Pz.Kpfwg. VI
- 5 Verwendung und Anbringung des Einheitsgerätes (Fuchs)
- 6 Tätigkeit zum Inbetriebsetzen des Schwungkraftanlassers
- 7 Höhenrichtaufsatz
- 8 Die Bordsprechanlage (mit Skizze)
- 9 Das Boehringer-Sturm-Ölgetriebe
- 10 Bedienungsanweisung und Störungen des Turmschwenkwerkes
- 11 Beschreibung der Trennwand des Pz.-Kpfwg. VI (mit Skizze)
- 12 Die selbsttätige Löschanlage
- 13 Schaltgetriebe und Auspuffkrümmerkühlung
- 14 Abschleppen bei Motor-Getriebe-Laufrollenschaden
- 15 Gliederung einer schweren Panzer-Kompanie
- 16 Erfahrungen im Wintereinsatz im Osten (Ofw. Beyer)
- 17 Zusammenwirken der Pz.Kpfwg.-Besatzung
- 18 Waffentechnische Hinweise für die Besetzung
- 19 Aufbau der zerlegbaren Verladebrücke für Pz.Kpfwg. VI (mit Skizze)
- 20 Das Schießen von Pz.Kpfwg. Tiger mit 8,8 cm KwK.
- 21 Visierbereich der Pz.Kpfwg.Kanone für 2 m Zielhöhe
- 24 Panzerschießlehre (Unterlagen Putlos)
- 25 Das Maybach-Olvar-Getriebe und deren Betätigung bei Notschaltung
- 26 Die elektrische Abfeuerung
- 28 Kurze Beschreibung des E. M. o. 9 mR. Merkblatt über die Ausbildung am Pz.-Kpfwg. Tiger, Ausbildung und Einsatz der schweren Panzer-Kompanie

Bestellen bei Pz.Ausb.Abt. 500, Paderborn

Putlos:

- 57 Zusammenwirken der Kpfwg.Besatzung
- 58 Pz.Schießausbildung am Sandkasten
- 65 Das Schießen mit der 8,8 cm KwK
- 321—75 Gerätebeschreibung zur 8,8 cm KwK 36
- 322 Waffentechnische Hinweise
- 323 Praktische Hinweise
- 324 Schulschießübungen mit KwK 8,8 cm 36
- 374 Pz.Schießausbildung Teil A

Bestellen bei der Pz-Schießschule in Putlos bei Oldenburg, Holstein

Bilder: UT für Pz.Kpfwg. Tiger

Fahrgestell

- UT 656/1 Laufwerk
- UT 656/2 .—. (Motor)
- UT 656/3 Wechselgetriebe
- UT 656/4 Steuerung
- UT 656/5 Lenkgetriebe
- UT 656/6 Leitrad mit Kettenspanner
- UT 656/7 Kraftstofförderung
- UT 656/8 Kühlanlage
- UT 656/9 Turmschwenkwerk
- UT 656/10 Höhenrichtmaschine, Geschütz- und MG-Lagerung
- UT 656/11 Turmschwenkwerk und Pz.Führerkuppel 8,8 cm KwK
- UT 656/12 Geschütz, Rohr im Schnitt
- UT 656/13 Luftvorholer
- UT 656/14 Wirkungsweise des Luftvorholers
- UT 656/15 Rohrbremse, Wirkungsweise der Rohrbremse
- UT 656/16 Sicherheitsschalter zur Rohrbremse
- UT 656/17a Verschluß, Teile der Bewegungseinrichtung
- UT 656/17b Verschluß, Verschlußkeil
- UT 656/18 Gesamtplan der elektrischen Abfeuerung

Bestellen bei Heereszeugamt Kassel

Berichte sind zu richten an: Dienststelle 10131 G

Doppel an OKH/Inspekteur der Panzertruppen, Berlin-Wilmersdorf, Fehrbelliner Platz 4
Fernruf 86 71 41 App. 2736
Ortsruf 87 93 51 App. 2736
Querruf J2 8071 App. 2736

Driver
Gustav, the Offroad Rover
You are driving a tank that has few enemies, but also few brothers. It is up to you whether it becomes a raptor ready to spring or a dead wreck.

Motto: Little things add up to completeness,
but completeness is not a little thing.

Motto: Kleinigkeiten machen die Vollkommenheiten aus,
aber Vollkommenheit ist keine Kleinigkeit.

The runner needs two hours to get ready for the start.

2 Stunden braucht der Rennläufer, um sich für den Kampf fertigzumachen.

Sonst nützen das beste Gerät und das härteste Training nichts.

Otherwise the best equipment and the best training mean nothing.

START

ESSEN
EATING

SCHMIEREN
OILING

WARMLAUFEN
WARMING UP

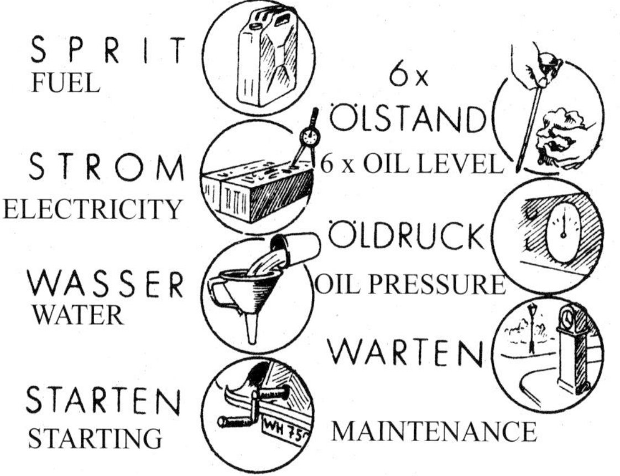

The Tiger driver needs two hours to get the tank ready to run.
Otherwise he'll flop because of a little detail.
Avoiding is better than healing. So think of these points before every start:
Fuel—electricity—water—starting—6 x oil level—oil pressure—waiting

Motto: Oh Friend, gasoline has two sides.

**Motto: Oh Freund, zwei Seiten hat der Sprit.
Mal fährst Du und mal fliegst Du mit.**

Sometimes you drive, sometimes you fly with it.
Gasoline is a fuel
When it is turned to gas, mixed with air in small amounts, and ignited, it drives the Tiger, all 60 tons, down the street with just little explosions, as a child fills a tire with just little puffs.
With one liter in the tank you can drive 200 meters.
The power of a giant is in it, but it is divided over half a minute like a massage, and the Tiger likes that.

Sprit

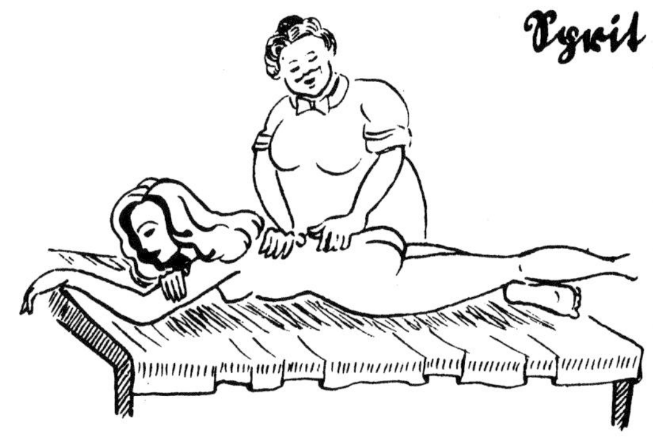

Gasoline
Gasoline is explosive
If the same liter flows into the hull instead of the carburetor, then it is turned to gas by the engine heat, the gas mixes with the swirling air, and is exploded all at once by a spark or heat.
This liter blows up your Tiger, so that the engine cover and your roof are blown upward farther than you can throw a stone. The tremendous power unites in one k.o. punch, and even a Tiger can't stand that.

Darum:

Therefore: Gas up—but don't let anything spill.
Otherwise the Tiger burns or blows up.
Attention! When the fuel runs out—immediately switch to the reserve tank. When the reserve runs out—immediately stop and turn off the motor. 30 seconds' work!

Otherwise the fuel pump and lines will empty, and no fuel will flow after you fill up: Unscrew the air filter and housing, remove the hollow screws from the carburetor, let the electric pump run until fuel comes (don't let it flood). Put everything back together.
One hour's work!

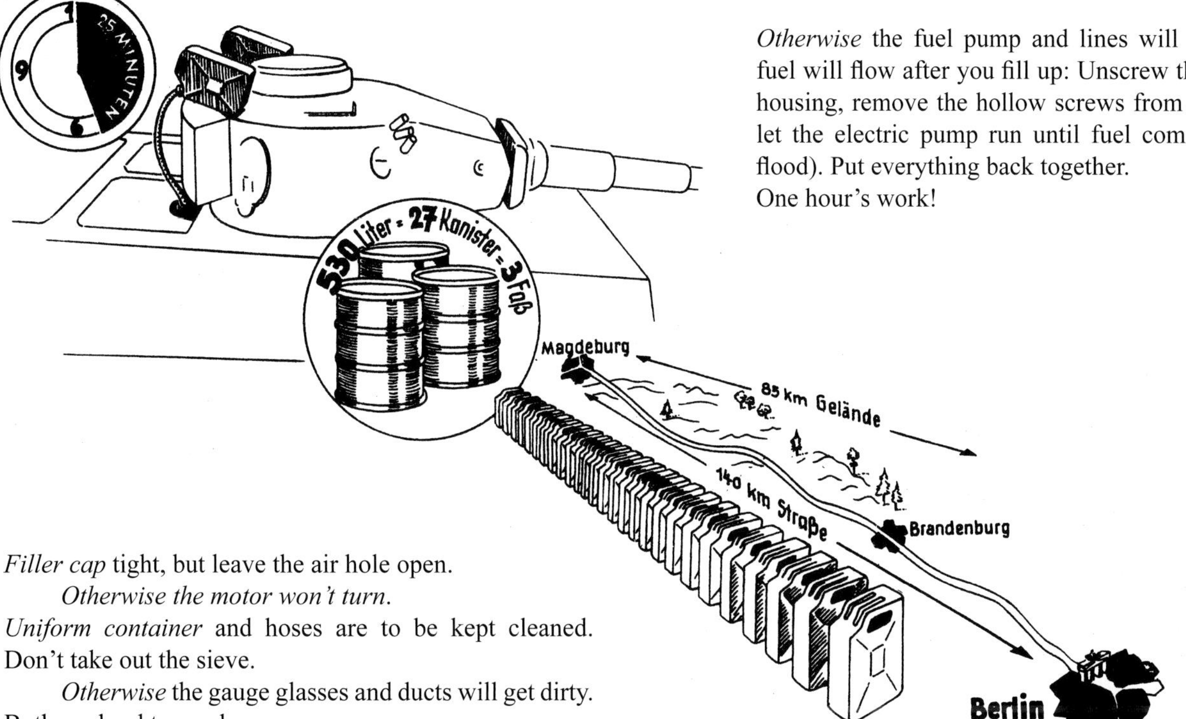

Filler cap tight, but leave the air hole open.

Otherwise the motor won't turn.

Uniform container and hoses are to be kept cleaned. Don't take out the sieve.

Otherwise the gauge glasses and ducts will get dirty. Both are hard to reach.

Clean the gauge glasses of dirt and water. Don't damage thickenings. Rather, change them put in clean. Tighten the casing nuts.

Otherwise the Tiger burns or blows up.

Check fuel lines
and pumps for thickenings. Handle lines and connections with feeling. Don't force thickened lumps (then they'll come loose while driving).

Otherwise the tiger burns or blows up.

The carburetor
Carefully clean and blow through the main jet, check to see if the float needle moved right back up after being pushed down (it must hang there motionless or be damaged).

Otherwise it will backfire when idling.

When there's a fire,
the warning lamp by the driver's visor lights up. The system sprays extinguisher fluid (if it doesn't, the loader must push the fire-extinguisher button, and you must at once turn off the motor and fuel, not step on the gas as in other vehicles.

Otherwise the extinguisher gases that were supposed to put out the fire will be sucked up. The fluid itself does not extinguish.

Spray jets must be sprayed by the heat sensors for cooling.

Otherwise the system will empty itself at once at the first flame. It is built to run 5 to 7 seconds.

The heat sensors
And lines must not be damaged or bent during work. Replace the extinguisher with a new one if the pressure sinks below 4 atmospheres. Check the seals,

Otherwise you'll have to get by with the hand extinguisher.

Causes of fires
Are always fuel or oil in the hull. Check the lines as soon as you can.

Otherwise it will blow up all over again.

Moral:
When fuel drips out of your fuel line,
You'll get the nicest explosive effect.

Motto:
Who takes good care of his batteries
will be rewarded richly.

They are your best friends
They crank up your motor when there's shooting outside, they fire your shells, they suck the smoke away! You can see in the dark, keep your direction in smoke, understand each other in the greatest noise, and hear and speak 10 km away.

Give out a round often,
So they can run at full speed!
Keep them warm
A charged battery freezes only at -65 degrees,
A flat one at -10.
That happens very easily, for tension and content decrease very quickly when it is really cold.

Fill with distilled or boiled water, or melted snow if necessary in winter, until the plates are covered by a finger's breadth. Keep the clamps acid free, well tightened and greased.
Otherwise the battery gets dirty or messy.

In the winter, start by turning the crank; that is cheaper than running down and recharging the battery!
If the tension sinks below 1 volts, or if you leave the tiger in the cold a long time—take out the batteries and take care of them.
Otherwise they'll burst!
12 volts! Don't let them sink below 11 volts! When you check, put one pole of the voltmeter on the body, the other on the distance light bracket. Turn on the light. If you check with the liquid tester, mark 1.285 is charged, mark 1.15 is uncharged. Don't make any short circuits, don't squeeze.
Otherwise the plates will bend.

Moral:
It is an old, old story:
Who is really full won't freeze much.

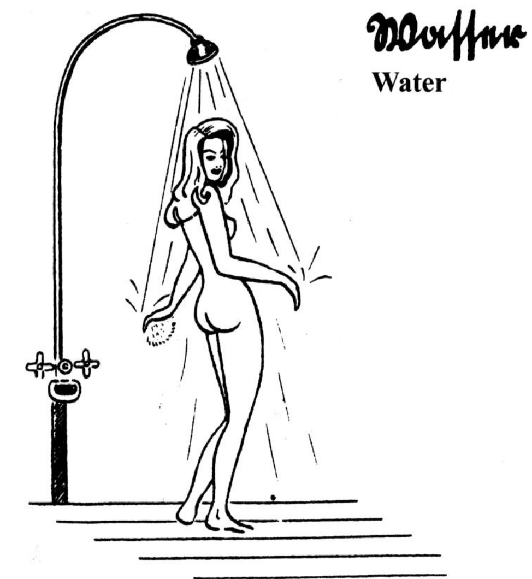

Motto:
The water's power does good
In case you thought of Glysantin [anti-freeze].
Water is a means of cooling
It flows around the housing endlessly like a fresh shower and takes the heat, that arises from burning and rubbing, away to the radiators. In winter, it also stores the warmth as a battery stores power, and thus keeps the motor ready to start.
Your Tiger needs 120 liters. At 85 degrees it feels just fine.

Water is an explosive
When it freezes into ice, it expands by 10%. If the walls can't bend, they are broken by force. Ice breaks stone and iron.
The 120 liters then become 132 liters, and there's no room for them, even in a Tiger's stomach.
Therefore:

When you are thirsty, give the good animal something to drink too, and make it clean water. If you can get the cooling protection *Akorol*, put it in pure, but carefully: Akorol is poisonous. Like a Steinhäger, it prevents rust and calcium buildups.

95 degrees—Attention! That is too hot already. Now the oil stops lubricating, and you can look for a new motor. It's better to stop at once and check

In winter, they mix grog with something stronger. Mix your cooling water with Glysantin in cold weather.

Here is the famous recipe from the Ice Bar in Sa Ukalt:

2 liters of Glysantin to	3 liters of water.
To -20 degrees, then	48 liters of Glysantin
	+72 liters of water equal
	120 liters
to -40 degrees, the opposite	72 liters of Glysantin
	+48 liters of water equal
	120 liters

Constantly check the cooling system, because Glysantin dissolves all deposits. But don't mix Glysantin with Akorol.

Therefore, fill it up until the sieve bottom is reached. Check the tube holders and pipes, especially the lowest ones, which link The radiators.

1. Do you have enough water in the radiator?
2. Are the ventilators turned on?
3. Do the sliding couplings work?
4. Is the oil cooler sealed?

Otherwise: The engine will seize.

Otherwise: The engine will burst.
So open the filler cap, let the hot water out through a rubber hose to the drain valve. Before refilling, rinse the cooling system and seal the drain valve shut. After a week turn it off hot, let it stand three hours so rust and slime settle, refill it through a linen cloth, also fill the water after working on the engine.

Otherwise: The radiator will leak.

Moral:
The Tiger drinks the water just
As gladly as you drink berry wine.

Motto:
The long-distance runner leaves himself time,
Whoever starts hastily, doesn't get far.

Starten
Starting

Before the start, the ski racer carefully checks the seat of the shoes and the positions of the bindings. Millimeters can decide everything.

That is the Firewall
Das ist die Brandwand

Before starting, carefully check the positions of all levers. One look must tell you whether everything is in order. They are all vitally important.

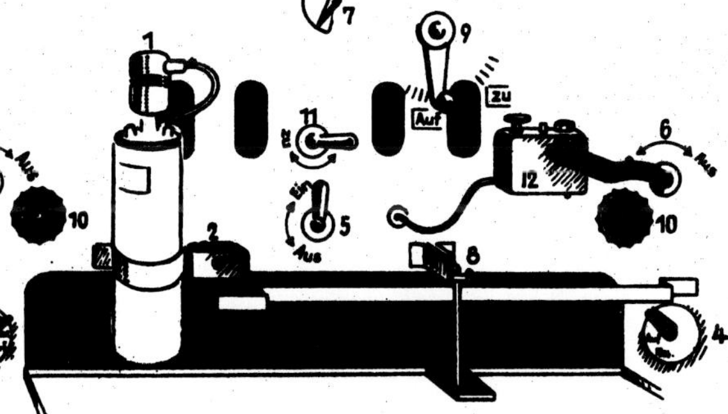

Fire extinguisher system
Safety kit

3. Bottom hatch	up	so gases can escape, also keep the rear hatch open, so fresh air comes in from above. Close only before fording, in mud, and before combat.	*Otherwise* the Tiger will explode.
4. Fuel gauges	up	Fuel tanks empty one after another. When the fuel runs out, shut off the engine at once.	*Otherwise*—see Fuel.
5. Battery main switch	in	It shuts off all users.	*Otherwise* you can't start.
6. Ventilator switch	on "land"	The ventilators are shut off for U-turns.	*Otherwise* the engine overheats.
7. Air outlet	on "land"	The fuel tanks are ventilated into the engine compartment.	*Otherwise* into the open.
8. Extractor	down	It throttles the air in the outlet channel between the gearbox and the fans.	*Otherwise* the gearbox gets hot.
9. Outlet blower	on "land"	It guides the hot gearbox air to the vents or into the engine compartment.	*Otherwise* the motor gets hot.
10. Ventilation throttle	open	It leads the hot engine air to the vents.	*Otherwise* the motor gets hot.
11. Slider	closed	Open only at the same time as the front scoop.	*Otherwise* it will stink in the fighting compartment.
Fuel pump	in	So the carburetor already has fuel when you start.	*Otherwise* the battery will run down.
Shift lever	in neutral	Lever forward, drive forward; lever back, drive backward.	*Otherwise* it will drive at once.
Ignition key	in	Don't turn, shut off other users.	*Otherwise* the battery will run down.
Clutch	step down	So the starter won't need to turn the gears.	*Otherwise* the battery will run down.
Starter button	push	Better longer and with longer pauses.	*Otherwise* the battery will run down.
Starter button	let go	As soon as the engine starts.	*Otherwise* the starter will be damaged.
Choke lever	back	when the engine runs evenly.	*Otherwise* the spark plugs will get sooty.
Gas lever	turn on lightly	Let engine run slowly 5 minutes, so test light flickers. Don't race the engine.	*Otherwise* it will stutter.
Clutch	let up	so the gears become hand-warm.	*Otherwise* you won't be able to shift.
Gas	give	Let it warm up, raising it from 1000 to 1500 rpm.	*Otherwise* the spark plugs will become sooty.

In the winter

The oil becomes hard and stiff. The shafts stick in their bearings, the pistons stick to the cylinder walls. It takes the strength of a bear to separate these parts and keep them moving until the oil becomes warm and liquid. Although the tiger starts at once with the electric starter, even at -20 degrees, start it with the hand crank. Spare the batteries.

Otherwise you can't start when the bullets are flying.

When it is very cold,

One Tiger can warm another. The hot cooling water of the one engine is pumped into the cold engine and its cold water is warmed. Afterward, check carefully to see if the engine is running normally.

Otherwise the Tiger may fly into the air.

Ventilators

Should be shut, so the engine warms up faster, so watch the thermometer closely.

Otherwise the engine will boil over like a pot of soup.

Spray fuel in

When the crank can't do the job.

Otherwise you'll lose confidence and time.

In the tropics

And in summer heat, set the ventilator fan at high speed.

Otherwise the motor will overheat.

Crank starting

Turn the hand crank clockwise. Push the crank in quickly and hold it until the motor starts, then let it go! If the pinion doesn't keep turning, crank again. Don't crank when the motor is running!

Exchanging cooling water:

A. Fill hoses.
1. Turn off the engine.
2. Screw hoses onto the red attachment.
3. Switch off cooler via the intake chokes.
4. Turn off cooler, remove radiator screws.
5. Let motor run, hold hose high, press tappet on free end of hose until water comes.
6. Replace lacking water and Glysantin.

B. Transferring:
1. Turn off engine when it reaches 60 degrees.
2. Attach hoses so that a red one is always attached to a green one.
3. On the warming motor, push choke in, ventilator out, cooler screws off.
4. Let motor run first at 2400k, then 2000 rpm, until the other motor reaches 50 degrees.
5. Turn off motor, choke out, ventilator in, close cooler screws.

Switch lever

Of the ventilator drive is removed and screwed back on in "increased cooling" position.

Moral:

A little turn and a hot drink
Will start even the iciest one.

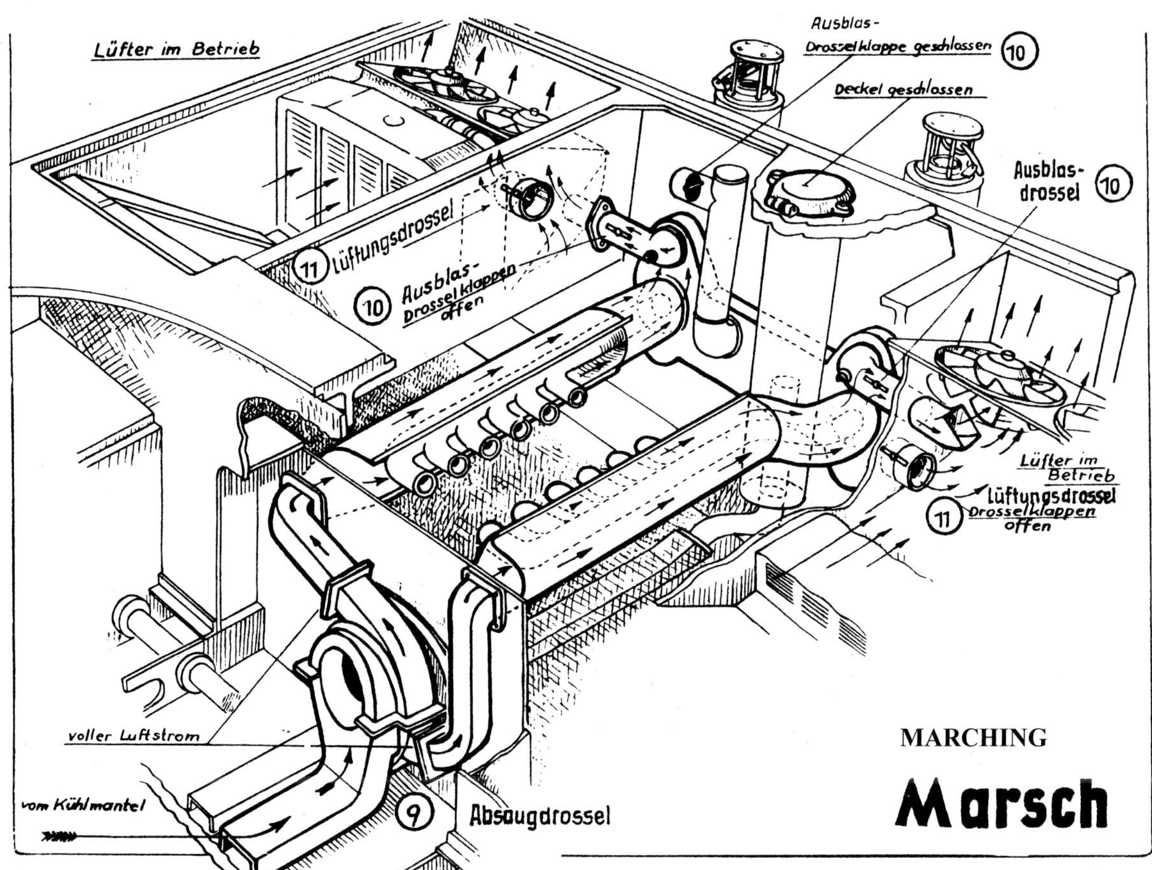

Motto:
The oil here is the sun's enemy,
But to the Tiger it's a joy.

Check the Oil Six Times

Oil is a lubricant

When you rub your hands together, they get hot. You don't need to rub them fast or with too much power. But if you put real skin oil in between, they stay cool.

Your machine turns 3000 times a minute with 700 HP. It would get burning hot, and all its moving parts would seize; you wouldn't drive one kilometer if oil didn't absorb the heat and rinse it away. Too little oil is dangerous.

Oil is inflammable

When it leaks from the lines, is thrown out by shafts, drips from faulty seals and mixes with gasoline, it burns red hot and sets pools of gas and other things in the hull afire.

Too much oil is dangerous.

Therefore:

Where to fill?	What to fill?	How much to fill?	Otherwise what happens?
1. Motor	28 liters of motor oil	Between upper and lower marks	The spark plugs will get oiled; you'll use much oil and many motors
2. Gearbox	30 liters of gearbox oil	Till the stick just Goes into it	You can't shift or steer.
3.Final drive (right)	6 liters of gearbox oil	Remove small (not big) checking screw	Filling too much or too little is bad.
4. Final drive (left)	6 liters of gearbox oil	Fill until oil runs over	
5.Turret drive oil	5 liters of gearbox below opening	Fill until one finger	You can't turn the turret.
6.Ventilator drive	7 liters of gearbox oil	Only to highest mark with tank stopped	It will be thrown at the exhaust mantle

Oil level
Too much oil is just as bad as too little. With motor running (1000 rpm) and at least 50 degrees warmth, measure and top off, best again after driving 5 kilometers.

Otherwise the oil won't Be the right amount.

Don't lose oil
Be sure seals are solid, tighten filler and drain screws, Check lines, trace every drip, notice sprayed or thrown oil, clean hull bottom through bottom hatch.

Otherwise the Tiger will burn.

Change oil
Before and after winter, at prescribed mileage and after repairs.

Otherwise you'll need a New motor.

In the winter
You can drive safely with *Wehrmacht* (Winter) motor Oil to -30 degrees. Under -30, draw off 4 liters of oil from hand-warm motor, add 4 liters of gasoline, and run motor at medium speed a short time to mix them.

Otherwise the motor will seize.

After driving 3 hours
The gas evaporates when the motor is over 60 degrees. You can drive on, but before you shut down, replace the evaporated gasoline. If it's not all gone, check with the blower gauge.

Otherwise it won't turn over the next morning.

Wehrmacht gearbox oil 8 E (green) is good down to -40, Thus doesn't need to be thinned.

Moral:
The Tiger owes its powers to
The right high pressure of its juices.

Motto:
The Tiger [tank] owes its powers mainly to the correct high pressure of its fluids.

Oil Pressure
The right amount of oil alone is not enough. Oil in the sump is just as useless as beer in the cellar if the pressure is lacking to pump it up to the thirsty consumers' hot, dry throats. Only then does the place come alive. Only then can you shift up and down smoothly, steer smoothly, and turn the turret like a weathervane.

The oil pressure gauge
Must show a pressure of at least 3 atm when the motor is idling and 7 atm when driving. If a line breaks or is clogged, or the bearing play is too great, the pressure drops. Then you must shut off the motor at once. *Otherwise the motor will seize.*
You must clean the oil filter at every oil change; it's better to do it more often.

1. Unscrew lid, take out filter packet.
2. Loosen wing nuts, draw out filter and tension plates singly.
3. Clean plates and housing thoroughly with gasoline.

Attention! Gasoline is leaded and not good for your skin.

4. First put in a filter plate, then alternating tension and filter plates, and press down Firmly with end plate and wing nut.
5. Insert packet, screw lid on, don't forget pressure screw!

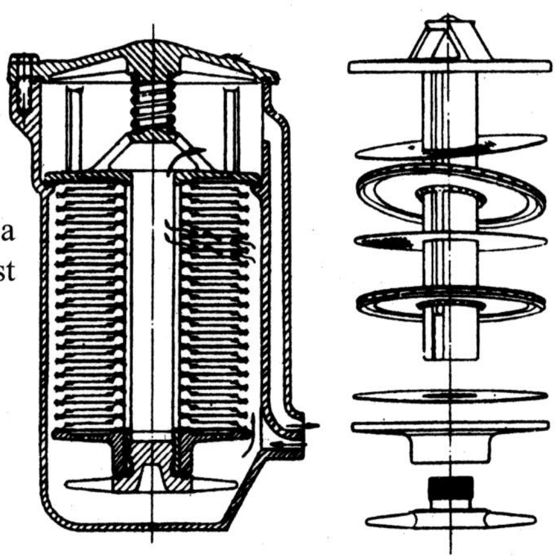

Moral: For life as well, the principle is good:
The pressure makes the atmosphere.

Maintenance

Before the race, the skier makes a couple spurts and half a circle to keep warm. Who starts cold gets muscle tears but no performance.

Before driving, the Tiger driver lets his motor run 5 minutes in summer, 15 in winter, until the cooling water reaches 50 degrees, the final drives are hand-warm, and the oil pressure reaches 3 atu. *Otherwise* the bearings are ruined.
So give some gas and let the motor run between 1000 and 1500 rpm. Don't let it idle.
Otherwise the spark plugs will pick up carbon.
Don't be lazy waiting for the time, but wait on the Tiger!

A. Lubrication

Motto: The movie star just greases her skin,
The driver greases the chassis.

Those who take good care are superior to others. Better more often and more thorough. Put on "day" and "night cream." *Otherwise* you'll have trouble with the storekeeper.

Moral: You'll find, even if a lot of dirt sticks on,
The nipple in the lubrication scheme.

Motto: The air, through its pressure, gives
The right sound in digestion.

Dust is your enemy
If you drive 7 kilometers, your wide tracks stir up dust from 1 hectare or 4 more of ground.
You will be seen from afar and lose your most effective weapon—surprise

Dust is your deadly enemy
While you drive these 7 km, your Tiger uses 170,000 liters of the same dusty air that you inhale.
It must inhale as much dust in 7 km as you would in 10 days if you were riding on the dustiest spot on the rear of the tank.
Your two air filters must stand all that; they are your only weapons against this deadly enemy.

The air filter

Catches the dust just as flypaper catches flies. But when it is full, it no longer works. The air comes into the cylinder almost unfiltered, the fine dust is ground up between the piston and the cylinder wall and scratches endlessly. With wear, gas and oil consumption increase because the pistons are loose in the cylinders.
The filter also lets too little oil through; then the motor draws in more fuel, which pushes the oil off the cylinder walls. Again fuel consumption increases with wear, this time because of insufficient lubrication. The two increase together, and soon you break down and need a new motor.
You can drive your Maybach engine 5000 kilometers in action if you give it clean air to breathe. Otherwise you won't get 500 kilometers.

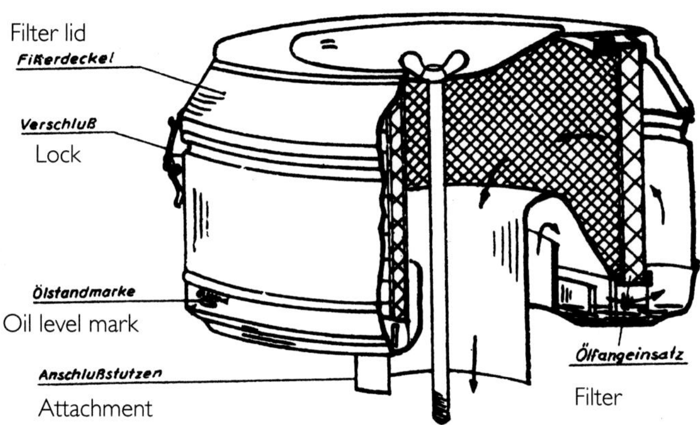

Therefore:
After every dusty drive, clean the air filter! Loosen the wing nut, lift the filter from the intake, down from the armor, locks off, lid off, filter out. Clean filter and housing in gasoline (caution - poison!) and dry well. Fill with used motor oil to the red mark. Replace filter, make sure it is well sealed. Put lid on, set filter smoothly and tightly on the intake, and fasten with wing nut...and don't forget the pre-filter!

The 4 Double Carburetors

They feed your motor loyally, but they demand *caution* and *feeling* from you! Don't bore and fuss at them with needles or thread, but work with wood chips and small pliers; don't screw the lid on too tightly!

Clean them often and be very sure that
The fuel level is right (drain by unscrewing the main line);
The air intake is set so you can read 38 or 40 from above;
The ring lies properly on the air intake (neither too high nor too low);
The choke flaps close firmly;
The floats don't get bent, and their mountings are working;
The rids fit smoothly into the accelerator;
The side hole of the idler and all the lines in the carburetor are open.
Otherwise the motor will jerk and stutter.
Avoid extra air with
Faultless seals and sealing surfaces.
Otherwise the motor won't run smoothly.
Think about idling.
Screw pairs of air screws all the way in together, and then back them off until the motor runs smoothly: determine the idling speed with the limiting screw on the air intake.
Otherwise the motor will start badly.

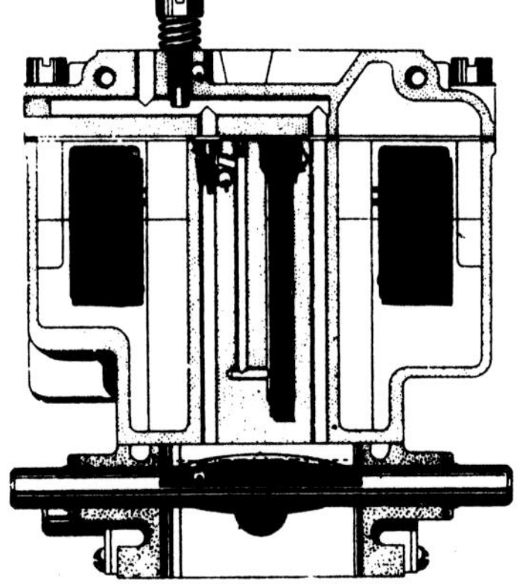

1. Idler jet (size 65)
2. Brake air duct (size 150 to 200)
3. Fording pipe
4. Idler air screw
5. Float
6. Choke flap

The right fuel level in the float housing

Take off the lid and put the first joint of your index finger on the edge of the float housing. Your fingertip must get wet.

Otherwise you'll look a long time for a fault.

Your *Guardsman* in the motor is the rpm regulator;
It helps you when the tiger is to pull better;
Warns you when you drive stubbornly, and don't look at the oil pressure gauge;
Brakes your temperament when you race the engine.

For up to 1900 rpm you will drive with only four carburetors at the *first stage*. It is in the front part of the double carburetor, and is easy to recognize by the connection to the choke flap.

When the motor runs faster, the four other carburetors are opened by flow regulators and oil pressure to the *second stage* with the engine speed between 1900 and 2800 rpm.

When it goes over 2800 rpm, they close again.

If the motor has too little oil pressure, a cutoff prevents higher engine speeds. - You should drive your sick Tiger only to the workshop.

Jet Reminder

A false idler jet takes revenge,
So take careful note: sixty-five!
Be sure to learn, for the first stage:
One-five-zero, two thirty-five;
For the second, notice without surprise;
Two twenty-five and two hundred!

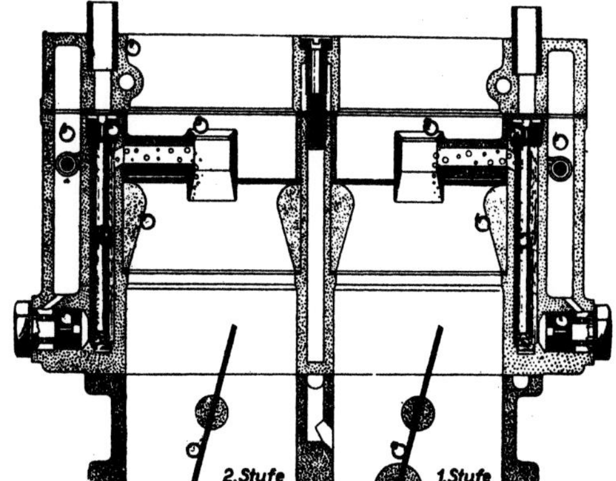

1. Main jets (size 235-225)
2. Brake air ducts (size 150-200)
3. Fording pipe
4. Air intake (size 38-40)
5. Middle sprayer
6. Float housing
7. Lid
8. Choke flaps

Moral:
When your mill groans and hisses,
It's the carburetor, nothing else.

Motto:
For performance there will only be power
When it is produced at the right place.

C. Gearbox

The gearbox is a highly trained, noble saddle horse. A light touch, and it changes its pace with secure and fast self-assurance. You must maintain it properly and keep the linkages clean, otherwise it will buck like a thoroughbred whose harness is on wrong, and whose chinstrap is badly fitted.

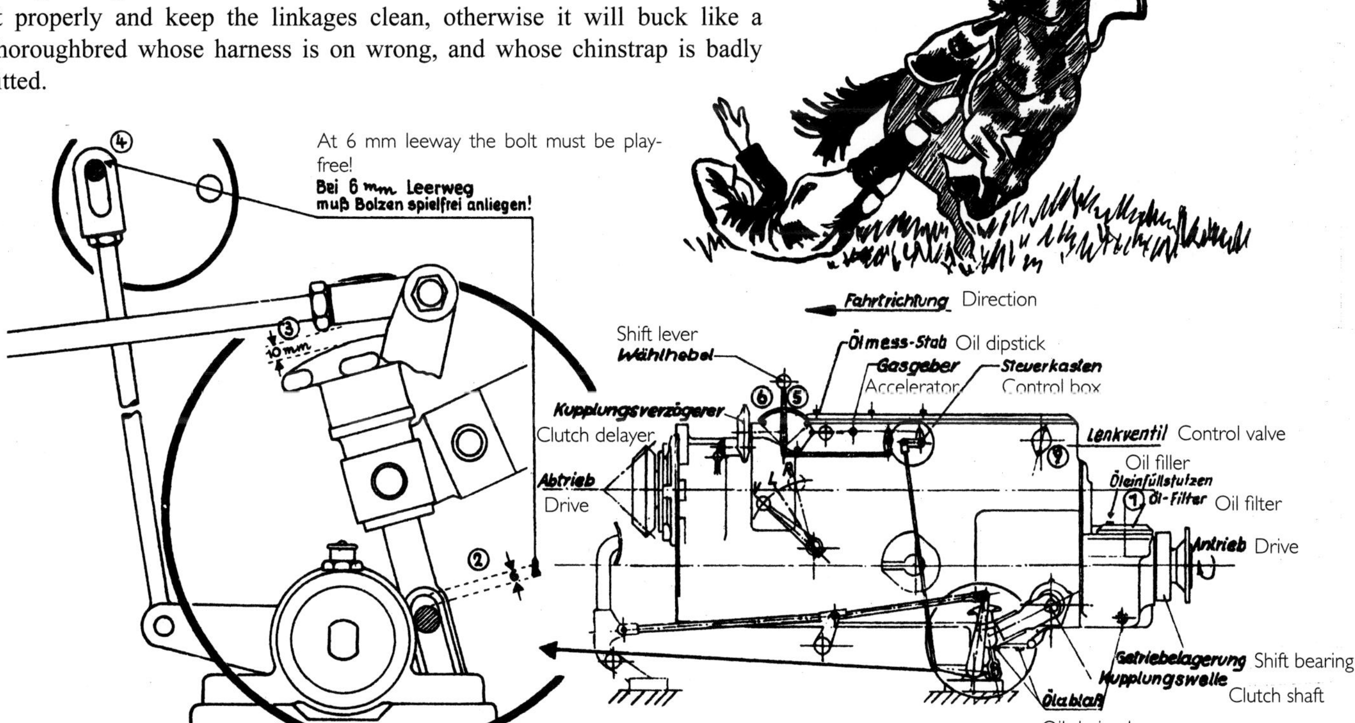

Therefore:

Transmission:

1. Check the oil level, clean the oil filter.
2. Turn lock nut to right until the clutch is released only after a dead movement of 6 mm. Make yourself a measuring stick 6 mm wide.
3. Set the foot-pedal striking point so that the lock nut allows a movement of 10 mm upward.
4. The angled lever to the steering box must be play-free when the clutch pedal has moved its free 6 mm (see #2 above).
5. Attach the lever to the accelerator shaft so that the motor reaches its highest speed when you push the gas rod to its contact by hand.
6. The rod of the gearshift must engage the gear securely.
7. Oil the rods and make them easy to move, so they return to their resting places quickly and surely.
8. The Telekin connections to the steering levers must always have some play.
9. Clean the steering valve if you have steering trouble. The sealing surfaces are rid of bits of dust when you push the valve plate in.
10. Tighten the attachment screws of the gearbox. *Otherwise* you cannot shift.

Jack shafts Often tighten flange nuts *Otherwise* they'll fly around your ears.

The brake lining cannot be replaced, as it is glued on, not riveted. You must change the whole disc, lining and all. Besides: Loosen the jack shaft and lever, take the brake off the brake carrier, loosen the screws of the lid with the brake housing, remove the lid. Check often with the special wrench (21 E 2799 U 15), and replace the [simmer] ring if oil comes through the brake holder.

Otherwise they'll get hot and smoke.

Final Drives Check seals. If oil is thrown out, they soon have to be replaced. *Otherwise* a new final drive will be needed.

When your Tiger goes 33 km/h, it has the same force as your *Panzergranate* 40 shell that flies at a speed of 3300 km/h.
When you step on the break, then this force has to be overcome by the brakes. The Tiger stops after covering 12 meters.
When the armor piercing shell hits, the armor plate must withstand all the force. Twenty millimeters of steel are penetrated. A braking path of 20 cm is not enough.
The brake lining must therefore withstand what 20 mm of armor cannot. Think of that when you use the brakes!
Therefore
You must, when braking, set a play of 13 mm on the lever. You can insert a "spy" into the viewing hole when the brakes are released. If the play is too great, then put the rod in one hole farther on.

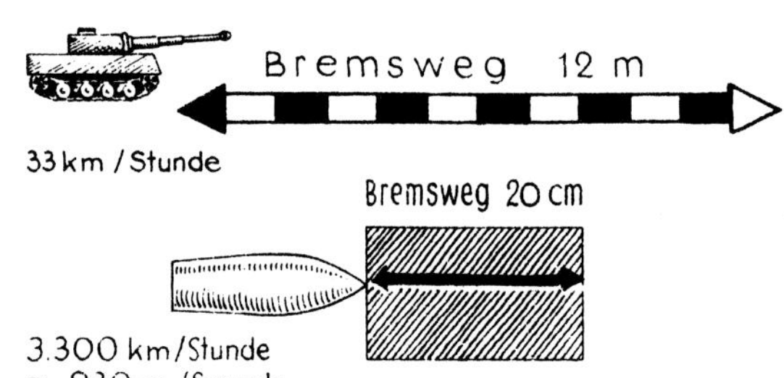

Stunde = hour, Secunde = second, Bremsweg = braking distance

Motto:
When a track is broken, one thinks,
If I had only checked it!

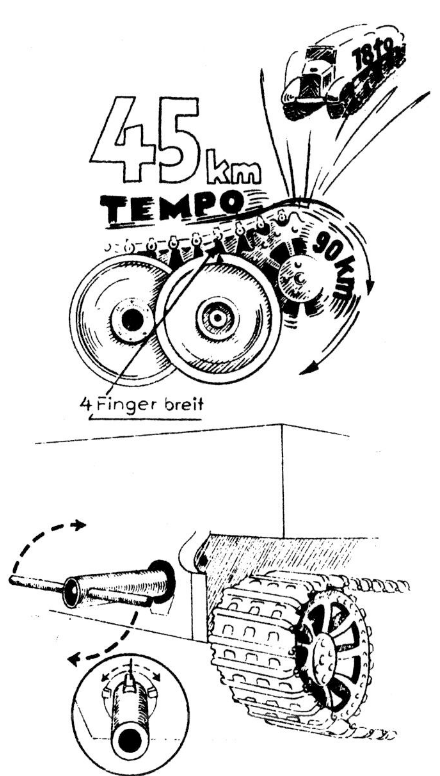

Track tension is extremely important!
The track runs forward on top at twice the tank's speed, thus at 90 km/h when the Tiger is going 45. If you don't keep the track properly tensed, it will hit against the drive wheel on braking and steering like an 18-ton tractor that falls from a height of 4 meters. It should hang four fingers above the first road wheel. Take notice when adjusting the track and don't tighten it too much!
Otherwise the motor must give out.
Check the *bolts and nuts* of the drive wheel, leading wheel, and road wheels, and tighten them; protect or change securing plates.
Otherwise the wheels will come off.
In the winter all the road wheels have to turn. Thaw them with the brazing lamp.
Otherwise you'll lose the bands.
Pay attention to loosened or torn bands, unsecured bolts, torn wheel rims, broken torsion bars, and cranks; replace them promptly.
Otherwise the damage will get worse and worse.
Torsion bars are the Tiger's springs. You must not damage their polished outer surfaces. It is like a love affair with them. If it has a little tear at first, it will soon break. Don't throw tools at it, don't pull any heavy or sharp tools over it, and don't climb on it with nailed boots.
Otherwise you must go to the workshop.
Putting on offroad tracks: Clean flanges completely of color, rust, dirt, and ice, and lubricate them very thinly. Mount wheels, attach crosswise bolts tightly, and secure them. Detach loading tracks under the leading wheel on one side. Drive the tank forward until the track is off the wheels. Lay the offroad track out ahead of it. Drive the tank forward until the track end is just ahead of the first road wheel. Wrap a cord three times around the drive wheel, tie the track on, brake the other drive wheel firmly with the steering lever, pull the track on, fasten and tighten the track, then do the other side the same way.

The loading tracks are put on in exactly the same way. The outer road wheels can then be taken off easily, because they hang free.

Bolts and track links can be changed easily under the leading or drive wheel. Don't put all the new links on together, but divide them.

Change the *toothed rings* of the drive wheels when the forward edges are worn out.

That is not a caterpillar,
Nor a centipede.
That is your Tiger from below.

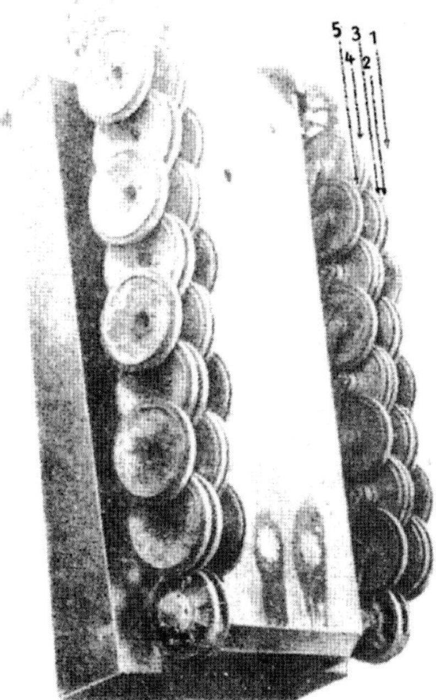

Here is an overview of the jobs, wrenches, and special tools that are needed to change a road wheel, drive wheel, leading wheel, or rim.

Road wheel row	1	2	3	4	5
How do I prop up The swing arms?	Put block before inner road wheel of arm to be propped. Drive onto it. **1**			Open track. Use winches to Lift one side of tank above track spur height.	
	Best done with 2 solid support plates, 2 3-ton hydraulic jacks, lift one side on blocks. **2**				
How many road wheels must come off?	1	3	4	8	13
What special tools Do I need?	27	27	27	10(2799/S) 70 50 C 2798 US **4** Pin M 39x1.5 Screw 18x35	15(2799/S) 70 50 C 2798 US **5** Pin M 39x1.5 Screw 18x110
How many rollers Must come off?	1 Outer rim	3 Inner rim	3 leading wheel drive	wheel drive wheel	5 5
What special tools Do I need?	27	27 2798 U10 Screwdriver **3**	22 50 C 2798 U5 pins M 39x1.5 pipe with 15 mm inner diameter, 75 mm long **6**	50, 46 wide wrenches Push drive wheel off with pushing screw. Remove screws M 14x90 piston with spring. C 2798 U3 with spindle & nut, wrenches 27, 46, head screw 50, remove catch, remove divided ring, replace felt ring **7**	

Moral:
When it's dark as inside a cow,
Cold, damp, and dirty too,
Block and winches sunk in the swamp,
Hammer and wrench cannot be found,
when bars break, arms hang,
three rollers are missing, five stick,
then one thinks in his gloominess,
"What would the designer do here?"

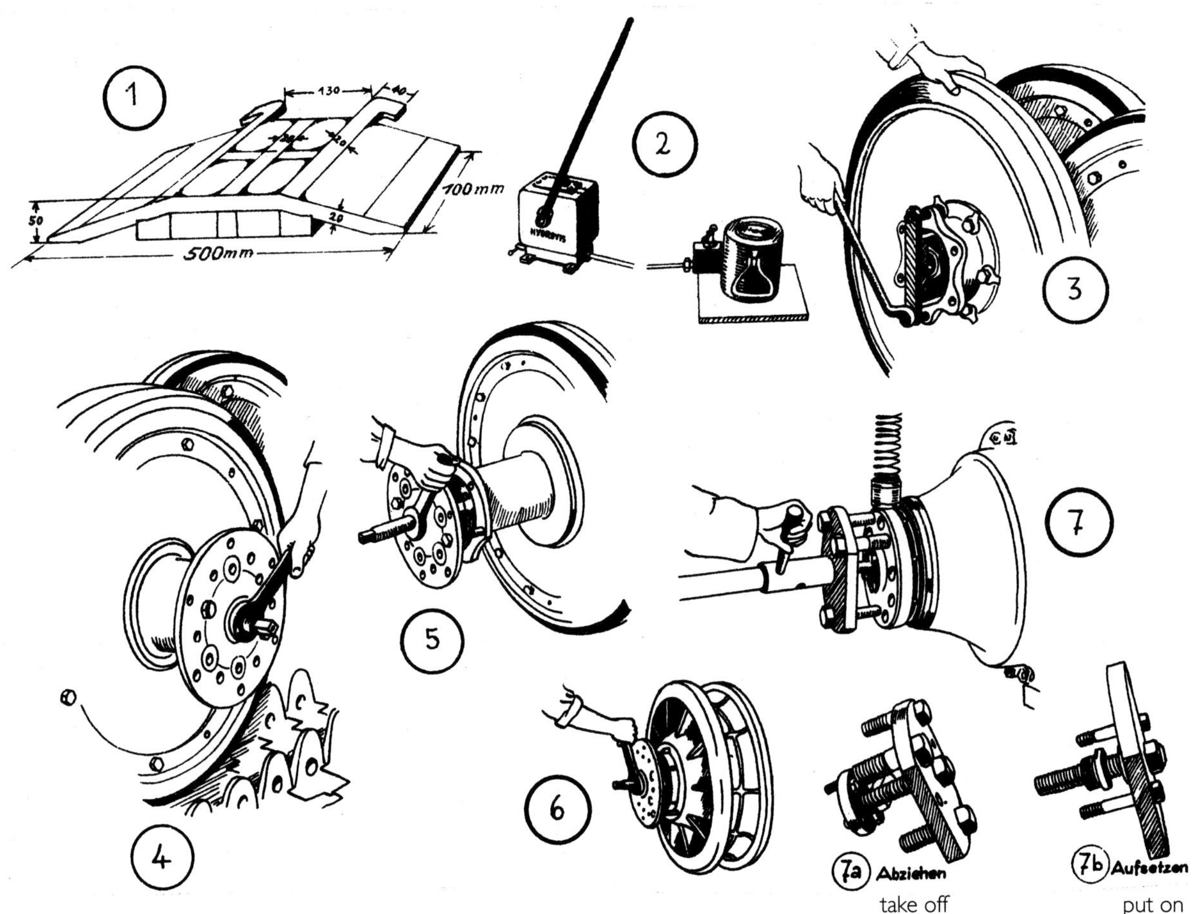

Motto:
The Tiger is, when you think of it,
A vehicle that's easy to steer.

Driving, but with Understanding

26 revolutions in a minute in ¾ time is what an elegant man makes in a Viennese waltz. Then the music melts into your ear and blends with the balanced movement. Slower is boring, but if you turn too fast, then you get dizzy and your partner falls to pieces from the heat.

2600 revolutions in a minute in four strokes is what the Tiger loves. Then he puts out the most power for his fuel. Your sense of rhythm, your ear, and your tachometer tell you when you have brought your partner to the right speed.

Never push it over 3000 rpm, or it will get too hot. The water boils, the oil stops lubricating, the bearings, pistons and valves burn out...

Therefore drive with your head, not with your other end!
Always note the engine speed **1** water temperature **2** and oil pressure **3** (p. 40)
Find the right road, but keep the direction,
Slide right in, but move from the spot,
Observe, but read the control panel,
Radio. But listen to motor and gearbox!

On the march — Turn cannon to 6:00 position and lash it down.

Houses and walls — Don't drive by them. The ruins look better in the weekly newsreel than on your rear end. All the dust is sucked in through the ventilator, and the radiator is covered and no longer cools. The motor overheats and breaks down.

Maps, paper, baggage, junk	must not block the light grids or disturb the gun when it turns.
Marshes, swamps,	dark places, high grass—avoid them. Better to take roundabout routes. Check the terrain on foot. Take a man piggyback, stand on one leg. If the ground holds, it will hold the tank. Drive smoothly, don't get stuck. Another Tiger will tow you out. Anchor a line, hook in The tracks, tow yourself out!
Corduroy road	It must be 3.5 meters wide, and all logs 15 cm thick, or you'll break through or tear loose.
Rivers	Hard beds and firm banks are needed. Where other tanks ford, the Tiger can make it. Shut off engine and prepare for underwater driving: bottom vent closed, pump on.
Bridges	Check on foot, prefer fording. Stop before bridge, point Tiger so it can cross without steering, pick a low gear, don't shift, drive slow, give gas when you are 5 meters on the other side.
Ditches and craters	Drive straight, avoid wet spots.
Woods	Tiger knocks down trees up to 80 cm diameter with bow angle. Don't drive on them. In too-narrow passages, drive zigzag with one side free.
Mines	Drive track, get back on track, don't steer, remove mines when possible.
Snow	Dry new snow to 70 cm is no problem.
Ice	Throw a track link ahead of the track, drive curves, don't steer, drive on crust at right angle. Keep one track in a ditch or edge. Branches or sand don't help much.

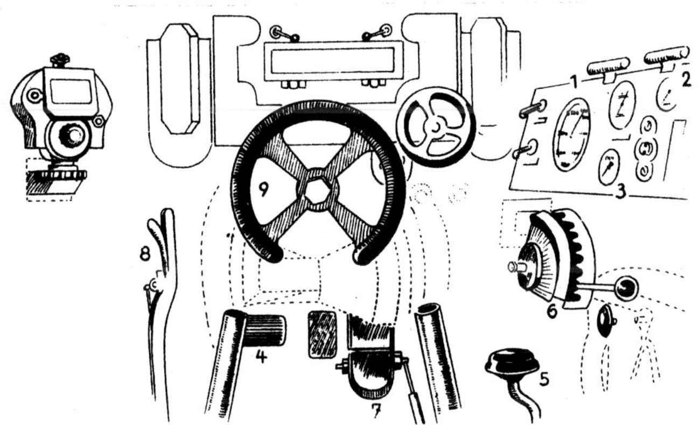

This is your problem seat.
You must know it well, so you can find all the levers and switches in the dark or in your sleep, like the light switches or the doorknob at home, or...oh, you know.
The driver's visor
Keep it active! Sometimes it sticks in winter or under fire. Loosen the 4 recessed screws in the body, remove the lid, and turn the out-of-center boxes to the left until the wheel movement is big enough.

Approaching 1st-4th gears (5th-8th gears forward impossible)	**4.** Declutch **5.** Direction lever **6.** Shift lever at 1-4, now shift. **7.** Give gas, let clutch in slowly	One gear is always engaged. If it is suitable for approaching, you don't need to shift.
Shifting *8 speeds*	Lever before grid Engage gear	Don't declutch or come off gas. 1-2 gears can be skipped if gearbox is warm. *Note the engine speed!*
Downshifting Engage gear	**8.** Lever before grid Handbrake by feeling	You don't need to double-clutch. 1-2 gears can be skipped if gearbox is warm. *Note the engine speed.*

Curves	**9.** Shift down before the curve. As you feel it, make a big or small arc. With each gear you can make one big and one small arc. The smaller the curve, the lower the gear must be. If it doesn't make it—use the hand brake and shift.
Turning on the Spot	Shift down to 1st-3rd gear. Declutch. Steer right or left. Push the big knob on the gearbox.
Stopping	Shift down to 4th-1st gear. Hand brake. Declutch. Direction lever to 0. Let the clutch in.
In reverse: 4 gears	Declutch. Direction lever to back. Shift lever before grid. Shift into gear. Give gas. Let clutch in slowly.
Command to Fire	Declutch. Put on hand brake.
"Position"	Shift to second gear.
"Brrrreakfast"	Steer to the rrrright, or
"Noontiiiime"	to the left siiiide.
(*see "meals"*)	Observe—calculate range—report—observe.
(*see "Estimation"*)	
Emergency Shifting	Direction lever to 0. Shift into gear with key. Declutch. Direction lever to forward. Give gas. Let the clutch in.

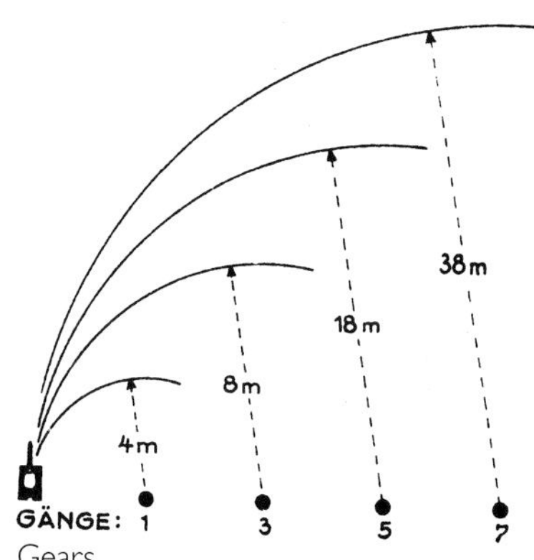

The direction lever cannot be moved to 0 or back as long as a higher gear than 4th is engaged. If you are in 5th to 8th gear—declutch—shift down. Reverse has only 4 gears.

Test and mark 10:30 and 1:30 positions. Commander and gunner advise by radio.

The position of the three shaft ends for the chosen gear can be found on the gearbox.

Moral:
Like everything that one may, but not must,
Driving is usually a pleasure.

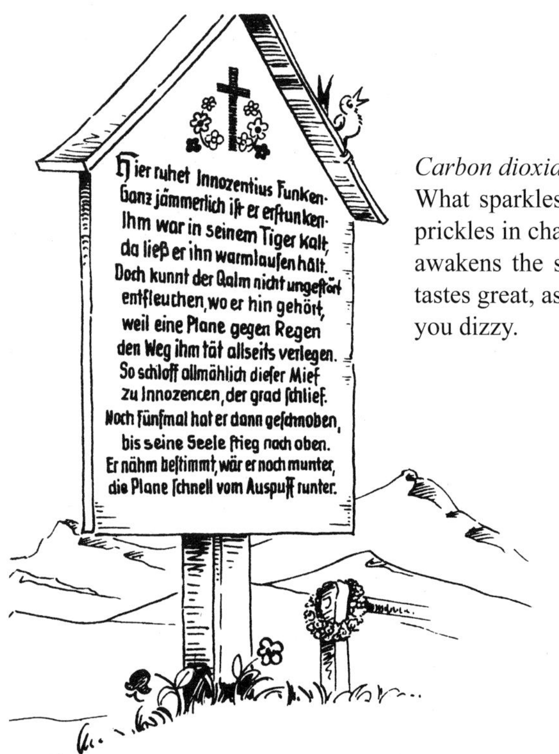

Epitaph on Sign: Here lies Innocentius Funken. He perished very miserably. He was cold in his Tiger, so he let it run warm. But the smoke could not escape undisturbed, as he had heard, because a canvas to keep off rain covered its path on all sides. So this gas gradually closed in on Innocentius as he slept. He inhaled just five more times before his soul went upward. If he were still alive, he'd take the canvas off the exhaust quickly.

Abstellen

Shutting down

Carbon dioxide (CO_2) *is lively*
What sparkles in soda, bubbles in beer, or prickles in champagne is carbon dioxide. It awakens the spirit of life, smells sour and tastes great, as everyone knows, and makes you dizzy.

Carbon monoxide (CO) *is deadly*
There is also CO in exhaust gas; it's very nasty stuff. You don't see it, don't smell it,
Scarcely taste it. You just slowly get tired, unconscious, your breath rattles a few
Minutes, and then you turn blue.

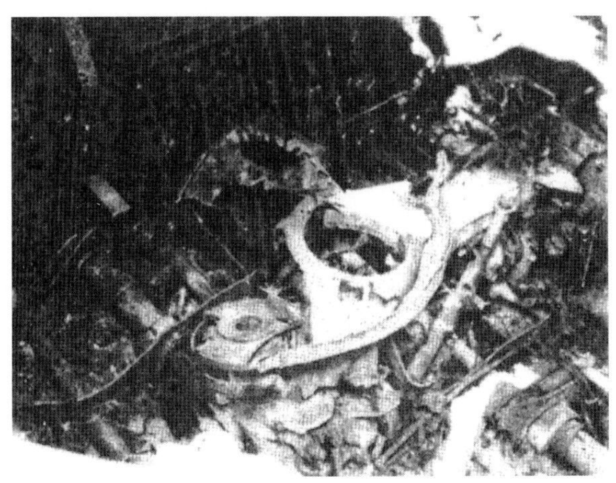

But sometimes it goes fast.
From a leak in the exhaust pipe, CO gathers in the hull. You're not thinking of anything bad, and you press the starter in the morning, suddenly the whole tank jumps, and you jump with it. A small spark from a badly insulated cable can blow up the whole tank.

Ventilation is the only way to deal with it. CO is heavier than air and flows slowly to the deepest place. You must make use of that.
Therefore:
When you shut down, put both air scoops up, open hatches, doors, and windows, close both fuel fillers, turn off ignition. If it doesn't stop—full gas, battery main switch at 0.

Otherwise the Tiger will blow up.

In winter, don't stop on smooth ground. Cut branches, boards, thick straw, planks, wooden walls, or hedges underneath
take chunks of ice or mud out from between the road wheels, move something every two hours; alternating warmth (melting) and cold (freezing) is especially dangerous.

Otherwise it will freeze!

Thin the oil (see 6x oil level) and remove batteries when you shut down for a long time (see Electricity). Shift into the gear you'll want to start with. A cold gearbox won't shift. Hold the clutch pedal down so that it stays declutched and doesn't freeze together.

Otherwise you can't drive away.

Moral:
The tank can stand its own exhaust
No better than a soldier can.

Recovery

Motto: With calmness, caution, and thought
Recovery is soon accomplished.

Just as you help your comrades in any situation, you must also bring your steel friend home when it breaks down.
If need be, a Tiger comrade can get you moving, but avoid that.
It's better not to undertake an attempt to move on your own. You'll harm the motor and running gear; it's not worth it—

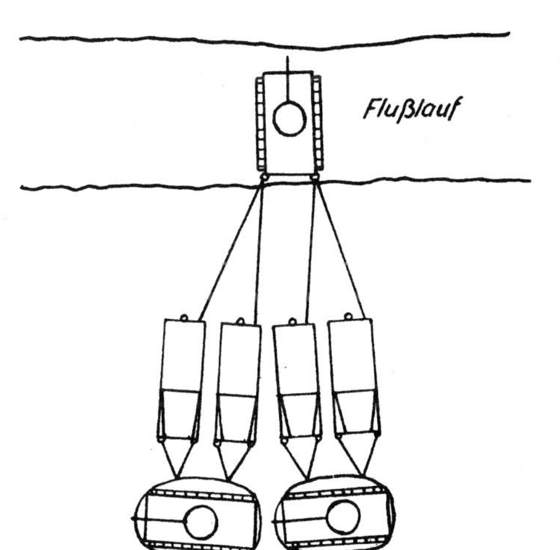

Rather
Avoid that and talk to specialists! Meanwhile, prepare for towing; here's how:

Gustav	
Releases or opens tracks,	*so that* obstacles to towing are removed
Looks after the running gear.	
Disconnects the final drives,	*so that* the final drive is disconnected
but the brakes work.	
Puts the screws back in.	
Hülsensack and Piepmatz	
Move obstacles from in front of	*so that* towing will be easier
The hull and tracks	
Schnellmerker	
Has looked for anchoring points for the towing vehicle	
and gotten out the right tools:	
Crowbars the towing rods, S-hooks,	*in case* towing is done with a winch
cables, winches	

Don't get carboned and butter bread, otherwise you'll get one on the roof! Tell the recovery vehicle driver at once about the tank's damage and ability to be towed.
And then, everybody get busy!
When the tank is free, it can be towed away in tandem.
Pay attention like a hunting dog, especially at bridges, fords, or narrow roads.
Keep in contact with the towing machines, help out with directions,
Otherwise you'll ram your comrades, or the tank will get stuck again.

Moral: Recovery is very troublesome,
But at the same time, necessary.

Motto: Even General Guderian
Sometimes travels on the train.

Loading
Verladen

Loading goes smoothly and quickly when you carefully prepare everything:

Brake the flatcar (SSyms) and brace both ends.	*Otherwise* the tiger will land on the rails.
Put loading tracks on the Tiger, stow the extra road wheels, and fold up the skirting plates.	*Otherwise* it will endanger rail traffic.
Choose end-loading ramps to load the Tiger, Lay out both offroad tracks side by side, and Drag them onto the vehicle. Wrap the loose ends. When the tank is on the car, don't forget to brake it and block both ends.	
During the trip, often check whether The brakes are on firmly, The wooden wedges are still nailed in place, The tank is in the middle of the car.	

Moral:
Loading is child's play
For one who has experience.

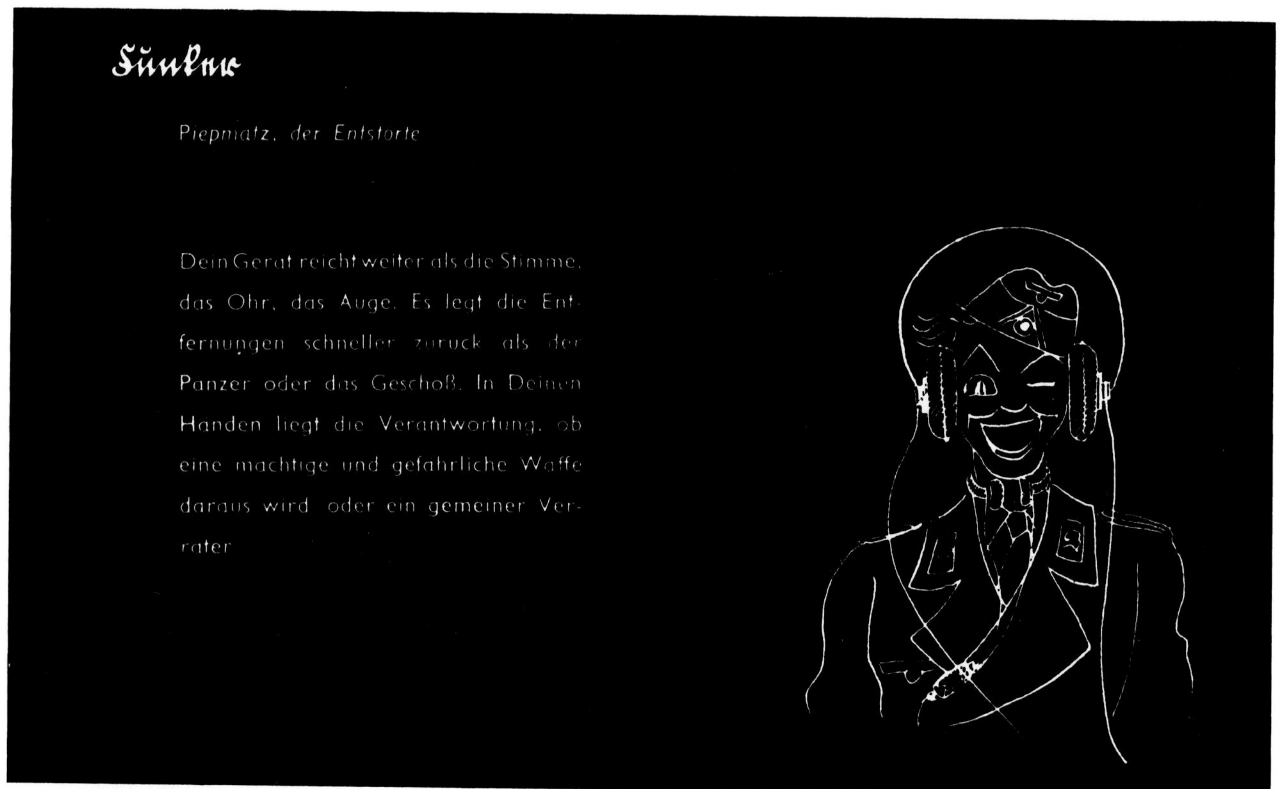

Radioman
Piepmatz, the desensitized
Your radio reaches farther than your voice, ear, or eye. It conquers distance faster than the tank or the shot. The responsibility of being a mighty, dangerous weapon or a common traitor is in your hands.

Motto: Often the right radio message
Gives an attack a good outcome.

The right mood and volume are often decisive for your future. On the other hand, laughable happenings, false position, lacking connection, or unsteady contact can spoil everything. Stay on line!

The Radio

Das Gerät

Always

1.Insert the cable to the transformer, and the one to the antenna, in their sockets.

2.Make sure that the switches are on "off" when the sets are not in use.

3.Check the connections to the battery (+ on +, - on -) via connection box 23, the groundings in the baseplate and transformer to the radio on a stiff seat. Look out for poor contact and worn spots.

Before use,

Plug in all the wires just as you see them in red on the drawing.

To use the receiver

Set	2 on high volume
Check at	4 if the scale lights up
And at	5 if the test lamp is on
Set	6 on "0"
Turn	7 to the ordered frequency And stop there
Set	8 on "far"
Turn	6 to highest volume
Set	8 to "near" if it is too loud
Turn	2 back if it is still too loud

After using

2 Turn the switch to "0"

1 and stick the cables in the resting place

To use the sender

Set	2 on "Tn"
Check at	4 if the scale lights up
and at	5 if the test lamp is on
turn	7 to the right frequency
press	9
turn	10 so long,
until	11 is farthest to right
does	11 swing when you use the microphone
place	2 on "Tg sounding" if you want to use Morse code.

Moral: The smart one always plugs in two frequencies on his radio.

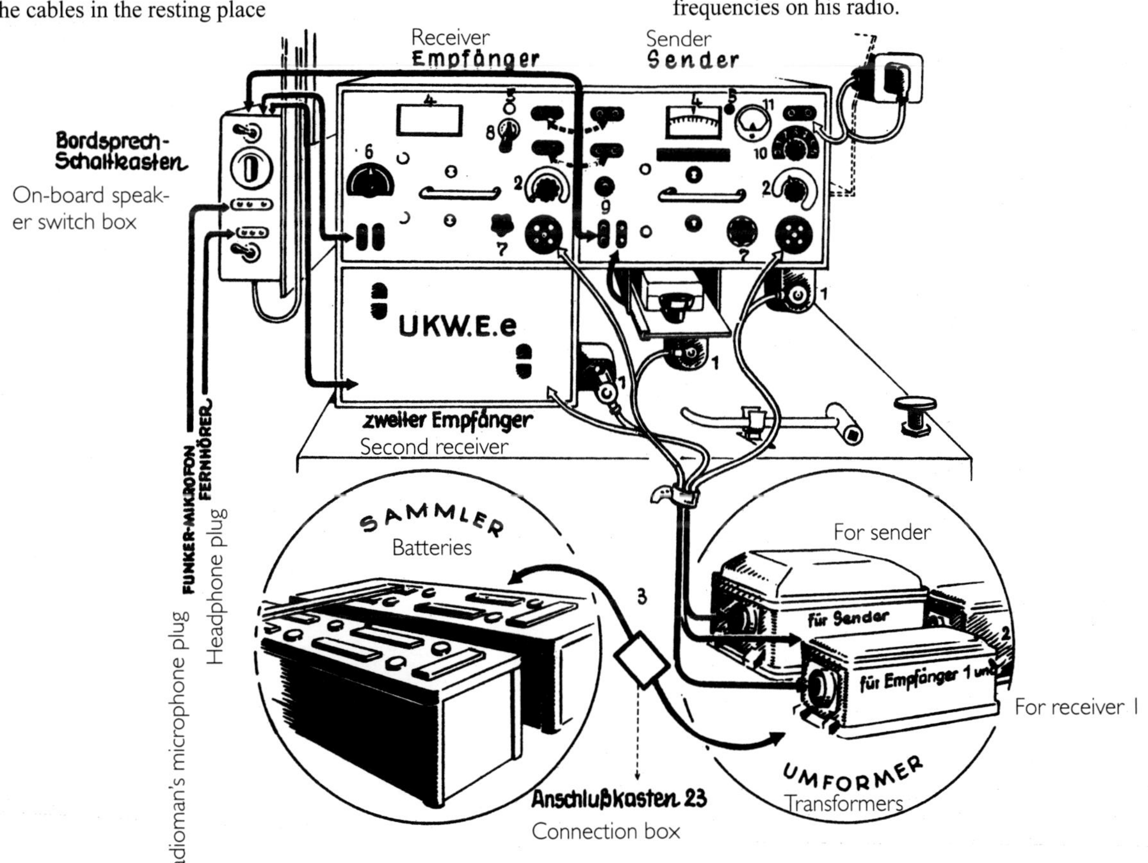

Motto: Telephone and radio
Aid faster communication.

The On-board Speaker

Das Bordsprechen

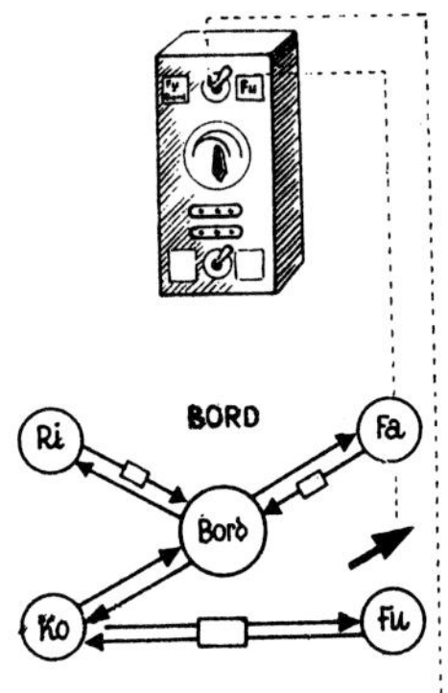

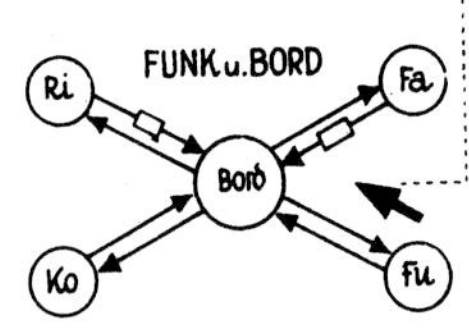

The four speakers are shown here in X form, sending and receiving by arrows. When the sending arrow goes through the microphone button, then it must be pushed while speaking.

This is the on-board speaker box with its two switches. With the upper one you can reach two different settings when speaking. The lower one can stand where it wants. The receiver is turned on; the sender is not. If you have no receiver, connect the 5-fold cable from the transformer to the speaker box.

1st case: "On board"

Tank commander! You can hear and speak without pushing your button. Therefore you must pay particular attention, because all that you say is heard. If you want to let off some curses or talk with the grenadiers, you must either take away the microphone or unplug it, or have the whole system shut down by the radioman.

If you want to tell the radioman something, you must push down your button.

Gunner and driver! You always listen, too. If you want to speak, you must push your buttons.

Radioman! You can speak with the commander only when you push your button.

2nd case: "Radio and on board"

Radioman! If you want to be connected with the on-board talking, turn the upper lever left to "Radio and on board." Like the commander, you then hear everything, and can speak without pressing your button.

Moral:
The on-board radio works sometimes
As well as in the "Femina."

Motto:
The radio traffic would be indescribable
With a radioman who was a woman.

Sending and Receiving

Empfangen

Here 2 x 2 cases are possible, because the lower lever is also involved. For the time being, we'll leave it to the right, on:

A."Tank Commander + Radioman Receivers 1 & 2"

1st case: "On board"

Radioman! You can send and receive by setting the operation type switch on "Tn" or "Receive," while the commander, gunner, and driver converse undisturbed.

If the commander wants to listen to what comes in, or wants to send, then you or he must push the button. Then you will also hear what comes in or is sent out. The commander is shut off from on-board speaking for the time being.

Here the on-board traffic is black, the radio traffic red.

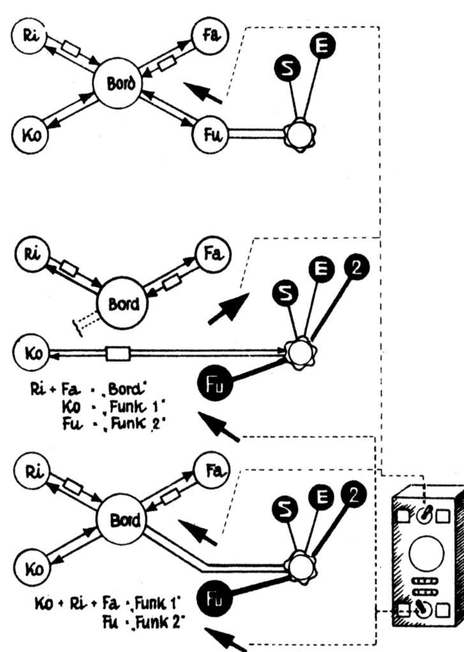

Here the meanings are:
Thick black arrow: receiver 2
Thin red arrow: receiver 1

2nd case: "Radio and On board"
If the whole crew is to hear, push the lever left to "Radio and on board."
All 4 are now linked with each other, all 4 can now send. The gunner and driver must push their buttons. Now listen very carefully and shut your mouth.
B. "Commander receiver 1, radioman receiver 2"
1st case: The upper lever is to the right on "board"
In vehicles with Fu 2 and Fu 5, you must listen to both receivers. That is also not difficult.
But if two messages come in simultaneously, then quickly press the button and move the lower lever left to "Commander receiver 1, radioman receiver 2".
Then you get only receiver 2, while receiver 1 goes to the commander, or
2nd case: to the whole crew, if the upper lever is at left on "radio and on board".
[lower left] [lower right]

Moral:
Thin black arrow: on-board traffic
So think fast and switch like lightning,
Or the lightning will strike your seat.

Loader
Hülsensack, the unbounded
Sixty tons of steel and 700 horsepower have only one task of protecting and moving the weapon that you operate. If you fail, then everything is in vain. Prove yourself, then you will help destroy a lot of enemy tons and horsepower.

Motto: Often one does not right to the shot
Because it doesn't have to, as you do.

The Fiancée from the Ammunition Factory

Die Braut aus der Munitionsfabrik

Don't unpack too early!
Don't insert, but lay lovingly on a blanket.
Don't damage the wrapping, but deliver it.
Don't let dampness, dirt, sun, or frost get in!
Don't throw and dent like the masons.

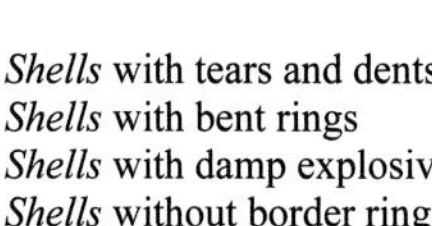

Shells with tears and dents — Out!
Shells with bent rings — Out!
Shells with damp explosive — Out!
Shells without border ring and closing plate — Out!
Caution!
Check, clean, don't oil!
Tighten loose detonators by hand!
Ignition screws must not stick out!
Attach head detonators by hand!
Don't take head detonators apart!
Straighten loose and twisted shells!
Ammunition with impact detonators gives short circuits!
Attention!
Clamp shells firmly in the holders!
Reposition in advance!
Don't hit the leading ring when loading!
Tank Shell 39 is black with a white point!
Tank Shell 40 is black!
HL Shell is gray.
Explosive Shell is yellow!
Set time fuses only with a wrench!
After unloading, get back to O.V... *or it will fail!*
Get rid of duds and casings!

Moral:
Whether blond or black, white or gray, cherish them like your fiancée.
Then the effect is tremendous. "A finger's touch and she's on fire!"

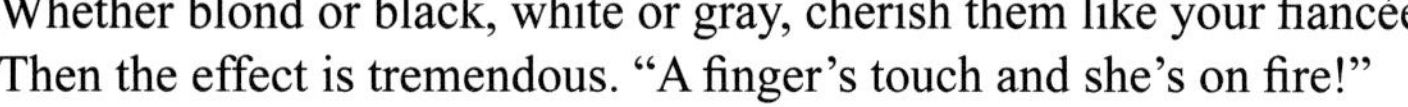

Die vielseitige Kanone

The Many-sided Cannon

Motto:
An obstacle in the cannon's barrel
Occurs, thank God, only rarely.

In advance
Test your electrics, take care of the ammunition, clean the breech, make sure all moving parts move, and un-oil the barrel before firing, but oil it heavily in back when it is hand-warm again. *Otherwise the gun won't fire!*
Attention
Remove muzzle cap, with ice also the kind you can shoot through.
Remove camouflage and twigs from the muzzle.
Look through the barrel during firing pauses.
Check at night with a flashlight.
Remove bits of explosive and residue.

Unload hot barrels in firing pauses. *Otherwise the gun will fire to the side.*
Don't fire
When the muzzle brake is loose or shot away—it works like a sail and absorbs 70% of the recoil.
When the barrel brake loses oil, it works like a shock absorber and absorbs 25% of the recoil.
When the recuperator loses air or does not work. It works like a door-closer and absorbs 5% of the recoil.
When the recoil gauge is at "firing pause." Push it forward after every shot.
When the splint on the opening lever is gone or loose. *Otherwise the cannon will shoot backward.*
Meanwhile: for experienced gunners and also. *Otherwise the cannon will shoot forward.*

Moral: The tank man doesn't like to believe,
Instead of meeting something, go to it yourself!

Motto:
The 8.8 ignites like a light.
Some of them never fail.

The Long Wires

Die lange Leitung

Problem with:	Cause:	Cure:
Shell chamber	Verdigris or dirt on the shell	Load new
Ignition screw	Unusable (may have sunk in)	New screw
Striking bolt	Too short, or broken off	New striking bolt
Bridge	Broken spring	New bridge
Small block	Not reached from bridge	Move gun forward. Fill air at 55 At. (4.4 liters of oil)
Push button plug	Cable shoe loose	Repair plug
Signal lights	You can fire if the bulb is burned out or fallen out	New bulb Straighten bulb spring
Oil seal	Barrel brake loses oil (contents: 5 liters)	Check seal, tighten screws, refill with oil
Bosch plug	Cable sticks, plug not all the way in	Text box and plug, new cable, straighten spring.
15-amp. Securing	Look for short circuit, Cable stuck	New securing by driver.
40-amp. Securing	Flak ammunition, wire worn through	Replace impact igniter with glow igniter screw.
Battery	Clamp loose or dirty	Clean, attach, grease.
Help with problems to 15 amp securing	Trigger light doesn't burn, signal lamp burns.	Switch on emergency battery.
" to Bosch plug	(same as above)	Plug cable into turret light plug, remove with loader's securing.

Test: unload cannon, hold trigger, put one pole of test lamp on flat mass, other on wire.
Caution! Don't cause a short circuit! Test wiring to cannon until lamp goes out. The flaw is shortly before that!
Attention! When the oil seal has switched off, you must not fire.

Moral: Many a man bit the green grass because he forgot the wire route.

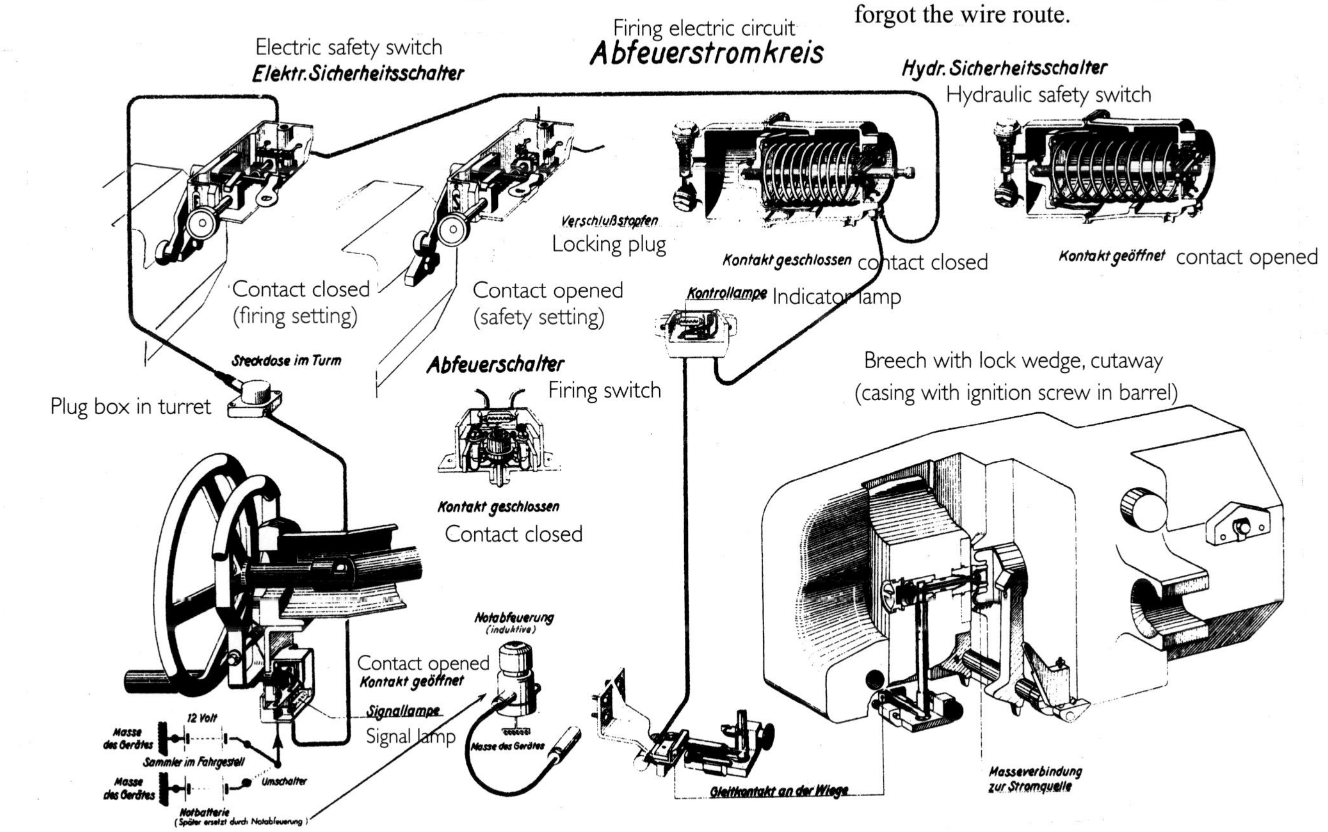

Firing electric circuit
Abfeuerstromkreis
Electric safety switch
Elektr. Sicherheitsschalter
Hydr. Sicherheitsschalter
Hydraulic safety switch
Verschlußstopfen
Locking plug
Kontakt geschlossen contact closed
Kontakt geöffnet contact opened
Contact closed (firing setting)
Contact opened (safety setting)
Kontrollampe Indicator lamp
Steckdose im Turm
Plug box in turret
Abfeuerschalter
Firing switch
Breech with lock wedge, cutaway (casing with ignition screw in barrel)
Kontakt geschlossen
Contact closed
Notabfeuerung (induktive)
Contact opened
Kontakt geöffnet
Signallampe
Signal lamp
12 Volt
Masse des Gerätes
Sammler im Fahrgestell
Umschalter
Notbatterie (Später ersetzt durch Notabfeuerung)
Masse des Gerätes
Gleitkontakt an der Wiege
Masseverbindung zur Stromquelle

Motto:
The messy guy—if he gets to shoot—
Brings obstacles to great pleasure.

The Five Ways to Eliminate Obstacles

Die 5 Mittel gegen Hemmungen

Shells
With dents, tears, rust, or pushed-in shots Out!
Use only German ammunition straight out of the package, not suspicious Russian jettisoned ammunition (explosive ammunition). Check every shell, clean it, don't oil it.
Belts
With stepped-on, bent or rusted pockets Out!
With broken-off or bent claws Out!
With worn-out connecting lashings Out!
Do it like the skiers!
Dip the belt in boiling paraffin, shake it off well, let it dry. It will last through a medium-sized campaign. Keep it neat, the claw must fit into the groove, put it together neatly, the nose must fit exactly into the window.
Machine gun
Put it together right.
Test the closing spring (front to medium inserter). Check the bolt spring (3 windings over the bolt end). The bolt nut must fit in audibly. Don't put the upper part of the feeder in the wrong way.
Oil
Only on movable parts and lock combs. Put sulfur on it, or better, some motor oil. Remove oil from the barrel, clean the lock combs.
Installation Otherwise you'll have obstacles!
Without stressing the MG. The fork must reach smoothly over the pins on the housing. Position the trigger rods with a lock nut, so the MG will shoot sustained fire. Tension lever forward so the catch doesn't break. Empty cartridge bag.

But before you install it...

Put your hand on your heart and ask five questions;
Question 1: Are the jacket and barrel bent, does the recuperator rod work?
Test 1: Cock the MG, muzzle-fire damper off. The barrel must allow you to push it back to the firing position easily with your finger, and must move forward again at once.

Question 2: Does the MG fire sustained fire?
Test 2: Step on the trigger. Pull the lock and let it move forward. It should be caught only when the trigger is released, but then at once.

Question 3: Is the lock ready to move?
Test 3: Breech off with locking spring. Breech must be easily movable with tension lever.

Question 4: Will the breech lock completely?
Test 4: Let the breech move forward, cover on, front surface of the breech housing must join with the angle of the bottom part of the feeder.

Question 5: Do feeding, pushing out, pulling out, and ejecting work?
Test 5: Put a few cartridges with bullets set on them into the belt. Let the shots move forward and pull back. Cartridge must be ejected properly.

New! Fast readiness to fire:
When loading, the breech remains forward!
You can feel very good about loading.
If the safety fails, no shot can be fired.
Put in the belt so that only one shot is advanced.
Don't force the cover.
When you want to shoot, you need only finish loading.
Wrong!
This distance shows that the breech is not locked.
Right!
These two edges must come together.

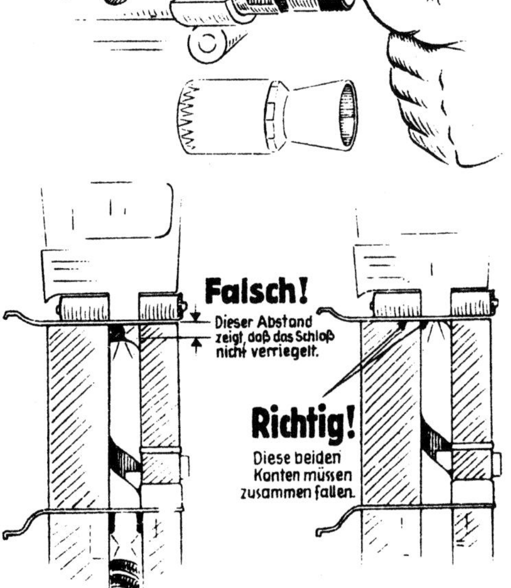

Moral:
In addition to the bullet belt,
Make sure the sprayer tracks neatly.

Motto: A donkey can tell by its tail
Whether it's wet, windy, or hot.
At the butt of the light MG
The soldier learns where the problem is.

The Donkey Barometer

Das Eselbarometer

If the tail is dry and does not shake	Nice weather
If the tail is dry and shakes	Wind
If the tail is damp and does not shake	Rain
If the tail is wet and shakes	Storm
If the tail cannot be seen	Fog

You can tell just as simply what is wrong with your MG if it has a problem!
Pay attention: Foot off the trigger
Right tension lever back, and pay attention:
Set safety at left
Right cover up, and pay attention:

1. Where is the breech?
2. What is ejected?
3. What is in the breech rail?
And now look...

The MG-Barometer

Das MG-Barometer

Where is the breech? **Wo steht das Schloß?**	What is ejected? **Was wird ausgeworfen?**	What sticks? **Was hemmt?**	What helps? **Was hilft sofort?**
vorne In front	Patrone angeschlagen	Versager	weiter schießen
	Patrone blank	Schlagbolzen	Schloßwechsel
	nichts	klemmender Gurt	Gurt nachziehen
		Ausstoßer	Schloßwechsel
		Zubringer	Gurt ziehen
fast vorne Near front	Patrone blank	verspanntes MG	Kralle lösen
		Verriegelungsstück	Laufwechsel
	nichts	verbeulte Patrone	Laufwechsel
	Was macht die Patrone?	**What does the bullet do?**	
mitte Center	Patrone klemmt, Lauf frei	schlechtes Gurten	weiter schießen
		Ausstoßer	Schloßwechsel
	Patrone klemmt, Hülse im Lauf	Hülsensack	Hülsensack leeren
		Auszieher	Schloßwechsel
		Patronenlager	Laufwechsel
	Patrone klemmt, Bodenreißer im Lauf	lose Bolzenmutter	Schloß- u. Laufwechsel
		Verschlußsperre	Laufwechsel
	Hülse klemmt, Patrone im Lauf	Auswerfer	Schloßwechsel
fast hinten Near back	Patrone nicht ausgestoßen	verbogene Tasche	weiter schießen
		Verbindungslasche	weiter schießen
		Schloßbahn	reinigen
		krummer Auswerfer	Schloßwechsel
	Patrone eckt	eckender Gurt	weiter schießen
		Zuführeroberteil	weiter schießen
hinten (gefangen nach dem 1. Schuß)		kurzes Gestänge	von Hand abziehen
Schloß steht nicht still	(wenn es stehenbleiben soll, Gurt festhalten)	klemmend. Gestänge	von Hand abziehen
		verschmutz. Abzug	oft durchladen
		Abzugsstollen	das andere MG

What was wrong? **Was war schuld?**

Deine Schuld:
- **Schmutz** – reinigen, entölen, ölen, Graphit
- *Schlamperei* – nachgurten, geraderichtet nachstellen
- Ermüdung – lahme Federn längen

Nicht Deine Schuld:
- **Bruch und Verschleiß** – neues Teil aus dem Ersatzteilkasten od. Waffenmeist.

Moral: You see, my friend, when it doesn't shoot,
That you are usually to blame.

Motto: Lllleft—sllllowly
Rrrright—rrrrapid!

Mo-Fa-Fu-La-Ba

Mo=Fa=Fu=La=Ba

Outside: Motorluke: close and bolt hatch
Fahrerluke: close driver's hatch tightly
Funkerluke: close radioman's hatch tightly
Lampen: lights out
Bahn: way clear

Inside:	Gunner	Unlash gun
1	Driver	Start engine
	Loader	Set swing path Lllleft—sllllowly Rrrright—rrrrapid
2	Radioman	Place selector lever on turret
3	Loader	Lift emergency lever of gearbox
4	Gunner	Swing by stepping on rocker backward—left forward—right
	Gunner	Aim with both aiming machines
	Driver	Give gas if it's to be fast

Schalthebel zum Schwenkgang
Shift lever for aiming apparatus
Liquid drive
Flüssigkeitsgetriebe
Plate clutch
Lamellenkupplung
Emergency lever Nothebel
Schwenkwippe Swinging balance
MG-Abzug MG trigger
Drehbühne
Revolving stage
Mitnehmer
Lifter
Shift lever
Wählhebel
Kupplung
Clutch
Getriebe
Gearbox
Gestänge
Rod

Motto: In many, the turret stays back
At home with his understanding.

Moral: Backward—left
Forward—right

Roof Damage

Der Dachschaden

Problem	Cause	Help
Turret won't move from foot	Clutch doesn't move	5. Let motor run, loosen clutch!
	Clutch rod too short or too long	6. Loosen nut on rod and adjust fork!
	Rod came out at ball pan	7. Connect ball pan and edge it!
	Lifter raised over drag ring carrier	8. Remove bell and position claw of carrier!
	No oil pressure	Refill oil!
	Rocker rod loose	9. Hook rod in, new safety splint!
Turret stays at 4:00 or 8:00 position	Turret sticks on motor hatch	Turn turret to 12:00 by hand and pull on gun with rope. Close hatch.
Turret moves only to Right	Spring under rocker is too long	4. Adjust spring or set rocker horizontally!
Turret moves faster One way than other	Rocker rod is too short or too long	9. Shorten or lengthen rocker rod!
Turret swings, does Not stop	Clutch and rod are stuck	6. Shut off motor and loosen rod!
	Compensating gear of Pressure spring is twisted	5. Release shaft and pressure nut of gear, detach clutch so as not to damage needle bearing, put spring in straight, install clutch!
Emergency lever Does not work	Lever turns on shaft, safety rod is bent	3. New safety rod!

Moral: Who has a brain swings elegantly—
Who doesn't, forces it by hand.

Richtschützen

Holzauge, der Unfehlbare

Das Schießen ins Schwarze ist eine Kunst, aber keine Schwarzkunst. Damit Du besser schießt als Dein Gegner, hast Du die schärfere Waffe und den scharferen Verstand.
Mit der 8.8 kannst Du einer Mücke den rechten Eckzahn wegschießen, hier lernst Du, wie:

The Gunner

Wooden-eye, the Infallible
Shooting into the dark is an art, but not a black art. So you shoot better than your opponent, you have the keener weapon and the keener understanding.
With the 8.8 you can shoot a gnat's right eye-tooth out. Here you learn how:

Motto: You'll never learn aiming or shooting
Before you have digested this.

The Mil

Der Strich

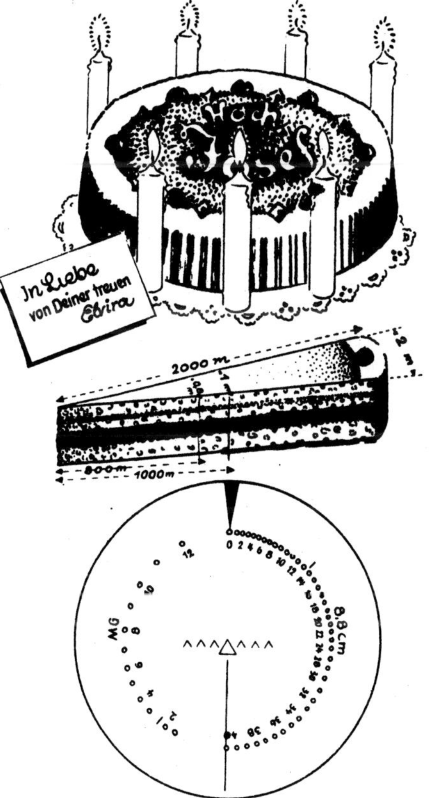

Hülsensack's fiancée Elvira gave him a big birthday cake, a huge thing two kilometers in diameter.
Every man in the division was to have a piece of it. Hülsensack divided it into 6400 pieces.
Those were really remarkable pieces of cake. If one stuck the point of one into his mouth, one had hardly anything between his teeth, because it was so thin, but farther back it got wider and wider. It was *1000 meters long*, and *one meter wide* at its outside end.
Elvira would have been glad to bake a cake in which every piece was 2000 meters long. They would have been 2 meters wide at the outer end. But the field post refused to accept it.
For such a piece of cake, you can easily calculate the width if you know the distance from your mouth.

At 1000 meters it is 1 meter wide,
At 2000 meters it is 2 meters wide,
At 800 meters it is 0.8 meter wide, etc.

The very smart people say the width is always 1/1000 or 1 0/00 (one promille) of the distance from your mouth.

Such a piece of cake is what we call a mil.

Four mils, for example, are as much as four pieces of cake side by side.
Be careful! Here are the thorns in your telescopic sight.

The points of two thorns are exactly 4 mils from each other.
If you aim over them, then it is just as if you looked along the edge of your cake.
If there is a house beyond them at 2000 meters, right between two points, then you know: "Aha!"

1 thorn space is	4 mils
1 mil (at 2000 m) is	4 mils x 2 = 8 meters
The house is 8 meters wide	Isn't that a killer?

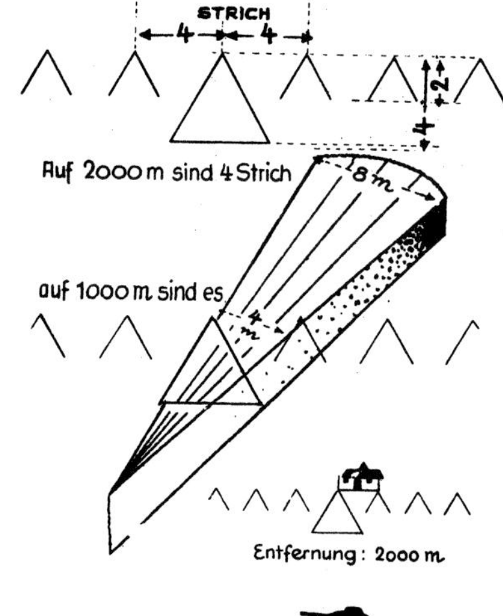

Question: A tank is 500 meters away, it extends over 3 thorn spaces How wide is it?
You calculate: 3 spaces at 4 mils = 12 mils.
1 mil at 500 meters = 0.5 meter. 12 mils x 0.5 = 6 meters.
Answer: The tank is 6 meters long.

Question: How high is the tank?
You calculate: Given that it is three times as high as one thorn space.
3 x thorn space height at 2 mils...
Oh, you can do this by yourself later.

The very smart people know that there is also a mil division in a telescope, which one can work in the exact same way. But also in your thumbs! Stretch your arm out; then your thumb is just 40 mils wide. One thumb spring measures 100 mils (look with one eye and then the other, always over the same edge of the thumb).
Then you can give the target sizes exactly with the naked eye at five mils, and astound everyone. Try it!
So: *If you know the distance, you can also figure out how big your target is.*

Moral:
You like to be close to your sweetheart.
By estimating, you divide near and far.

Estimating

The middle one is just right!

Estimating the range exactly—nobody can do that.
"Measuring"—many learn that.
Setting one's visor right—everybody learns that!
You must learn to estimate up to 1200 meters, give or take 200 meters. If 500 is the right distance, your estimation must be between 300 and 700 meters. That is really not an art. Over 1200 meters, estimating is more like guesswork.

Estimate shorter	Estimate longer
For dark targets.	For bright targets.
When it's dark and blurry.	When it's bright and lively.
In restless, foggy air.	With a bright background.
When the sun and reflections are in your eyes	With the sun, over flat land.
	Through the telescopic sight.
	If you can't see what's between you and your Target.

Estimate twice: 1. The target is definitely closer than X meters (for example, 900 m)
2. The target is definitely farther than Y meters (for example, 500 m)

And take the median between the two estimations (for example, 700 meters)
Only the *driver* and the *commander can estimate correctly*, because they can see directly with their eyes. Through the telescopic sight it's not so good.
1, because the sight magnifies everything two and a half times.
2. because you cannot estimate correctly using just one eye.
Close one eye and have a comrade hold a finger half a meter in front of your nose. Now try to use your index finger to push it away quickly from the side.
Attention: Don't hold your own finger up, and don't look first with both eyes.
But the *gunner* and the *commander* can "measure" with the telescopic sight and optics. You will soon learn that, too.

If you have time, do it this way:

The Tank Commander
Measures or estimates the distance — see "measuring"

The Driver
(needs more time) reports his distance — see "Estimating"

The Tank Commander
Calculates the "median" — see first grade, elementary school

The Gunner
(has meanwhile measured or estimated)
Reports his distance — see "Measuring"

The Tank Commander
Calculates the "median" again and orders the right distance see "Order to fire"

The Gunner
(the distance is not the right range) sets the range see "Exact Range"

900 | 1300 → Tank commander 1100
1000 | 1600 → Driver 1300
800 | 1000 → Gunner 900
Tank commander + Driver → Report → Median 1200
Median + Gunner → Report → Right Distance 1050
Command
Right Range Set 1200

But you always have time
For when you shoot blindly, that costs much more time, more shells, and betrays your position before you can get results.
3 times 2 eyes see more than two—you estimate exactly as 100 meters.
3 times the commander must calculate—that's why he gets paid more.
3 times he reports or orders—that's what the speaker is for.
Practice is everything.
Attention: the right distance is not the right range!

Motto: Even masters measure, for you can't
Rely on eyeballing.

Moral:
Shorter, unclear, dull, in the dark,
Haze, restless, sun sparkles!
Bright sunshine, clear and cheery,
Even, between, optics—farther!

Measuring Das Messen

When a painter wants to measure a distance exactly, he compares the size of the pencil with the model.
You can compare the size of the thorn with the target! For if you know how big your target is, you can use the mil to figure out how far away it is.
Take care: The Russian tanks are all three meters wide. If we assume that it is exactly that wide and will stretch over 1.5 thorn spaces, then you can say, "Aha!"
1.5 spaces at 4 mils each = 6 mils
6 mils = 3 meters
1 mil = 3/6 = 0.5 meter
0.5 m x 1000 = 500 meters
If it is placed diagonally, then you cannot reckon with length and width; then you take the height. The M 3 is 3 meters high. If we assume that it looks in the optic as it does in the drawing, then you calculate:
3 thorn heights of 2 mils each = 6 mils
6 mils = 3 meters, etc.
In the telescope, the mil divisions look like this:
Task: Figure out how far away this truck is!
Here are some measures:
Attention: the right distance is not the right range!

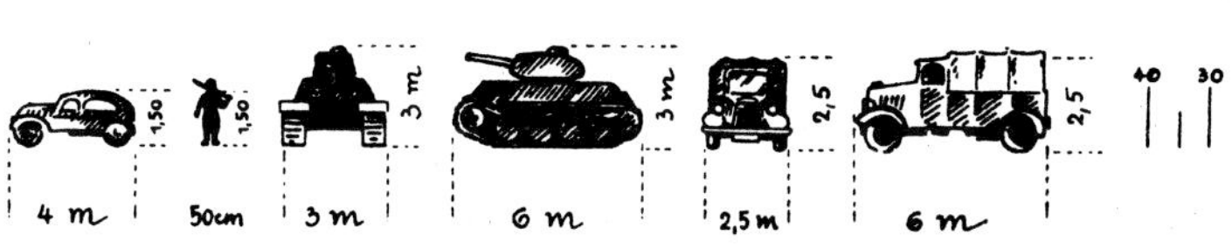

40 30 20 10 0 10 20 30 40

Moral:
Instead of how far it is to the target,
Estimate what it is in mils and meters.
You divide the meters by the mils,
Then times 1000 and you've measured right.

Motto: Save ammunition; a wagon load
Will be enough for a Knight's Cross.

The Seven Good Ones

Die guten Sieben

Pistol: out of hatches, at guests on the rear.
MP: out of hatches, at trenches and nests in dead space.
Eggs: out of hatches, at holes and hidden targets.
Launcher: when it's urgent, when you're hemmed in, when you have to retreat quickly, when it gets scorchy and stinky.
Bow MG: up to 200 meters, at man, horse, or vehicle.
Turret MG: to 400 meters at man, horse, or vehicle (and if there are several, even farther, at houses, or to nail the enemy to the ground for your infantry.
Tank gun: Explosive shells:
Without delay (o.V.): Gives splinters 20 meters to either side and 10 meters forward. Proved against antitank and other guns, massed targets, nests, smashes shields, tears tires, tracks, visors, sets fires, tips vehicles.
With delay (m.V.): Hits mines vertically, penetrates and blows up wooden Bunkers, houses, dugouts, woods, and young tanks.
Ricochets hitting flat on firm ground: bounces off, flies 50 meters farther, and then explodes 4 to 8 meters over positions that you can't see and fire on in other ways.
Armor-piercing Shell 39: Hits tanks and loopholes to 2000 meters.
Armor-piercing Shell 40: Hits heaviest tanks to 1500 meters (dispersion). Use only when 39 shell won't penetrate. Attention! There is more power behind it! *From 600 to 1100 meters you must make the range* 100 meters less; from 1100 to 1500 meters, 200 meters less.
HL Shell: Against heaviest tanks to 1000 meters (great dispersion). It Blows big holes but flies slowly. Thus, you must always set *the range ¼ farther than otherwise!* (for example, not 600 m, but 750 m). Don't use it if camouflage, twigs, or nets are in front of the target; otherwise it will go off too soon!

Attention: The right distance is not the right range.

Moral: So shoot less often but hit more!
That will please Reich Minister Speer.

Motto: Like this picture of a woman,
Many targets seem incalculable.

Elvira wird erschossen

Elvira Gets Shot

Little-used ranges for a target
500 distant, 2 meters high,
On hand in 6 usable sizes.

The right distance is not the right range?
The men of the Tiger didn't want to believe that. Hülsensack had acquired a two-meter-high placard of the loved Elvira and set it up as a target 500 meters away. They wanted to clobber it; every man wanted to take Elvira down with one shot.

Driver Gustav took the range as 475, had Elvira sitting on the main thorn, aimed half a meter to the left, as is proper—shot too short—at exactly 25 meters.

Radioman Piepmatz took range 500 and scored a direct hit on her world-famous toenails.

Then Hülsensack, the loader, came up (he was trained at the third level), spat on his hands, took range 700, fired—boom—and the shot went right through her coveted navel.

Gunner Holzauge shook his head, for at range 700 the shot should have gone too high. He went all out, took range 1000, and hit the top of her head.

Tank Commander Schnellmerker took range 1100 and shot over her head. At that range, the magic was ended.
Range 25 meters too short, no direct hit! Range 500 meters too far, direct hit!!!!!
The layman is astonished; the specialist just smiles!

Moral: The right estimation often doesn't bring
The direct hit that you hoped for.

Motto: For the old tank man, it's very much
A question of the seat of the shot.

Hülsensack Always Scores

Hülsensack trifft immer!

The tank gun fires point-blank. Thus, the shot goes right to the set range and no farther.

If you know the distance exactly and shoot with range equal to distance, then you hit the stopping point.
But you never know the distance exactly. If you estimate even 25 meters too short, then the shot will go into the dirt 25 meters in front of it, as with Driver Gustav.

The trajectory of the 8.8 is wonderfully stretched. You only need to crank the barrel up a little higher to shoot much farther. Then with the far range you'll hit your near target as long as it is high enough. *With range 1000, for example, you'll hit all targets between 0 and 1000 mm that are two meters high.* Isn't that wonderful?

Shooting at Elvira with 1000 range is, of course, not very sure, for if she were just a few centimeters shorter, the shot would go over her, like Commander Schnellmerker's.

You have many usable ranges for one target! The smallest of them in the distance; all other are higher. You can hit Elvira with 6 different ranges: 500, 600, 700, 800, 900, 1000.

Don't set the range equal to the distance. For if you estimate just 25 meters too short, you'll shoot 25 meters too short. Do it like Hülsensack, take the median, then you'll hit the middle of the target, the navel.

Then he can try estimated distances of 200 meters either way and still hit. Hülsensack always scores, for he never makes bigger mistakes when he estimates.

Moral:
The old boys usually set the optics
Farther than they estimated.

Hülsensack's Navel Range Law

Das Hülsensack'sche Nabelweitengesetz

Motto: $V_{Navel} = E + \frac{\frac{H}{2}}{\frac{E}{1000}} \cdot 100$

That is the only thing that you don't need to notice.

A. If Elvira were twice as tall, then twice as many ranges would be usable.
The navel range is than 1000.
You can be off by 500 meters up or down.
B. If the target is too small, for example, the toenails, then only one range (500) is valid,
the exact distance: Gun nests, tanks in ambush, loopholes, weak spots on tanks, such
as the turret (so the shot hits vertically) must be attacked thus. You can't estimate
wrong.
C. If Elvira moves farther away, then fewer and fewer ranges are valid.
D. Finally only one is left: Range equals distance.

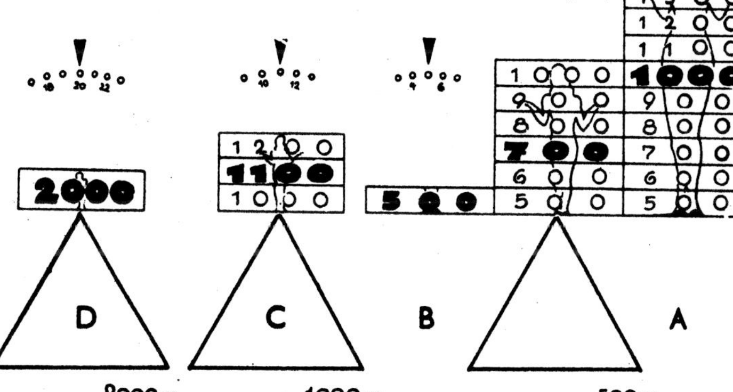

If the target is very small, or it only looks small because it is far away, then the number of usable ranges is also *small*, because the target is only a few mils high, or none at all.
Only *small* estimating errors are allowed.

If the target is *big* or looks *big* because it is close, then the number of usable ranges is also *big*. *Big* estimating errors are allowed.

How do I find the right range?

1. Estimate the distance.
2. Estimate the height of half the target (navel) in mils by comparing it with the thorn (or the height of the whole target, and take half of it)
3. Half the target in mils times 100 meters

Count to the distance too.
Then you have the navel range
and hit the navel.

By how much can my estimate be off?

Mils times 100 meters

That's how much you can estimate too near or too far, and still score.

Motto: Like Max Schmeling with his right
Is a bullet in the fight.

Always and everywhere, set up the target from below, until it sits up.
Attention!
The tank gun always fires ½ meter, the MG 1 meter to the right,
Because the tank gun is ½ meter and the MG one meter to the right of the optics.
Therefore always aim the tank gun ½ meter, the MG one meter *to the left!*

Under 1200 meters

You cannot shoot next to it if you work neatly with the *navel range*.

Over1200 meters

You usually must set the range at the exact distance. Since you never know it precisely, you fire

Too near or too far.

Then you must change your range, as it was false, even by only 50 or 25 meters. *Don't change the stopping point,* for that matters little from 1200 meters on. Only if the shot

Goes left or right

beside it, may you *move the stopping point to the side.* If it is more than two mils, then take the next mil on which the target is sitting.
If you don't hit with the first shot, you have either dug yourself in or not adjusted the weapon.

You are to blame, not the gun.

Up to 2000 meters, the gun fires point-blank. Only at 3000 meters does it fire one out of three shots to the side. At 4000 meters, only every 4th shot hits (dispersion).

So always ask yourself whether firing at great distances is worthwhile.
After every heavy fire—barrel high, breech open, ventilating and cooling, in the winter put the muzzle cap on.
Moisten the ground before the muzzle; otherwise it will raise dust.
In the winter camouflage this spot, for it will turn black.

Example:

1. fewer than 600 meters	
more than 400 meters	Median = 500 m
2. Target height is 4 mils	
Navel height thus 2 mils	
3. 2 x 100 m	= + 200 m
Navel range	= 700 m
Allowed estimating error	
2 x 100 meters	= 200 m
Valid, therefore, are all estimates	
Between 500 m + 200 m	= 700 m
And 500 m – 200 m	= 300 m

Moral:
It is easy to compare
The mil height and the navel height.
Take the distance, and you add
mils times a hundred to it.
A hundred meters for the mil
Is the most you'll be off.

Shoot, but with Understanding

Schießen, aber mit Verstand

Moral:
Have the sun in your back,
the wind at your side,
Fire only when stopped,
Then you'll score and be happy.
Holladiria, holladirio!

Knife or Fork?

Messer oder Gabel?

Motto: Is the knife or the fork right?
You must eat, that's important.

One eats with a fork, *the other with a knife.*

You must be able to work with both! From 1200 meters on, they don't always score, especially the explosive shells. Now the tank gun has to help. It fires a measuring stick into the country for you, and you can use it to measure your target.

Be careful: Fire at your target only one shot with a range equal to 100 meters *less* than the estimated distance. This will definitely fall too short.

If you can see the terrain behind the target Then fire a fork:
For the second shot, add 400 meters. It will go behind the target. Now a measured area of 400 meters is there. You must divide it into 4 sections and can measure just how many meters from the first shot are left.
The third shot must score!

If you can see only the terrain in front of the target, then fire a knife:
For the second shot, you may add only so much that it hits before the target. Between the two spots you again have a stretch that you can measure how many meters there still are to the target. Using the knife calls for ability.

The third or fourth shot must score!

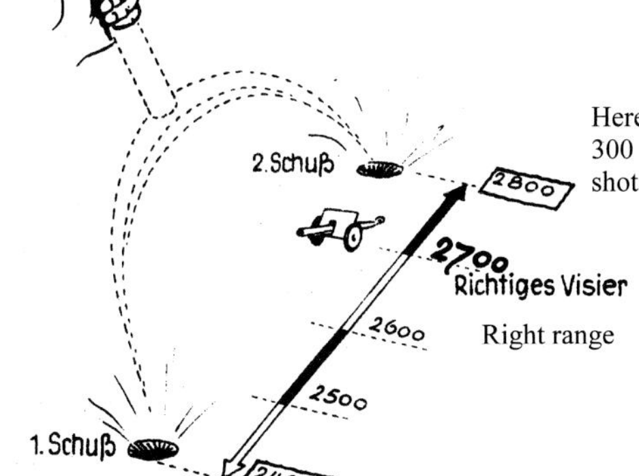

Right range

Here you must add 300 meters to the first shot.

2700 Richtiges Visier

Right range

2.Schuß

2600

2500

1.Schuß

2400

Here you must still add 100 meters to the second shot.

Moral: Until twelve hundred, shoot the navel.
Beyond that, use the knife or fork.

Allowing for Speed

Der Vorhalt

Motto: It's easy to hunt what runs,
If you know what to allow for speed.

The five men of the Tiger had obtained some cherries when the furlough train stopped, and now they began to spit the pits at the telegraph poles. That was great. The train moved ahead slowly. At first they scored; then everything went past behind the pole. They were all surprised. Then Hülsensack the loader made his mouth into a howitzer barrel, closed one eye, looked over his nose a good distance before the pole, fired powerfully and—boom—off went the shot, right at the pole. The faster the train went, the farther ahead he aimed.

Is your target under 200 meters—aim at it!

If one goes by your nose *between 200 and 1200 meters—aim ahead!*

For when you aim exactly, the man has already moved a few meters while your shell is flying. *It hits the spot where he was, not where he is.*

First you must estimate how he is moving:	slow	medium	fast
	10 km	20 km	30 km
And then move the main thorn ahead,			
With armor-piercing shells 39 and 40	3	6	9 mils
With explosive shells	4	8	12 mils

Example: A truck rolls by at medium speed.
"MG 20 shots—10 o'clock—600—truck—8 mils ahead!"
Always work with the next thorn on which the target will land.
That's what they are there for, and always let them run into the big thorn.
If it doesn't drive straight, but obliquely past you, then take half the allowance.
Example: A tank goes by at an angle, at medium speed.
"Tank 39—one o'clock—600—tank—3 mils ahead!"
If your target is over 1200 meters—stop, for you would fire too much ammunition at moving targets.

You can see the amount of allowance easily with the...

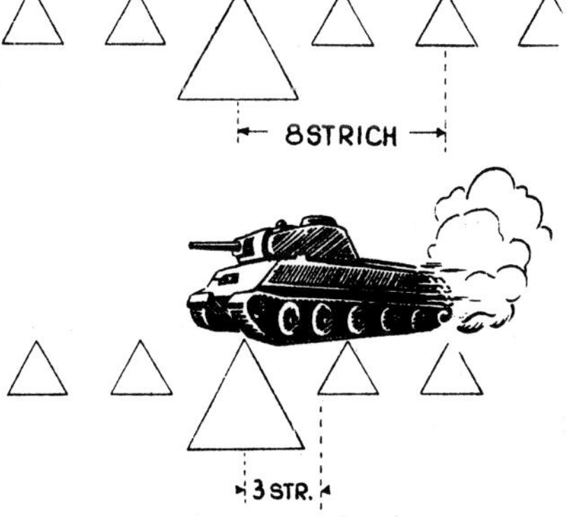

Moral: 9 and 6 and 3-
Use them for tanks.

12 and 8 and 4-
That's what we explode.

Motto: If you use your optics for the purpose
Of adjusting a flyspot,
And then fire cleanly and coolly,
You'll still shoot to the side.

Adjusting

Das Justieren

Always lash your weapons down for marching. In spite of that, they will be moved by vibration. Adjust them yourself, for you know your weapons!

First the tank gun: Here you need cord and insulating tape or grease.
1. Tape a cross of cord across the muzzle.
2. Take the striker out.
3. Take the range of a distant target through the barrel.

Then the right telescope:
1. Set the right focus.
2. Set the gun visor at zero.
3. Remove the protective cap from the optics.
4. Adjust the main thorn to the traverse of the target.
5. Adjust the main thorn to the elevation of the target.

Then the left telescope:
1. Set the gun visor at 1000 meters.
2. Turn the right telescope to the target.
3. Swing the thorn to the left.
4. Set the right focus to the left.
5. Change the eye distance until the two crosses meet.
6. Adjust the auxiliary thorn to the traverse of the target.
7. Adjust the auxiliary thorn to the elevation of the target.

The emergency visor is now adjusted strictly to 1000 meters. You can now hit all targets two meters high between 0 and 1000 meters. Over 1000 meters you must go into the target or let the target disappear.

Finally the turret MG: Here you need a case with a hole, Hülsensack always carries them with him.
1. Bottom plate off. Take the lock out. Put the case in the barrel.
2. Set the MG visor at the adjustment mark between 200 and 300 meters.
3. Aim the right telescope at the target over the main thorn.
4. Adjust the MG to the target through the hole in the case bottom and the mouth.
5. Check by firing.

Bow MG: Check by firing.

Moral: Adjust the tank gun often,
Then you'll fire with success, otherwise not.

Panzerführer

Schnellmerker, der Rechtzeitige

Dein klares Denken, Dein sicherer Befehl geben erst der Panzerung Leben, der Geschwindigkeit die Richtung, dem Geschoß die entscheidende Wirkung. Du haltst die Hand voller Trümpfe, nur lerne spielen!

The Tank Commander
Schnellmerker, the Punctual
Your clear thinking, your sure command give life to the armor, direction to the speed, the decisive effect to the shot. You hold a hand full of trumps; now learn to play!

Motto: From way back when until today,
One commands the shot to hit the target.

The Command to Shoot

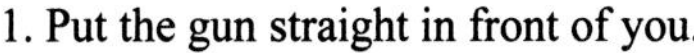

1. Put the gun straight in front of you.
2. The piston to the left foot.
3. The shell out of the pocket.
4. The shell on the barrel.
5. The loader out.
6. Shorten the loading rod before you.
7. Go to it, 1-2-3.
8. The stopper rod out of the pocket.
9. The stopper rod in the mouth.
10. Bite off the stopper.
11. Stopper on the barrel.
12. Loader on it.
13. Go to it, 1-2-3.
14. The spring before the cap.
15. The gun in the swing.
16. Clean out the ignition hole.
17. The spring on the cap.
18. The powder horn out.
19. "Powder on the pan".
20. Powder horn in place.
21. Make a grim face.
22. Cock the hammer.
23. Get set.
24. Aim well.
25. Give fire.
26. Pray for help.
27. Fire.

In the Thirty Years War, 27 commands were necessary to fire a shot. That is why it took so long. Besides, the commands were different in various regiments. Some didn't get by with fewer than ninety commands!
Make it short: Press your will into an order of eight commands!

Motto: 27 big jobs still remain—as this chart shows—
Not even including the small ones. Practice is everything!

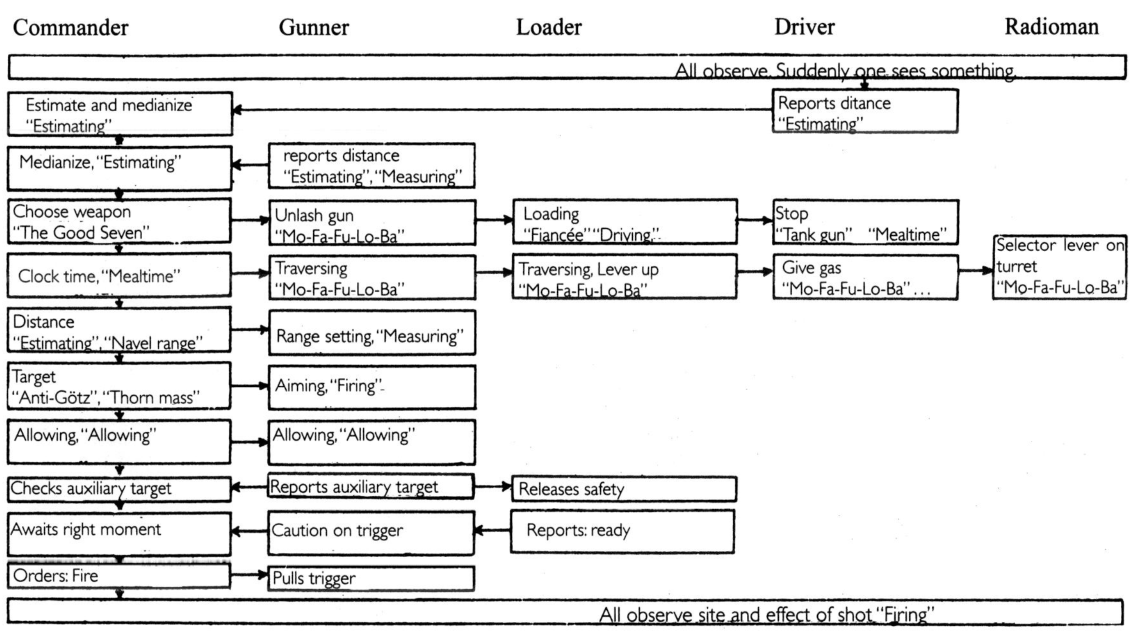

The words in quotes refer to the applicable chapters, the titles sometimes shortened.

Moral: Tank—white—close by coffee—
1050—Gen'ral Lee
6 mils allowing—another at right
Ready—fire—they won't get any farther.

Motto: The mealtimes don't just keep
The soldier alive, but the tank, too

The Mealtimes

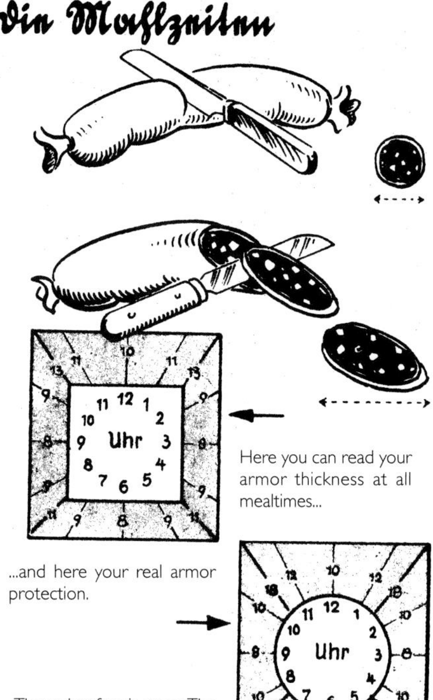

Here you can read your armor thickness at all mealtimes...

...and here your real armor protection.

The red surface is armor. The numbers are centimeters.

Your tank is at the gun mount 12 cm,
In front 10 cm,
At the sides and rear 8 centimeters thick. Nobody ever was before!

But you yourself can make him much thicker!

When Mother slices the sausage vertically, then you get a slice just as wide as the sausage is thick.
But if she cuts it diagonally, then the slice is twice as wide!
Here it's about the sausage—it's now or never!

If you let your tank be fired on squarely, then it is *ten centimeters thick*, and withstands all calibers up to and including 7.5 cm.
But if you place yourself *diagonally* and let them shoot diagonally, then it is *13 centimeters thick*. A shot that strikes diagonally can penetrate much less than one that strikes squarely. Thus, these 13 cm protect you against diagonal shots as a tank 18 cm thick would be protected (if you want to cut the sausage diagonally, you need a sharper knife).
So diagonally your armor protection is really 18 cm thick, and withstands all calibers up to and including 15.2 cm.
Then you absolutely cannot be penetrated!
You see that when you turn your tank from 12:00 to 1:00, it becomes 2 cm thicker.
To penetrate these 2 cm, your enemy must be 1000 meters closer.
One centimeter of armor weighs as much as 500 meters of combat distance!
If you place the tank diagonally, it will be as if you had moved your enemy four kilometers farther away at one stroke.
From there he can shoot as much as he wants.

The best positions toward your enemy are at
10:30, 1:30, 4:30, and 7:30.
According to those times, we call them mealtimes.
The syllable "time," for clear understanding, is always drawn out l o n g—Middaaaay).
They are easy to remember, as they are mealtimes.
Driver: For placement, always turn right or left until the enemy is at the breakfast or lunch position. (Try out, note the direction.)
Gunner: Always fight dangerous targets in mealtime positions (read the turret setting from the clock face, help the driver).
Commander: Approach dangerous enemies diagonally. Take diagonal position so the enemy is in a mealtime position (read target position from clock face, help the driver).

Moral: At "mealtime," even at 15.2—
All you'll get is a scratch at most.
The enemy finds that disgusting,
But for you, my friend, it's a pleasure.

The Cloverleaf

Das Kleeblatt

Motto: If the enemy steps on this cloverleaf,
It can be dangerous for you.

We see the Tiger from above.
At what distance can the T-34 with its long 7.62 cm gun penetrate me?
At 12:00, under 500 m
At 12:30, under 300 m
At 1:00, I am safe
At "Midday" I am safest
At 2:00, under 500 m
At 2:30, under 1300 m
At 3:00, under 1500 m
At 3:30, under 1300 m
At 4:00, under 500 m
At "Coffee" I am safe, etc.

Put our clock on it

And enter these distances.

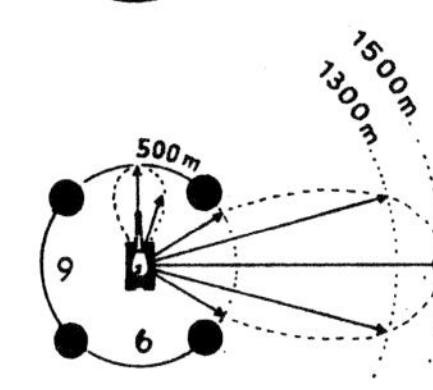

If the enemy stands in the cloverleaf, I'll get penetrated.
If he stays outside, I am safe.
At the "mealtimes" the Tiger can't get knocked out.
Tiger men!
It is up to you whether the Tiger is safe or not.
Enjoy your mealtime!

If we do that for all the hours, and link the end points of all the safe distances, that makes a cloverleaf.

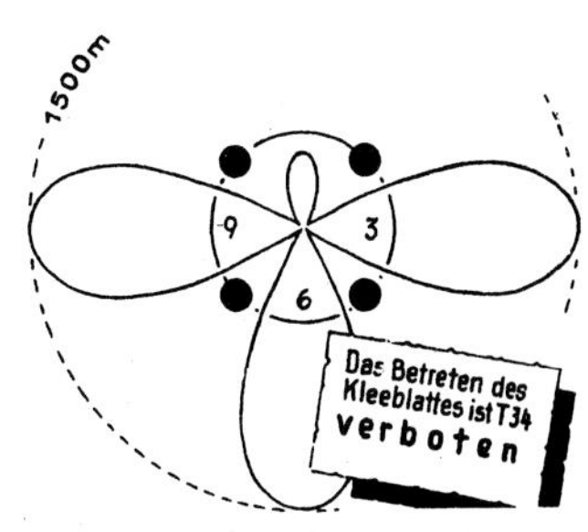

If the enemy is really standing in the cloverleaf, then don't do it in your pants, but turn the Tiger to "mealtime." Then the enemy is right outside again. If two fire on you, then turn the one to "mealtime" and knock out the other one.

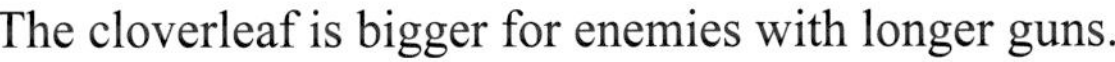

The cloverleaf is bigger for enemies with longer guns.
For enemy weapons that penetrate less, it has just three leaves, because your front is safe at any distance.

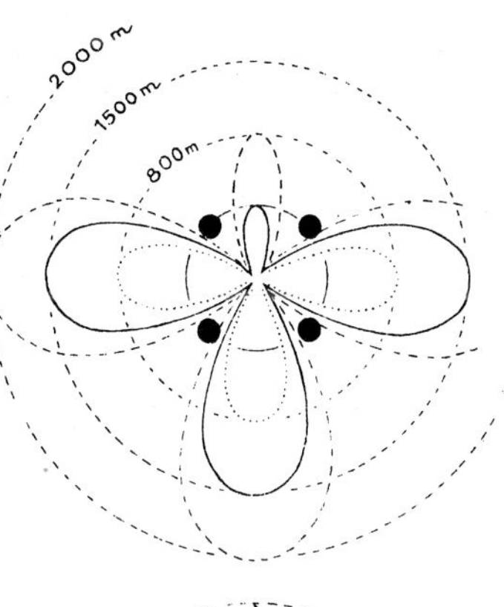

A number of its own
You must make a note for every enemy tank, for then you know exactly how big your cloverleaf is!
For the T-34 with the 7.62 cm long gun it is **15**.

1500 meters is how long the three big leaves are!
(Because the tiger is equally thick at the sides and rear).
Still 1000 meters shorter than the big leaves, thus here

500 meters is how long the short leaf is
(because the Tiger is 2 cm thicker in front).

The very smart people
Can also work out for 2, 4, 5, 7, 8, and 10 o'clock how close they can let the enemy come without being penetrated.
This distance is likewise

1000 m shorter than the big leaves
(because the Tiger is 2 cm thicker there).

The extremely smart people
Can also do that for 11 and 1 o'clock.
The distance is

1000 m shorter than the small leaf
(because the Tiger is 2 cm thicker there than in front).

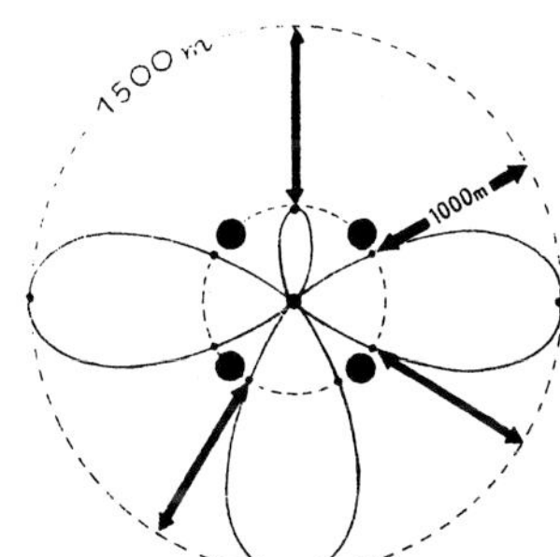

Moral: If such a guy stands on your clover,
Then play a trick and throw him out.

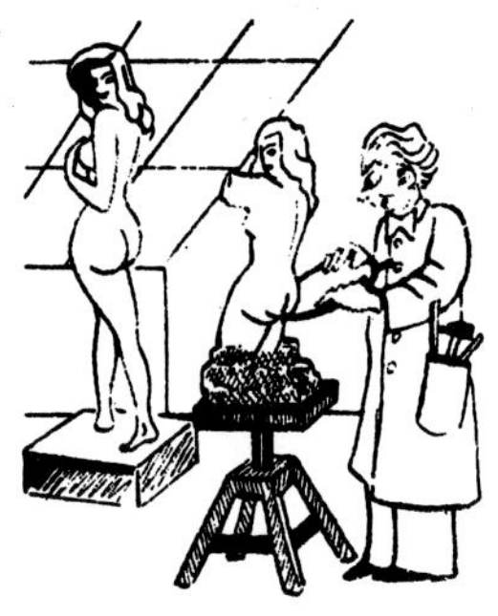

Motto: The moderate shoots a lot,
The master shoots with measure and purpose.

The Prick Measure

Das Stachelmaß

The sculptor compares his model with his work! If the plastic fits exactly between the two points of the gap gauge, he knows that it has the right mass.
The tank man compares the enemy with the prick measure! If the T-34 (front) fits exactly between the two peaks of the prick measure, then he has the right mass to fire on. Then you know
1. *That you can penetrate him, and*
2. *what the distance is.*
You can penetrate the side or rear of all enemy tanks within 2000 meters. That is easy to see. Their fronts are all thicker. You must then come closer or let them come closer—the T-34, for example, to 800 meters. The distance varies for all tanks. Study the tank fire chart in the pocket of this book!
The prick measure tells you when you are at shooting-down distance. For the T-34, for example, it is 43.
4 = *prick measure-front:* The T-34 must be 4 mils wide, so that you can shoot it down through the front (or must fit between two points). Then it is
800 meters wide.
3 = *prick measure-side:* The T-34 must be 3 mils wide, so you can penetrate its side.
It is then 2000 meters wide.
Prick measure-rear is always half the side mass, here about 1.5 mils. It is then 2000 meters wide.
For very smart people:
If an enemy tank turns from "side" to "mealtime," then it becomes at most 10% wider as a target. These 10% errors are reckoned in. You must then fire on the middle of the turret, so that your shot hits squarely.
Moral: The mass of the points shows you
That you can beat him, and when.

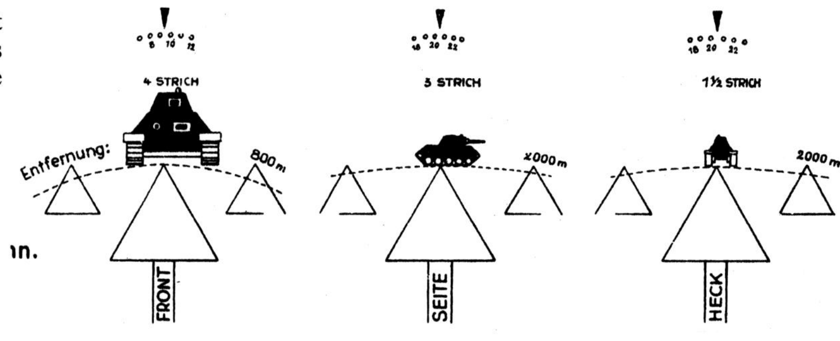

Motto: The warrant is as well known to you
As your girl's picture and phone number.

The Warrant

Steckbrief

Every wolf cub knows the Spitfire and the He 111.
Every boy can tell a Ford V-8 from an Opel Kapitän at 500 meters. The old foxes recognize the DKW 250 by its sound.

Then you will probably learn to differentiate and recognize the enemy tanks. Hurry and bend yourself over the tank recognition chart in the pocket.

Notice their appearance and the following five warrants:

T-34	15	8	43
KW I	9	4	84
Churchill III	7	15	24
Lee	8	20	13

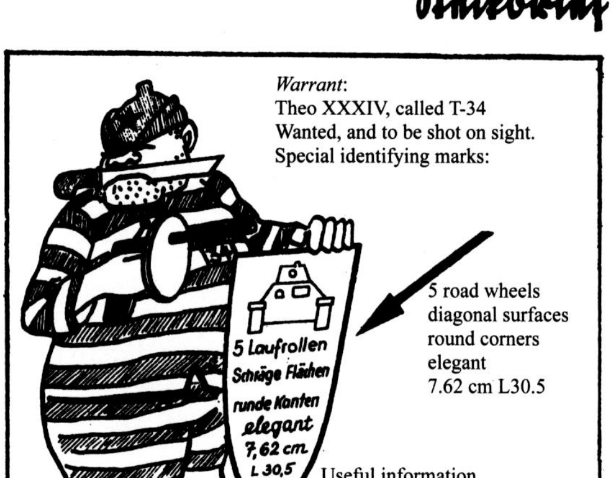

Warrant:
Theo XXXIV, called T-34
Wanted, and to be shot on sight.
Special identifying marks:

5 road wheels
diagonal surfaces
round corners
elegant
7.62 cm L30.5

Useful information
T-34 15 8 43

T-34	15	8	4	3
Type	Cloverleaf	Range	Prick measure front:	Prick measure side:
	I'll penetrate	*I penetrate*	4 lines	is the T-34 wide at 2000 m,
Your poor enemy	side and rear at less than 1500 m, front always at 1000 m less, so here from 500 m, at mealtimes never!	front at 800 m, side and hear of all tanks at 2000 m.	is the T-34 wide at 800 m.	rear is still half the side briar patch, so here 1 1/2 lines

Moral:
Often the exact number is pleasant, or also unfortunate.

Are you in credit or debit?
Who will give whom a beating?

Anti-Götz

Motto: Whoever reaches farther smashes
The other easily on his roof!

With your iron fist you can keep your opponent at a distance and knock him out without letting him even chew on you.
You are farther away from him than he is from you!
The Anti-Götz is the space between your cloverleaf and your reach.
Be careful!
You can penetrate the T-34 front at 800 meters,
The T-34 can penetrate your front only at 500 meters.
Anti-Götz: Between 500 m and 800 m
You can shoot him down, but he can't shoot you down!
You must try for this combat distance!
If you are at "mealtime," then you can't lose the round!
You bring more weight and more reach into the ring.
You'll always beat him. Isn't that a killer?

The five charts in the pocket show you your possibilities in a tank duel. They include the cloverleaf, prick measure, warrant, and Anti-Götz for your dangerous opponent. Look at them long enough, and read the chapters often enough, so that every chart appears before your eyes if you even murmur the warrant, just as you see the picture in your breast pocket at once when you think of "her."

And the moral of the story is:
I can get you, but you can't get me.

Panzerklau

The Tiger Claw

For every shell that you fire,
Your father has paid 100 RM taxes,
Your mother has worked a week in a factory,
The railroad has traveled 10,000 kilometers!
Think of that before every shot!
Explosive shells fired at unknown targets "on suspicion," at targets that could be shot down with a machine gun, are a crime.

Armor piercing shells fired at useless distances, at shot-down tanks, or fired with poor aim, just make nicks in steel!

Tiger men! Save!
Make use of the thick armor! Go!
Rolling is cheaper than MG!
MG is cheaper than tank gun!
Deliver cartridges and packing cases!

The Tiger drinks fuel by the canister.
Every liter has to be brought 3000 kilometers.
Tiger men! **Save!**
Be spaing with each liter!
Don't run the motor needlessly!
Do you know when the next fuel will arrive?

The Tiger, with all that goes with it, costs 800,000 RM
And 300,000 man-hours of work. 30,000 people have to give a whole week's pay, 6000 people have to toil for a week, so you can get a Tiger. They all work for you.

Tiger men!

Bibliography

Aders, Erwin, *Memoiren* (unpublished)
Boelcke, Willi A., *Deutschlands Rüstung im Zweiten Weltkrieg*
Carius, Otto, *Tiger im Schlamm*
Chamberlain, Peter, & Chris Ellis, *Profile: Panzerkampfwagen VI Tiger I (H)*
Crow, Duncan, & Robert J. Icks, *Encyclopedia of Tanks*
Feist, Uwe, *Tigers in Action*
Fey, Will, *Panzer im Brennpunkt der Fronten*
Guderian, Heinz, *Erinerungen eines Soldaten*
Halder, Franz, *Kriegstagebuch*
Icks, Robert J., *Tanks and Armored Vehicles*
Magnuski, Janusz, *Wozy Bojowe*
Munzel, Oskar, *Die deutschen gepanzerten Truppen bis 1945*
Mellenthin, W. W. von, *Panzer Battles*
Nehring, Walther K., *Die Geschichte der deutschen Panzerwaffe 1916-1945*
Ogorkiewicz, R. M., *Armour*
Oswald, Werner, *Kraftfahrzeuge und Panzer der Reichswehr, Wehrmacht und Bundeswehr*
Schausberger, Norbert, *Rüstung in Österreich 1939-1945*
Scheibert, H. & C. Wagener, *Die deutschen Panzertruppe 1939-1945*
Senger und Etterlin, F. M. von, *Die deutschen Panzer 1926-1945*
Spielberger, Walter J. & Uwe Feist, *Panzerkampfwagen VI Tiger I and II Königstiger*
Spielberger, Walter J., *Der Panzerkampfwagen VI and its variations*
Spielberger, Walter J., *Profile: Panzerjäger Tiger (P) Elefant*
Spielberger, Walter J., *Die Kraftfahrzeuge und Panzer des österreichischen Heeres*
Stoves, Rolf, *die 1. Panzerdivision*
Tiger-Fibel, *Generalinspekteur der Panzertruppen 8/1/1943 (Dienstvorschrift 656/27)*

Abbreviations

a/A	old type, old version
A (2)	Infantry Department, Ministry of War
A (4)	Field Artillery Department, Ministry of War
A (5)	Foot Artillery Department, Ministry of War
A 7 V	Traffic Department, Ministry of War
AD (2)	General War Department, Section 2 (Infantry)
AD (4)	General War Department, Section 4 (Field Artillery)
AD (5)	General War Department, Section 5 (Foot Artillery)
AHA/Ag K	General Army Department, Vehicle Section
AK	Artillery Design Bureau
AKK	Army Vehicle Column
AlkW	Army truck
ALZ	Army freight train
AOK	Army High Command
APK	Artillery Testing Commission
ARW	Eight-wheel vehicle
A-Typen	All-wheel drive vehicle
BAK	Anti-balloon cannon
Bekraft	Fuel Department, Field Vehicles
BMW	Bavarian Motor Works (company)
Chefkraft	Chief of Field Vehicles
(DB)	Daimler-Benz (company)
DMG	Daimler Motoren-Gesellschaft (company)
Dtschr.Krprz.	German Crown Prince
E-Fahrgestell	Uniform chassis
E-Pkw	Uniform car
E-Lkw	Uniform truck
Fa	Field Artillery
FAMO	Fahrzeug-und Motorenbau GmbH (company)
Fgst	Chassis
FF-Kabel	Field phone cable
FH	Field howitzer
FK	Field cannon
Flak	Anti-aircraft gun
F. T.	Radio-telegraph
Fu	Radio
Fu Ger	Radio set
Fu Spr Ger	Radiotelephone
g	Secret
Gen. St. d. H.	Army General Staff
Gengas	Generator gas
G. I. d. MV	General Inspection of Military Vehicles
g.Kdos	Secret command matter
gp	Armored
g RS	Secret government matter
gl	Off-road capable
GPD	Gun Testing Commission
Gw	Gun vehicle
(H)	Rear engine
Hanomag	Hannoversche Maschinenbau AG (company)
HK	Halftrack
H.Techn.V Bl	Army technical manual
HWA	Army Ordnance Office
I. D.	Infantry Division
I. G.	Infantry gun
In.	Inspection
In. 6	Inspection of Motor Vehicles
Ikraft	Inspection of Field Vehicles
ILuk	Inspection of Air and Field Vehicles
K	Cannon, heavy gun
KD	Krupp-Daimler (companies collaborating)
K. D.	Cavalry Division
KdF	Kraft durch Freude (Strength Through Joy Nazi organization)
K. d. K.	Commander of Motorized Troops
K. Flak	Motorized anti-aircraft gun
Kfz.	Motor vehicle
K	Small
KM	War Ministry
KP	Motorized limber
(Kp)	Krupp (company)
Kogenluft	Commanding General of the Air Force

Krad	Motorcycle
Kr. Zgm.	Towing tractor
KS	Fuel
Kw	Motor vehicle, or combat vehicle
KrKW	Ambulance
KOM	Motor bus
KwK	Tank gun
l	Light
L/	Caliber length
le	Light
le FH	Light howitzer
le FK	Light cannon
le F.H.	Light howitzer
le. I.G.	Light infantry gun
le. W.S.	Light Military Tractor
LHB	Linke-Hoffman-Busch (company)
l. I. G.	Light infantry gun
Lkw	Truck
LWS	Land-water tractor
m	Medium
MAN	Maschinenfabrik Augsburg-Nürnberg AG (company)
MG	Machine gun
MP	Machine pistol, submachine gun
MTW	Personnel carrier
Mun.Pz.	Armored ammunition vehicle
n	Revolutions per minute (rpm)
n/A	New type, new version
NAG	Nationale Automobilgesellschaft (company)
(o)	Stock, trade, civilian
Ob. d. H.	Army High Commander
O. H. L.	Army High Command
O. K. H.	High Command of the Army
O. K. W.	High Command of the *Wehrmacht*
Pak	Antitank gun
P. D.	Armored Division
Pf	Engineer vehicle
Pakw	Personnel car
Pz. F.	Armored ferry
Pz. Kpfwg.	Armored combat vehicle, tank
Pz. Spwg.	Armored scout car
Pz. Jg.	Tank destroyer
Pz. Bef. Wg.	Armored command vehicle

(R)	Tracked vehicle
R/R	Wheel/track drive
(Rhb)	Rheinmetall Borsig (company)
RS	Tracked towing vehicle
RSG	Tracked mountain vehicle
RSO	Raupenschlepper Ost (Tractor East)
RV	Communication
Sankra	Medical vehicle
s	Heavy
sFH	Heavy howitzer
schg.	Able to run on rails
Schlp.	Towing vehicle
schf.	Amphibious
Sd. Kfz.	Special motor vehicle
Sfl.	Self-propelled gun mount
Sf	Self-propelled gun mount
S-Typen	Rear wheel drive vehicle
SmK	Pointed shell with core
SPW	Armored troop carrier
SSW	Siemens-Schuckert-Werke (company)
s. W. S..	Heavy *Wehrmacht* towing vehicle
StuG	Assault gun
StuK	Assault cannon
StuH	Assault howitzer
Tak	Antitank gun
Takraft	Technical Dept., Inspection of Motor Vehicles
TF	Radio frequency
Tp	Tropical version
Vakraft	Test Department, Field Vehicles (WWI); Test Dept., Inspection of Vehicles (*Reichswehr* & *Wehrmacht*)
ve	Fully desensitized
v/max	Maximum velocity
V	Muzzle velocity
VPK	Technical Vehicle Testing Commission
Vs. Kfz.	Test vehicle
VKz	Test vehicle
ZF	Zahnradfabrik Friedrichshafen (company)
ZRW	Cogwheel vehicle
Zgkw	Towing vehicle
WaPrüf	Weapon Testing Office
Wumba	Weapon and Ammunition Procurement Office
wg	Amphibious